Social Development in the World Bank

Maritta Koch-Weser • Scott Guggenheim
Editors

Social Development in the World Bank

Essays in Honor of Michael M. Cernea

Editors
Maritta Koch-Weser
Earth3000
Bieberstein, Germany

Scott Guggenheim
Edmund Walsh School
Georgetown University
Washington, DC, USA

ISBN 978-3-030-57425-3   ISBN 978-3-030-57426-0 (eBook)
https://doi.org/10.1007/978-3-030-57426-0

© The Editor(s) (if applicable) and The Author(s) 2021. This book is an open access publication.
Open Access This book is licensed under the terms of the Creative Commons Attribution 4.0 International License (http://creativecommons.org/licenses/by/4.0/), which permits use, sharing, adaptation, distribution and reproduction in any medium or format, as long as you give appropriate credit to the original author(s) and the source, provide a link to the Creative Commons license and indicate if changes were made.
The images or other third party material in this book are included in the book's Creative Commons license, unless indicated otherwise in a credit line to the material. If material is not included in the book's Creative Commons license and your intended use is not permitted by statutory regulation or exceeds the permitted use, you will need to obtain permission directly from the copyright holder.
The use of general descriptive names, registered names, trademarks, service marks, etc. in this publication does not imply, even in the absence of a specific statement, that such names are exempt from the relevant protective laws and regulations and therefore free for general use.
The publisher, the authors, and the editors are safe to assume that the advice and information in this book are believed to be true and accurate at the date of publication. Neither the publisher nor the authors or the editors give a warranty, expressed or implied, with respect to the material contained herein or for any errors or omissions that may have been made. The publisher remains neutral with regard to jurisdictional claims in published maps and institutional affiliations.

This Springer imprint is published by the registered company Springer Nature Switzerland AG.
The registered company address is: Gewerbestrasse 11, 6330 Cham, Switzerland

Michael Cernea

Introduction

From the Editors: Scott Guggenheim and Maritta Koch-Weser

Despite the global success of development in reducing poverty, hundreds of millions of people still live in abject poverty and danger, in shanty towns and favelas, or in rural communities and tribal lands. They live in poorly governed or conflict zones that have been shelled to pieces, and they suffer from climate change, famine, crime, and corruption.

"Putting People First", Michael Cernea's mantra first published in his seminal book of the same name, rings even more true now than ever. The phrase originated at the World Bank, more than 40 years back, when that institution was at its most significant as the world's largest and leading development finance institution. "Putting People First" became a movement.

This book documents how concepts and strategies from applied social science can be used to improve the quality of international development and thereby people's welfare and life prospects. The book recapitulates and presents voices from the time, decades ago, when social specialists first joined an international development institution, the World Bank. They were guided by Michael Cernea, the World Bank's first social scientist. This book presents the story of how change in a large development agency became possible.

But the essays contained in this book are of more than historical interest. Social development continues to matter if we are to make progress in solving some of the world's major new social challenges—from internal and international migrations to ethnic, cultural, and religious divides, to collaboration on managing the global commons—our shared climate, water, oceans, and biodiversity.

To Our Readers

This book is assembled for development practitioners who care to make a difference. We hope that our book makes a contribution to the continuous search for social strategies that will reach people on the ground most effectively. Perhaps, the most important lesson from the experiences recounted in this book is not about understanding the reality "out there." Michael Cernea's genius lay in his ability to use the structures and vocabulary of the World Bank itself to generate a willingness to bring social specialists into the core of World Bank thinking and operations.

Social practitioners continue to work at the World Bank—but many more will now be working out of national development banks and agencies in emerging economy countries, in bilateral finance institutions in higher income countries, or in non-governmental organizations, consultancies, and academia. They will face many of the same challenges that Michael and his colleagues did. We hope that this book helps them find their own way through them. The book is also written for the aspiring practitioners among you, students engaged in development-oriented studies who are now at the outset of their careers.

Uses

The goal of this retrospective is to provide some insights for building a social development agenda for the future. If you want to find out how to orchestrate the introduction of new ideas and skills in the daunting and resistant context of large bureaucratic organizations, then you may be fascinated by Part I of this book, which shows you how Michael Cernea went about turning the World Bank leadership's general curiosity about social development into a strong and supportive constituency of senior managers who became convinced of the value of social analysis. As top-level support grew, Michael and his colleagues began to embed social development into the normative structure of the Bank, removing it from the realm of the outlying curiosity and instead making it part of the routine ways in which the World Bank manages its policies and programs.

If you want to envision what development anthropology practice means, where it is a needed and indispensable element of development team work, and what kinds of contributions it has made—you will be interested in Part II. The essays in this section describe personal professional experiences, real life cases from different regions, which will help you understand how this first generation of the World Bank's social development practitioners turned social knowledge into development practice. You will find that this is not a facile parade of successes and failures, but rather a carefully differentiated assemblage of demonstrative regional and sectoral experiences. Some of them may resonate with you and your own focus of work today.

In Part III, we portray for the 1970–2000 period one of the most contentious and thought-provoking challenges in social development—involuntary displacement and resettlement, mostly in connection with large dams and irrigation infrastructure. The controversies that swirled around resettlement marked a major turning point for both the Bank and its social development staff. We give extra room to this topic because it will stay with you, the next generations of practitioners, for a long time, involving not just the technical language of development programming but fundamental issues of ethics, rights, and responsibilities.

Origins

While we now hope that this book may become a useful reader for practitioners and academic programs, it was initially only modestly intended as a "Festschrift" for Michael Cernea, the decades-long thought leader on social development at the World Bank. Special credit goes to our colleague William Partridge, who led the way to the 2011 Bieberstein symposium honoring Michael Cernea. Most of the contributors to this book came together then, exchanging experiences and following up with their own write-ups. Some in our social science core group—among them Gloria Davis, Shelton Davis, and Jonathan Brown—were no longer alive, but they left us small texts or oral histories, which we include here to commemorate their fundamental contribution. And some have watched the processes we describe from outside the prism of the World Bank—Robert Wade's portrait of the India-Narmada project is a case in point – providing a close-but-distant portrayal of the controversies and issues at play.

> **The Bieberstein Meeting, May 2011**
> The contributors to this book came together in Bieberstein, Germany, to celebrate the work of their former World Bank mentor and colleague, Michael Cernea. Michael Cernea's seminal 1980 book *Putting People First* and the policies on involuntary displacement and resettlement, cultural heritage, indigenous peoples, and more, which he managed to mainstream at the World Bank, had long become quality standards in development work worldwide.
>
> Since the early 1970s, Michael Cernea pioneered social analysis and planning in international development work with singular foresight, tenacity, and success. At the World Bank, Michael Cernea introduced and mentored a community of social development professionals throughout all of the Bank's regions and sectors, many of whom went on to become senior professionals in the Bank and other development institutions. He also was the first to succeed in getting social development codified in the World Bank's governing policies and operational procedures, enabling changes which improved the quality of development for millions of people the world over. His importance for development was recognized by his disciplinary colleagues when they awarded him
>
> (continued)

their highest honor, the Malinowski award (included here). The social development framework that he built at the World Bank continues to have relevance for today's practitioners the world over.

All of the participants in the Bieberstein group had been inspired by Michael Cernea at some stage of their careers. They included his managers, colleagues, and professional friends from the academic community at large. Over their professional lifetimes they had walked many roads together, and they now wanted to look toward some of the evolving challenges in development anthropology as they began handing over leadership to a new generation of social development practitioners.

Editors Note: Part 1

The goal of this first section is to describe how changes to the World Bank's overall sense of mission opened a first door to social development. Robert McNamara's forceful declaration in the early 1970s that the overarching goal of the Bank was to end poverty led to a major shift in the demand for Bank skills, first primarily for economists, but soon also with a tiny opening for a first non-economic social scientist. Even so, the resistance to social specialists was high, and had there not been pressure from the very top, the likelihood of Michael Cernea getting a job offer to become the World Bank's first professional sociologist would have been very low. **Leif Christoffersen** describes the Bank management's initial puzzlement at President McNamara's decision to hire a sociologist, and then the challenge of finding one. **Charles Weiss** tells a fascinating story of about how quickly the economic establishment closed ranks against the thought of hiring any more than its one lone sociologist. Nevertheless, they were eventually overruled by a coalition of senior managers worried about single-discipline hegemony. **Huw Evans**, a member of the governing board for both the Bank and the IMF, similarly describes how initial resistance to social development was overcome by senior management's belief that the Bank needed a broader disciplinary skills mix to understand how social processes affect economic outcomes —along the lines **James Wolfensohn**, World Bank President in the 1990s, later describes. Proving how much it took top-down pressure to pry open the doors to social analysis, we have included the request from four World Bank Board members to the Bank's two senior vice-presidents to take a more strategic and operational approach to introducing social assessment to all aspects of the World Bank's work. **Ismail Serageldin** was the World Bank vice-president charged with putting together the first fully institutionalized system for environmental and social sustainability, which became both anchor and advocate for an institutional approach to social development policy. As manager and former skeptic, **Jonathan Brown** describes how he became "a convert"—based on his discovery of social assessment's value for the projects in his unit early on, as the top-down reform began to percolate throughout the system. The section concludes with a contribution from Susanna Price, who uses the Asian Development Bank's experience with social analysis to show how once the World Bank's walls had been breached, the principles for social analysis were taken up and adapted by other big development banks.

Social Development Work—Live—Editors' Note

The contributions in this section take the reader on a journey across many of the domains of development anthropology and sociology, as it grew up within the World Bank. Largely written in autobiographical mode, these contributions portray the early work, challenges, and results of applied work carried out by development anthropologists at the World Bank. Portraying his own professional trajectory and explaining the positions that he has stood for since coming to the World Bank in 1974, **Michael Cernea**'s 1995 Malinowski lecture provides the point of departure. **Maritta Koch-Weser's** personal account in "Anthropology at Work" portrays her 20 Years as A Development Anthropologist at the World Bank, providing live examples of project and policy challenges in social development work across the world's major regions. **Gloria Davis** was the World Bank's first full Director of Social Development. The extract from her oral retrospective retraces social development's emergence as an institutional part of the Bank. **Scott Guggenheim** describes his personal journey as he went from Michael Cernea's understudy to becoming the team leader for a very anthropological national community development program in Indonesia, a model that in turn has inspired other countries to think of communities and their role in development. **Shelton Davis**—a founder of Cultural Survival International before he joined the World Bank—illustrates in his article the internal policy argument for valuing cultural diversity in World Bank member countries, and, especially, the need for safeguard policies relating to indigenous peoples. **Amir Kassam**, a senior scientist in the Consultative Group on International Agricultural Research (CGIAR), describes the advent of social science research in the agricultural research realm. Finally, **William Partridge's** contribution is a candid, autobiographical discussion of resettlement-related challenges, and obstacles faced by field-focused social scientists in the application of several of the World Bank's Safeguard Policies.

Editors Note Part 3

The displacement of people by large-scale development projects proved to be a turning point for social development in the World Bank. Michael Cernea's *Risk and Reconstruction Model for Resettling Displaced Populations* gave an analytical foundation for understanding why development-related displacement would have such devastating effects on poor people unless effective mitigation strategies were designed, financed, and carefully carried out.

Unfortunately, while the World Bank had produced a policy on resettlement as early as 1982, all too often it was honored more in the breach than in its observance. By the mid-1980s, international criticism of the human and environmental costs imposed by large-scale infrastructure development was already on the rise, but it took the debacle of the **Narmada Sardar Sarovar** project, beautifully described by Robert Wade in his contribution to this section, to galvanize World Bank management into action. We have included an extract of the subsequent **1994 Bankwide Resettlement Review**, led by Michael Cernea, which revealed that the human impact problems illustrated by Narmada were being repeated across the World Bank's portfolio. Proposing large-scale reforms to how projects involving resettlement were designed, reviewed, and managed, the Bank committed to ensuring that the costs of development in the projects that it financed would no longer be disproportionately borne by the poor. **Guoqing Shi, Fangmei Yu, and Chaogang Wang** illustrate how the dialogue on resettlement between the Bank and China led to big improvements to China's own framework for resettlement, while **Hari Mohan Mathur** describes how the post-Narmada clean-up built resettlement capacity within the Indian social science community.

Acknowledgments

Over the decades, social development at the World Bank has come to involve many outstanding colleagues. We wish to express deep respect and gratitude for their respective pathbreaking work in the field, and their thought leadership mainstreaming social development work. The list of names is long and legend, individual as much as "esprit de corps" team achievements, and includes, in alphabetical order: Arbi Ben Achour, Sabina Alkire, Arjun Appadurai, Dan Aronson, Jeffrey Balkind, Michael Bamberger, David Beckmann, Esra Bennathan, Lynn Bennett, Grazia Borrini, Jonathan Brown, Javed Burki, David Butcher, John Butler, Gonzalo Castro, Robert Chambers, Wang Chaogang, Shaojun Chen, Maria Donoso Clark, John Clark, Nat Coletta, Elena Correa, Maria Correira, Cynthia Cook, Maria Cruz, Gloria Davis, Shelton Davis, Jacomina de Regt, Philippe Dongier, Kreszentia Duer, Neville Dyson-Hudson, Judith Edstrom, Cyprian Fisiy, Paul Francis, Ashraf Ghani, Daniel Gibson, Maninder Gill, Christiaan Grootaert, Daniel Gross, Shi Guoqing, Anthony Hall, Steve Heinemann, Steven Holtzmann, Michael Horowitz, Fred Hotes, Saad Ibrahim, Malcolm Jansen, Narpad Jodha Singh, Arielle Klein, Conrad Kottak, Alcira Kreimer, Ayse Kudat, Mauro Leonel, Francis Lethem, Sam Lin, Judith Lisanski, Madeleine Maillieux Santana, David Marsden, Katherine Marshall, Meena Meenkshy, Maria Clara Mejia, Betty Mindlin, David Mitchnik, Augusta Molnar, Elizabeth Monosowski, Caroline Moser, Josette Murphy, Andrew Norton, William Partridge, Stan Peabody, George Psacharopoulos, Richard Reidinger, William Reuben, Lawrence Salmen, Ellen Schaengold, Thayer Scudder, Teresa Serra, Norman Uphoff, Jorge Urquillas Rodas, Warren van Wicklin, Michael Walton, Aubrey Williams, Susan Wong, Michael Woolcock, Mishka Zaman, Chaohua Zhang, and many more.

Contents

Part I Growing Social Science Demand at the World Bank

The Important Contribution of Social Knowledge to International
Development... 3
Leif E. Christoffersen

The Road to Achieving a Critical Mass of Sociologists and Anthropologists
in the World Bank.. 27
Charles Weiss

Address to the World Bank Sociological Group.................. 41
Huw Evans

Working Together at the World Bank for Broadening the Development
Paradigm.. 47
James Wolfensohn

Social Analysis in the World Bank............................ 57
Huw Evans, Eveline Herfkens, Ruth Jacoby, and Jan Piercy

Social Sciences at the World Bank and the Broadening of the
Development Paradigm....................................... 59
Ismail Serageldin

The Direct and Major Operational Relevance of Social Assessments... 81
Jonathan C. Brown

Social Analysis in Project Lending: Writing New Rules and Changing
Old Practices.. 97
Susanna Price

Part II Social Development Work—Live

The 1995 Malinowski Award Lecture: Social Organization and
Development Anthropology.................................... 119
Michael M. Cernea

Anthropology at Work... 147
Maritta Koch-Weser

Social Development (Excerpts from Her 2004 Oral History).......... 167
Gloria Davis

Putting People First in Practice: Indonesia and the Kecamatan
Development Program... 177
Scott Guggenheim

The World Bank and Indigenous Peoples........................... 191
Shelton H. Davis

The Need for Social Research and the Broadening of CGIAR's
Paradigm.. 205
Amir Kassam

Fighting Poverty, Combatting Social Exclusion................... 223
William L. Partridge

Part III Involuntary Resettlement

The Risks and Reconstruction Model for Resettling Displaced
Populations.. 235
Michael M. Cernea

Muddy Waters: Inside the World Bank as It Struggled with the
Narmada Irrigation and Resettlement Projects, Western India....... 265
Robert H. Wade

From Onlookers to Participants: How the Role of Social Scientists
Has Changed in India's Development in the Last 70 Years.......... 315
Hari Mohan Mathur

Social Assessment and Resettlement Policies and Practice in China:
Contributions by Michael M Cernea to Development in China........ 329
Guoqing Shi, Fangmei Yu, and Chaogang Wang

Part IV Retrospective and Outlook

A Retrospective: Michael M. Cernea (1934–) 347
Anthony Bebbington

List of Publications 355
Michael M. Cernea

Part I
Growing Social Science Demand at the World Bank

The Important Contribution of Social Knowledge to International Development

Leif E. Christoffersen

This essay has a twofold purpose. I will first reflect on how the contribution of sociology and anthropology enrich the practice of economic development and broader sustainable development aimed at reducing poverty. As a start, I will be reflecting on the context and reasons why in the early 1970s the World Bank decided to create the first in-house position of a professional sociologist within its central staff. The selection process we undertook was quite dramatic.

Further, this essay attempts to describe how from a tentative experiment starting at the individual scale, a process emerged that built a strong and respected community of development sociologists and anthropologists that has become influential in the World Bank.

With the benefit of hindsight, we now see more clearly that over the last 40 years the Bank's expanding community of professionally trained social specialists has collectively pioneered and produced enduring changes in the Bank's thinking, policies, operations, and ethics. They brought a distinct body of social knowledge and methods that they practiced and advocated both in-house and internationally. Under their call for *Putting People First*, they substantially broadened the Bank's development paradigm.

The scope and impacts of these changes, in particular in the formulation of social development policies and in defining many operational guidelines, have benefited not only the World Bank. They spread further into the international development community, as well as into the national policies and legal systems of many developing countries.

L. E. Christoffersen (✉)
Alexandria, VA, USA

© The Author(s) 2021
M. Koch-Weser, S. Guggenheim (eds.), *Social Development in the World Bank*, https://doi.org/10.1007/978-3-030-57426-0_1

Crossing the Rubicon Towards Social Knowledge

The process of creating this new professional group started in the early 1970s, when the Bank for the first time allocated a regular position to a rural sociologist.

Before discussing the recruitment process, let me just briefly describe the historical and policy context for the poverty-reduction approach of the World Bank (hereafter referred to as the Bank), which included the creation of a Rural Development Division in 1973. At the 1944 Bretton Woods Conference, its founding member governments wanted the Bank to focus on investments for "productive purposes, including the restoration of economies—and the encouragement of the development of productive facilities and resources in less developed countries." As young professionals at the Bank in the 1960s, we were constantly reminded that the key purpose of the Bank was to further economic development. Economic growth was the key policy objective.

During the late 1960s and early 1970s, many critical voices, both inside and outside the Bank, were concerned with the inequalities in the sharing of benefits from foreign aid projects and programs. Most of these benefits seemed to accrue to the upper political and business strata in the recipient countries—those among the upper 20% of income groups. This concern coincided with political development in higher income countries, many of which had established programs directly addressing lower income groups, as, for example, the War on Poverty under President Lyndon Johnson in USA.

Inside the Bank, I recall many discussions about whether we could address domestic poverty given our institutional requirement to justify such projects in economic terms. A large number of senior managers and staff, as well as influential members of the board, felt that the Bank's main purpose was to reduce income disparities **among** countries and not **within** countries.

The Bank's clients in developing countries felt comfortable with projects emphasizing favorable economic benefits, pointing to the Bank's Article of Agreement. Many did not think it prudent to accept loans for projects emphasizing social issues, including income redistribution. The economic impact of social issues was difficult to measure. National inequalities were considered primarily a domestic issue; a matter of national budget priorities and hence a matter of national sovereignty.

Despite some opposition, Robert McNamara (Bank president from 1968 to 1981) managed to broaden its policy and operational focus to include distributional aspects of economic growth. McNamara was influenced by Harvard professor Hollis Chenery, who co-authored a seminal study on economic development titled Redistribution with Growth. Chenery joined the Bank as Vice President for economic policy and research.

Within the Bank, some policy advisers supported this new direction of operational policy. Among these, Mahbub ul Haq was particularly effective in encouraging McNamara to pay attention to the distributional implications and thereby the social dimensions of economic growth.

Chenery opened up a new perspective for McNamara in that policies promoting economic growth could be pursued in tandem with social concerns about the distribution of economic benefits.

The conclusion of *Redistribution with Growth* noted: "*distributional objectives should be treated as an integral part of development and growth strategy—(one) should concentrate on the definition of relevant socio-economic groups in different types of countries, on their production, savings, and consumption activities, and on the interrelationships among the groups.*" Moreover, "*the effectiveness of policy measures and government investment programs in alleviating poverty is greatly affected by the leakage of benefits to people other than the intended recipients. The mechanism of leakage and the relationships between reducing leakage and efficiency in GNP terms need to be explored.*"[1]

Working in McNamara's office at that time, I remember his excitement about the ideas associated with a highly respected Harvard economist. Members of his top management team were encouraged to read this book. Poverty alleviation was in many high income countries considered a welfare function that was difficult to justify in terms of economic costs and benefits. How could the Bank get involved? To which extent was it constrained by its Articles of Agreement?

Another outsider also influenced the Bank's leadership. Robert McNamara had met Montague (Monty) Yudelman earlier at an OECD meeting in Paris where he was presented with Yudelman's empirical field research on small famers in Africa. It showed that unleashing the productive potential of small and poor farmers could produce significant economic growth and that this objective could be done in parallel with seeking poverty reduction. The idea that small farmers could be economically productive was not generally accepted internationally. McNamara saw the strategic importance of this argument and invited Yudelman to join the Bank, where he soon became Director of its Agriculture and Rural Development Department

Pioneering thinkers such as Mahbub ul Haque, Chenery and Yudelman, opened up new vistas for the Bank. It was possible to address income inequalities and poverty reduction within an economic growth perspective.

This unleashed a lot of dynamic creativity. McNamara's address to the 1973 Annual Meeting in Nairobi presented a novel framework for a broad involvement in poverty reduction. The Bank was lauded by its members for its pioneering stance. Widening its focus in this way, the Bank began to confront poverty issues, which over time have increasingly become a central objective of international development.

In 1973 the Bank created its first global Rural Development Division mandated to help clients design and experiment with new projects and programs. I was given the task to lead that new Division. We would test how the Bank's novel poverty-reduction policy could be implemented. The main focus was projects directly benefitting the lower income groups in rural areas of developing countries. Inter alia it would test the merits of wider approaches embracing several sectors such as

---

[1]Chenery, Hollis, Montek Ahluwalia, Clive Bell, John Duloy, Richard Jolly (1979) *Redistribution with Growth*. NY. Oxford University Press, pp 270.

integrated rural development projects focusing on *poverty groups*. More generally, by testing and assessing new types of projects we would seek to identify those that were most effective, for later replication throughout the Bank. .

For the Bank these were untraveled roads, exhilarating times and ambitious approaches. Hence, under Yudelman's leadership, the Agriculture and Rural Development Department (AGR) increased considerably its role in the Bank on matters of both policy and operational guidance..

Three challenges arose immediately. First, for reasons already mentioned, there was considerable opposition to this policy, both inside and outside the Bank. The creation of a new operational division was meant to test how this new concept could best be designed and implemented in the Bank's rural development operations, and thereby demonstrate results that might stem such concerns and opposition.

Second, a debate soon emerged about the institutional requirements of the wider approach to rural development such as integrated rural development, a concept that rather quickly turned out to be very popular with many other donors. Should poverty oriented projects be pursued in a single sector, such as agriculture, that could be implemented by existing institutions in the country, or could multiple sector objectives be pursued under an overarching project structure that could help assure effectiveness and efficiency? The latter often meant that new institutional structures had to be created or, if already established, the integrated project had to rely on institutional structures that had little operational experience.

Third, as a direct consequence of this new thinking, the question arose as to whether the Bank had expertise beyond engineers, economists, financial analysts and technical specialists, that could put into effect policies and projects that addressed these wider concerns about socio-economic groups and the interrelationships between different income groups in a country. While the Bank had been open to multidisciplinary approaches since its beginning, it had not employed sociologists and anthropologists on its staff. When we planned staffing of the new division, this discrepancy was noted.

After a long and exacting search, we recruited a sociologist in 1974, the Bank's first in-house expertise of such kind. Within a single decade, by 1985, that first step snowballed: the Bank had further recruited and was employing tens of such professionals.

Due largely to its community of social specialists, the World Bank became the first agency in the multilateral development bank community equipped to use and incorporate knowledge and insights from non-economic social sciences in a widening series of its tools and products. These ranged from operational methods, to planning and incorporating a new content in projects, to carrying out social research, to publishing studies and books, and even *crafting innovative social policies new to the Bank*. Cumulatively and gradually, these growing additions helped the Bank broaden its focus on economic development and poverty issues within the larger sustainable development perspective. After a major effort to recruit environmental expertise in the 1980s, the Bank was staffed to address the concept of sustainable development, which remains a guiding principle of the Bank.

The projects in which the Bank invested its massive financing became transfer vehicles not only for financial resources but also, over time, a vehicle for new principles, new domestic social policies, and better approaches to *self*-development in the borrowing countries. We didn't anticipate then that the initiative for incorporating social knowledge and skills would take the impressive extent that non-economic social sciences—and the functional role of social specialists—have played over time. They have proven indispensable for integrating social development with economic development and environmental sustainability.

All this, however, is not to pretend that bringing social science knowledge into the World Bank's operations at large has been a smooth and easy process, with no hurdles, push backs, and sometimes shocking reversals and failures. It was, in reality, an uphill battle all the way: a battle with past routines, a battle with entrenched concepts and narrow theories, a battle with old mind-sets and habits. And that battle was carried out not only at the Bank's headquarters, but also in the makings and the implementations of field projects in our member countries.

However, a fruitful interaction of *economic* and *social expertise* became possible under the pioneering policy for reducing poverty that Robert McNamara institutionalized into the Bank's thinking, financial investments, and ethos. The body of non-economic social science knowledge was germane and became integral to that new goal orientation imprinted on the Bank by its pursuit of poverty reduction. The battle for absorbing and asserting that knowledge in practice has continued subsequently, and seems to continue today as well.

A New Orientation and Our Search for New Skills

The start-up challenge facing the new Rural Development division was to assemble a staff with a skill composition consistent with its novel mandate. We wanted to recruit at least half of the staff from within the Bank. This would get the new division a core of seasoned Bank staff that was well grounded in its operational methodology. The other half would be "new blood," to be recruited from outside.

When I mentioned to McNamara that the new poverty reduction projects would require new skills, and involve new risks, and that some may end in failure, his response was that failures would be acceptable as long as we gained valuable new knowledge and lessons. However, failures without drawing lessons, and thus not gaining new knowledge, would not be accepted.

Our poverty focus on a specific population segment—the 'target group', often defined as the poorest 40% of the population—forced us to question whether we had staff with "people skills", not just the agro-technical and economic skills. We needed people well versed in issues related to rural institutions, community organizations, rural coops, rural credit, marketing groups, farmer behavior and psychology.

During these deliberations, the idea emerged that we should recruit a rural sociologist. The Personnel Department was asked to begin a search and compile a list of some 10–15 world-level rural sociologists. The recruitment unit responded positively to the task.

One of the candidates was a rural sociologist from Romania. The CV of Michael Cernea was quite interesting and came with strong references from respected scholars outside his country. For his research and scholarly writings, the umbrella organization of European Sociologists had elected him as Vice President of the European Society for Rural Sociology. Moreover, a world-level social science think tank at Stanford University in Palo Alto had previously invited him for a year as fellow in residence in the US—at the Center for Advanced Studies in the Behavioral Sciences (CASBS). However, we were hesitating because he lacked work experience in developing countries. His fieldwork was from within his own country. Romania had recently become a World Bank member, and its socialist type of agricultural system was different from most of our member countries. Therefore, his candidacy was not obvious. In the first round we didn't give him priority on our short list for interviews, and I placed his CV file at the bottom of my pile.

We began to interview various candidates. Yet one after the other appeared unfit for our needs. Some were only interested in research limited to their discipline. Multidisciplinary teamwork was not high among their habits. Others came with an already made up mind about the World Bank and took a rather lecturing posture, seemingly anticipating to instruct the Bank rather than to work cooperatively with its staff. Yet others wanted just short-term engagements before returning to academic life.

One by one, the pile of CVs got smaller. Michael Cernea's name came up again. I took new interest in that candidate. We found his publications and read a couple of his articles on rural cooperatives. He had researched and written on issues similar to some we were facing in African countries, such as Tanzania or Algeria, which were experimenting with socialist agriculture. When interviews with other candidates failed, this candidate became more interesting. At least he warranted an interview. We tried to contact him in Bucharest, where he was a social researcher at the Institute of Philosophy of Romania's Academy of Sciences.

The "Present-Absent" Candidate

Prior to this point, in the fall of 1973, the Personnel Department sent one of its staff to Bucharest to discuss with the Ministry of Finance the recruitment of some Romanian specialists to the Bank, as Romania had become a new member of the World Bank. The Ministry was preparing files, while our recruiter had the name of only one potential candidate, namely Michael Cernea. But we did not know whether or not he would be interested in working for the Bank.

Upon arrival in Bucharest, the Bank's representative phoned Michael Cernea and inquired—on a non-committal basis—whether in principle he might consider working at the Bank in Washington. Cernea's answer was affirmative. The recruiter promised more information and indicated that the Ministry of Finance would arrange a preliminary interview. He told Cernea to expect a phone call in the next couple of days.

This, however, proved not to be that simple. When our recruiter was told that Cernea was out of town, he was surprised, since he had received Cernea's assurance that he would be waiting for the call. The Bank recruiter asked the Ministry to search again over the next 2–3 days. The Ministry promised, but the recruiter was again told that Cernea "was not in town—he was out of the country", definitely unreachable. Our colleague was puzzled, but had to accept the response.

To his credit, however, our colleague remained skeptical about Cernea's alleged sudden travel. Before departing Bucharest, he placed another call to Cernea to check if he had returned. Cernea responded immediately and said that he had been waiting each day "glued to the phone", but he never got any call. The recruiter, stunned, had his doubts confirmed. He realized that he had been lied to and told Cernea that he was prevented from meeting him. He would report to the Bank what had happened.

Later, another recruitment mission to Bucharest planned to contact Cernea. The staff member asked to interview Cernea. The next day he got the response he feared: "Sorry, Dr. Cernea is out of the country." But this time he was forewarned; he pressed his counterparts to find out where Cernea could be reached abroad, for the Bank to contact him there. Expecting more misinformation, he was surprised to get a precise answer: "Dr. Cernea is at the World Congress of Sociology in Canada."

Meeting Cernea for the First Time

The secretariat of the World Congress did indeed confirm that Cernea was a registered participant, invited by the American Sociological Association (ASA) as an international guest. This was my first chance to talk to Michael directly. Most surprised by my call, he said that he wasn't part of Romania's official delegation to the Congress, but came on a tourist visa due to the invitation and ticket sent him as a foreign guest-scholar. I invited him to Washington for an interview, but he said that he didn't have a USA entry visa, only a visa to Canada.

By that time, and after having unsuccessfully interviewed many other candidates, I was determined to meet this candidate in person. I decided to fly there myself and the next day I was in Montreal. My first talk with Cernea was long and interesting. He had in-depth knowledge about agriculture, Romanian peasants, cooperatives, and peasants' economic motivations. He sounded different from many of the candidates I had interviewed. He impressed me with his practical vision on rural sociology. In Romania the tradition of rural sociology, referring to his own village empirical monographs, were partly akin to what in the west was done by anthropologists. Most interesting to me was his description of what he called the "action-and-social-reform" theory and practice. It was used by Romania's rural sociologists aiming at better livelihood at the village be level. He regarded such improvements as a worthy purpose of sociology. This part in particular caught my attention because Cernea appeared to conceive sociology's usefulness in an activist perspective, oriented to practical problem solving , and not merely to describe, analyze, and teach. He was not 'lecturing' me about his knowledge, he appeared driven to seek solutions.

I felt optimistic about his likely "operational value" to development work. In my response, I conveyed my preliminary conclusion that he might indeed be helpful to us. Before coming to a firm conclusion, I wanted my colleagues to meet with him. Would he be agreeable to give a seminar in Washington, so that we could listen to him first hand? He readily agreed.

A Seminar, More Interviews, and a Consequential Decision

Since Cernea didn't have a visa to enter the US. I told him that the Bank would definitely arrange this though the State Department and let him know the border point where the visa would be waiting for him. We agreed, the Bank obtained the visa for Cernea, and he came to our headquarters.

The first day after arriving in Washington Cernea gave a lecture/seminar for the full staff of the Rural Development Division. He presented the paper he had just given at the World Congress, a chapter of the book he had published in Romania earlier that year (1974) on agricultural production cooperatives. His paper was about the "peasant family's private plot in collective farms" in Romania. Reporting his research data, he explained the capacity of the family unit as a structured mini-social-organization able to mobilize even fragmented scraps of the family members' labor resources that were not used by the collective farm: the elderly, the children, the adults' time after returning from the collective farm's work. And he revealed the causes of their success: personal motivation; healthy economic self-interest: what the family produced on the small family plot was allowed to belong to the family, rather than to the collective farm. The family's capacity to self-organize and commit to intense work, he argued, led to much higher productivity per unit of land. He gave empirical data about yields achieved on the tiny family plot per unit of land, which were spectacularly higher than the yields of the collective farm. Cernea offered insights and hard data. All this had the marks of a solid comparative empirical study, with an intriguing causal analysis. We asked challenging questions and the give-and-take discussions were rich.

The next day we prepared a morning schedule with four or five teams, each consisting of two division members, to interview Cernea for some 30–40 min each. I chose not to attend these sessions, since I had talked to Cernea enough myself, and also didn't want my presence to affect the discussions. Thereafter each team gave me its feedback. They were impressed and all supported hiring him

When the last interview was over, I informed Cernea of the outcome of the interviews and offered him the job of rural sociologist in our Division. I explained again that it was a new experiment for us all, not just for him. He would be the first in-house sociologist. He could bring his family to Washington, but he should be prepared to travel a lot to our projects on different continents. Our job offer covered a 3-year period, with the possibility of extensions.

Cernea accepted on the spot; he could barely hide his emotion. We were happy and relieved as our long search had ended. It seemed to all of us that we had finally found the right person. It was such a significant step for us that I informed our President, Mr. McNamara, that we finally found and hired a rural sociologist for our experimental Rural Development Division.[2]

.... And yet, this soon turned out to not be the end of our recruitment saga

Unanticipated Obstacles

Opposition to hiring our hard-found sociologist unexpectedly popped up and threatened our plans. The problem arose when we began to prepare his recruitment papers as a regular staff. This was 1974 and Romania was the only World Bank member-country from the Eastern European bloc. Fortunately the Bank, unlike the UN, has no country quotas for staff recruitment. No country can itself appoint its nationals to the Bank. Rather, the Bank has a statutory right to interview, recruit and hire any national of a member country, except of those working in a Government position (to avoid brain drain). Nonetheless, Romania's Government had submitted a list of persons they would like to see hired for Bank jobs. The Bank was prepared to examine those candidates as well, but had no obligation to hire candidates restricted to that list. Thus, the Bank was fully within its right to hire outstanding professionals outside the Ministry's proposals.

Now that we had found Cernea, and the Personnel Department was ready to hire him outright. But then he told us that he was afraid that the Government might not release his wife and two teenage children to join him in Washington, if he was hired without a nod from Bucharest. Therefore, the Personnel Department telexed to the Ministry of Finance that they had found Cernea in Canada and that the Bank decided to hire him. In parallel, Michael immediately informed his family and the Director of his Institute requesting a leave of absence, and asked friends back home to help arranging for his family to join him.

On our side, we, in fact, were eager to send Cernea right away on an important mission to Tanzania and Mauritius. Tanzania was in the midst of creating a rural village program of a semi-socialist type called *Ujamaas* and we needed Michael

---

[2]We learned that Mr. McNamara was very pleased with our courageous step. One of the Bank's Vice Presidents, Shahid Javed Burki, recalled McNamara's reaction in a note he published later. Burki wrote: "When I was [in 1974] the Secretary of the World Bank Policy Review Committee chaired by Robert McNamara... at one of our meetings McNamara entered E-1227, his conference room, sat down, looked at the assembled Vice Presidents, and banged the table—something he always did when he wanted to make an important announcement. He said '*Gentlemen, we have taken an important step. We have just hired the first social scientist. He is a Romanian and his name is Michael Cernea.*'" (Shahid Javed Burki, *One Memory*. In vol: Gloria Davis, Andrew Steer, and Warren van Wicklin III (eds). *Michael Makes His Mark: The Life and Times of a Change Agent in the World Bank*. Social Development Department, World Bank: Washington, DC. August 1998, p. 1.

immediately to help prepare the project where the cooperatives would play an important part. We hadn't yet received the expected support from Bucharest, but we got Cernea a visa and sent him to Tanzania as part of that project mission. We assumed Romania would come around.

However, no response came from Bucharest. Our mission to Tanzania returned and Cernea phoned Bucharest. The answer he got was clear: the authorities were opposed, and his Institute declined giving him leave of absence. He was told to return to Bucharest to "explain why he wanted to work for the World Bank".

Personal Support from Robert McNamara

That sounded bad. It was more than a refusal—it was a threat. Cernea was very worried. He knew that, should he return, he would not be allowed to come back, and he would be punished. We too became concerned. It was ironical that, after so many candidates we declined, we could not hire the one candidate we definitely wanted to have.

We decided to explore the matter with Romania 'diplomatically', through the Bank's Vice President for External Affairs, and in the meantime send Michael on a project identification mission in Algeria. But that exploration also confirmed the opposition of Romania's authorities. When the team returned from Algeria, we informed Cernea about the impasse.

His performance in the field in two different countries, each with different types of agriculture and geography, confirmed our assessment that indeed he could be highly useful as a sociologist to our work. Although these were Cernea's very first steps into Africa and into the Bank's operational work, he performed surprisingly well. In Tanzania, he felt the need for more time to talk to the farmers to decipher and assess the functioning of the *Ujamaa* cooperatives. He offered to remain overnight in a village hut for more interviews. His request was respected, and our team picked him up on its return, after 24 h. It turned out that indeed his night talks with villagers around a fire brought much unanticipated information and useful insights for our project. In short, beyond his good seminar in the Bank, testing him in the field also worked out very well. The Tanzania team leader, Scott McLeod, reported very positively on his professional usefulness.

To overcome the obstacles with Romania's Government and Cernea's research institute in Bucharest, the Bank then tried to break the impasse through an extraordinary step. Cernea informed us that when he had been invited to the US by that high-status Stanford think-tank for social scientists, the Stanford Center for Advanced Behavioral Sciences, as a Resident Fellow for 1970/1971, Romanian authorities also rejected this request. He got permission to go only after the Stanford Center's Director wrote a personal letter to Romania's President, Nicolae Ceausescu.

Deciding to use a similar strategy, I went to see our World Bank President, Mr. McNamara, and asked him whether he would agree to send a letter to Ceausescu. He knew already about Michael Cernea's recruitment, supported it, and readily accepted. With the approval of the Bank's European Department, I drafted a letter jointly with a colleague from Personnel, John North. McNamara signed it. For this article, I got a copy from the Bank's archive. Here it is:

> **International Bank for Reconstruction and Development**
> **Washington, D.C. 20433**
> November 5, 1974
> Honorary President of the
> Academy of Social and Political Sciences
> Nicolae Ceausescu
> Bucharest, Romania
> Dear Mr. President:
> I recall our past meetings in Bucharest and in Washington... You may perhaps know, Mr. President, my deep concern that development assistance be directed increasingly at the lower income groups in the developing countries, particularly through integrated rural development programs, in areas of rural poverty. A new Rural Development Division has been established in the Bank and it is staffed with a group of experienced, high-level experts.
> I am particularly pleased that we are actively seeking to have a distinguished Romanian scholar, Professor Michael Cernea, Member Correspondent of the Romanian Academy of Social and Political Sciences in Bucharest, join us as the Rural Sociologist in the Rural Development Division.
> In this connection, I am writing to you in your capacity as the Honorary President of the Romanian Academy of Social and Political Sciences to consider the release of Mr. Cernea, on a 3-year leave of absence basis, to join our staff. We are convinced that Professor Cernea would contribute to our understanding of rural development problems and would enable us to share with the developing world some of the impressive results which Romania has achieved in its rural progress.
> As Honorary President of the Academy, you may be as proud as I am that a Romanian scientist, Professor Cernea, can participate so prominently in our rural development work.
> Sincerely,
> Robert S. McNamara
> President

To our astonishment, Ceausescu didn't respond to Mr. McNamara. Romania's Government didn't have a case for opposing the hiring, since the Bank was in its right to employ him. They were blackmailing Michael to return, keeping his family hostage.

We discussed the matter again. It was clear to all of us, as I wrote later for the record in a formal memorandum, that *"Romanian authorities obstructed the Bank's hiring procedures. However, the Bank was committed to prevail over these obstructions.*"³ Romanian officials were sounded out repeatedly by staff of the Bank's European Department. There was no give. Stony silence. Meanwhile, Cernea heard from his family that authorities were making their living conditions difficult.

Bank management firmly decided to keep Michael Cernea. He was told that the Bank couldn't intervene politically to press for his family to be freed. He accepted this and said that he would deal with that himself. He would get legal help to negotiate his children's way out, and if it became necessary, he would go public with the entire hostage-keeping story. The Bank didn't need to inflame the conflict further and could afford to let *"the official dispute calm down. But substantively and materially, he was our staff member from the outset."*⁴

For 'extracting' his children, Michael received legal help from several American scholars and academic colleagues he had come to know earlier during his year at Stanford. They succeeded in gaining the support of some of the highest-level US political personalities[5] who intervened officially to get his children out of Romania. It took some 16 months until the happy news arrived that his hostage family was allowed to leave Romania and join him in Washington by end of 1975.

Michael's work in the Bank and life in Washington had finally normalized.

Work Across the World's Meridians

However complex our hiring Cernea had been, the real-life test of what a sociologist could achieve as a newcomer to the complex fabric of the Bank's daily work was still ahead of him. We hoped for the best, but only practice and time could prove if our hopes would pay off.

During his first year and a half in the Bank Cernea enthusiastically agreed to undertake back-to back project missions in Africa, Asia and Latin America. He needed to learn the different segments of the project cycle. He went to Tanzania's Kigoma, Mwanza and Shenianga provinces for the projects' preparation and appraisal; to Mauritius for project supervision and for finding training options to integrate jobless people in income generating work; to India's rice-bowl—West

---

[3]Leif E. Christoffersen. *Hiring of Mr. Michael M. Cernea*, Office memo to Mr. Ian Hume, Director Personnel, Sept. 14, 1989.

[4]Leif E. Christoffersen, *Memorandum to Ian Hume,* Ibid.

[5]One of his colleagues-scholars at the Californian think tank was a prominent legal authority and US attorney—the Harvard Law School Professor Alan Dershowitz. He and one of his former graduate students, a young lawyer by then, Daniel Segal, did the legal work necessary in Washington DC for extracting Michael's family from Romania. That legal and political work was carried out independent of the Bank. It was a hard-fought process. The decisive support for Michael's family reunification came from the United States Senate, with the personal involvement of the former US Vice President, senator Hubert Humphrey and Senator Henry Jackson, who agreed to act in Michael's split-family case. The US Senate placed Michael's case on a "list of family unification issues" and became the sponsor and negotiator with Romania's Government, successfully obtaining release and freedom for Cernea's family.

Bengal, Bihar and Orissa states—on an agricultural sector-mission to identify the constraints to raising production, tasking him to study farmers use of agricultural credit; in Latin America, to Mexico's nation-wide innovative PIDER program for helping in setting up its monitoring and evaluation system; and so on.

Cernea immersed himself with passion in activities totally new to him. A defining moment was, for me, when one of our senior agronomists, Peter Nottidge, with decades of experiences in Africa, requested that Cernea be assigned to his forthcoming project mission. When I asked what motivated this request, he said in his gruff way that Cernea "*can solve problems*". That request told me that Michael and his brand of knowledge had made a break-through.

The RD Division's experiments with poverty reduction were rewarding in large measure because we had assembled a multidisciplinary group. The "artisans" of our Division's successes were excellent in their fields, such as David Turnham, Peter Nottidge, Andrew Mercer, Scott McLeod, Olivier Lafourcade, Don Martinusen, Gus Schumacher, Maritta Koch-Weser, Ted Davis, Paulos Abraham, Tudor Kulatilaka, Francois Falloux, Mike Furst, Phyllis Pomerantz, Ben Thoolen, Jim Edgerton, Dan Lindheim, Claes Lindahl, Musa Ahmad, Michael Baxter and others. They brought Cernea into their work programs and he was learning from all of them. Multidisciplinarity was our hallmark, part of our innovation in staffing. Together we embarked on new pioneering fields for the Bank.

Cernea's integration in the Bank's work was advancing well, but this didn't mean that it was free of obstacles, prejudgments, résistance, and clashes with entrenched mind-sets. As a newcomer he had first to get a footing, gain confidence in himself, make sure that his work fitted into the main stream. With each field-mission his conviction was confirmed that social knowledge was indispensable for inducing development. He was in constant search for project 'niches' in which sociological knowledge was needed, yet was not being used. However, he also encountered pushbacks. He discovered that there were also institutional and structural limits to what he himself could do.

In our division's projects he was identifying 'social issues and recurrent social variables' that were ignored or underestimated. He was happy that improvements he proposed were seriously discussed in the division, often resulting in changes or additions in project design and implementation. He broadened our understanding of rural development.

Decisions to Bring More Social Specialists into the Bank

Since many other Bank units were interested in work on poverty reduction, it was suggested that they too use sociologists for their projects. Cernea was advocating that social specialists be hired as in-house staff, and that the divisions that were skeptical could start by employing sociologists and anthropologists as consultants for specific projects, missions, seminars, and select those who confirm effectiveness. A few cases followed. The Bank's Young Professional Program—for the first time in its history—took the step to allocate a slot to a rural sociologist, and hired Jacomina de Regt, a young rural sociology graduate from the Netherlands. From 1977 a German-Brazilian anthropologist, Maritta Koch-Weser, did outstanding work on short-term assignments for food projects in Brazil; she was first hired as consultant, was also sent to a complex Bank project in Brazil (Polonoroeste), performed very well, was hired full time as staff, and over time advanced to a stellar career in the Bank in both social and environmental work. Another early recruit was an American anthropologist, Gloria Davis, who had considerable field-experience with Indonesian irrigation villages for her PhD. The chief of the Bank's Agricultural Division for Indonesia, Amnon Golan, realized that she knew more than the Division's irrigation engineers about how farmers negotiated their shares of water increments and how irrigation systems and their tertiary canals functioned *at the farm level*. Earlier he doubted the merits of employing such expertise. To his credit, he soon offered her a staff job in his Division.

Cernea thought these steps were good, but too slow, and too few. The vast majority of Bank projects were not subject to social analysis. It was imperative for the Bank to create an in-house *critical mass* of social specialists. The 3–4 sociologists then working in the Bank was a "minuscule" number given the Bank's operational magnitude. They were only applied in the agricultural sector. Instead, an entire "cohort" was needed, not yet as a 'special unit' in the Bank's center, but staff spread out in the various operational units Bank-wide. It was important that they constantly interacted with economists and technical specialists and applied the use of social knowledge in our projects.

One of Cernea's most successful institutional initiatives for building a 'critical mass' of social specialists in the Bank was taken in 1978. Approaching the Bank's Senior Advisor for Science, Charles Weiss, he asked him to support his plea to bring *social* science knowledge in the Bank, not only knowledge from technical sciences. Weiss, working in our Vice-President's front-office, was asked to help involve such expertise in more sectors than agriculture. It was important to create more social capacity in the Bank for dealing with the major social and cultural dimensions and issues of all the Bank's lending sectors. Weiss was receptive. It led to a meeting convened by Mr. Baum of all Central Policy directors to discuss the Bank's needs for more inputs from other social sciences than economics alone. The content and outcome of that meeting were reflected in a memo widely distributed to senior and middle level managers in the Bank's lending sectors and in Personnel. (The full story on that key meeting is told by Charles Weiss article in this book). It became a turning point in hiring trained social specialists throughout the Bank.

Subsequently Cernea took the initiative to start an internal "*Bank Sociological Group*". Its main objective was to bring together the Bank's few trained social specialists with other Bank staff to discuss the social architecture of Bank projects deemed as major successes, or projects that were recognized as having failed embarrassingly. Despite its informal status, the Sociological Group had regular meetings advertised throughout the Bank and open to all Bank staff. There were open discussions and a number of outside social scientists were invited to lecture on social issues of specific interest to the Bank.

Over time Cernea was instrumental in helping recruit systematically, one after the other, highly competent social scientists. Among them were both young talents and scholars with established status. To name just a few: Scott Guggenheim, whom Cernea brought into our Division as his research assistant, then over time became one of the Bank's top social scientists; William Partridge, a leading anthropology scholar in USA; the social anthropologist Ashraf Ghani (now President of Afghanistan); Dan Aronson (lured away from teaching at Canada's pre-eminent McGill University); Dan Gross, who left his Professorship at Columbia University to work in the Bank; Warren van Wicklin (trained in political sciences, who created the Bank's first database on people displaced by all Bank projects); Cyprian Fisiy (a young Cameroonian double PhD, who was able to learn his way through various Bank assignments and 15 years later became the director of the Bank's central Social Development Department); and many others.

Cernea also made social knowledge *more directly and more easily available to all Bank staff.* He invested much of his time in training the Bank staff at large: he initiated training courses for staff on the social issues of projects; invited many outside academics who had done their independent research on Bank-financed projects to present their findings and discuss them with groups of Bank staff working on the same countries and sectors; and kept rosters of potential social consultants and making their names available to managers and project team leaders. One such example was the respected Norwegian sociologist, Gunnar Sørbø, who specialized on Sudan and the Horn of Africa and who was director of the Christian Michelsen Institute in Bergen, Norway. His services were used repeatedly over several years by the regional agriculture division for that part of Africa.

Moving from Individual Projects to Policy Work

From working initially exclusively on individual projects, Cernea shifted gradually to producing guidelines, methodologies, and to proposing policy norms that would involve the use of social knowledge. This started with an internal paper that outlined an ambitious "model" to explain to Bank operational staff what, when, and where a sociologist or anthropologist could contribute to the Bank's most typical practices and project stages. That model was titled *"Entry Points for Sociological Knowledge in Each Stage of the Project Cycle."*. Seminars were offered for the Bank's regional staff. His paper was published outside the Bank. A prolific writer on social issues, many of Cernea's papers were published by the Bank's Publication Department. He edited full-sized books on social issues in Bank projects , such as participation, farmers learning behavior, land tenure changes, etc. He encouraged other members of the Agricultural and Rural Development Department to write papers for these books about their own experiences. Later on he included his "Entry Points" model in his major Bank book, *Putting People First: Sociological Variables in Rural Development*, which came out some years later (1985). This book was a success for the

Bank at large: it highlighted the Bank's pioneering role in addressing the role of people in projects and project's social-cultural variables.

During the mid/late 1970s the Bank decided, as part of its strategy for reducing rural poverty, to finance national agricultural extension systems to increase the productivity of poor farmers in Asia and Africa. Regional staff asked us to develop a comprehensive monitoring system for extension projects, to compare impacts and facilitate transfer of experience. We gave that task to Cernea. Together with a reputed statistician, Dr. Ben Tepping, Cernea went out to field-observe these extension projects, consulted with local researchers, and produced in 1977 the World Bank's first large M&E system on extension, a book-size publication explaining options and methods to assess the impacts of novel agro-information on farmers. We liked this study, published it,[6] and sent it to countries with extension projects. That was Cernea's first Bank publication. Next he initiated and edited two books on spreading research findings to farmers.

This experience convinced us of the value of Bank-wide instruments, able to achieve a multiplied use and social impact. While continuing project-focused fieldwork, Cernea turned to initiating other Bank-wide guidelines with social content.

The next Bank-wide policy tool arose from an explosive issue that surfaced in a totally different part of the Bank: a social disaster in a dam project in Brazil that forcibly displaced some 65,000 people. The disaster was caused by the project's omission of any social planning for people's resettlement. The dam's construction was completed, the sluices were closed, and water was let to flow into the still populated area of the would-be reservoir. The impending catastrophe in this Bank-supported project made headlines around the world. Cernea sensed the broad relevance of that huge social disaster, as the epitome of overlooking the social content and impact of an infrastructure project. He used to define this syndrome as the typical "original social sin" on projects, that was the pattern that kept exasperating him about many projects, even those of lower profile than a dam. This sin was 'committed' everytime, he said, when crucial issues of a *social nature* inherent in infrastructure projects, were overlooked by Bank staff in the initial project concept. Usually, the Bank's staff had all the requisite *technical* and *economic* competence, but they were neither trained on key social issues, nor required by the Bank to recognize social processes intrinsic and germane to their project. This pattern repeated itself in many projects, allowing social issues to fall between the cracks from the outset. The social "vacuum" either exploded later, such as in Sobradinho Dam, or undermined the project's technical success and people's livelihoods. In the Sobradinho case, the absence of social planning caused a catastrophe for the tens of thousands of people being uprooted. It brought international blame that shook the Bank. The Bank's President was utterly distressed, both because this mega-disaster caused great harm to poor people and also because it produced an international outcry against the World Bank.

---

[6]Michael M. Cernea and Benjamin J. Tepping, (1997) *A System for Monitoring and Evaluating Agricultural Extension Projects.* Washington DC: World Bank.

Cernea sensed the pattern behind this individual project case and talked to me and to Monty Yudelman, volunteering to write a set of social guidelines—not for the Brazil project, it was too late for that—but for all future projects causing similar forced displacements. We encouraged him. Our department took charge of issuing the draft guidelines, circulated them for comments by regional infrastructure staff and also alerted them to create safety nets for poor rural people victimized by displacement. After several months of staff debates, we sent the re-drafted text to Warren Baum, our Vice-President for Bank project policies, fearing his famous "red pen" that marked all papers he read. Yet this time we got few marks. Baum sent the document to McNamara, who promptly approved it and commended our Department for it. He decided that it should be issued not as technical optional guide, but as a Bank Operational Policy on involuntary resettlement.[7]

This was the Bank's first explicit social policy. It placed a firm check on well-known and repetitive long-term harm, mandatory for all Bank projects involving displacement. It was the world's first-ever policy instituting rules for providing the social protection justly due to forcibly displaced people. By extension, this policy became mandatory also to all countries seeking Bank funding for projects involving displacement. This was a deep policy breakthrough for the Bank. Until then no multilateral development bank or developing country had any normative system for displacements.

Writing that policy became a turning point also in Cernea's tenure in the Bank. It made him aware of the *multiplier* impact of involving sociologists in policy work. After having been promoted earlier to "Senior Sociologist," he was now appointed as the Bank's "Social Advisor". This was a new position on the Bank's job-list that considerably increased his influence; as Senior Adviser he had to clear all draft staff appraisal reports (SARs) with big social implications and risks before financing approval by the Bank's Loan Committee.

The Bank's adoption of its resettlement policy gave an impetus to regional Bank divisions to recruit more trained social specialists, in order to carry out the work required by this policy. In turn, Michael involved other Bank anthropologists in policy producing work. An interesting example is the process through which the Bank's next social policy—on indigenous populations—was prepared and adopted. One of the newcomers to the Bank was the anthropologist Sheldon (Sandy) Davis, hired for his known scholarship on indigenous populations. Davis, together with an environmentalist, Robert Goodland, prepared a draft policy, to which Maritta Koch-Weser and Cernea also contributed. That draft went through internal rounds of Bank staff discussion, and only after being "vetted" (informally) by the Bank's Sociolog-

---

[7]World Bank, *Operational Manual Statement 2.33. Social Issues Associated with Involuntary Resettlement in Bank-Financed Projects.* February 1980. Washington DC. [OMS (*Operational Manual Statement)* was the acronym used at that time for the Bank's formal policies guiding operational work.]

ical Group was sent to the Bank management in 1982.[8] It contributed in turn to broadening the Bank's attention to the social issues of development. Thereafter, it was replicated by ADB, IADB, and some bilateral aid agencies, exercising positive influence far beyond the World Bank's own lending.

As Social Adviser Cernea critiqued the absence in such reports of a structured social analysis of a project's area population, its needs and its social organization. There was a paradox between the Bank's proclaiming the poorest as its main target group, while the Bank's appraisal rules didn't require either its staff or the borrower to carry out such social analyzes neither during project preparation nor at project appraisal. This 'policy vacuum' made him an ardent spokesman for changing the Bank's *general* appraisal methodology. He elaborated and submitted a 'content outline' and Bank 'procedures' for the new type of analysis he saw as indispensable to the Bank: the *social analysis of the impacted population under each project*.

This was a systemic demand, and a bold one. It asked for modifying the very 'production model' of the Bank's hundreds and hundreds of projects. The effort to persuade management this time took longer than in the case of the resettlement policy. In many professional organizations there is a constant competition for intellectual jurisdiction over issues; hence, the need to build professional alliances for promoting changes in set models and practices. Many staff defended the existing appraisal methods. Cernea was able to find intellectual allies for such reform in unexpected quarters. Some of the Bank's top economists opened up to this idea. The Senior Policy Adviser in our Vice-Presidency, Herman van der Tak[9] took interest. He became a supporter of the proposal for introducing "social analysis" in the Bank's operational policy and also recommended the inclusion of a related analysis—*institutional analysis*—in the model for appraisal work. In turn, the Bank's Sociological Group became a key support tool for reforming appraisal methods. It proved to be effective in challenging old mind-sets, in open discussions. Project team leaders were invited to present their projects, selected either as success cases, or because they failed on social reasons. The debates were exciting, sometimes heated. Bank staff of various specialties became regulars of the brown bag lunch seminars. Cernea also obtained a departmental budget to invite a large number of outside distinguished scholars in anthropology and sociology to give lectures for Bank staff on key social issues and on their own recent research findings.[10] The Sociological

---

[8] World Bank. OMS 2.32 *Tribal Populations in World Bank Financed Projects*. Washington D.C.

[9] Herman van der Tak had earlier tried to change the way the Bank calculated the "rate of return" of projects by proposing the concept and methodology for calculating a "social rate of return"; yet this did not gain traction in the Bank (see Herman G. van der Tak and Lyn Squire, *The Economic Analysis of Projects,* Baltimore: John Hopkins University Press, 1976)

[10] Among the eminent outside academics scholars who were invited to speak on social issues in poverty reduction projects were anthropologists, sociologists, political scientists, such as Frederick Barth, Robert Chambers, Neil Smelser, Neville Dyson-Hudson, Michael Horowitz, Conrad Kottak, David Maybury-Lewis, Theodor Downing, Thayer Scudder, Walter Coward, Norman Uphoff, and Bank Board members, as well as other well-known scholars. Equally, Cernea persuaded many of the World Bank's most senior managers to meet, speak to, and engage in discussion with the

Group's meetings were oriented to project methodology and 'good practices': they discussed participatory approaches, and focused on themes which were then captured in the title of the celebrated book: *"Putting People First: Sociological Variables in Rural Development"*.[11]

Eventually, in 1983, the Bank's management was persuaded to appoint a working group to re-examine the norms for project preparation and appraisal. The result was the full rewriting of the Bank's policy on project appraisal. The new normative Operational Manual Statement nr. 2.20 (January 1984) included two fully new sections: one drafted by Cernea on the "Sociological Appraisal" of projects,[12] the other written by van der Tak and his economic adviser, Arturo Israel, on "institutional analysis", asking for the evaluation and build-up of borrowers' capacity.[13]

The adoption of social analysis as a Bank norm influenced the substantive paradigm of our work by changing the Bank's concept of what a development project should be, how it needs to be built, and what it must accomplish. This adoption itself embodied the success of a robust intellectual in-house debate for change. The conceptual change was accompanied by an operational methodology. Given the decisive role of appraisal, the broadening of the appraisal's scope triggered *content changes* throughout the full project cycle: project design, preparation, implementation, supervision, and evaluation for the Bank's investments.

The normalizing of social analysis had a deep impact beyond the Bank's headquarters.

It sent an important message to borrowing countries on how their own approaches to project preparation and management needed to be improved and conducted. Effects became gradually visible on modifying not only the Bank's but also borrowers' staffing patterns for work on various components of Bank projects: indeed, to carry out the new operational work requirements (e.g., demographic surveys,

---

members of his "Bank Sociological Group." Among them: Ibrahim Shihata, Warren Baum, Ismail Serageldin, Wilfred Thalwitz, V. Rajagopalan,; and Bank's Board's Executive Directors—Hugh Evans (UK), Jean-.Daniel Gerber (Switzerland), E.Herfkens (the Netherlands). Such sessions were home for challenging questions raised to the Bank's senior managers by our rank-and-file staff social specialists. This proved also to be an effective in-house social strategy for "staking the social ground": it "voluntarily compelled" some of the highest persons in the Bank's system to pause, think, and look from the perspective of a social specialist at what the Bank was—or was not—doing. The social community was gaining reputation as a solid professional group apt and ready to engage the Bank' senior managers in paradigmatic, theoretical and operational issues of the Bank's work.

[11] Michael M. Cernea (Ed.) *Putting People First: Sociological Variables in Development Projects.* New-York-London: Oxford University Press, 1985, 1991, 2nd ed.

[12] World Bank, *Operational Manual Statement 2.20. Project Appraisal- 1984 Jan. (it replaced the prior OMS 2.20 with same name that was unchanged for a dozen years).*

[13] For a detailed description of the long uphill battle inside the Bank to introduce social analysis as a key component of the World Bank's procedures, a much more complete account than I can offer here is given in Michael Cernea's own paper: *A Landmark in Development: The Introduction of Social Analysis* (see the book: S. Price and K. Robinson (Eds.): *Making a Difference*. Berghan Books, 2015.

consultations, resettlement plans, promoting organized local participation, etc.,) additional professional staff with trained social knowledge became employed. Overall, mandating the norm of social appraisal became one of the crucial steps in moving the Bank to broader informed and planned *social* development.

Cernea and his colleagues' work for crafting and promoting these and several other World Bank social policies changed the course of the World Bank's work on important recurrent processes inherent in development. There were other social policies that were proposed and developed by the collective effort of these professionals. They are discussed in other chapters of this volume (see for more details Ismail Serageldin's paper). The Bank's social policies were innovations in development work that were replicated also by other MDBs and bilateral aid agencies, and some even by huge private sector banks, that became known as the Equator Principles Banks. The very presence of an expansive and energetic community of sociologists and anthropologists at the World Bank, their activities and publications, became more widely known and publicly recognized.

A meaningful recognition of the impact that social scientists working on development programs came from the world's largest scholarly anthropological society: in1988, the American Anthropological Association (AAA) gave Cernea the "*Solon T. Kimball Award*" for pioneering work, "*to honor your outstanding contribution to applied anthropology and public policy ... and to expanding the scope of anthropology in development, advancing the cause of 'Putting People First'* ". This was most meaningful for the Bank institutionally, coming from scholars who in their research output tended primarily to see mainly flaws and failures in our projects.

A Group Process That Led to Collective Products and Institutional Success

Michael Cernea and I became close friends, and I remain proud that we brought him into the Bank. His colleagues and Bank managers recognized and honored his leadership as a "change agent" (see the telling publication by Davis, Steer, and van Wicklin[14]). In closing this essay, I would like to single out four characteristics of his and his social specialists group's work that carry wider significance for bringing social knowledge into development practice, namely: the ability to insert new specialized knowledge within a multi-disciplinary institutional framework; the ability required from sociologists to work well within teams and help organize collective efforts towards the pursued goal; activism, the ability for solving, not only lamenting, problems; and a capacity to derive general policy-level conclusions and norms from fieldwork experiences.

---

[14]Gloria Davis, Andrew Steer, and Warren van Wicklin. *Michael Makes His mark: The Life and Times of a Change Agent in the World Bank.* Washington DC: Social Development Dpt., World Bank, 1998.

First, as Cernea did effectively, I think that sociologists must seek to find *"natural entry points for sociological knowledge"* in both projects and policies; it's important to grasp what a project is able to achieve and, both, to communicate and to listen to the reasoning of colleagues with different expertise and perspectives, be they economists, engineers, agronomists, lawyers.

Second, sociologists must be good team builders and workers, not lone rangers. They must be able to understand the nature and potential of the institution in which one works, not just one's narrow task. Cernea rightly sensed that the Bank *must* have an in-house critical mass of trained social specialists and worked hard to find and bring-in suitable ones, who would have, as he likes to say, "both good brains and a firm moral spine." He became the leading architect in building up the size and the functions of the Bank's staff of social specialists. The Bank's community became *the world's largest group of development sociologists and anthropologists working under a single institutional roof.* It was their convergent effort that led to collective products and to collective successes. The Bank's recently published audit report (2014) counted within Bank staff the highly impressive number of 373 social specialists and environmentalists,[15] among which the number of social specialists forms the majority: 200. In the new post world-war era of post-colonialism and international development-cum-aid, the Bank became, historically and indisputably, the world's pioneering institution that first built in its midst the distinct capacity of a critical mass of social specialists and absorbed productively a novel body of social science knowledge additional and germane too to economic sciences and economic development. Sooner or later, all other MDBs followed our model incorporating within their own structures groups of trained social and environmental specialists, thus gradually broadening the paradigm of their development interventions.

Third, sociologists must have a problem-solving orientation. They must go beyond reporting weaknesses and criticizing faults to creatively well thought options and problem-solving mechanisms; Cernea called this "finding functional alternatives". Dissecting past errors provides insights retrospectively, yet the harder challenge is to conceive doable solutions to inherent ongoing risks. Finding solutions calls for social inventiveness, weighing if planned actions "fit", and for the capacity of anticipating even the famous 'unanticipated consequences'.

The last and crucial characteristic we must search in social specialists is the ability to think in policy terms, not just local "fixes"—both existing policies and those not yet existing but needed. Cernea *introduced groundbreaking social policies in development.* Their theoretical spring-board was the Bank's 1970s reorientation to poverty reduction, our broadening of the economic paradigm beyond economic growth alone to include distribution, the crafting of safety measures and participatory methodologies into managed development. These were the areas where the entire social community's presence and work in the Bank have made transformative and

---

[15]Mouhamadou Diagne. Report on an Advisory Review of the Bank's Safeguard Risk Management. June 16, 2014; http://pubdocs.worldbank.org/en/317401425505124162/iad-draft-report-advisory-review-safeguards-risk-management.pdf

enduring contributions. These policies had a paradigmatic international influence, had effects that rippled and today endure far beyond the Bank, having led to replications in other agencies and in developing countries too. The writings of our Bank social specialists have gained world-wide circulation and international audiences; they enriched and continue to influence research on the social dimensions of development.

In a recent conversation Cernea credited some coincidences that led him to be recruited by the Bank. I disagreed with my good friend. The key point is that he possessed some rare qualities, which we had been hard pressed to find. His professional competence, militancy for change, analytical and writing skills, team-spirit and capacity to lead, explain more than apparent 'coincidences'. He was the social scientist we were looking for, and we were never disappointed.

We were then, and are now, proud of the pioneering contributions of the Bank's sociologists in their totality to international *social* development. I've recently come across an authoritative confirmation offered by the President of the International Rural Sociology Association, Prof. Joseph Molnar; on behalf of his global scholarly organization. He wrote: *"Sociologists at the World Bank have successfully introduced many theoretical propositions, methods, and action-principles, derived from sociology, in the formulation of development policies, yet not without struggle. Their efforts have influenced countless investment programs aimed at poverty reduction, food production, rural and urban development, environmental protection, and overall—at improving peoples' livelihoods"*.[16] Indeed, they early advocated the broadening of the Bank's social knowledge and development paradigm and supported also the incorporation of environmental analyses. The Bank's orientation to *social* development increasingly received other global validations. Soon after the first environmental "Earth Summit", Rio-1992, the Heads of States of all UN countries re-united in 1995 in Copenhagen to embrace together the common goal and commit their countries in their first *"World Summit For Social Development"*.

Leif E. Christoffersen grew up in Norway, pursued undergraduate studies at Edinburgh University in Scotland, and graduate studies in international economics at the Fletcher School at Tufts University in the US. In 1964 he was recruited to the World Bank under its Young Professional Program. Over the following 28 years he served with the World Bank in Washington D.C., mostly in management positions related to agriculture, rural development and the environment. At the time when Michael Cernea was recruited from Romania, Christoffersen served as head of the global Rural Development Division. Since leaving the World Bank he has served as Senior Adviser to the Norwegian University of Life Sciences and led the Norwegian Research Council's program committee on multilateral development. From 1989 to 2004, Christoffersen chaired the Board of the GRID-Arendal Foundation in Norway, which provides support to the UN Environmental Program on environmental information systems, technology and communications. He has served as chairman of the Board of Scandinavian Seminar College in Denmark and as member of the board of directors of EARTH University in Costa Rica. He was team leader for several independent institutional evaluations for large organizations carrying out global programs, such as IUCN (the

---

[16] Joseph Molnar, in vol. *"Themes for the Third Millennium: The Challenge for Rural Sociology in an Urbanizing World."* Washington D.C.: World Bank. 2000.

World Conservation Union) in Gland, Switzerland, the Global Environment Facility in Washington D.C., and the UN Food and Agriculture Organization in Rome. More recently he served on the International Advisory Panel of RUFORUM, a network organization being owned by and serving African universities.

Open Access This chapter is licensed under the terms of the Creative Commons Attribution 4.0 International License (http://creativecommons.org/licenses/by/4.0/), which permits use, sharing, adaptation, distribution and reproduction in any medium or format, as long as you give appropriate credit to the original author(s) and the source, provide a link to the Creative Commons license and indicate if changes were made.

The images or other third party material in this chapter are included in the chapter's Creative Commons license, unless indicated otherwise in a credit line to the material. If material is not included in the chapter's Creative Commons license and your intended use is not permitted by statutory regulation or exceeds the permitted use, you will need to obtain permission directly from the copyright holder.

The Road to Achieving a Critical Mass of Sociologists and Anthropologists in the World Bank

Charles Weiss

A succession of dominant academic and applied disciplines influenced the intellectual paradigm, policies, and lending operations of the World Bank before, during and immediately after the presidency of Robert McNamara. The account that I document below about one part of this disciplinary succession and intellectual expansion of the World Bank's outlook is based on the author's work in the Bank between 1971 and 1985, during which time I served as the Bank's first Science and Technology Adviser.

This position was located in the front office of the Bank's vice president for policies and projects. My job was to promote innovative applications of science and technology in the projects financed by the Bank, and to develop ways to use its investment lending for building local scientific and technological capacity in the developing countries.[1] This essay focuses on what is usually called 'McNamara's time' at the World Bank, which until today remains in my view (as well as in the ranking of other veteran staff members, and of some Bank historians) the most remarkable period in the history of the World Bank.

In this essay, I distinguish three broad phases in the succession of professional disciplines that influenced most strongly the Bank's intellectual framework. The first phase was the pre-McNamara era between 1945 and 1970, which was dominated by engineers and financial specialists. The second broad phase was the decade of the 1970s, characterized by a profound substantive shift in the Bank's thinking and in its

---

[1] For a fuller treatment of these activities, see Charles Weiss, Science and Technology at the World Bank, 1968–1983, *History and Technology*, 22, 81–104 (2006), and Charles Weiss, The World Bank's Support to Science and Technology, *Science*, 227, 261–5 (1985).

C. Weiss (✉)
School of Foreign Service, Georgetown University, Washington, DC, USA
e-mail: weissc@georgetown.edu

staff composition, with economics becoming the preeminent science and economists becoming the predominant professional group in the Bank. Within the large group of economists, a more granular analysis would also distinguish a division into micro- and macro-economists. Due to the microeconomists' close involvement with technical specialists in the design of "project packages" and the formulation of sectorial policies, they initially had a stronger influence in the Bank than their macro-economic colleagues.

The third phase started in the early 1980s, when the advent of structural adjustment programs shifted established the dominance of the macro-economists. But this third phase also saw the gradual formation of a new professional group, the Bank's community of professional social and environmental specialists located and embedded across the Bank throughout the operational staff. The presence and influence of the Bank's first staff members with expertise in sociology and anthropology started quite late, only in the mid-1970s. A few pioneers and forerunners of this new community gained some place inside the Bank's headquarters in the 1970s, with McNamara's direct support. But only in the 1980s did they gain some critical mass and the kind of positions on the Bank's organogram that afforded them intellectual power and influence over the World Bank's processes and products. Their roles in the Bank started to have a gradually growing impact on the Bank's overall model of doing business—its development paradigm—during the third of the phases outlined above, the decade of the 1980s and beyond.

The World Bank hired its first in-house sociologist, Michael Cernea, only in 1974, followed by very few other trained social specialists over the next 4 years. They were: Gloria Scott; a young professional, Jacomina de Regt; Maritta Koch-Weser, who started in 1977 as a consultant; and Gloria Davis. Only during the third phase did the hiring of social specialists pick up pace and begin to move gradually toward gaining the critical mass they needed to work at the Bank's larger scale, rather than only intervening project-by-project.

This essay describes in detail a single critical moment in 1979–1980 that gave a deliberate impetus toward creation of a critical mass, roughly at the passage from phase two to phase three. I am proud to have been part of this event.

McNamara's Knowledge Revolution

On becoming President of the World Bank in 1968, Robert McNamara inherited an organization whose major function was to lend for infrastructure projects in its member developing countries, using much the same standard technology and project design as would be normal in advanced countries. Its lending was limited to a billion dollars a year, the most his predecessors thought that world financial markets would be willing to allow it to borrow. The operating staff that McNamara found in the Bank—the staff concerned with the lending program and the projects for which the Bank lends—consisted mainly of engineers and financial analysts.

Throughout the 1970s and early 1980s, techno-economic analysis was both the Bank's greatest operational strength and also its greatest operational weakness. It gave rigor and objectivity to the evaluation of projects and the analysis underlying sectorial policies. At the same time, it created an intellectual atmosphere and organizational culture in which the non-economic social sciences, specifically applied sociology and anthropology, were not seen as areas of knowledge needed for the activity, objectives and mission of the Bank.

The most important change initiated by Robert McNamara shortly after he became President was to re-orient the World Bank's policy and programs toward the major objective of reducing poverty in the developing world. No financial institution had ever before tried to fight poverty on such a global scale. He announced that a major objective of the Bank would be to fight poverty in its borrowing countries, first through a new program of multi-component "rural development" projects, predominantly in agriculture, and later through a program of "urban development," chiefly low-cost housing. No one knew precisely how to meet this exciting challenge, but the staff embraced the new objective and its moral underpinnings, and were willing to try.

To achieve the new objective of reducing poverty, McNamara put his indelible imprint on the Bank with a series of revolutionary changes. He increased the lending portfolio to some $16 billion and the staff to 5700. They brought to the borrowing countries, most of which had only recently freed themselves from being colonies to become independent countries, a high degree of professionalism, honesty and freedom from motivations of private profit.

McNamara's deeper and subtler changes in the disciplinary composition of the Bank operational and development policy staff were three-fold: first, to embed economists at all levels of the Bank; second, to recruit smart, ambitious, under-30-year-old "young professionals" with training in economics or management (almost never in engineering, technology, or the non-economic social sciences) to spearhead his new initiatives and to challenge experienced, older professionals to think in new ways; and third, to staff the Bank's project divisions—the staff directly responsible for identifying, preparing, appraising, and supervising projects, and evaluating them after their completion—in such a way that technical experts (agronomists, infrastructure engineers, urban designers, etc.) were required to work together with applied microeconomists in what became known, somewhat grumpily, as "creative tension."

Within each regional staff, these operating departments were organized in parallel in two types of divisions: "program" and "project". The first were staffed mostly by macroeconomists, whose function was to analyze a country's economy and draw up broad plans for the size of its lending program, identify the sectors (agriculture, industry, etc.) in which priority lending was to be provided, and the broad outlines of possible projects for Bank financing. The Bank's largest units were the project divisions that oversaw the preparation and design of projects by the borrowing country, carried out with more or less help from Bank staff and consultants, depending on the country's level of expertise. The Bank then appraised these projects through missions comprising economists and technical specialists, but very seldom, at that time, a social or environmental specialist. The project divisions were also in charge of supervising project implementation on the ground by the borrower's agencies, while the program divisions were responsible for making sure that the Bank's projects added up to a coherent strategy and met the lending targets for each country, the latter being one of McNamara's most important management goals and his key measure of success.

Project plans drawn up by technical experts for consideration for Bank lending were subjected to an increasingly elaborate discipline of cost/benefit analysis, resulting in an unmatched level of sophistication in techniques of quantitative, techno-economic cost/benefit analysis. The scope of this analysis was construed quite broadly, as long as project costs and benefits could be expressed quantitatively and translated into money equivalents. The quantified benefit of a project, for example, might have consisted of the value of increased rice production resulting from an irrigation project, the value of the time saved by commercial truckers resulting from the construction of a road, or the value of the increased earnings of the graduates produced by an education project. If the calculated benefits of an investment, suitably discounted, exceeded its discounted costs, it was considered to be beneficial at the scale of the entire society.

The Bank's economic and technical specialists were able professionals, often world-class experts with many years of senior experience in their respective specialties, giving the Bank staff the sobriquet of an 'army of colonels.' Their economic and technical analyses gave rigor and objectivity to the evaluation and justification of projects, and blocked many a resource-wasting boondoggle from being approved for financing.

However, this techno-economic approach also had its severe downsides, which at that time were not yet perceived or regarded as such. For instance, the unilateral use of cost/benefit assessment at the level of the entire society was devoid of an equally necessary distribution analysis. (Some Bank economists[2] actually worked out techniques for this purpose, but these were never put into practice on a substantial scale.) This prevented the Bank from assessing what proportion of the benefits were accruing to the poorest, or more generally, how the gains and the pains of the projects it financed were distributed within the country's population. Without this kind of analysis, the Bank's ability to assess the effects of the projects it financed on poverty was unequal to its ambition of reducing poverty.

Development Policy: A Quasi-monopoly of the Economist ?

The Bank's organizational culture and disciplinary perspectives were substantially limited by the anomaly that the non-economic social sciences, specifically sociology, anthropology, political science, and social psychology, were not regarded as

---

[2]Lynn Squire and Herman van der Tak, *Economic Analysis of Projects* (Baltimore: Johns Hopkins Press for the World Bank, 1975), available at http://documents.worldbank.org/curated/en/954731468156870423/pdf/794880PUB0Econ00Box377372B00PUBLIC0.pdf

areas of knowledge needed for the activities, objectives and mission of the Bank. Its emphasis on costs and benefits that could be monetized and quantified encouraged the tendency to overlook, or directly neglect, important adverse social and environmental effects that were hard to monetize, as for example the human costs of population displacement by infrastructure or the environmental costs of loss of biodiversity. Feeding into and reproducing this overly narrow view was the almost exclusive emphasis on recruitment of staff with expertise in economics or with senior experience in a specific area of technology. A generalist on the Bank staff—especially a young generalist—tended almost always to be an economist. Indeed, the hiring of young staff with training in applied science or engineering was specifically discouraged.

This narrowness entailed a cost at the policy level. The formulation of new operational policies and guidelines that controlled the areas in which the Bank would lend for projects, and the intellectual framework for the resulting operations remained almost entirely the guarded province of the Bank's economic staff. Few subjects were deemed worthy of serious attention unless their importance could be justified with economic arguments. Economics was the sovereign body of knowledge that claimed jurisdiction over the policies of the Bank, and it was economics that controlled the pattern of all the Bank's policy analyses. In the terms of organizational theory, economics was the dominant discipline, causing the Bank's understanding of the complexities of development at the grassroots to suffer limitations that should have been unacceptable both in the Bank's theory and in the Bank's practice.

This one-dimensional approach relegated to secondary importance (or worse, to complete ignorance and neglect) dimensions and factors studied by non-economic disciplines like sociology and anthropology, and limited the potential contributions of environmentalists and social specialists. Recommendations coming from such disciplines were more difficult to quantify and monetize. Social and environmental impacts were also longer run in nature and hence vulnerable to discounting. Again reflecting the dominance of economic concepts, poverty was defined strictly by income levels and income distribution. Considerations of democracy, of the agency of the project area's population, and human rights were excluded, by the then-dominant narrow interpretation of the Bank's charter—the "articles of agreement"—that only economic considerations should guide its policy and lending decisions.

The models that dominated the economic discipline in the 1970s and later had important blind spots. First of all, many development economists were trained and socialized to believe that liberalization, privatization, "getting prices right," and "letting the market work"—the core of what eventually became the Washington Consensus—were all that was needed for successful development. If these principles were implemented, so the received wisdom went, other imbalances would be straightened and fall into place.

At the same time, important bodies of knowledge relevant to inducing development—environment, health, and education, to name but a few—were themselves in early stages of conceptual development, while the capacities of disciplines like anthropology and sociology to use their knowledge in an applied manner were also incipient. They had their own reverse blind spots, especially regarding economic variables, and lacked operational translations for applying their insights to practical situations. This meant that the concepts and approaches that advocates would have needed in order to demonstrate the importance of these fields to Bank operating and policy staff were underdeveloped and at a disadvantage to compete organizationally with the dominant discipline of economics. They were therefore in a weak position to challenge the ruling economic paradigm. The recognition that economic growth could also have serious adverse social and environmental impacts, especially in developing countries, was also very limited or absent.

On the positive side, the pressure to meet the economic arguments put forward by the Bank and by financial officials in developing countries also resulted in advances more in the economic than in the non-economic disciplines. Once Bank economists and their outside colleagues became convinced of the importance of a subject—often as a result of outside pressure—they made important contributions in laggard disciplines of applied economics. Some members of neglected disciplines also tended to build bridges to the economic profession from their side. Pressed to demonstrate the economic validity of their concerns, sociologists and anthropologists gained new appreciation for the economic causes and impacts of the social changes they predicted or observed. Anthropologists learned to characterize the destruction of cultural heritage, or the failure to provide adequate compensation to farmers displaced by an irrigation project, as externalities that must be recognized as a real part of a project's cost.

Entrepreneurial Advisers in Social Disciplines

Environment, sociology, and to a lesser extent women's issues presented the danger that a project that neglected them could produce a well-publicized disaster, with concomitant, unwelcome negative repercussions on the Bank's reputation and ability to get funding. In 1970, the Bank took the positive step of creating an Office of Environmental Affairs under James Lee, which aimed to use for Bank-financed projects environmental standards proposed by the US Environmental Protection Agency. Lee's office reviewed the design of projects being considered for funding in an attempt to ensure compliance with these standards, which was more than other development assistance institutions did at the time.[3] But the Bank did not have an overall environmental policy able to inform the attention to the environmental impact of individual projects and was still far from incorporating environmental considerations into its country analyses. The Bank's staff at large was inadequately educated not only on social matters but also on environmental matters; many still

---

[3] See, for example, Robert E. Stein, *Banking on the biosphere? : Environmental procedures and practices of nine multilateral development agencies* (Lexington MA: Lexington Books, 1979).

regarded environmental protection (and Lee's office) as a constraint, a passing fashion, or even an obstacle rather than as a worthy objective.

The first Bank unit that decided to search for and appoint a professionally credentialed sociologist was the experimental division created by McNamara to test new models for projects aimed to reduce poverty. That Department was led by Montague Yudelman, Leif Christoffersen and Don Pickering, and included some of the Bank's best agricultural specialists and economists. They felt that in order to reach and understand the poor, the Department would also need a professional trained in social sciences, capable of translating sociological theory for applied purposes in real-life project situations, and being intellectually action-oriented (the long search for such person is described in this book's essay by Christoffersen). Michael Cernea became the first ever sociologist on the Bank's full-time staff. Indeed, as I learned later, when he was hired his recruiters and colleagues called him the "Ambassador for Sociology," and said that he had to demonstrate that this social science was useful to the Bank. (I had had a similar challenge when I was hired as the Bank's first Science and Technology Adviser.) Nonetheless, to begin with, Cernea was initially offered a term contract. Only after he was able to prove that his sociological knowledge was valuable for practical purposes was he tenured. For a few years, he remained the Bank's only in-house staff sociologist. It took some time until, slowly, the idea that other sociologists might be brought in began to be contemplated.

A Request for Help on the Issue of Critical Mass

My responsibility as Science and Technology Advisor in the Bank's center was to be alert to new developments in science and technology that could be relevant to the Bank's work, and then to facilitate bringing the new knowledge to the attention of Bank staff that could evaluate and use them.

At that time, however, anthropology and sociology were not on my screen. Social science disciplines other than economics were not seen at all as part of the knowledge used by the Bank. Yet I welcomed the first hiring of a sociologist. For me it symbolized not just a new individual staff member, but also a new Bank window opened to a still unused domain of science knowledge and research.

As time went on, I heard about some of the new things that Cernea was doing in the Bank's poverty reduction projects, and some times also met with him, to keep up with developments. One of these, for instance, was the design of a system for monitoring and evaluation of an entire category of Bank projects in India and other countries (on agricultural extension and its impact on farmer behavior). This was the first design of its kind in the Bank and was issued as a World Bank publication–rather unusual for a young staff member who had joined the Bank only recently. I also knew that he was cultivating allies among like-minded staff wherever they could be found, convening informal meetings of these staff to discuss issues of shared concern, inviting outside anthropologists or sociologists to give seminars on projects they were researching, or publishing articles about, and advocating for the use of more social specialists in the Bank's projects. It was much as I had done myself, on relevant new development in science, when I was establishing my role as the Bank's first Science and Technology Adviser, and continued to do thereafter.

Toward the end of 1978, Michael approached me, proposing a talk over lunch about sociology in the Bank. He had a plan and wanted to enlist my help. Cernea was content and optimistic about his own work, but he was rather upset that the hiring of other social specialists in the Bank was for all practical purposes blocked by inertia. He pointed out the contradiction between the increasing interest at the center of the Bank for sociological competence, on the one hand, and the unwillingness of the Bank's regional departments to allocate slots to hiring sociologists, on the other. He described specific obstacles he had encountered and without mincing words said that there were more than a few prejudiced middle-level managers who were openly opposed to dealing with what they termed "soft sciences" and "warm-hearted but cloud-dwelling people", who—as they believed—had little tangible to contribute to a hard-nosed economic agency like the World Bank.

Cernea had reached the conclusion that, to the contrary, the Bank needed to purposively go out and hire more social specialists because, he said, the kind of social issues and problems on which he had to work in his Division's projects were present, more or less, in multiple other comparable projects across the Bank. But there were no trained social specialists in those other Divisions and no willingness to hire staff with such professional profile. He explicitly argued that 'a minimum critical mass of professionally trained social specialists needed to be created in-house to work day in and day out to address the many social and cultural issues confronted by the Bank in every development project'. Only sociology and anthropology could provide such knowledge and skills for what he termed as "financially induced and managed development." Undeterred by the resistance he met, he asserted his firm belief that the Bank "needed social specialists in most Bank projects, and at every key stage of the project cycle". In sum, Cernea directly asked me point blank if, in my capacity as Science and Technology Advisor, I could support his advocacy for more applied social scientists in the Bank.

It became very clear why he had asked for our lunch. He had a point. I did not have any advice on the spot, though I was left with the sense that he was right; he had clearly come up against a textbook case of the syndrome familiar to students of the diffusion of innovation processes.

I could only empathize, and I promised to think about what he had said.

In December 1978, over Christmas vacation, I wrote a two-page memo to Warren Baum, the Bank's Vice President for Projects and Policies and its champion for project quality. My memo recommended that the Bank increase the proportion of staff trained in non-economic social sciences, especially anthropology and sociology. To support my argument, I made a metaphoric reference to the process of "adaptive radiation" that Charles Darwin observed among the finches of the Galapagos Islands. I also made two pragmatic organizational suggestions: that sociologists be diffused throughout operational departments, not only located in the center; and that recruiting should be encouraged through the higher levels in the Bank's regional vice-presidencies if this was necessary to overcome the hesitation or reluctance of mid-level managers.

Below are excerpts from my Jan. 3, 1979 memo to our vice president, Mr. Baum, in which I articulated my argument; I also ensured, in line with Bank rules, the prior agreement of the Senior Economist and Policy Adviser, Herman van der Tak, Baum's deputy and my immediate manager and mentor. Below are key excerpts from my memorandum, fortunately preserved, titled 'Disciplinary Balance of Bank Staff':

> The Bank's highly skewed composition by discipline is one of its major long-run internal problems. The preponderance of Bank staff, both at working and managerial levels, are economists and engineers (in the general sense of applied technologists, to include agronomists, highway planners, etc.) Moreover, a generalist—especially a young generalist—is in the Bank almost by definition as economist. [...]
>
> The Bank needs more than engineering and economic insights. And it is remarkable how many it does succeed in getting. This phenomenon has an interesting analog in evolutionary biology. In the field studies that provided the empirical basis for his theory of evolution, Charles Darwin found that the finches, the only major group of birds to have colonized the Galapagos Islands, had evolved in many directions to fill ecological niches that elsewhere were filled by owls, eagles, sparrows, etc., a process now known as adaptive radiation.
>
> By the same process, the Bank has evolved economists and engineers who do their best to think and act like sociologists, anthropologists, political scientists, ecologists, technologists, students of administration, etc. [that is, to substitute as best they can for the specialties the Bank was chronically lacking]. That this has happened is a tribute to human adaptability, and has produced many useful results. But it is not the same as having real interaction among staff trained in different disciplines. On the contrary, it inspires false confidence that economics is the only knowledge that really matters, and that other disciplines can be "picked up."
>
> The root of the problem lies in the Bank's pattern of external recruitment plus its policy of promotion from within [...].

I also warned Mr. Baum against the typical counter-arguments he might hear opposing the hiring of regular in-house staff by citing the routine work-around of occasionally employing outside consultants. I wrote further:

> It will be protested that:
>
> a. The Bank employs consultants of other disciplines, when they are needed.
> b. The application to development projects of disciplines other than economics and engineering is not based on a firm conceptual foundation.
>
> 'a' is true but is not a sufficient counter-argument. Sociology is not a specialized discipline to be embodied in a single adviser, or brought in on call to work on problems defined by others. Sociologists should be widely diffused throughout the operational departments of the Bank. So should ecologists. If this need is not perceived at the level of the operating divisions, recruitment should be carried out at higher levels in the regions.
>
> 'b' is the statement of a problem, not an excuse for inaction. The Bank, and the developing countries in general, need professionals trained in other disciplines who have a strong familiarity with the needs [of the client countries]. If these people do not exist in sufficient numbers, the Bank should make special efforts to give them the necessary experience, through participation in Bank missions, research projects, EDI courses, or

even training fellowships to work as quasi-staff members. The cost to the Bank will be repaid [...] by the new dimension they will bring to Bank work, even as they are being trained, and as an investment in the quality of future projects.[4]

The Response of Senior Bank Management

Baum's response to my memo was faster and more far-reaching than I had expected. He circulated my memo to the Directors of all sector departments in CPS, and convened a meeting for discussing the issue. In fact, I shouldn't have been surprised, because his record on this issue was consistent: he had from the outset personally supported the hiring of the first full-time sociologist into the Central Projects Staff (CPS), of which he was the head.[5] He was also aware that Michael Cernea's department was very satisfied with his work, so my memo met a very receptive ear. He asked that I lead the meeting discussion with my memo's argument that employing a significant number of trained social specialists throughout the Bank would enhance project quality. Preparing for the meeting, each director had to focus—in some cases for the first time—on the role of the non-economic social sciences in the operations for which they had responsibility, and to consult with their staff on the use of professional social knowledge in their operations. And, of course, being familiar with the tight way Mr. Baum ran our vice presidency, the Directors knew that he would ask them to report on their follow-through.

The debate that followed was memorable. Fortunately, I have the written minutes of that January 9, 1979 meeting, written by my colleague Sushil Bhatnagar.[6] In what follows, I'm using these minutes extensively.

My argument began with an undisputable fact: the almost total absence, with one exception, of trained social specialists on Bank staff. Further, I also argued that when economists try to substitute and speak for sociological disciplines, it is not the same as having "real interaction of staff who are trained in different disciplines and are able to look at a given situation from different perspectives",[7] due to their different knowledge lenses. As a result, "sociological or technological issues too often surface

---

[4]Charles Weiss to Mr. Warren C. Baum (through Herman G. van der Tak). *Disciplinary Balance of Bank Staff*. Office Memorandum, January 3, 1979.

[5]The same perspective led Warren Baum to write, jointly with Stokes Tolbert, a comprehensive book on investing in development, which contained a strongly worded argument in favor of carrying out social assessments in all projects. (See Warren C. Baum and Stokes M. Tolbert, *Investing in Development* (Baltimore: Johns Hopkins Press, 1985.)

[6]Sushil K. Bhatnagar (Office of the VP Project Staff) to Department Directors and Projects Advisory Staff in Central Projects Staff. "*Disciplinary Balance of Bank Staff.*" Office Memorandum, January 9, 1979. Present in the meeting were: Messrs. Baum, van der Tak, Aklilu, Fuchs, Gordon, Jaycox, Kanagaratnam, Lejeune, Rovani, Sadove, Tolbert, Willoughby, Yudelman, Dosik, Hardy, Lee, Lethem, Morse, Raizen, Ray, Weiss, Bhatnagar. (3 pages.)

[7]Charles Weiss, in Sushil K. Bhatnagar, idem. page 1. (All further quotations in *italics* are from Sushil's Bathnagar's memorandum with minutes for the World Bank's files.)

late in the project cycle or are not seen at all, while policy papers and research proposals do not benefit from a truly multi-disciplinary review"; and I placed into discussion the proposal that the Bank recruit young sociologists or "technologically oriented generalists" just as it recruits young economists.

More than I expected, virtually all the directors of the Bank's central sectoral departments (just one exception) embraced my argument. Some indicated that they were incorporating at least some sociological insights into their work and took the opportunity to shine before Mr. Baum and their peers. Others defended themselves, invoking the limited manpower with which they had to accomplish their core tasks.

Montague Yudelman, the director of the Agriculture and Rural Development Department and a McNamara protégé, pointed out that his department was the only Department in CPS that had a professional sociologist as a full time staff member. He gave a pretty detailed and highly favorable description of Cernea's initiatives in his Department, and also reported that Cernea he "provides direct operational support to regional divisions for sociological issues in projects" The work of Michael Cernea, he said, "has raised staff consciousness regarding such issues as the 'culture of poverty,' compulsory resettlement, and the institutional premises to community cooperation" through a series of well-attended sociological seminars offered by invited scholars in anthropology and sociology on such subjects as irrigation, land settlement, livestock and pastoral populations, small size credits, agricultural research, etc.[8] He further reported that "Cernea also has developed a roster of consultant sociologists and anthropologists (available from him on request) and organized a handful of staff members who are trained in sociology—most of whom make little use of their training on the job (!)—into an informal 'sociological group' for the exchange of work-related experience."

Kim Jaycox, the director of the Urban Projects Department, who like Yudelman had been specially tasked by McNamara to develop an innovative approach to alleviating poverty, reported that local sociologists were being used effectively as consultants in the urban sector. Jaycox suggested that general anthropologists (as distinct from those defined mainly by their specific country knowledge) were suitable primarily for work such as development of guidelines and standards and for developing staff sensitivities to social and cultural problems. He proposed that the Bank develop "stables" of available anthropologist and sociologist consultants with experience in important areas of Bank work. Jaycox agreed that "a narrow disciplinary mix meant narrow project design and late recognition of externalities." Aklilu Lemma, the director of the Education Department, supported Yudelman and Jaycox and added that in his opinion, this last point was a major long-run problem of the Bank.

---

[8]Several of these commissioned papers, authored by outside social scientists and enriched after being discussed in open seminars with Bank staff, are included in the volume: *"Putting People First. Sociological Variables in Rural Development"*: (New York: Oxford University Press, 1985; 1991 2nd ed.)

Stokes Tolbert, the director for tourism projects, supported the memo's assertion that the Bank should have staff who were able to identify and define broad sociological issues and who could assess the qualifications and supervise the work of non-staff sociological consultants who were hired to work on the design and supervision of specific projects. Other directors agreed with the importance of sociological issues, but were more inclined to stress the importance of raising the consciousness of Bank staff through reviewing projects and holding seminars, rather than by hiring staff with specific training in sociology.

The main dissent from this viewpoint came from Chris Willoughby, the director of transportation, who said that he did not believe that inattention to sociology and anthropology was a serious problem for the Bank. He argued that the Bank already had many staff members with "broad training" and that the transportation staff under his supervision were well equipped to deal with the broader aspects of Bank-financed projects.

At the meeting's end, Baum summarized the discussion with firm conclusions: "The Bank needed more exposure to disciplines like sociology and technology (broadly construed) and . . . the demand for experts in these areas would increase as staff were more exposed to these perspectives and grew to understand their relevance to Bank work."

Copies of the minutes of the meeting were sent to all members of the Bank's top management, including Mr. McNamara's personal assistant, Caio Koch-Weser, and to all the Bank's Operational Vice Presidents: Messrs. Stern, Baum, Barletta, Benjenk, Chadenet, Chaufournier, W. Clark, Hopper, Husain, Wapenhans, Weiner, and Gabriel, as well as to the director of Bank Personnel Dept., Mr. Jennings, to William Clark, the Head of Public Relations, and to the official liaison with the Bank Executive Directors, Mr. Hattori. This was the routine pattern of distribution for the minutes of all meetings of CPS directors. Its importance in this instance lay in the fact that the policies decided in the meeting would lead to changes in recruitment policy, and that there were likely to be specific follow-up measures to assess both implementation and impacts.

Baum was clearly determined to push the Bank forward on this issue. After some time, CPS established a recruitment committee chaired by Michael Cernea and given the mandate to help the Personnel Department to recruit and hire social specialists from outside the Bank by interviewing the individuals identified and selected by the Personnel Department and assessing their professional quality and suitability for Bank work. That committee had the authority to endorse or reject these candidates on professional grounds.

The Road to Critical Mass

Warren Baum's support mattered much in the Bank of that time. He understood that the Bank needed to treat in a professional manner the social dimensions and determinants of development, and not only the economic and technical drivers of development. For this, he agreed that it was not enough to have a few heroic pioneers doing their best to spread the gospel of sociology and anthropology to a staff of thousands of seasoned economic and engineering professionals. Nor was it enough to sporadically use temporary consultants, nor to resort to economists ready to improvise and substitute for social science professionals, despite their lack of training in non-economic social sciences.

On the contrary, spreading ideas inside a large scale bureaucratic organization required an uphill struggle against the prevailing Bank economic culture in order to pursue a broader vision of *social* development, including but not limited to economic growth. It required the creation of an in-house "epistemic community" that spread the understanding of new concepts across the institution along pathways of communication not dictated by the formal organizational structure.[9] The new epistemic community attracted the attention of independent researchers who published studies that described it in the literature as a textbook example of the impact of informal networks in changing the intellectual culture of a large and well-established organization.[10] In time, the ideas and policies that they promoted also spread to other development assistance agencies and influenced their operations.

Almost immediately after this meeting, the Bank's readiness to recruiting such specialists as regular staff increased. The Bank had already identified a number of social specialists that could do good work, and had employed them as consultants. Among this ready pool of new recruits was, for instance, Maritta Koch-Weser, who since 1997 had been successfully and repeatedly employed for 3 years as a consultant; now, in 1980, she received an expedited offer to become a regular staff member. The quality and creativity of her work made her a leading anthropologist in the Bank, and she later rose to high managerial responsibilities. Another excellent former consultant, the cultural anthropologist Shelton (Sandy) Davis, was hired in 1980 as a regular staff; he was to become the in-house champion of attention to indigenous communities inhabiting lands in which the World Bank-financed development projects. As more anthropologists and sociologists became Bank staff, the reasons for recruiting similarly trained and talented professionals became more convincing to skeptics.

As is described in other chapters of this book, throughout the 1980s this group pushed up energetically, step by step, a number of important social policies, and thus prodded the Bank to broaden its development paradigm from purely "economic growth" or "economic development" to the concept, language, policies and practices of "social development." Due to the prominence of the Bank and its intellectual leadership among MDBs and other development aid agencies, this broader social development model spread, to the ultimate benefit of poor people in the developing countries. The prompt and energetic response of Warren Baum to the memo I had

---

[9]See Peter M. Haas, Epistemic communities and international policy coordination. *International Organization 46*(1), 1–35 (1992).

[10]See Kardam, Nuket. 1993. "Development Approaches and the Role of Policy Advocacy: The Case of the World Bank", *World Development* 21 (11): 1773–786.

written as a result of Michael Cernea's initiative had broken a bottleneck to the achievement of a critical mass of anthropologists and sociologists in the World Bank and in other development assistance institutions.

Charles Weiss has an AB in chemistry and physics, summa cum laude, and a PhD in chemical physics and biochemistry, both from Harvard University. He was appointed in 1971 as the Bank's first Science and Technology Advisor, and served in this capacity until 1985. From 1985 to 1997 he was a Principal of Global Technology Management, Inc., and taught at the Woodrow Wilson School of Princeton University, the School of Advanced International Studies of Johns Hopkins University, the University of Pennsylvania, and the Foreign Service Institute of the U.S. Department of State. Dr. Weiss became Distinguished Professor of Science, Technology and International Affairs (STIA) at the Walsh School of Foreign Service at Georgetown University in 1997, serving as the Director of STIA until 2006. On his retirement in 2014, the annual medal awarded to the outstanding STIA graduate was renamed in his honor. He now holds the title of Distinguished Professor Emeritus. Dr. Weiss was elected a Fellow of the American Association for the Advancement of Science (AAAS), and was also a Visiting Scholar with the Center for Science Diplomacy. Dr. Weiss has published several books, most recently: Structuring an Energy Technology Revolution (MIT Press, 2009), and Technological Innovation in Legacy Sectors (Oxford University Press, 2015), both with co-author William Bonvillian, and Science, Technology and the World We Want (Oxford University Press, 2021). Dr. Weiss has published articles and lectured on a broad range of topics, including innovation policy, scientific uncertainty, environmental policy, and science and technology in developing and emerging economies. He has lectured at numerous universities, including Harvard, the University of California (Berkeley), the Massachusetts Institute of Technology, Jawaharlal Nehru University (Delhi), Makerere University (Kampala, Uganda), the University of Sao Paulo and the Graduate Research Institute for Policy Studies (Tokyo).

Open Access This chapter is licensed under the terms of the Creative Commons Attribution 4.0 International License (http://creativecommons.org/licenses/by/4.0/), which permits use, sharing, adaptation, distribution and reproduction in any medium or format, as long as you give appropriate credit to the original author(s) and the source, provide a link to the Creative Commons license and indicate if changes were made.

The images or other third party material in this chapter are included in the chapter's Creative Commons license, unless indicated otherwise in a credit line to the material. If material is not included in the chapter's Creative Commons license and your intended use is not permitted by statutory regulation or exceeds the permitted use, you will need to obtain permission directly from the copyright holder.

Address to the World Bank Sociological Group

Huw Evans

Introduction

I feel myself to be an outsider amongst you: I am a macroeconomist by background, having worked in the UK Treasury for many years. Yet I have become convinced in my time at the World Bank of the importance of understanding the social context of the Bank's work, and the social impact of Bank lending, especially because of the UK ODA's experience in this field. As an Executive Director at the IMF too, I have gained important insights into how that institution uses its Board more effectively, with more cooperation, and much greater partnership between the Board and management.

Why Does the Bank Need Social Analysis?

Let me explain a little more about why the Bank needs social analysis. Firstly, I start from the position that the Bank's mandate is economic development: other social objectives as such are outsides its mandates. While most of our governments have signed up to a range of social objectives unilaterally or as part of international agreements, it is not the job of the Bank to help countries achieve all of them. It is the Bank's job to help poor people improve their standard of living, and more generally to promote economic development. Article IV, section 10 states that "only economic considerations shall be relevant to their [i.e. our] decisions". I am convinced that this apparently narrow focus is one of the reasons why the Bank has many successes.

Some of my colleagues who represent borrowing countries sometimes get concerned when we talk about social issues in the Board, because they fear that the Bank will try to impose social norms. The Bank must be interested in social relations insofar as they relate to economic development. A clear understanding on this will go a long way to reducing resistance in the Board to the examination of social issues. For example, this chair pressed for a long time to get agreement to a policy on gender, not as a goal in its own right, but because it is clear that the different roles of men and women affect the success of development assistance, and the different access to resources of men and women affects their access to development investments. Thus, putting more investment into education without addressing the barriers to women's participation would be economically, as well as socially, inefficient. Once the evidence for this was clearly presented to the Board, the policy received broad support. It would never have achieved this if we had based our arguments on women's rights alone, important as these are.

Increasingly, external criticism is focusing on social rather than environmental impacts; e.g. resettlement; indigenous groups; health user fees etc. This has already proved damaging to the Bank: e.g. Oxfam/Christian Aid etc. get a lot of publicity in the UK for campaigns criticizing the social impact of World Bank adjustment lending, not all of it valid. The Bank needs to learn from the past and develop social procedures now, to defend the Bank from vulnerability to criticism in this area. This will be good for the Bank's clients, in terms of better assistance, as well as good for the prospects of maintaining shareholder support for the Bank.

We need social analysis to understand economic processes, and the impact of economic change. This is partly an issue of project quality: the social dimension affects project outcomes. It can help identify whether and how a project can contribute to development; it can help set realistic objectives; it helps to identify appropriate activities to meet objectives. It is also partly a duty of care: the Bank must avoid unintended adverse social impact. Social analysis reduces the risk of encountering unforeseen adverse consequences, and of negative impact.

There are similar reasons for doing environmental analysis: both to improve project quality and sustainability, and to avoid adverse impacts. The Bank ignored both environmental and social impact for most of its history. As a result, it came under damaging criticism for adverse environmental impact. This undermined support for the Bank. It belatedly improved environmental procedures, but too late to avoid lasting damage to the Bank, as well as to some borrowers.

What Needs to be Done

The Bank has so far responded piecemeal, with separate Operational Directives on different social issues, e.g. resettlement, indigenous peoples, gender. This sometimes is burdensome on Task Managers, and confusing for the Board, management, staff and clients alike. For example, it is ridiculous to mandate social assessment in relation to biodiversity, but not elsewhere. We need to consolidate and encapsulate all social issues into a single Operational Directives and document for doing the social analysis we need. I would hope that a Bank Operational Directive would make social analysis a mandatory part of the project preparation and appraisal. Note that I include gender in this. I do not think it helpful to separate this out from other social relations. Much as we lobbied hard to get an OD on gender, I would gladly rescind it in exchange for an overall OD on social assessment.

In the Bank, we need a single central department, charged with developing the policy, monitoring its implementation, and promoting best practice. I commend the work of Gloria Davis, Michael Cernea and others for pioneering much of this in the Bank, but I have always been uncomfortable with having one Vice-President responsible for poverty, social policy, and gender, and another responsible for resettlement, indigenous peoples and so on. I suspect that this has contributed to the Bank's piecemeal approach. It certainly does nothing to help the Bank present a clear message on social issues.

But as in other disciplines, the bulk of the work needs to be done in the context of actual programmes and projects. That means that we need staff in the regions to provide social analysis for country programmes: planning the Country Assistance Strategy, undertaking ESW and policy dialogue, and designing and supervising operations.

In order to carry out this work, we will need more social analysis; something we have argued for in the Board for a long time, and in my role as a Personnel Committee member.

Too often, we have been dissatisfied with the management's response, which points to social analysts employed under various Trust Funds, including internal Trust Funds like the FIAHS fund. We have never been satisfied with this approach, even though we appreciate the specific contributions of these funds. Indeed, the UK has financed a Social Analyst slot until very recently, when Andrew Norton returned to ODA. But reliance on additional funds is a symptom that the activity is not yet regarded as a priority for regular budgetary resources. However we may get by in the meantime, we will not solve the skill-mix problem until we solve the budget problem: getting managers to allocate their budgets to hire social analysts as regular World Bank staff.

But let me sound a note of caution. If we take a historical perspective on the Bank, we can see that there have been successive phases of dominance by different disciplines. The IBRD was set up by bankers, who would review financial proposals. This quickly gave way to a Bank of engineers, who designed infrastructure projects, which are a lasting monument to their technical expertise. Eventually, the engineers gave way to economists, when it became clear that the client economies could not afford to maintain all this infrastructure. We still have now an economists' Bank. This is obvious from the relative numbers of economists versus other staff. This is emphasized by our central research department being called "Development Economics Vice Presidency," and our training institute as an "Economic Development Institute."

There may be some amongst you who look for the dawning of a new age, when the economists are dethroned by the social analysts. I do not expect this to happen, nor do I think it would be a good thing if it did happen. As I said at the beginning, the Bank is fundamentally about economic development. Economics will always be a core discipline at the Bank, though I think there are far too many macro-economists, when the business of the Bank is far more micro.

What is needed is not a change in the core discipline, but an end to hegemony by one discipline. We must avoid financially unsound loans, which do not build lasting infrastructure. It is what led to fine infrastructure, but which after being built could not be maintained. Equally, we must avoid economic reform programmes which are not socially sustainable, or projects, which hurt the poor they are trying to help. I fear that dominance by social analysts would lead to excellent participatory processes, but the activities might be economically and technically unsustainable, scarce resources might be wasted, and the debt might not get serviced. Instead, the Bank needs to become a truly multi-disciplinary organization.

Introducing social analysts into the Bank does not mean turning out the economists. It means finding a better balance between complementary skills. Let me say a little more about how this can be done.

How to Achieve This

In the Bank we see too much emphasis on preparing a blueprint, and then defending it against criticism, often even against the real-world critique that it is not working. The Board has become a kind of *viva* exam: at the end of the long months of writing the dissertation, the task manager defends it against a range of questions. If he acquits him or herself well, he or she sits back in satisfaction at a job well done. It can and should be a much more cooperative process, as I know from experience at the IMF Board. It is difficult to bring different disciplines into this way of working, since the project is framed within the context of the discipline from which the Task Manager comes. Too often, the economist is brought in to validate a design prepared by the engineer. Likewise, it would be a danger if the social analyst is brought in only to 'right a paragraph' on the project prepared only by the economist.

I have been glad to see efforts in many parts of the Bank to move away from this kind of project cycle. One element of this is the emphasis on participation: once we accept that we need the input of all stakeholders, we have made a huge leap in the direction of opening up the design and appraisal of the project. Stakeholders will raise social issues, whether we like it or not.

The second element is the process approach. Moving away from seeing a project as a blueprint helps open up the scope for responding to social realities.

The third element is multidisciplinarity. That means drawing together all the relevant professional perspectives and evaluation. If we can get social analysts 'onto the team', then they can play a constructive role, rather than being seen as another layer of criticism and review with which the task manager has to contend.

As a member of the Budget Committee, you would expect me to have given some thought to the cost of all this.

As I said earlier, this is a cost, which the Bank must accept on its regular budget, not palm off onto trust funds, whether internal or external. That is why we have not supported indefinite continuation of the FIAHS fund. However valuable the specific activities it has financed, it should be no more than a pump-priming exercise. Allowing it to become permanent will keep social analysis in the category of add-on, rather than internal core cost. The only way social analysis will get funded from the regular budget is if managers, as budget holders, see it as a priority for use of scarce resources.

The key to this is accountability. Jim Wolfensohn has rightly placed a lot of emphasis on this. So do I.

I fully support recent efforts to develop monitoring indicators of project performance. Task managers should be clearly accountable for the achievement of project objectives. The objectives should encompass social impact, which should be monitored during implementation and evaluated after project completion. Only when managers are held accountable for the development effectiveness and social impact of their projects will they take social analysis seriously. And that means investing resources in social analysis.

Role of the Board

I would like to hear from you how you think, as a Board member, I can help this process along, but let me offer a few initial thoughts.

We have seen increasing Board concern about social issues. With Jim Wolfensohn, we have a President who is strongly committed to social issues. The Task Force in which many of you are involved, provides an opportunity to present management and the Board with workable proposals. I'm sure that there is a lot of creative thinking going on at the moment as part of this process. Like Eveline Herfkens, I strongly advise you to explain to your management and to the Board why taking full account of social impact leads to better projects.

But again, let me inject a note of realism. What we are discussing is not all that novel, though it may be new to the Bank. Many donor agencies have incorporated social analysis into their work for many years. In the UK, ODA has had Social Development Advisers for nearly twenty years, and has had a separate Social Development Department and Chief Social Development Adviser for four years. Most importantly, it employs sufficient social analysts in its country departments to ensure that they are fully engaged in project teams and country strategy teams. I welcome the efforts that the Task Force is making to draw on this experience. So let us not go overboard in designing something new and untried. Let's simply aim, as a modest first step, to bring the Bank up to the industry standard.

Part of the reason I say this is that I am conscious that there is a lot of change going on in the Bank. Many staff, and some Executive Directors, may question whether this is an issue which we need to press ahead on now. We can convince them it is, if we propose something attainable. So we all have a role to play in persuading our colleagues that this is an issue which, like the environment, will not go away; that we ignore it at our peril; and that the result of neglect will be poo portfolio performance, and continued and justified external criticism.

Now, I will continue to play my part in the Board in emphasizing the importance of social issues, and holding management to account for the development effectiveness of the Bank's portfolio. But we all have a part to play in convincing managers of the contribution of social analysts to improving development effectiveness. It must not be seen as a special interest clamouring for attention. Instead, we must bring to managers' attention—whether from above or below—the contribution that social analysis can make to project quality, and to avoiding damaging impacts on the poor.

A final word. When people appear on talk-shows, they always have a book to promote. Some of you may have seen this already. It is a Guide to Social Analysis, prepared by ODA. To the professional social analysts amongst you, it may seem fairly basic. But its aim is to explain in practical ways how social analysis can contribute to project design and appraisal. It is required reading for all social analysts working on ODA projects. You may find it useful in your work, or may want to put it on the reading list of task managers you work with. There are order forms here, for anyone interested.

April 1996

Huw Evans trained as an economist and serving for many years with the UK Treasury, Huw Evans represented the United Kingdom on the World Bank Board between 1994–1997.

Open Access This chapter is licensed under the terms of the Creative Commons Attribution 4.0 International License (http://creativecommons.org/licenses/by/4.0/), which permits use, sharing, adaptation, distribution and reproduction in any medium or format, as long as you give appropriate credit to the original author(s) and the source, provide a link to the Creative Commons license and indicate if changes were made.

The images or other third party material in this chapter are included in the chapter's Creative Commons license, unless indicated otherwise in a credit line to the material. If material is not included in the chapter's Creative Commons license and your intended use is not permitted by statutory regulation or exceeds the permitted use, you will need to obtain permission directly from the copyright holder.

Working Together at the World Bank for Broadening the Development Paradigm

James Wolfensohn

I accepted with great pleasure the invitation to contribute to this volume intended to honor Michael Cernea, one of the most outstanding colleagues that I had the good fortune to work with during my years at the World Bank. Michael was the leader and spokesperson of the Bank's initially small but continually growing community of sociologists and anthropologists, a community that was on the front line of my efforts to broaden and strengthen the Bank's focus on effective poverty reduction.

After some personal recollections on how I encountered Michael Cernea and the social group, I will talk about some of the key ideas and principles regarding my work at the World Bank. For this part of this essay, I think that it would be best to not rephrase into the language of today what I said publicly then, because the original language conveys the political messaging I would use to convey strategy to staff.

My First Meeting with the Bank's Senior Sociologist

My first encounter with the Bank's senior sociologist was totally unplanned. It was as spontaneous as could be on both sides. Shortly after I started my work at the Bank, I was told that I had to attend an event which a card carrying anthropologist would describe as a modern tribal ritual. The "tribe," in this case, was the World Bank's staff, and that day's ceremony was a ritual meant to honor the "elders of the tribe," people who just passed the mark of having served 20 years on the Bank's staff. It sounded to me like a reward not only for performance but also... for endurance.

The ritual required the Bank's President to bestow on each of those survivors a huge and shiny SEIKO desk-clock, adorned with a small plaque engraved with two

---

J. Wolfensohn (✉)
Wolfensohn & Co, LLC, New York, NY, USA
e-mail: James@wolfensohn.com

names: one of the survivor, and the other—mine! I objected to having my name there since I was still in my early weeks at the Bank and was still just a new face to all of those veterans. But I was told that it was a long tradition, a custom that must be respected even by a new president. In essence, I thought to myself, I'm being politely let know that however highly placed on the World Bank's totem pole I am, traditional ways of the Bank are not going to be easily changed ... Well, this wasn't quite an auspicious beginning for my own plans to transform the World Bank. So, I didn't succeed in getting my name off that plaque. I submitted to the tribe's ritual, solemnly giving to each of these good, long-serving veterans a... Japanese desk clock.

Yet teasing apart, I must say that I was glad for the opportunity. I did want to know some of the Bank's veterans. In those days of my debut, I felt still like the Bank was the proverbial huge elephant, which one has to look at from all sides to get a grasp of its entirety.

Once the ceremony ended, there was a little treat and get-acquainted talk. Not much time passed, until a fellow button-holed me, and said, "Mr. President, I am glad to meet you for the first time personally. If you don't mind, I have a question to ask you." "Shoot," I replied, "what's your question?" "Well"—he said—"I have followed most of the speeches that you gave over the last few weeks while you were meeting with the Bank's departmental staff. In one of those speeches you used a concept that stood out for me, because it was quite new and unusual in our Bank vocabulary." "What was it?" I asked.

"Well, as a 'veteran,' he said, "I've been working in the Bank now through five presidents before you. I've listened to a lot of speeches, but none of them used one surprising, entirely non-economic concept that you spoke about." "Well, what was that term that shocked you?" "The term was '*social justice.*' You spoke about social justice as you talked about the Bank's mission of reducing poverty, promoting sustainability, advancing equity, and so forth. All of these other terms are part of our routine jargon. Your new idea made us sit up and listen. 'Social justice' is something all of us believe in but nobody has the courage to say, at least not in this institution. Why did you say that? And what do you mean by it?"

> Well, why are you surprised? Of course, we have to support and promote social justice. Frankly—I added—I wanted to use another word, one that comes from the Yiddish language. You probably don't know it. That word was Mitzvah—I couldn't find a perfect translation, but it means the obligation to do "good deeds". What I really wanted to convey was that part of the Bank's mission, in my view, is to work to make better for people, and to bring more good into our world that is so full of contrasts, poverty, inequality, squalor, famine, tragedy. So, this is what I meant. But now tell me, so who are you? What's your name? Why did you react to this particular term?
>
> I am Michael Cernea, a sociologist, the Bank's Senior Sociologist and Adviser for Social Policies and Sociology. And the term Social Justice is very much on my mind too, because the Bank's social policies are meant to repair situations where people are not treated well.
>
> Ah, you are a sociologist, Adviser for Social Policies? I am glad that you are here!
>
> "You know", I told him, "before coming to the Bank I was given a stack of briefing books almost five feet high. I was very conscientious and went through all of them. But never ever did I find in them anything saying that the Bank has a Senior Sociology Advisor

who deals with social policies. If this is your job, you've got to help me. Tell me a bit about what you do and what are our policies."

The fellow was very happy and started to talk, saying that the Bank has many social specialists, he wasn't the only one, that they are working both on projects and to apply and improve on the Bank's several social policies, and so on. What he was saying was interesting, but there were other people waiting around us that wanted also to talk with me. So, I told him, *"Michael, what you are telling me is highly interesting. But this reunion is hardly the place to discuss these issues. Would you please put all that you have to say into a note? Tell me how the social parts of development are being addressed in the Bank. Send your note to my chief of staff, Rachel Lomax. I'll read it and find a way to continue this discussion."*

A week later, my chief of staff handed me a long memo, "from Michael Cernea, the Social Policy Senior Advisor." The memo was indeed highly interesting and frank. It described what social specialists were doing in the Bank, but it was also very candid in describing difficulties, lack of sufficient resources, resistance, and a specific list of what he thought we had to do. It was more than what I had expected. I thought "I must follow this up."

Each Monday morning I had a routine meeting with all of the Bank's Vice Presidents in order to discuss our priorities for the week and to listen to what they had to bring up from each of their domains. I felt that this was a good place to bring up the social dimensions of our Bank Work. I took Cernea's memo, told the meeting how I got it, and then I read to them several paragraphs from that memo, with my comments. My message was that these were very important issues. I said that I was surprised that according to that memo, there were many things which needed to be done, but that there was not enough concern or resources. I asked the Vice Presidents to read Cernea's memo for themselves, and told them that I would personally address those issues.

As I learned subsequently, most VP's immediately called Cernea's office and requested copies of his memo to me.

I asked my Chief of Staff to invite Michael Cernea to a lunch with me, and to bring along three or four other social specialists working in each of the Bank's regional Vice Presidencies. The meeting took place the following week. It revealed a series of issues, which indeed were highly important for the Bank's work at large. Those issues and the lack of a sufficient commitment to address them resonated with me because many of them were along the lines which I myself thought the Bank should be following.

The meeting with Cernea took place two weeks later. I had invited Caio Koch-Weser, one of my two Managing Directors, and also the Bank's Vice President for personnel, because my thinking was that we needed to strengthen the group of the Bank's social specialists. Michael brought along five of his most prominent colleagues, sociologists and anthropologists, each working in a different operational region of the Bank. I think he brought along Gloria Davis, Maritta Koch-Weser, William Partridge, and Ayse Kudat. I asked Cernea and his colleagues to bring up the most important issues and to be specific in their proposals. I learned much about what the Bank was doing—and also what it was *not doing*—about the social and cultural aspects of development.

What they said was factual, important, and frustrating, in that so much of what they described was reflecting an institution hemmed in by its own rigidity. I assured them that I would follow up. I said that I will appoint a Bank Task Force and ask it to produce, in 60 days, a report about the Bank's work on the social issues of development and how they were treated by the Bank. On my side, I promised them that if their report would be constructive and with good proposals, I would take it to the Bank's Board and get the Board to intensify support for doing what was needed on the social side of our development tasks.

At Caio Koch-Weser's suggestion, we decided to also ask one of the Bank's VP's, Javid Burki, to be co-chairman of the task force together with Michael Cernea. We thought it was useful to have a joint task force of social specialists and economists. The report was ready in about 3 months. It was titled *Social Development Work in the World Bank*. I brought it to the Board, being very candid about my own opinions regarding the need to strengthen the Bank's social work, and I asked the Board to also be constructive in their proposals.

We had a good debate. The Board meeting was indeed supportive, and we decided to allocate a special budget for a series of measures for strengthening and enlarging the Bank's community of social specialists so that we could put the best proposals into action. I successfully convinced the Board to create what we called a "strategic compact," namely, to allocate $12 million from Bank resources to strengthen the Bank's group of staff professionally trained to deal with social development. This financial input had very positive effects. We hired a new cohort of social specialists who were distributed within the Bank's regional Vice Presidencies. Their role was to help the Bank's technical staff better identify, at the level of many individual projects, what could be done to increase the social impact of a good number of projects.

We also took steps to support and improve our professional expertise through the creation of sectoral "professional networks" among our staff. Further, I have given personal strong support to the creation of a "Social Development Network". Not everybody in the Bank's management supported the creation of this 'sectoral network.' One of the most senior Bank Vice-Presidents opposed its establishment. I had to overrule him and the Social Development Network was created. Creating this network was intended to give the social community a bigger organizational voice, making the community of socially aware staff stronger and larger, and able to give increased support to the other sectoral networks.

A few years later the Bank's Operation Evaluation Department evaluated the impact of that strong financial support. Their review validated the effort and went even further, saying that the Bank still needed to improve its attention to the social dimensions of development projects.[1]

Discovering "Social Assessments"

Another significant episode that I vividly recall from my early weeks as World Bank President is the first meeting that I chaired of the World Bank Board of Executive Directors. By coincidence, that meeting also had a significant "social moment." That day's agenda included the approval by the Board of an infrastructure project in a "transition economy"—the Azerbaijan Republic—for improving and rehabilitating the water supply system in the capital of the country, Baku.

I listened with great interest to the comments of the Board members intended to improve the quality and access of water necessary for the population of Baku. In preparing myself for this first meeting, I had carefully read two documents on this project that were distributed in advance to every Board member. The main document was the staff's appraisal report containing the full description of the project's content, implementation approach, and financial arrangements. The second document was titled "*Social Assessment of the Azerbaijan Baku Project*".[2]

That social assessment was authored by a Bank Sociologist, Dr. Ayse Kudat, who wrote it together with a local Azerbaijani social researcher. The document gave me convincing information about Baku's population and its difficulties in the period following the disintegration of the former Soviet Union. It described the water supply crisis that Baku was going through at that time, and it gave detailed information about the population of Baku, its characteristics and needs, and the ways in which the population would benefit from the improvements and rehabilitation of its water supply.

During the Board meeting, while I was listening to the questions and comments made by various executive directors, I noticed that all of the questions and comments referred to the Appraisal Report. None of them referred to the social assessment,

---

[1] About the impact of that social development report of 1996 on the overall work of the Bank. See also the publication: Gloria Davis. Social Development Network in the World Bank, 1973–2002. Paper No. 56, March, 2004.

[2] The social assessment to which Mr. Jim Wolfensohn refers had been authored by a World Bank Sociologist, Ayse Kudat, and a local Azerbaijani social researcher, Ahmed Musayev. It was subsequently published in a special volume by the Bank as a part of a set of nine social assessment studies devoted to issues sustainable development. The book's title is *Social Assessments for Better Development: Case Studies in Russia and Central Asia*. Edited by Ayse Kudat and Michael M. Cernea. (World Bank 1997). (Note by the present volume's editors). (Regarding this set of Social Assessment, see further in this volume the paper by Jonathan Brown, who comments from the perspective of a World Bank Technical Division Chief about the usefulness of social assessment for the Bank's work for in Russia and other central Asian countries formerly part of the Soviet Union).

which had also been distributed to every member as an independent annex to the Appraisal Report.

When the Board meeting ended and my turn came to sum up the conclusions in the Board's discussion and decision, I recognized that, in fact, I was still a novice in the ways in which Bank projects were being prepared, described, justified, and presented to the Board. In my conclusions, I supported Bank financing for the project. But I also felt that I needed to be frank and make one critical comment about the unfolding of the Board's discussions. That comment was to express my own reaction to the two documents. Of course, I had read the Appraisal Report, assured myself that it was correct in its economics, and paid tribute to the staff who prepared the project. However, I also said that during my preparing for this first Board meeting, the document which turned out to be of most interest to me personally, was not the Appraisal Report itself, but rather its annex: the "Social Assessment," because it gave me more of an understanding of what was going on for the people of Baku. It was that social assessment that convinced me fully that the project is not only necessary, but a clear priority for the population, and so the Bank was certainly taking the right step in offering financing for this project. I commented most appreciatively on the social assessment, congratulated its authors, and I also said that I would like to see more such social analysis in every future project addressing similar issues. I also took the opportunity to announce to the Executive Director and everyone else present that I was determined to give my strongest support to the Bank's concern with the social and environmental dimensions of each project.

Fighting Corruption

Within days of my arrival to the Bank I was told by the general counsel, in great secrecy, "Don't mention the 'C' word." So, I asked, "What exactly *IS* the 'C' word?" He replied, "Corruption."

That statement surprised me to no end. I was coming from the private sector. I knew well from that experience not only how rotten corruption was, but even more how its rottenness could kill many worthy and healthy activities. Nor could we ignore the resentment and anger that corruption produces. Wasn't the Bank listening to the people?

I did not listen to the Bank's general counsel. I had no intention of not raising publicly the issue of corruption. One of my earliest public statements as President of the World Bank became known as my *"cancer of corruption"* speech, given at the annual meetings of the World Bank and the IMF:

> Let's not mince words: we need to deal with the cancer of corruption. In country after country, it is the people who are demanding action on this issue. They know that corruption diverts resources from the poor to the rich, increases the cost of running businesses, distorts public expenditures, and deters foreign investors. They also know that it erodes the constituency for aid programs and humanitarian relief. And we all know that it is a major barrier to

sound and equitable development. Corruption is a problem that all countries have to confront. Solutions, however, can only be home-grown. National leaders need to take a stand. Civil society plays a key role as well. Working with our partners, the Bank Group will help any of our member countries to implement national programs that discourage corrupt practices. And we will support international efforts to fight corruption and to establish voluntary standards of behavior for corporations and investors in the industrial world (JW original quote).

One of the Bank's accomplishments for which I am very proud is that during my tenure at the institution's helm, the Bank went on to support more than 600 anticorruption programs and governance initiatives developed by its member countries.

The Centrality of People

A high point during my work at the Bank was that I had so many opportunities to visit developing countries and meet poor people whom the Bank was aiming to assess and free out of poverty.

In my first 16 months on the job, I visited over 40 countries. Elaine, always a sensitive and wonderful advisor, joined me in most of these visits. We spent long evenings exchanging impressions and thoughts on what we had seen and heard during those days. We met with government leaders and with business and nongovernmental organizations. But it was our conversations with the ordinary people, the poor and the disadvantaged, that made the biggest impression on us. I have learned that they do not want charity; they want opportunity. They did not want to be lectured to; they wanted much more to be listened to. Like all of us, they want a better life for themselves and for their children. What I have seen in country after country is that, when they are given a reasonable chance, the results are truly remarkable.

My interest in the people explains another key idea that led to many strong statements I made inside the Bank and repeated again and again to others, which was (and I am going to use again citations from my prior statements):

> It has been my strong belief that we will not make development sustainable and inclusive unless we put people at the center of the development process. This means a much greater focus on country ownership and participation, a better appreciation of local conditions, and more attention to the role of culture (pp. 122–123, from JW Printed Papers).

> Economic growth is essential, but not sufficient to ensure the reduction of poverty. We have learned that we must put poverty front and center. We have learned that we must take the social and structural hand in hand with the macroeconomic and the financial. We have learned that, for development to be real and effective, we need local ownership and local participation. Development cannot be done only by investment in infrastructure planned by big engineering companies or Western capital (pp. 158–159, from JW Printed Papers).

The Bank Needs a New Development Paradigm

What I learned from these encounters with many different people at the grassroots translated soon into an overall idea that the Bank should decisively broaden its development paradigm. The thinking which was prevailing when the World Bank was initially established, defined the central objective of the Bank to be "economic growth." However, as was famously said, *"people do not eat GDP."* The poorest people do not immediately or directly benefit from economic growth, and the simple and passive "trickle down" idea that had been advertised as the solution to poverty seemed less and less convincing.

My intensive meetings with people and activists in so many countries led me to the idea that the Bank needs to broaden its development paradigm from "economic growth" into a model which included much more the kind of things which people need and aspire to for their immediate livelihood needs. This is what made me decide to use my Second Annual Address to the Board of Governors as a forum for advocacy for enlarging the Bank's framework.

In that 1996 Address, I began by outlining the progress achieved in the past year on our six main priorities: IDA replenishment, debt relief, partnerships, the private sector, post-conflict reconstruction, and building a results culture at the Bank itself. But in addition, and no less importantly, I explained my thinking on moving the World Bank to re-thinking its approach to poverty reduction, to move from "growth with redistribution" to a more complex model that incorporates governance, social and sustainability matters in its analysis and operations:

> Essential for our strategy is the need for a broader, more integrated approach to development—a new paradigm, if you will. Poverty reduction remains at the heart of everything we do. But the magnitude and complexity of the task are daunting. Reducing poverty clearly involves the interplay of a number of issues: macroeconomic policy, private sector development, environmental sustainability, and investments in human capital, especially girls' education and early childhood development...Without the social underpinnings, it is difficult for economic development to succeed—and virtually impossible for it to be sustained.
>
> The lesson is clear: for economic advance, you need social advance—and without social development, economic development cannot take root. By designing more participatory country strategies and programs—reflecting discussions not only with governments but also with community groups, NGOS, and private businesses.

Reducing poverty cannot be done by economic growth alone; it requires broader-based social development. Quite apart from macroeconomic and financial policy, a functioning legal system and a functioning justice system that works are poverty projects, as are good governance and fighting corruption. We have just seen in Indonesia, the Republic of Korea, and Thailand that those hit hardest by an economic crisis are the poor. The poor benefit from proper financial supervision and control, an independent central bank, well-functioning capital markets, and social safety nets. Can one distinguish building roads, or a power grid, or a water supply system, or a judicial system, or good governance from poverty reduction? These are the questions which evaluators need to address. (JW).

Development is not just about technocratic fixes. Development is about getting the macroeconomics right, yes, but it is also about building the roads, empowering the people, writing the laws, recognizing the women, eliminating the corruption, educating the girls, building the banking systems, protecting the environment, and inoculating the children. Development is about putting all the component parts in place, together and in harmony (JW).

I think I am going to finish here. After all, this entire volume is dedicated to the effort of the Bank's community of social specialists to broaden the World Bank's paradigm. Probably the most adequate end to this essay could be to recall the brief speech that I gave at Michael's celebration when he retired from the Bank. Fortunately, I don't need to recall the speech word by word, because it was preserved in a small Bank publication, that three of Michael's closest collaborators—Gloria Davis, Andrew Steer, and Warren van Wicklin—compiled out of written tributes and congratulatory letters and messages, and the Bank printed as an elegant publication, titled: *Michael Makes His Mark: The Life and Work of a Change Agent at the World Bank*:

> Well, Michael, if you are the first and oldest sociologist in the Bank, I am the newest. But one of the advantages of being a president is that from my office you can more easily deal with the sort of problems that you had. And so it is that since I've been here, without really knowing a thing about the theoretical background of a sociologist, or having a fraction of the knowledge that you or anybody in the room has, I started with an idea that I regard as being really quite obvious: that we are here because of people. And we are here because we care about social justice. And we are here because the success of the development projects that we do must be measured in terms of their social impact.
>
> You have done a great job for this institution, trying to keep our staff focused on critical social issues. This is allowing me to now point to many of the achievements of the Bank in terms of our own history, in terms of our own perceptions of the importance of people and the importance of the social aspects of the work that we are doing for development.
>
> I came from the middle of an argument about Bosnia to join you here, simply because I wanted to meet a few people who make sense, and who care about the sort of things that have kept me going. So I have come really to say to you and Ruth—thank you for what you have done. And to say, on behalf of the non-sociologists in the Bank, that the World Bank is a much better place because you have been here.
>
> James Wolfensohn (Reproduced from the publication, "Michael Made His Mark: The Life and Work of a Change Agent at the World Bank" Edited by Gloria Davis, Andrew Steer, Warren van Wicklin. 1998. World Bank, Social Development, Washington D.C.

James D. Wolfensohn was President of the World Bank Group between June 1, 1995 and May 31, 2005. Universally considered one of the Bank's most influential and effective presidents, Mr. Wolfensohn is best known for defining the Bank's mission to be one of fighting global poverty and helping the world's poor forge better lives. Under his leadership, the World Bank broke new ground in the global development community, including landmark initiatives to combat corruption, advance debt relief, preserve the environment, and give attention to the role of women in development.

Open Access This chapter is licensed under the terms of the Creative Commons Attribution 4.0 International License (http://creativecommons.org/licenses/by/4.0/), which permits use, sharing, adaptation, distribution and reproduction in any medium or format, as long as you give appropriate credit to the original author(s) and the source, provide a link to the Creative Commons license and indicate if changes were made.

The images or other third party material in this chapter are included in the chapter's Creative Commons license, unless indicated otherwise in a credit line to the material. If material is not included in the chapter's Creative Commons license and your intended use is not permitted by statutory regulation or exceeds the permitted use, you will need to obtain permission directly from the copyright holder.

Social Analysis in the World Bank

Huw Evans, Eveline Herfkens, Ruth Jacoby, and Jan Piercy

1. The World Bank's mission has important environmental and social implications. These issues are of acute concern to our shareholders, as well as to civil society in both developed and developing countries. We believe that the World Bank now has moved significantly towards procedures and expertise to address environmental dimensions of its work. However, we are very concerned at the slow progress in establishing equivalent strengths in social analysis, which is essential to the Bank's objective of reducing poverty in an equitable and cost-effective manner.
2. Social issues have recently achieved a more prominent place on the international development cooperation agenda. We welcome the World Bank's renewed commitment to social development, including the Bank's active participation in the Social Summit (Copenhagen) and Women's Summit (Beijing). We are very appreciative of the President's own commitment to social issues, which he stated so clearly in his speech to the Annual Meetings, and in the recent Board discussion of evaluation results.
3. We acknowledge that much has been done in recent years to address specific social issues, such as resettlement, indigenous peoples, participation. However, this has been piecemeal. The Bank does not systematically ask the relevant questions on the social impact of its work, nor does it allocate adequate budget resources or deploy enough staff with the right skills. As a result, the Bank is facing increasing criticism for the adverse social impacts of its work, which it is ill-prepared to address.
4. With your new responsibilities for operations, we look to you for action on this important issue. Specifically, we recommend that you:

E. Herfkens · R. Jacoby · J. Piercy
Retired, The World Bank, NW Washington, DC, USA

(a) Issue an Operational Policy and Bank Procedure instructing the conduct of Social Assessments where appropriate for all operations (investment and adjustment): we note that OP/BP 10.04 (issued in April 1994) indicates that an OP/BP 10.06 on Sociological Criteria in investment operations is due to be issued, but over a year and a half later, this still has not occurred;
(b) Consider consolidating the Bank's social analysis expertise in a single focal point instead of spreading it between two central vice-presidencies;
(c) Meet the commitment to expand the social sector skill base, by establishing a cadre of social scientists in each region to carry out social analysis in country activities.

5. We also hope that you will promote more systematic social analysis in Economic and Sector Work.

Huw Evans trained as an economist and served for many years with the UK Treasury. He represented the United Kingdom on the World Bank Board between 1994–1997.

Eveline Herfkens. Prior to representing the Netherlands group on the World Bank Board between 1990–1996, Eveline Herfkens had served as a member of the House of Commons of the Dutch Parliament from 1981–1990.

Ruth Jacoby joined the World Bank Board in 1994 and served as the Chair of the Committee on Development Effectiveness (CODE).

Jan Piercy was appointed to the World Bank Board by US President Clinton in 1994. Prior to joining the World Bank, she had been Senior Vice President of Shorebank Corporation in Chicago, a bank holding company designed to promote economic development in disinvested urban and rural areas.

Open Access This chapter is licensed under the terms of the Creative Commons Attribution 4.0 International License (http://creativecommons.org/licenses/by/4.0/), which permits use, sharing, adaptation, distribution and reproduction in any medium or format, as long as you give appropriate credit to the original author(s) and the source, provide a link to the Creative Commons license and indicate if changes were made.

The images or other third party material in this chapter are included in the chapter's Creative Commons license, unless indicated otherwise in a credit line to the material. If material is not included in the chapter's Creative Commons license and your intended use is not permitted by statutory regulation or exceeds the permitted use, you will need to obtain permission directly from the copyright holder.

Social Sciences at the World Bank and the Broadening of the Development Paradigm

An Essay in Honor of Michael Cernea

Ismail Serageldin

I joined the World Bank in 1972 as a 'Young Professional', recruited right after my graduate studies at Harvard. Over the years the Bank entrusted me with diverse jobs and responsibilities, mostly in the Middle East and Africa regions, regarded as the most difficult. This broad spectrum of assignments exposed me to many types of the Bank's activities, each one a school for understanding complexity and a place of experiential enrichment.

The World Bank's First Vice-Presidency for Environmental and Social Matters

However, as I'm now summoning my recollections, I have no hesitation to state that the most challenging and gratifying assignment I received during these years was when the then President of the World Bank, Mr. Lewis Preston, gave me the task to organize a new Vice Presidency—the Bank's first Vice Presidency for Environmentally Sustainable Development (ESD), My new task was to participate in implementing the designed expansion of the institutional architecture of the World Bank by building and inserting a new Vice Presidency—new both by content and by its functions—inside and outside the Bank, into the fabric of our daily work.

This happened in October 1992. We spent the next 2 months selecting and redeploying staff. The ESD Vice Presidency started its operations on Jan. 1st 1993. This assignment was at the moving frontiers of development goals and knowledge. Consistent with its Bretton Woods charter, the World Bank had been known as a giant economic and financial agency, supporting development projects.

I. Serageldin (✉)
Library of Alexandria, Shatby, Alexandria, Egypt
e-mail: is@bibalex.org

But the Bank's reorientation in the mid-1970s toward poverty reduction, revealed for all of us new and complex social realities and institutional requirements, which called for fundamental new policies and new knowledge.

During the 1980s, the Bank did make major steps toward a new development paradigm by adopting several original—indeed, pioneering at the international level—social and environmental policies and by introducing significant new practices, to which I'll refer in much detail further

Step by step, these pioneering new policies had incrementally broadened the Bank's conceptual and action paradigm. There were also initiatives taken by individual managers, of which I was one: a significant organizational innovation, for instance, was my decision to create in the Africa Region a distinct unit devoted to the "Social Dimensions of Adjustment"; another example was the international conference I initiated on "The Cultural Dimensions of Development". I was not the only manager to take such steps. But of course this was not enough to change the dominant paradigm in the Bank. Indeed, the Bank's internal organizational structure hadn't been simultaneously re-adjusted to its evolving goals and to its advances towards a new social development paradigm.

The pioneering work done by Michael Cernea in formulating a totally new Bank policy to openly confront the pathologies of forced expropriation and displacement, was a great service he did to the Bank itself, as well: he positioned the World Bank, in this respect, ahead of the entire international aid community. Remarkably, the Bank was equipped with that essential social-cum-environmental policy in 1980. That was fully 10 years before the Rio Earth Summit, and 15 years before the 1995 Social Development Summit in Copenhagen. That was a decisive reversal of the dysfunctional previous treatment of an entire category of social processes, but not yet a broad reorientation of the Bank's dominant development paradigm. That would come only by the reorganization launched by the Bank just after the time of the Bruntland Report and the Rio Earth Summit.

Indeed, shortly after Michael's success in writing and introducing the Bank's first social policy on resettlement, the Bank's social staff recommended and obtained the adoption in 1982 of the first Bank policy on Indigenous Populations adversely affected by development projects (Shelton Davis, Maritta Koch-Weser, and Michael Cernea). Further, after 2–3 more years of 'internal lobbying', Cernea also succeeded in 1984 in convincing the Bank's leadership to improve the operational policy and methods of project preparation and appraisal by introducing for the first time sociological analysis as mandatory for all the Bank's forthcoming projects, not only for certain categories of projects. The generalization of social analysis was achieved through a basic policy document (OMS 2.20 for Project Appraisal-1984) elaborated jointly by the Bank's lead sociologist working hand-in-hand with three other very senior Bank policy staff: an economist, a financial analyst, and an institutional specialist, to integrate all four key analyses used by the Bank for approving its investments.

The decisive events of the 1980s in broadening the Bank's development paradigm turned out to be those associated with the Sardar-Sarovar Dam project that was being financed by the Bank in India. Known as the Narmada project, it was severely criticized for its impact on the poor displaced by the project. Without discussing here India's primary responsibility, the shortcomings in the Bank's work were due not to a policy blunder, but to a deep internal organizational weakness. Indeed, policy-wise the Bank had a correct and robust policy framework. Michael Cernea was the first inside the Bank who sounded the alarm in 1982, during Narmada's project appraisal. He succeeded in postponing approval by the Bank's Loan Committee for one full year, to allow India the time to prepare a "rolling resettlement plan", since none had been prepared until then. But it was the Bank's lack of a central structure capable to ensure operations' consistency with policy that was the Bank's disabling inner organizational gap (see Robert Wade's chapter, this volume, for a documented description of how the Bank's regional operational Irrigation Division chief deliberately resisted and circumvented the Bank's policy, ultimately pushing the Bank into the Narmada fiasco). Wade's retroactive analysis depicts amazingly well how the Narmada case was not a case of absent policy, but a failure of the Bank's organizational structure to achieve consistency of some Bank staff's behavior and their adherence to policies that were already on the Bank's books. The Environment and Social Development (ESD) Vice-presidency was Lewis Preston's correct solution to filling the Bank's organizational gaps, to avoid actions inconsistent with Bank policies, and to promote best practices among the Bank staff.

My new task became to create a new component inside the Bank's institutional architecture, organically inserting a new Vice Presidency – the ESD, new both by substantive content, and new by its functions in the Bank's internal processes and in its external attributions. In addition, the ESD Vice-presidency included two other central departments: The Infrastructure Department and the Agriculture and Rural Development Department, together with the task of leading, on behalf of the Bank, the CGIAR research consortium.

Working with the World Bank's Professional Sociologists and Anthropologists

The ESD's creation in 1992 became possible also because the Bank already "possessed" an intellectually strong body of professional sociologists and anthropologists whose driving force and leader for over a decade was Michael Cernea (see Leif Christoffersen's essay, this volume, on Cernea's recruitment history). He indeed became sociology's most successful and creative 'Ambassador' for the Bank, and probably for international development aid agencies, beyond what anybody could have anticipated at his recruitment.

Indeed, the Bank was still slow and resistant to the new body of knowledge that Michael Cernea was showing and underlining. It took no less than 3–4 more years for the Bank to hire just only one rural sociologist as "young professional", Jacomina de Regt, and two other anthropologists, Maritta Koch-Weser and Gloria Davis, both outstanding, who were to also have brilliant professional careers at the Bank. Cernea was tenaciously fighting that initial snail-pace growth and kept advocating intensely for creating a 'critical mass' of professional social specialists and for placing them not only in agricultural divisions but in all of the Bank's sectors. He reached up to Bank senior managers and leading economists, like Warren Baum, the Bank's Vice President of the Central Policy Staff (CPS), Herman van der Tak, the CPS principal economist, Charles Weiss, the Bank's Senior Adviser for Science, and Montague Yudelman, Michael's Department Director, who after becoming familiar with his work became strongly supportive of Michael's initiatives.

Finally, a turning point in the Bank's hiring of social specialists occurred after Warren Baum convened in 1980 a key meeting of all OPS Program Directors, which was also an outcome of Michael's lobbying and networking (on this non-routine meeting, see Charles Weiss's essay, this volume, on how "a critical mass of social specialists" was created in the Bank.).

The 1980s decade indeed registered an accelerated and massive hiring of professional social specialists, and also a diversification of their work on the social variables of new sectors, beyond agriculture. They introduced changes into the Bank's project designs, in analytical appraisal methodology, and in implementation practices. When the ESD Vice-presidency was created in 1992 it inherited for its social work the precious "asset" of a tested community of social specialists that during the prior 12–14 years had built a substantial foundation of social policies (of which I'll soon talk in detail). Relying upon and enabling further this already existing in-house community of development sociologists and anthropologists, the new Vice Presidency was able to build, expand, and consolidate further.

Building the Case for Using Social Science and for Converting Knowledge into Policies

Further in this essay I will outline my perspective on the essential contributions of this community of social experts to the Bank's work, both before the existence of the ESD Vice-presidency, and thereafter, particularly contributions to the Bank's mission to reduce poverty and to counteracting development's risks and pathologies.

My own strong concern for social issues, as well as my collaboration and friendship with Michael Cernea, extend over a long professional timeline. We met at the World Bank decades ago and engaged in some common activities many years before ESD existed. It appeared that we both thought that the economic model being used by our institution was too narrow to deal with much of the broad set of essential variables of development, made even more complex by the very goal of reducing the dismal poverty that was devastating the developing world. Broadening the Bank's guiding paradigm required that the Non-Economic Social Sciences (NESS) play a much bigger role than they had in the Bank's structure and treatment of development issues. In the new ESD Vice Presidency, I had the pleasure to work directly with Michael Cernea, to appreciate him as a scholar, a professional and a colleague, and above all, as a human being. We remained friends after his retirement and after I left the World Bank in 2000 to become Egypt's Founding Director of the Bibliotheca Alexandrina (BA), which seeks, in the third millennium, to recapture the spirit of the Ancient Library of Alexandria. For 8 years Michael Cernea has been a member of the Board of Trustees of the Bibliotheca Alexandrina, and one of its very active instigators of social science conferences at the BA too. At the time of this writing, Michael remains a very active member in the Committee of Advisors to the Library's Director. Our close friendship and collaboration continues to this day.

In our years at the Word Bank, we found ourselves fighting on the same side of many issues. When I became the de jure patron of the Non-Economic Social Sciences (NESS) in the institution, Michael was the leader of the growing Bank community of social specialists. From a population of one (himself) in 1974, when he was brought into the Bank, the number of professional social specialists grew to some 160 staff in the mid-1990s. This was, as he rightly pointed out, the largest group of non-economist social scientists working together on development under the same institutional roof anywhere in the world. Furthermore, their work allowed them to be constantly in the field, gaining experiences that few of their colleagues based in academic establishments could match.

Michael's Challenging Theoretical Argument

After his first years in the Bank, during which he had understood *what* the Bank does, and *how* it does it, Michael had the intellectual courage to formulate a challenge to what he had observed. That was not just a challenge on the nuts-and-bolts of putting one or another project together, but rather a theoretical challenge, a paradigm-level challenge, that was bold and surprising for a newcomer to make. He challenged the institution's one-sidedness in using the knowledge available from only the economic sciences. More explicitly, he critiqued the Bank for *not* taking into its mainstream thinking and practices the existing storehouse of knowledge offered by such social sciences as anthropology, sociology, social psychology, which are studying how the people whom the Bank defines as its "target population" live, act, think, interact, organize themselves for mutual help, for collective actions, and aspire to bettering their lives. He contended that not only actionable social knowledge was being omitted, and in this way, key dimensions of reality were being overlooked in the Bank's policies and projects, to the detriment of the Bank's clients and self-defined goals.

This was not a lightweight challenge. Michael had been brought into the Bank's house with a practical, yet narrow mandate: to help the work carried out on the experimental new type of integrated "rural development" projects with which the Bank was aiming to reach the rural poor. His initial given assignment was work on project after project, piece meal. He did this job well, but also did more: as he understood gradually better the World Bank, he was not content with just challenging one or another project or component. Michael challenged the institution's overall philosophy as one-sided and incomplete, and its methodology as obsolete, by not embracing and renewing its approaches in light of existent social knowledge germane to the Bank's development daily work.

Cernea constructed his challenge thoughtfully and systematically. Over a period of a few years, he prepared a full book, coherently argued, in which he not only raised fundamental questions but also constructively articulated feasible alternatives to the Bank's ongoing routines and conventional wisdom. He involved in that book other well-reputed scholars too, and titled his book unusually, as a manifesto: Putting People First (Cernea 1985).

The basic tenet of the book was that *"People are—and should be—the starting point, the center, and the end goal of each development effort."* And the book's subtitle explained conceptually what he meant, what the book was all about: *'The Sociological Variables of Development Projects.'* Making good on the book's title and subtitle, he articulated clearly his theoretical platform in the first chapter of that seminal book, unambiguously titled: *'Using Social Science Knowledge for Development Projects and Policies.'*

In the Bank's intellectual climate at that time, his whole idea-set was daring. He questioned the dominant position of economics in the Bank's thinking to the detriment of other forms of knowledge and expertise. He pleaded for the purposive use of non-economic social science knowledge for conceiving, inducing, planning, and managing development; and he didn't shy away from bringing up again and again ethics, explicitly invoking the Biblical commandment: "do not do unto others, what you don't want to be done to you". He also felt comfortable in discussing theory, and he launched his key challenge to the Bank starkly. Literally, the opening first sentences of his book's first chapter declared, without mincing words:

> Several scientific disciplines, particularly economics, preside over the processes of planned development. But...sociology and social anthropology have not been called on by the Bank to serve extensively. Yet planning is a knowledge-based exercise. But the storehouse of knowledge and knowledge-generating methods amassed within the social sciences has been largely overlooked by the World Bank for several decades.

Cernea's critique of the dismissal of social science knowledge (except economics) produced by other social sciences germane to development work, continued unsparingly. In his constructive critique, he reminded the World Bank and all his book's readership, (which soon became international) of an unpleasant fact, namely the reasons for failure of many development projects. The premise of his reformist advocacy was a fact of elephantine size. The fact that a good number of projects registered failure was, obviously, not a novelty. But he pointed to a category of causes that had not been considered until then, declaring clearly that:

> Repeated failures have plagued many development programs that were—and largely because they were—sociologically ill-informed and ill-conceived.

Being also a realist, Michael also conceded upfront that recognizing such a knowledge deficit, and overcoming it, will be "uncomfortable for development agencies" and would entail difficult intellectual clashes. Yet he insisted that, nonetheless, "addressing the social and cultural variables of projects" was indispensable, and will remain indispensable, for development effectiveness.

Michael didn't want his call for "*Putting People First*" to be only his personal argument. He invited a number of distinguished anthropologists and sociologists, the vast majority of whom had never worked before with the Bank, to produce a collectively articulated, mutually complementary, and factually documented argument. Moreover, he first invited each scholar-coauthor to the Bank to test their chapter with the Bank's practitioners by presenting their papers and reasoning in lectures, seminars and open discussions with the Bank's technical and economic staff. That strengthened each paper, which only became a chapter in the integrated book after going through an open debate inside the Bank. Furthermore, Cernea asked this roster of eminent scholars in social sciences to articulate what *Putting People First* means for project patterns in each one of some ten major economic development sectors or sub-sectors.

The book immediately made waves internationally. Such advocacy was unexpected from the World Bank and the book became an instant success for the Bank itself, not just for Michael. Book reviews were published in both developing and developed countries. The volume went into multiple print-runs. The then Director of the Bank's Publication Department invited Michael to become a member in the Department's manuscript review committee, to promote other comparable publications. Answering demand, a 2nd, enlarged edition of PPF, was printed. The book began to be translated and reached international audiences in five languages, including in China, Japan, Latin America, Indonesia, and France. Its seminal influence on the international development community and in Universities surpassed all expectations, and continues today.

Converting Social Science Knowledge into Social Policies: A Historic Progress

When I'm arguing that today social sciences are more important than ever in inducing development, I'm fighting the same fight like at the Bank, years, but this time from the tribune of the new Library of Alexandria. The message is the same that Michael and I fought for at that time: namely, to give space to the Non-Economic Social Sciences (NESS) in decision making, in policies, and in projects.

A historic series of institutional stepping-stones started in 1979/1980 with the writing and adoption of the Bank's first social policy, the policy on involuntary resettlement. This first step continued with the adoption of a sequence of Bank landmark social and environmental policies throughout the 1980s. The cumulative effect of these policies enlarged the Bank's theoretical and operational paradigm, contributing measurably to the Bank's gradual shift from its traditional economic growth doctrine toward the broader paradigm of social development. Implementing these policies demanded more in-house staff social specialists to expand the Bank's work and to assist the Bank's borrowers in absorbing these policies in their work preparing new projects for Bank financing.

Those new and pioneering social policies were:

- 1980: The policy on *Social Issues Associated with Involuntary Resettlement in Bank Financed Projects* (WB OMS 2.30 February)
- 1982: *The Policy on Indigenous (Tribal) People in World Bank Financed Projects* (WB OMS 2.34)
- 1984: *The Policy on Sociological Analysis at Project Appraisal (*WB OMS 2.20) introduced for the first time social analysis as mandatory for the preparation and appraisal of all Bank financed projects'. This policy was the first that brought up at the Bank's policy level the issues of women in Bank projects
- 1984: The first *World Bank Environmental Policy* (1984)
- 1986: WB Operational Policy Note. (10.08) *Involuntary Resettlement that substantively strengthened and broadened the Bank's first Involuntary Resettlement Policy*
- 1986: *The protection and preservation of Physical Cultural Heritage affected by World Bank financed projects civil works: chance finds* (WB OMS 1986)
- 1988: *Policy Guidelines for Implementing the World Bank Involuntary Resettlement Policy*. This World Bank Technical Paper consolidated and detailed the 1980 and 1986 resettlement policy documents; it was intended to make public for the first time the Bank's resettlement policy for increasing its impacts (Cernea, M: Policy Guidelines on Involuntary Resettlement. World Bank Technical Paper nr 80)
- 1989: World Bank OMS: "*Involving Non-Governmental Organizations in Bank Supported Activities*"
- 1990 World Bank. "*Primary Education: A World Bank Policy Paper*"
- 1991 World Bank. "*The Forest Sector. A World Bank Policy Paper*"
- 2001: *Cultural Heritage and Development. A Framework for Action in the Middle East/N. Africa*, The World Bank, Washington DC

Some of these policies marked a huge progress not only for the World Bank, but were also novel ideas replicated gradually by OECD countries' bilateral aid agencies and by the regional multilateral development banks.

The institutional and functional necessity of a specialized central Vice Presidency for dealing with the work requirements of this new body of social and environmental policies became increasingly obvious. This was needed for continuing this conceptual and guidance work on new issues such sustainability, social capital, and others. ESD Vice-presidency's influence inside the Bank resulted also from its capacity to bring up social, cultural, and environmental concerns at the top decision making levels of the Bank, due to which, the social and environmental policies were taken much more seriously into account by the Vice Presidents leading the Bank's large operational regional vice-presidencies of the Bank, within which the bulk of the Bank's staff at large is working.

By about mid-1990s, the World Bank's growing community of social scientists led by Michael Cernea, many recruited by him directly, had reached its peak intellectual power, institutional influence and numerical size inside the World Bank. Thus, the World Bank benefited from stellar rosters of staff anthropologists and sociologists, such as Gloria Davis, Maritta Koch-Weser, Shelton Davis, Scott Guggenheim, Deepa Narayan, David Butcher, William Partridge, Ashraf Ghani, Cyprian Fisiy, Cynthia Cook, Marlaine Lockheed, Stephen Heineman, Michael Bamberger, Augusta Molnar, Nat Colletta, Daniel Gross, Lynn Bennet, Dan Aronson, Chona Cruz, Stan Peabody, Paul Francis, Elena Correa, Jorge Uquillas, and others. As the leading development anthropologist scholar Thayer Scudder noted, Michael Cernea "*was the force behind the recruitment of additional social scientists that in time became the largest group dealing with development-induced resettlement*" (Scudder 2005).

In addition, numerous academics from universities and research institutes were invited to offer lectures to the Bank's staff—among them Fredrik Barth, Robert Chambers, David Maybury-Lewis, Neil Smelser, Shi Guoqing, Gunnar Sorbo, Thayer Scudder, Walter Coward, Hari-Mohan Mathur, Conrad Kottak, Theodor Downing, Hussein Fahim, Alf Jerve, Balaji Pandey, Warren van Wicklin III, Abdul Salam, Michael Horowitz, Caroline Moser, and uncountable others.

In turn, the activities and influence of the World Bank's community of social scientists working as development practitioners had also a radiating intellectual effect: it became a centrally located force, with growing world-wide intellectual influence that was unmatched in other multilateral development banks; a force that in turn provided support and interacted with large cohorts of sociologists and anthropologists in developing countries, who previously were latent "onlookers" (see Mohan Mathur essay, this volume) or involved only in teaching.

This tribute to the Bank's community of social specialists and social science scholars would be incomplete without my respectful acknowledgement of the value, richness, and originality of the vast body of research publications they created over years of working, thinking, and writing. This body is solidified knowledge. Without it, development anthropology and development sociology would not be the disciplines that they are today. Michael Cernea has been and remains an indefatigable writer, published then and today, known and studied in numerous countries. Together with him, scholars and writers such as Scott Guggenheim, William Partridge, Maritta Koch-Weser, Deepa Narayan, Lynn Bennet, Nat Colletta, Maria Clara Mejia, Anis Dani, and others produced a cornucopia of excellent evaluation studies, position papers, policy guidelines, innovative lending instruments, handbooks and sourcebooks, etc. The intellectual influence of this strong group of social scientists, remains felt today, through their writings, within both the international development and academic communities (see the annotated bibliography by Cernea and Adams 1994; Davis 2002).

The World's Largest Empirical Research on Development-Forced Population Displacement and Resettlement

In the wake of Narmada's globally resounding resettlement failure, Michael Cernea conceived a new and ambitious brain-child. Beyond the clash around the Narmada project that had "sucked-in" all management's attention, Michael remained concerned about the fundamental matter: the health of the Bank's entire ongoing project portfolio involving resettlement. Narmada's stormy events were not yet over when Michael went to the Bank's Senior Vice President, Ernst Stern, and proposed that the Bank undertake a review of its entire project portfolio to identify all ongoing projects plus those in the preparation pipeline that may have displacement effects and analyze whether there are other "hidden Narmadas" which might explode sooner or later. The kind of review he suggested was much more than a simple deskstock-taking. He recommended an action-oriented empirical field-research. Another novelty he proposed was for the review teams to not only *identify* projects-with-problems, but also to have the authority to initiate on-the-spot remedial actions for making such projects consistent with the Bank's resettlement policy. I gave that proposal my full support.

Bank management approved Michael's proposals. The Bank's President, Lewis Preston, appointed in 1993 a Task Force headed by Cernea with broad powers to analyze all 1986–1993 projects causing forced displacement. A Steering Committee, chaired by myself as the founding head of the new ESD Vice-Presidency, was to ensure the cooperation of all operational Bank Vice-Presidencies

Cernea worked closely with another eminent anthropologist, Scott Guggenheim. For the review's field activities, a strong segment of the larger community of social specialists was marshalled. The review covered almost 200 projects under implementation between 1986 and 1993, an analysis unprecedented for any other Bank issue. As Chairman of the Steering Committee, I worked closely with the Cernea-led Resettlement Task Force.

The Bank-wide review ultimately became a book-size study, with two print-runs (see Cernea et al. 1994/1996). This was not the kind of routine World Bank desk-review. That was an incisive analytical field-study, with unique features that elevated the study's caliber and results. First, it covered not just a selected small sample, but the largest ever collection of real projects (192 projects), enabling robust findings and substantiating credible generalizations. Second, it employed a competent research-and-action staff force, sent out to dozens of countries to empirically assess the real-on-the-ground-state of resettlement. Third, it had a capable, honest and uninhibited leadership in the central Task Force. Nominally, the central Task Force consisted of only four persons, named above; yet, at Michael Cernea's call, in practice virtually all Bank social specialists took part in one or another role.

As a result, the study produced new insights and strategic recommendations for the Bank and its member governments on their performance, failures, and on how to improve resettlement planning and livelihood outcomes. It also equipped the emerging social science domain of displacement/resettlement with a text-book methodology on how to analyze such processes, their risks and outcomes.

The Bank's Board of Executive Directors and the Bank's Management adopted all the Task Force recommendations—a genuine coronation of the Task Force's efforts. This reinforced the internal respect inside the Bank for resettlement operations. Following the study's recommendations, Bank management decided to increase further the number, role, and resources of the Bank's social staff. The study defined seven strategic priorities for the Bank's further work on resettlement. The Bank became more capable for providing hands-on assistance to our borrowing countries to minimize involuntary resettlement whenever possible, and carry it better when such resettlement was unavoidable.

Even the critics of the World Bank from the NGO community gave exceptional praise to the review's quality and candor. A book on accountability in development by Fox and Brown concluded that:

> The World Bank's 1993–1994 resettlement review set a still unmatched precedent in terms of rigor, comprehensiveness, transparency, and self-criticism. Inside reformers strategically used public transparency as a tool for increasing institutional accountability, defined as compliance with reform commitments... and was produced with strong support from the vice president for Environmentally Sustainable Development.

For myself too, I must say that my participation in the 1993–1994 study was a powerful eye-opener. It revealed weaknesses in the quality of some of the Bank's work that I did not suspect; nor were other senior Bank managers aware of them. I felt that due to the principled manner in which the analysis was conducted, particularly its field action-research method, the resettlement review set a model of trenchant and candid analysis of quality in Bank-financed projects, worthy of replication beyond resettlement. Therefore, while the task force members returned to their other duties, I brought up the issue of a "crisis of quality" in the inner discussions of the Bank's management. I felt that similar grave inconsistencies between Bank policies and practice may lurk beneath the surface in other sectors of Bank work. The example set by the resettlement study became my recurrent reference, a "proof" for my arguments. I wrote two memoranda on quality issues to the Bank's management team (Serageldin 1995a, b), in which I argued that the resettlement review gave us lessons and a pattern of how management should further analyze consistency in policy implementation, and that the work-style of the review should be leveraged towards further culture change inside the Bank. Verbatim, I wrote:

> I am encouraged to push in the direction of the Resettlement Review by its results. There, we had a 100% review of the portfolio and the pipeline. Sociologists, anthropologists, economists, and other specialists reviewed every report by the regional staff and participated in repairing problems as they found them. Regional management was reporting monthly to the President's office....

All these efforts not only improved standards, but also changed the culture in many of the Bank's Departments. At the retreat of the Bank's sociologists and anthropologists, which followed the Bank-wide Resettlement Review, they spoke of its effects on how the attitude in their department had changed not just about resettlement, but about other social issues. This prompted me to call for similar portfolio reviews in other sectors:

> Nothing less than this kind of systematic and intensive scrutiny, supported at the highest levels of management will be able to bring about the culture change needed in the Bank. (idem, 1995b).

I must add that it is to the credit of the Bank that it allowed such candid discussion of all issues within and outside its walls. The directness of the critique and the quality of the debate around its findings would be difficult to imagine in many other institutions, especially in many of the governments whose projects the Bank finances and supports.

The Emergence of the Impoverishment Risks and Reconstruction Model

Surely, the deepest foray made by this study was in conceiving the insightful model or pattern of multiple risks revealing and documenting the financial, economic and social risks of becoming impoverished, jobless, homeless, and marginalized are risks that confront the poor when they are exposed to expropriation of assets and physical displacement. To do so, it validated and applied the model conceived by Cernea (see Cernea 1997), defined by him as "The Impoverishment Risks and Reconstruction model", mischievously summarized in the acronym "IRR", which for most economists means "Internal Rate of Return" for the economic analysis of project investments. It is thus appropriate to give some thought to how the IRR model has enriched the theory and methodology of resettlement research The Cernea IRR model became the single most influential social science analytical tool in to reshaping the thinking on forced displacement and resettlement processes.

The IRR model had its theoretical and empirical origins outlined gradually before the review but this was the first large-scale test of the IRR model on the universe of the Bank's all projects ongoing then. Ultimately, this vast body of empirical evidence convincingly confirmed its explanatory power. The publication of that study was what placed the IRR model solidly on the map of international development social science as a tested tool for diagnosis, remedial planning, research and performance evaluation.

Which are the most common impoverishment risks from displacement? How can they be countered? Cernea's research deconstructed the empirical evidence and concluded that there are recurrent processes that give rise to impoverishment along eight main variable dimensions of poverty: landlessness; joblessness; homelessness; marginalization; increased morbidity; food insecurity; lack of access to common property; and social disarticulation (Cernea 1997; Cernea and McDowell 2000). In addition, affected people may face other risks as well, emerging from specific project/context circumstances, but these eight risks are most important and virtually ubiquitous, even though their intensity does vary in every case by sector or by other parameters like family size, gender, age, time, etc., as Cernea has explicitly stressed (1997). For instance, specialized research on displaced women has consistently confirmed the IRR model and its explicit assertion that women suffer more severe impacts than men and may be exposed to additional specific risks. When the risks of impoverishment aren't targeted through counter-risk measures included in the projects' context, it is certain that they will morph into real and economically detrimental effects on people's welfare.

A Self-Destroying Prophecy and Unprincipled Censorship

The operational effectiveness of Cernea's IRR model resides not only in its risk analysis, but also, and even more, it resides in the model's 2nd part. Indeed, the IRR's second "half" outlines the response strategy for each impoverishment risk, one after the other. These elements can effectively counter-act the risks outlined in the model's first part by *directing reconstructive actions* in the desired and needed areas. This part is not less important than the risks themselves: the two parts are germane to each other. The second part is modeling the processes of economic and social rehabilitation and improvement of the livelihood of the families affected by displacement. The IRR model's operational usefulness to practitioners anywhere would be limited if the model itself only revealed risks but said nothing on how these risks can be dealt with.

As Cernea has explained (see also his chapter on the IRR model, this volume) he embraced the argument of a giant of modern sociology—Robert King Merton. Merton famously deconstructed the paradox of "self-destroying prophecies" and argued that, under certain circumstances, some predictions (or prophesies) can change social behavior and can trigger actions that prevent the predictions from fulfilling themselves : hence, "self-defeating prophesies".

By using correct and strong concepts to inform project planners on how deeply toxic the risks inherent in forced displacement are, Michael aimed to determine those responsible for each project causing displacement to plan all needed to reverse and prevent impoverishment from happening.

Yet, even inside the IRR's intellectual home, its message did not enjoy an easy ride. I will turn to some of the in-house battles that the IRR model had first to fight and win inside the Bank in order to become an instrument publicly known and used in many other places beyond the Bank itself. I was a party to some of those battles. Now, decades later, I'm pleased to share some of my observations as an insider.

The model's description of displacement's intrinsic impoverishment risks scared some of our colleagues One concern about the review, expressed during its unfolding was related to fact that it asked for a transparent recognition and analysis of the risks imposed upon the displaced populations... Several attempted to silence it by questioning its "political usefulness" and "appropriateness." Mostly, they were scared by the model's candid terminology about risks, and they didn't want it included in the review's report to the Board and to the public.

Having to oversee the review process on behalf of the Bank's senior management, I had to respond. From the supervisor of the Team's work, I became their advocate in the management circles of the World Bank.

Surely, project documents mentioned some risks, but these were routinely macro-risks, foreign exchange risks, and supply risks. Some of our colleagues objected against what they saw as the Bank's communicating to the wide world that its own projects cause risks. Today, two full decades later, this may sound strange and would be labeled "concealment of risks." Effectively, they reacted negatively to the review's detailed articulation of the impoverishment risks from displacement as problematic in a major Bank review. The opponents claimed that the report will "alienate" many officials of the borrowing governments because they don't like to admit such risk to their own publics. Some termed the IRR concepts as "inflammatory" likely to confirm NGO's public criticism of the Bank based on the Bank's "own admission."

Cernea refused to accept such comments as valid and declined to compromise the review's analysis of impoverishment. He argued that the terminology was empirically documented and theoretically correct. Diluting the truth-telling through some rosier wording would undermine the goal of creating genuine awareness about the catastrophic effects of expropriation, uprooting, joblessness and other losses. The team argued that "keeping silent about risks" would not make the risks go away from Bank-financed projects. On the contrary, the unaddressed risks would only fester and would surface with added virulence because they were not recognized and tackled in a timely manner. I supported the team's position.

For a while, the battle for candor seemed largely won by the review's Task Force. But when the draft's chapters started to come in for management's review, its explicit and strong concepts —such as, "landlessness", "joblessness", "homelessness", "increased mortality and morbidity," and so on— caused a wave of objections.

Again, I supported Cernea and his team. In the end, the powerful logic of the model itself, the steadfastness of its proponent, and perhaps not least the backing by the review's Steering Committee, prevailed over defensiveness. The Task Force's review was published as written, uncensored. The evidence-based model of a typical pattern of impoverishment risks, including the counter-risk remedies it recommended, remained at its center.

Subsequently, after the Bank-wide study was completed, and its authors were congratulated by the Bank's Board, I returned to the "semantics" of the IRR model during a private conversation with its key author. Cernea gave me two reasons for his refusal to soft-pedal the impoverishment risks. I must say I not only endorsed but also fully liked his reasons and his steadfastness. He had both general and personal motivations.

First, Michael reminded me of his work as a sociologist during the dictatorial communist regime in his country of origin, Romania. That regime, he said, imposed not only official censorship over published writings, but also put a pernicious systemic pressure to induce self-censorship. That was very demeaning, and he had costs to pay for refusing to yield to censorship. Now he was determined to resist at the World Bank any notion of forbidding the discussion of new concepts. I couldn't support more his feelings, having had to fight censorship myself

Second, Michael emphasized that he had a purposive communication strategy, because he had to overcome a paradox intrinsic in the Bank's work. His choice of strong concepts in predicting displacement's fundamental impoverishment risks was deliberate, not accidental. He had for long concluded that the causation of new poverty through displacement did not receive the unvarnished exposure it needed. He therefore needed terms that would compel everybody's attention. Therefore, for the risks he identified empirically, he selected true and strong concepts to trigger the awareness of Bank staff and managers that making people worse-off was an unacceptable violation of development ethics and of World Bank normative policy, which couldn't be tolerated simply because the Bank-financed projects were "aimed to serve the greater good". Bank-financed projects are undermined by a perverse paradox: even while they do reduce poverty for some people, they can be causing harm and new poverty to some other people. So he said:

> But this is not an unsolvable paradox. I've seen and lived through forced displacement myself, with my family. The knowledge of displacement's ugly effects is in-printed in my own DNA, indelibly. by personal experience. I'm therefore determined to trigger intolerance to poverty creation, through all available Bank means: more financing; technical planning; moral reasoning; and—why not—correct strong precautionary semantics too. Moreover, through my IRR model I'm not just disclosing risks passively/contemplatively: but I'm also defining for each intrinsic risk the pragmatic strategy to prevent potential risk from becoming real impacts. Loudly branding impoverishment risks is like sounding the alarm: making them impossible to ignore is my prophesy-destroying strategy.

That was a memorable conversation which made me understand Michael better. This is why he refused to eliminate the concept of "impoverishment" from the name of his model and declined to employ softer concepts for defining the risks themselves and insisted on keeping them as he had labeled them. By now all people speak of the risks of "landlessness, joblessness, homelessness," and so on.

By his determination to call risks by their proper names without "beating about the bush", Cernea sought to expose the tragic reality of what is still frequently occurring in development practice. This was not intended to inflame criticisms of the Bank: it was aimed to mobilize the determination of his colleagues, and not least the agency of the risks' bearers, to confront and fight the ills that he unambiguously identified. That determination was aggravating to some in the short term, but it left its mark on many in the long term. I gave my full backing to the necessity of addressing these risks, and today, over two decades later, it is clear that the global resettlement literature has mainstreamed the risks of impoverishment, showing that forcefully exposing the unpleasant realities was the right thing to do.

During the quarter century that passed since the Resettlement Review, the IRR model went on to become a very impactful tool, the most employed internationally analytical instrument in social science research on resettlement. Its conceptual apparatus about risks has become current vocabulary, current currency. Far beyond the World Bank, it is used and validated in countless studies, books, handbooks, training manuals, reports, journal studies, international conferences, etc. (see earlier, footnote 1).

Knowledge Alone Is Not Enough. Political Will Is Indispensable to Stand Up Against Impoverishment

The science of handling population resettlement issues as a domain of social sciences has registered a massive enrichment in its conceptual apparatus and recommended methods. Looking back to when the first institutional policy on population resettlement was formulated, this domain was rudimentary, only incipient, undeveloped. Over a relatively short period of time, the progress has been exceptional. The impoverishment risks and reconstruction (IRR) framework has made its contribution to this growth, and new concepts and research trends are emerging.

Displacement failures today are increasingly being seen not only as unacceptable impoverishment pathologies but also as major aggressions against basic human rights. The conceptual vocabulary of human rights, which development agencies have long tried to avoid, is making inroads in resettlement theory being absorbed by scientists and activists into the argument for sustainable post-displacement reconstruction. Philosophers and ethics researchers are joining the ranks of displacement scholars; from their perspectives, they're questioning the morality of predicating the pursuit of profits for some (or even for the "public interest") on ruining the existence and livelihood of others, robbing Peter to enrich Paul (see, among others, Penz et al. 2011). Legal theory and legislation are advancing towards defining certain forms of forced population displacement as a "crime" punishable by laws.

Overall, no one can any longer claim today—be they governments of private sector corporations—that they didn't know about, nor that they could not anticipate the negative impacts and pathological effects from the forced displacement caused by a development project. Indeed, we now have a body of knowledge that is much more advanced than the level at which development projects and resettlement processes are implemented. The failures of timely post-displacement recovery are more frequent than successes, largely because the governments (or other entities) owning the projects are not willing to do the responsible planning and allocate the necessary financing. Though a complex process, involuntary resettlement is neither technically nor socially intractable; it can be conducted successfully. Thus, the ball is in the court of the governments, of the public agencies, and of private sector corporations which sponsor and own projects that cause expropriations and displacement.

My own involvement in international development taught me that the decisive factor is the political will of public aid agencies and the political will of developing countries' governments. The extent to which the government of each country has the political will to deal with involuntary resettlement sustainably is precisely the extent to which it will work or fail. Emphasizing this fact, a World Bank evaluation study went as far as to recommend that governments which do not have the political will and commitment to handle involuntary resettlement soundly should not be supported to embark on such project at all (Picciotto et al. 2001). This was a fair warning.[1] Commensurate financing, the quality of the reconstruction plan, and the extent to which impoverishment risks are deliberately counteracted, makes or breaks the success of resettlement.

There is no one single variable, no silver bullet that can resolve this conundrum. There is one central factor, though, that can connect all that is needed, and that is the presence of political will. This is necessary at both the level of the state, and of the private corporation, since nowadays displacement is caused by private and public projects alike. It is only when political will is exercised that the needed resources can be mobilized, including financial resources, and when there are better chances that the impoverishment risks inherent in forced displacement can be arrested before morphing into a range of painful social pathologies.

Yet unfortunately, political will isn't a constant and the philosophical outlook does not remain continuous: it sometimes changes from one government to the following one, changes with the succession of political leaders, or with managers of international public agencies. Even in an agency as stable as the World Bank changes can occur unexpectedly, largely reflecting the leadership style of the President of the Bank and his or her philosophy. Following the unexpected death of President Preston in May 1995, the Bank was lucky to get a dynamic leader in the person of James Wolfensohn. Wolfensohn was a strong advocate of keeping a focus on the fight on poverty, and was sensitive and very insightful on the non-economic dimensions of development, including social and cultural variables. I left the Bank to return to Egypt during his presidency.

Regretfully, after President Wolfensohn, President Paul Wolfowitz was appointed as Bank president in June 2005. He abolished the ESD vice-presidency, to the surprise of many Bank staff. That was a major setback to the ongoing progressive evolution of the Bank and of its social and environmental safeguard policies, described earlier in this paper, that already had gained broad international constituencies, including not only all other MDB's (the Multilateral Development Banks) but also of some 70–80 giant private sector banks that had adopted many of the same policies under the banner name of the "Equator Principles Banks". The Bank's central ESD staff was dispersed, diminishing the Bank's capacity to promote and monitor consistency of the projects' content and implementation with the Bank's statutory policies. The weakening of the Bank's central set up also facilitated subsequent further changes as well, expressed in the recasting and replacement of the cluster of ten explicit safeguard Bank Policies (BPs) and Bank Operational

---

[1] The proposal to give this warning to borrowers was made in 1994 by an Executive Director of the World Bank during the Board's discussion of the Portfolio Resettlement Review (World Bank 1994).

Procedures (OPs) with an environmental and social framework (ESF) and a set of standards (ESS) which were declared by the Bank as "binding" for all the Bank's borrowing countries. In effect, the bank was telling the countries/borrowers what was expected of them to do, but absolving itself of any responsibility if they did not follow the recommended policies and procedures. This was an enormous setback, as the Bank's specialized and highly qualified technical social and environmental staff, were dispersed into the regional staff teams, with little authority to review the risks associated with the proposed operations. The dispersal of the central staff weakened the critical mass of the Banks non-economic social staff, whereas such a critical mass had in the past been the source of much innovation and could in the future have continued to innovate in the application of new knowledge onto the thinking about development and linked that to actual performance in the field. It is to be welcomed that the past achievements were not totally lost, and that the broadening of the Bank's paradigm remained a reality, even if the implementation of that broadened paradigm was rather weakened in some areas.

I mentioned the episode described above in order to stress that progress hasn't occurred as an uninterrupted ascent. Every advance needed to be defended and strengthened continuously. And I am happy that the broadening of the Bank's social development paradigm had become already irreversible and under the drive and commitment of some individuals of excellence it continues to advance further.

Closing Thoughts on the Impact of the ESD Central Vice-Presidency on the Work of the World Bank

In addition to other important activities described earlier, the Bank-wide Resettlement Review was the first large Bank-wide activity under the aegis of the new ESD Vice-presidency it was to be followed by many other initiatives. The IRR model that it launched internationally, was one of Michael Cernea's most important contributions to the Bank and to development thinking generally. Inside the Bank, it was a triumph of how a central vice-presidency should work with regional operational staff and with borrowing countries on one of the thorniest processes in development.

The World Bank is remarkably well endowed in talent. The staff of the Bank are, by far, its most important resource. They bring exceptional professional skills to bear on the problems of the poor in this world. The Bank is also a place of innovation, where intellectual sparks fly and where the debate is forceful, professionally demanding, and characterized by a hard edge of intellectual rigor, and informed by pragmatism too. Many of the intellectual movers and shakers inside the Bank are seldom known outside the institution. They derive their satisfaction from having pushed the institution's process of conceptualizing and practicing development along the lines they think are right.

The existence of a solid group of social scientists in the central ESD vice-presidency enabled the Bank to place additional tasks on the shoulders of this precious human resource of the Bank. They had review functions to carry out, to ensure compliance with policies by Bank central and country based staff (sometime weakened by centrifugal tendencies). They also performed intellectual services beyond the Bank, such as participating in and organizing international social science conferences, and regularly inviting outside eminent scholars for lecture for the Bank staff. For example, the ESD vice presidency co-organized in 1995 and 1996 two consecutive international conferences with Oxford University. These two conferences resulted in two influential books.

During the last 5 years I had spent in the Bank, from 1996 to 2000, before returning to Egypt to revive in our modern times Antiquity's Library of Alexandria, the ESD Vice-presidency was a key actor in promoting and broadening the Bank's social development mission and paradigm. Those 5 years coincided with the first period of Jim Wolfensohn's presidency of the Bank. It was not a coincidence that Michael Cernea sought and succeeded in the first weeks of Jim's work's in the Bank to capture his attention and personal support to the work, role, and needs of the Bank's community of social specialists (see Davis et al. 1998). Michael's written proposals to Jim Wolfensohn lead to a full scale Bank-wide *Social Development Report* (World Bank, 1997) that was submitted to the Bank's Board, which then decided to institute a distinct "Social Compact" program and a very substantial financial allocation for further expanding the resources, staff, and activities of the Bank's social specialists. I engaged myself, with Cernea, Kreszentia Duer, Katherine Marshal, in organizing a series of international Conferences on the Bank's support and investment projects for preserving better the developing countries' material Cultural Heritage. Michael Cernea was then invited back from retirement to research and write the World Bank's first formal policy framework for the *Preservation of the Cultural Heritage of the Middle East and North African Countries* (Cernea 2001)

By the time Michael Cernea and I left the Bank, the institution was equipped with a groundbreaking set of policies, called the "Environmental and Social Safeguard Policies". These aimed to ensure that Bank staff worked with our member governments to try to ensure that each operation was as well-designed as it could be, and that the cynical concept of "tolerable collateral damage" would never be resurrected from history's garbage bin.

Development remains a complicated and often messy process on the ground, with the rich and powerful displacing the poor and the weak. The role of the Bank remains the same but does expand in depth and breath: to eliminate poverty, avoid producing new poverty risks, and eliminate any negative economic, environmental or social side-effects of the projects that the Bank finances.

Even inside the Bank, and despite its fundamental commitment to *social* development, we've also noticed periodic bouts of resistance by misguided managers or poorly trained individual staff to the institution's social and environmental safeguard policies. The Bank's in-built responsibility is to overcome such departures from its mission. This is why I must also say that I was surprised and unhappy when Mr. Paul Wolfowitz, who came to the Bank after the enlightened tenure of President Jim

Wolfensohn, erroneously decided to abolish the central ESSD Vice-presidency and thus undercut he Bank's actual policy and operational work on these core issues. This reduced the value of the Bank's investments to all countries, developed or developing. The Bank's organizational structure was weakened, not strengthened, by eliminating its central part, indispensable functionally to the social and environmental sustainability of its investments, with adverse effects in practice. I know that most of the work we had done remains integrated into the fabric and thinking of the Bank. The need to further improve the performance of its fundamental mission remains today as strong as ever.

I mentioned the episode described above in order to stress that progress doesn't occur as an uninterrupted ascent. Every advance needs to be defended and strengthened continuously. And I am happy that the broadening of the Bank's social development paradigm had been already irreversible and under the drive and commitment of some individuals of excellence it continues to advance further

My deep confidence, in this salute to Michael Cernea and his contributions, is that by now much of this knowledge has spread internationally and many countries and many development agencies are by now endowed with capable social scientists of their own, working on development. That will be the real legacy of the work of all the militant social specialists celebrated in this chapter.

My further hope is that new generations of social staff – with the same vigor as generations past – and applied social scientists in many countries will benefit from the new landscape being created by the revolution in science and technologies, and succeed in keeping the paradigm of social development constantly evolving to ensure that it benefits all the people. The enlightened practices of the few ought to become the current practices of the many.

References

Cernea, M. (1985). *Putting people first: Sociological variables in development* (1st ed., 2nd ed. 1991). New York: Oxford University Press.

Cernea, M. (1997) The impoverishment risks and reconstruction model for resettling displaced populations. *World Development, 25*(10).

Cernea, M. (2001). *Cultural heritage and development. A framework for action.* Washington, DC: World Bank.

Cernea, M. (2015). Landmarks in development: the introduction of social analysis in project appraisals. In S. Price & K. Robinson (Eds.), *Social assessment policy and praxis and its emergence* (pp. 35–59). New York: Berghahn.

Cernea, M. *Poverty risks from population displacement in water resources development.* Harvard University: HIID. Development Discussion Paper No. 355.

Cernea, M., & Adams, A. (Eds.) (1994). *Sociology, anthropology, development: An annotated bibliography of World Bank publications 1975-1993*. With a foreword by Ismail Serageldin. Washington, DC: World Bank.

Cernea, M. M., & McDowell, C. (Eds.). (2000). *Risks and reconstruction: Experiences of resettlers and refugees.* Washington, DC: World Bank.

Cernea, M., Guggenheim, S., Aronson, D., & van Wicklin, W. (1994/1996). *Development and resettlement. The bank-wide review 1987-1994.* Washington, DC: World Bank.

Davis, G. (2002). *A history of the social development network in the World Bank, 1973-2002*. WB Working Paper. Washington, DC.

Davis, G., Steer, A., & van Wicklin, W. (1998). *Michael makes his mark. The life and times of a change agent in the World Bank*. Washington, DC: Social Development, World Bank.

Penz, P., Drydyk, J., & Bose, P. (2011). *Displacement by development: Ethics, rights and responsibilities*. Cambridge University Press.

Picciotto, R., van Wicklin, W., & Rice, T. (Eds.) (2001). *Involuntary resettlement. Comparative prospective* (Vol. I and II). Washington, DC: W.B. Evaluation Series.

Scudder, T. (2005). *The future of large dams* (p. 22). London: Earthscan.

Serageldin, I. (1995a). *The crisis of quality: Reflections and recommendations*. Note to Bank Senior Managers. April 25. Processed

Serageldin, I. (1995b). *Detailed recommendations for improving quality management in the bank: Suggestions*. Processed. July 14.

Ismail Serageldin, Emeritus Director, Library of Alexandria in Egypt. He serves as Chair or Member of a number of advisory committees for academic, research, scientific and international institutions and civil society efforts. He is a member of the Institut d'Egypte (Egyptian Academy of Science), US National Academy of Sciences (Public Welfare Medalist), the American Philosophical Society, The World Academy of Sciences (TWAS), the World Academy of Arts and Sciences (WAAS), the Indian National Academy of Agricultural Sciences and the European Academy of Sciences and Arts. Previously he has been Vice President of the World Bank (1992–2000), former Chairman, Consultative Group on International Agricultural Research (CGIAR, 1994–2000), Founder and former Chairman, the Global Water Partnership (GWP, 1996–2000) and the Consultative Group to Assist the Poorest (CGAP) (1995–2000). He was Professor at the Collège de France, Paris, and Distinguished Professor at Wageningen University in the Netherlands. He has received the Order of the Rising Sun from Japan and the Legion d'Honneur from France and is a Commandeur of Arts and Letters of the French Republic. Serageldin has published over 100 books and monographs and over 400 papers on a variety of topics including biotechnology, rural development, sustainability, and the value of science to society. He holds a Bachelor of Science degree in engineering from Cairo University and a Master's degree and a PhD from Harvard University and has received over 35 honorary doctorates.

Open Access This chapter is licensed under the terms of the Creative Commons Attribution 4.0 International License (http://creativecommons.org/licenses/by/4.0/), which permits use, sharing, adaptation, distribution and reproduction in any medium or format, as long as you give appropriate credit to the original author(s) and the source, provide a link to the Creative Commons license and indicate if changes were made.

The images or other third party material in this chapter are included in the chapter's Creative Commons license, unless indicated otherwise in a credit line to the material. If material is not included in the chapter's Creative Commons license and your intended use is not permitted by statutory regulation or exceeds the permitted use, you will need to obtain permission directly from the copyright holder.

The Direct and Major Operational Relevance of Social Assessments

Jonathan C. Brown

Do international development agencies listen to the people they are trying to help? And if they listen, do they really hear? And if they hear, do they understand and follow up in ways that affect what we do?

In the mid-1990s development agencies are questioned by skeptics who contend that even if institutions like the World Bank want to listen to the people, they lack the means to do so, being trained in remote oases of learning in professions distant from what constitutes reality at the grassroots level of developing societies.

Indeed, development agencies face a major challenge in defining their roles and in mobilizing support at a time when the themes of the day are fiscal restraint (less money) and more discipline (fewer people doing more).

Some development agencies are responding to such criticisms by strengthening the quality of their technical, financial, economic, and environmental work. And they are reaching out to the people they are trying to help—the ultimate "clients" or main "stakeholders"—to work *with,* rather than *for* them.

This article was written in 1996 by Jonathan Brown, the chief of the operational division tasked to provide policy advice for investment lending for infrastructure, energy, and the environment to the Bank and to the new states emerging from the collapse of the Soviet Union (the Russian Federation, Azerbaijan, Kazakhstan, Kyrgyz Republic, Tajikistan, Turkmenistan, and Uzbekistan). Jonathan Brown was not what is usually understood by the term "social specialist," as he was highly trained in in economics with degrees from Yale and Harvard Business School. He was strongly supportive and creative in the use of analytical and social tools such as social assessments for projects, an alternative concept for "sociological analysis" required by the Bank's "project appraisal" OMS 2.20. Most of the "social assessment" studies to which this article refers were carried out by the Bank's Social and Environmental Division in the Central Asian countries headed at the time by Ayse Kudat, a Bank sociologist with vast international experience. This article appeared first in 1997 in the book titled *Social Assessments for Better Development: Case Studies in Russia and Central Asia,* edited by Ayse Kudat and Michael M. Cernea, published in the ESD Vice Presidency monograph series as a "work in progress for public discussion."

In the private sector this is called marketing, demand assessment, or testing consumer preferences. No private company would operate or launch a product without demand assessment and marketing. And even then, the number of bankruptcies and failed products testifies to the difficulty of successful market gauging. Among other international development agencies, such as the multilateral development banks like ADB, IDB, and AfDB, stake-holder consultation at the grassroots level is still an innovation yet to be accepted and insti-tutionalized. In the past, failure to consult ade-quately with stakeholders may have contributed to failure of project operations, but unlike private sector firms, the international development agencies themselves were not put at risk when their products failed. And to be fair, governments and their public servants were often as unwilling or as unprepared to consult with stakeholders as the international develop-ment agencies and their civil servants. While the private sector has spent much of the twentieth century expanding and deepening their "marketing procedures" so that marketing became an acceptable "profession," stakeholder consultation in development agen-cies doesn't yet have the reputation of a profes-sion—a status that economists, technicians, and financial analysts have achieved and toward which environmentalists are still struggling. Rather, stakeholder consultation and social analysis (separate from economic or technical analysis) are mistakenly seen as something anyone can do. This paper illustrates the contribution of social assessment—one mechanism for stake-holder consultation—used by the World Bank. It has improved the substance and process of pol-icy reform and investment projects in develop-ing countries and economies in transition. The case studies presented result from the work of the social scientist group in the Europe and Central Asia region of the Bank and cover the period of 3 years when social assessments were introduced in that region.

While it is accepted in principle that consult-ing the people—arguably the most important stakeholders in the development or transition process—should be systematically done by the World Bank, this consultation process is, in fact, rarely done. When it is done, it is often done superficially. And when it is done well, the findings are not always followed up. This has happened in part because consultation is rarely the result of a structured process performed by specialized professionals trained in the social sciences. This situation has persisted because there have been too few examples of successful social analysis to serve as guides. Therefore, many World Bank staff have not been prepared to spend intellectual and monetary resources on social assessments and local consultation.

The consultation process can be narrow or broad. At its most narrow—as often occurred in the past—a World Bank staff member talks with officials in a country and on this basis alone pol-icy dialogue or an investment project moves for-ward. At its broadest reach, the consultation process involves a wide range of stakeholders, including those people, groups, and institutions directly affected by the policy reform or invest-ment project.

The narrow consultation is easier—not much more effort is required than looking in a mirror. The broad consultation requires more time and resources and a professional approach. The social assessment—a systematic, sociologically and methodologically guided process of learning about stakeholders—is an important mech-anism for involving a full range of stakeholders. Social assessment is not the whole participation process but one input. For social assessments to gain credibility among World Bank staff and government officials—who are economists, financial analysts, technicians from many sec-tors, and even generalists—it is important to demonstrate that these "strange" products that result from the work of non-economic social sci-entists really do facilitate the process and improve the substance of the World Bank's basic products: policy reform and investment projects.

This chapter summarizes the relevance of social assessments to policy reform, investment projects, and lending for emergencies from the viewpoint of a division chief who is responsible for preparing, appraising, and supervising development projects and who is not a social sci-entist himself. It suggests reasons why social assessments have been more readily accepted in theory (by World Bank staff and governments) than in practice. Finally, the chapter will suggest institutional mech-anisms to facilitate the accep-tance of social assessments, either through per-sua-sion—the basic thrust of this book—or through institutional norms within the domain of good management and leadership.

Social Assessments for Preparing Policy Reform

It is believed that improving the welfare of peo-ple in developing and transition economies requires institutions and policies that encourage economic growth and allow for the sustainable development of essential services. Part of the policy theology is that reform is usually unpleas-ant and has to be forced on people by govern-ments, resulting in conflict. People are seen as part of the problem rather than as part of the solution.

Seeing people as the enemy of policy reform is nowhere more evident than in the debate over cost recovery, or who will pay for essential goods and services. The reform theology assumes that people will resist higher tariffs. But is it true that higher tariffs mean higher real costs for people in all cases? And even if this is true, will people object? Social assessments play a critical role in this debate. Their findings, as indi-cated in this book, have shown that higher tar-iffs can lead to lower real costs and that higher prices will be accepted by consumers if there is a credible expectation of improved services. Social assessments can give courage to govern-ments facing the need for cost recovery meas-ures by allowing the people to be supporters of reform.

During the preparation of the Baku (Azerbaijan) Water Supply Rehabilitation Project in 1994, water company officials and the World Bank team concluded that higher tariffs were essential to provide the financial resources necessary to put the Baku water company on a sound financial footing. However, discussions with the government over raising tariffs quickly became emotional. Government officials raised the specter of public riots, while the water company and World Bank team offered the gloomy vision of corporate bankruptcy.

The stalemate was broken as a result of the social assessment done as part of early project preparation. The social assessment found that although the public water supply service was inadequate *throughout* Baku, the low-income segment of the city's population suffered the most from the water situation. On average, households spent about seventeen times more on alternative water supplies than on their monthly water bills. The poor spent 7% of their income on coping strategies while wealth-ier citizens spent only 2%. The social assessment also showed that householders would be willing to pay substantially more than their current monthly water charge for better public water service. The poorest elements of the population were prepared to pay 6% of their income, a slight decrease from their current payments for coping mechanisms.

The water company and World Bank team found that a tariff level of about 4% of income for the poorest population segments was sufficient for the company's financial objectives. The government could argue that while this was an increase in tariffs, it was actually a reduction from the 7% this group was currently pay-ing for alternative water supply.

The social assessment was accepted in Azerbaijan because it was done by a team of World Bank and Azeri social scientists and was based on detailed surveys done professionally and presented in a user-friendly way, including public fora which were televised.

The role of social assessment in facilitating discussions of cost recovery was even more dra-matic in Turkmenistan during the early prepa-ration of the Urban Transport Project. Carried out in February 1995, before issues of cost recov-ery were even discussed with the government, the social assessment revealed a situation in Ash-gabat of poor service in public transport and of tariffs so low that there was no coin small enough for a passenger to pay a single-ticket fare. The result was an unsustainable and dete-riorating public transport system. The poorest quarter of households were compelled to spend 12.8% of their income on various mecha-nisms for coping with the lack of public trans-port or to make "extra" payments for using public transport when it was available.

The social assessment also revealed that 94% of public transport users would accept a 200% increase in tariffs if there would be real improvement in service. Tariff increases were immediately put into operation. The quick improvement in public transport service resulted in the poorest households paying higher fares but incurring lower real costs for transport when compared to the cost of their previous coping mechanisms. Raising tariffs lowered the real cost of transport and cost recov-ery was never an emotional issue during project preparation.

Turkmenistan's Urban Transport Project is the World Bank's first investment operation in this new member country. As part of project preparation the government has issued a *"Declaration on Urban Transport Policy"* an Action Plan setting out the policy objectives to be implemented during the project's lifetime, and an Operations Improvement Plan to sup-plement the list of improvements already imple-mented. It is unusual for a policy reform package to be prepared by a government before World Bank financing has been negotiated, espe-cially for a new member of the World Bank. There is no absolute proof, but one might sug-gest that the bank's social assessment turned urban transport consumers into allies of reform. It also emboldened the government, which was highly satisfied with the Bank's social assessment study, to take steps towards policy change.

Social assessments can be particularly helpful where cost recovery's impact on different popu-lation groups is more complicated. In the Kyrgyz Republic the World Bank provided a $20 million International Development Association (IDA) credit in June 1996 to fund a Power and District Heating Rehabilitation Project. Cost recovery was a contentious ·issue for the government, since social considerations and its policy of pro-moting domestic power use were the main rea-sons for keeping power and heat tariffs artificially low and the structure biased towards household consumers. The result was an unsus-tainable deterioration in the financial situation of the energy utility, inefficient and uneconomic energy consumption, and inequitable prices. A social assessment of proposed tariff increases was carried out during project preparation. The findings of the assessment indicated that the proposed tariff increase for electricity was feasible, while the increase for district heating was feasible only if a social safety net was introduced to protect low-income households. Households without access to district heating, and therefore relying on natural gas and coal for heat, also needed protection. The impact of the tariff increase on electricity could be mitigated by maintaining a reduced subsistence tariff for resi-dential consumers. The outcome was that higher tariffs were introduced where they were affordable, with a social safety net designed for those groups for which it had been demonstrated that the financial burden would be too great.

The important contribution of the social assessment was to provide a framework of facts, figures, and predictable outcomes that took the subjectivity and ideology out of the cost recov-ery debate.

The contribution of social assessments to policy reform can be broadened to encompass entire sectors engaging in major restructuring where the World Bank is supporting the reform program through a sector adjustment loan (SECAL), as the Russian coal case illustrates.

In June 1996 the World Bank approved a $500 million loan for Coal Sector Adjustment in Russia in support of the government's program to reduce the adverse impact of the coal sector on the federal budget by making possible the decrease and eventual elimination of sector sub-sidies, which in 1993 amounted to 1% of GDP; promote the long-term sustainability of the coal sector through the establishment of a com-petitive, commercial industry; support a restructuring program to reduce the size of the industry while increasing its efficiency; and cushion the socioeconomic impacts of the restructuring on coal miners, their families, and affected communities. The SECAL was accompanied by a $25 million loan for a Coal Sector Restructuring Implementation Assistance Project, which included:

- Support for stakeholders' participatory activities at the national, regional, and local level for government, coal industry, and non-governmental institutions
- Social programs to be implemented by local governments, nongovernmental and community-based organizations with continuous social assessment, and social impact monitoring of the coal reform program

- Improvements of the management of government subsidies to the coal sector to enhance transparency and financial accountability and to ensure that target groups received the level of subsidies for the purposes intended
- Assistance for commercialization and demonopolization of coal companies, environmental management associated with the coal industry, development of procedures for closing unprofitable mines, and for operation of the government's coal reform agency in the Ministry of Economy.

The social assessment carried out as part of the SECAL's preparation had a profound impact on the coal reform program by:

- Demonstrating (unexpectedly) that non-miners in coal regions were the largest group affected adversely by the coal reform program. In response, a major part of coal sector subsidies was reoriented to coal communities for the population at large rather than to coal companies for coal miners who had been a privileged economic group. In addition new mechanisms were devised to make the purpose, beneficiaries, and the distribution channels for subsidies more transparent and able to be monitored.
- Revealing that human settlements in the coal region have diverse characteristics with respect to demographic structure, income level, and labor force. This would appear to be self-evident but much of the reform agenda treated the coal sector as a monolith. The social assessment persuaded the government to recognize the local nature of many of the problems and of possible solutions for the coal sector.
- Demonstrating that the transfer of social assets from coal companies to local governments—an important objective of the coal reform program—was having adverse effects on local communities that were not previously anticipated. In response, coal subsidies for social assets were redirect from coal companies to coal communities.
- Showing that miners and non-miners had low trust in the government, in the coal industry, and in outside agencies such as the World Bank, but would trust a new institution representing of a broad range of stakeholders. The interagency Coal Commission and the Association of Coal Mining Cities, new institutions with broad stakeholder representation, became the vehicles by which many decisions were made. In addition pilot programs were created to channel loan funds for the first time in Russia to nongovernmental and community-based organizations, as well as to labor unions.
- Suggesting that measures to enhance workers' ability to move freely in search of alternative employment were seen by many coal miners facing job loss as more relevant than expensive job creation schemes whose funding and efficiency were questionable.

Difficult negotiations between the groups in Russia pushing for reform and those advocating the status quo—with control over nearly $2 billion in annual subsidies at stake—were affected by what the social assessment revealed about the coal mining regions and peoples' concerns, especially about the subsidy system and the pro-- cedures for closing mines. At one point in the negotiations over the subsidy system, the sup-porters of the status quo produced an elaborate justification for keeping the existing system. The advocates of reform pointed to the results of the social assessment this way: those who were sup-posed to benefit from subsidies had no trust in the existing system. The findings showed that it was not the reformers alone or an outside insti-tution like the World Bank proposing and supporting change, but the people themselves. The subsidy system was changed.

In addition, donor support, particularly from the World Bank, was facilitated because Russia could demonstrate that its coal sector reform program was cushion-ing the impact of reform on the most affected people, as the people them-selves thought relevant and appropriate when they spoke through the social assessment—their vehicle for stakeholder consultation. Experience from around the world has shown that reform of coal sectors is difficult, costly, and takes many years, if not decades, to happen. The social assessment gave World Bank staff more confidence that Russia's coal sector reform program was based on realities in the coal mining areas and responded to the real needs of people. The Implementation Assistance Project's funding of social monitoring ensured that the process of social assessment and stakeholder participation would continue to be part of the future reform agenda for coal in Russia.

Social Assessments Are Essential for the Bank's Sector Analysis Work

Sector work in the World Bank is designed to identify systematically the challenges, con-straints, and options for a country in a specific sector, based on that country's own situation—such as population, resources, and needs—and considering relevant worldwide factors. Sector work sets the framework for the Bank's invest-ment lending and policy dialogue in a sector as well as its identification of specific investment opportunities.

Given the scope and importance of compre-hensive sector studies, it would appear that social assessments should be key building blocks on which sector work is founded. Yet this has not been the case in the countries covered by this book, except perhaps for the Bank's poverty assessment studies. The explanation for this gap is the need for World Bank sector work to con-centrate on macroeconomic analysis for new Bank members and on sector issues for which reform options have been explored in other parts of the world and are thought to be trans-ferable to the countries of the former Soviet Union. Also, these countries' desire to borrow quickly for investment projects has meant that sector work and project preparation have in many cases been merged, rather than carried out in sequence. Still, sector reform is deeply country specific, and would benefit greatly from social assessment at the sector level.

The first draft of the Russia coal sector report, for instance, covered the coal industry as one national industry to be analyzed. The Russians requested the World

Bank team to do a second draft, assessing the industry coal basin by coal basin. The final report was a much more relevant document that served as an important basis for preparing the Russia Coal Social Adjustment loan. Thus a social assessment at the sector level proved to be, in this case, very useful for designing a major, sector-wide restructuring intervention. It is likely that this is true for all or most Bank and borrower programs, and that the use of social analysis in sector-wide studies and programs could be considerably expanded, both within the Bank and in other institutions.

When identifying constraints and reform options, sector work should investigate the social processes and factors that determine the current situation in the sector as well as the framework for realistic reform. As such, social assessment could have important contributions in:

- Identifying key sector stakeholders and proposing a framework for their participations as actors in sector reform
- Evaluating the impact of reform options on stakeholders, especially to gain their support where possible and to understand their opposition when it occurs
- Designing measures to mitigate adverse effects of sector reform proposals
- Identifying cost-effective interventions that could be undertaken immediately, the "win-win" actions that facilitate the implementation of sector reform in its early stage
- Determining whether a sector is appropriate for Bank investment operations given the Bank's social development and poverty reduction objectives, including the most appropriate target groups and geographic areas where these objectives can best be achieved.

The social assessment in sector reviews is a more systematic process of stakeholder consultation, especially in countries of the former Soviet Union, where the traditional institutions of civil society such as nongovernmental orga-nizations are not as representative of population viewpoints as they are in other parts of the world.

Utilizing of social assessment in sector reviews would go far in defining the social development agenda so that a social assessment would not have to be done in great depth for each investment operation in the sector.

Social Assessments and Investment Lending

The social assessments that our division has supported and used have had a profound effect on the focus and shape of our investment pro-jects in countries of the former Soviet Union. As a result, these investment projects are more appropriate for the people being helped, more efficient and financially viable, involve the peo-ple in ways that reduce investment costs and improve operational performance, and are environmentally more sustainable. This may seem an ambitious contention, but if true, it implies that social assessments can make as great a con-tribution to World Bank investment lending as the traditional economic, financial, technical, and environmental tools for evaluating projects. Consider, for instance, the Baku (Azerbaijan) Water Supply Rehabilitation Project for which a $61 million IDA credit was approved in June 1995. This project was originally conceived as the provision of pumping stations and spare parts so that the traditional water company operations could be "restarted." As a result of the social assessment, however, the focus of the project shifted substantially towards involving the consumers in the investment project.

The social assessment revealed the high level of water losses caused by leaks in households and in the distribution system. This resulted in the project's budgeting for a community-based repair and maintenance system for 180,000 households, as well as for a major network repair program. The social assessment also illustrated the need for a metering and billing pro-gram for households and industries as a means for improving the water company's finances and for promoting water conservation. A consumer outreach and awareness-raising program was designed to provide information on reducing water losses, to build public awareness about the scarcity of water and the need for conserva-tion, to show the importance of community par-ticipation in leakage repair programs, and to explain the need to pay for water and the advan-tages of metering for improved cost recovery.

The social assessment also showed that the water company had little knowledge about the preferences of its customers. Therefore, the project included establishing a consumer relations unit within the water company to deal with con-sumers as partners.

In Kazakhstan in 1995 the government and the World Bank initiated a detailed preparation for a Water Supply, Sanitation, and Health Project in the Aralsk and Kazalinsk regions, the parts of the country most affected by the deterioration of living conditions resulting from the Aral Sea shrinkage. A social assessment was carried out that showed that people's concern about water was in fourth place, behind income to buy food, cooking fuel shortages, and unpaid wages. As a result, project preparation was stopped, redirected, and begun with a wider focus on peoples' concerns, especially the contribution of water to economic activities such as gardening and raising livestock. Rather than start with a full scale investment project, the government and the World Bank decided to fund a small pilot project to test project design and implementation capacity. Thus, the major contribution of the social assessment in Kazakhstan was in reorienting project preparation before it had gone too far in a direction that did not respond to peoples' needs. In Turkmenistan the initial orientation of the Urban Transport Project was toward the provision of new buses and spares to raise the level of service. The social assessment done during project identification revealed a system in chaos, with 90% of users dissatisfied with the service, which was practically non-existent during the evening rush hour. The key problems were the behavior of drivers and the poor finances of the bus company. The social assessment identified a number of operational improvements and poten-tial solutions, including:

- Substantially raising bus drivers' salaries thus reducing their incentive to exploit the public in order to supplement their incomes. At the same time transport

supervisors were designated to ride on buses to monitor driver behavior, and fare collectors were added to buses. This "carrot and stick" approach to the key problem of driver behavior resulted in a marked improvement in driver performance and hence in better service to the public.
- Increasing the nominal fare by 200% and making other improvements in ticket availability. This improved bus company finances enough to keep more buses in service.

As a result of these reforms more buses were available for longer periods of time, allowing an improvement in bus scheduling, and satisfying a key complaint of consumers. Internal management and personnel policies were also improved.

In this way, the social assessment made possible real improvements in urban transport service more than 18 months *before World Bank investment funds were scheduled to become available.*

The Turkmenistan social assessment revealed that the findings of social assessments cannot always be acted on automatically and that they, in turn, must be subject to the other usual analytical criteria for investment lending: economic, financial, technical, and environmental. That social assessment showed, for instance, that consumers expressed strong preference for having a seat in public transport vehicles during rush hour. If acted on uncritically, this priority would have resulted in overinvestment, since few urban transport systems can afford to satisfy this demand. Furthermore, the social assessment's survey by city zones reported the need to improve the road systems in parts of the city. Although also a legitimate concern this need was not within the financial possibilities of the Bank-funded project.

Perhaps the most extensive use of social assessment occurred during the preparation of the Uzbekistan Water Supply, Sanitation, and Health Project. As part of an extensive stakeholder consultation process on the project design, five distinct social assessments on different aspects of the project were carried out. One of these covered Karakalpakstan and Khorezm—the two administrative territories most severely affected by Aral Sea Basin conditions—and were very helpful in directing the investments necessary for addressing the environmental and social consequences.

With regard to implementation arrangements, the social assessment and participation process helped convince people to change their view on some design options for the project. In initial meetings, people expressed strong preference for a self-managed water supply scheme because they believed that the local water company, Vodokanal, would provide poor service if it managed the plan. However, when the community received information on the advantages, disadvantages, and costs of the various schemes, they agreed with the experts' recommendation to link the community with the main supply pipeline operated by Vodokanal. This community consultation approach was a first experience for Vodokanal. While initially there was a hostile reaction from the community and apprehension from Vodokanal's perspective, the end result has been beneficial for all stakeholders.

The social assessment also changed the technical parameters of a key project including the definition of what is "acceptable" water quality. The government suggested that a water supply project would have to use low-cost investments such as shallow wells and handpumps. But the social assessment found that 68% of households complained of the salty taste of their main water supply. It was then decided to complement the social assessment with a salinity taste-tolerance survey. This survey found that the local population would tolerate salinity up to 2000 mg/l, and twice higher than Uzbekistan's own national standard of 1000 mg/l.

This finding had important cost-savings implications for the project: given resource scarcity, the project can make smaller investments in water quality to meet the 2000 mg/l tolerance level rather than the 1000 mg/l national standard. On the other hand, the survey demonstrated that shallow wells and handpumps, supplying water with salinity levels between 5000 and 7000 mg/l might appear to allow an acceptable investment pattern. But this appearance is deceptive from the consumer's viewpoint, because the water produced would be undrinkable.

The social assessment and the local consultation process also suggested that it was possible to test a lower water consumption design standard, which would permit reducing investments and operating costs of water distribution networks. The current design norm of 350 l per person per day has been reduced to 150 l per person per day, a change made primarily for financial reasons. This change might well have been rejected as socially unconscionable had the information supplied by consultations and social assessment not been available.

Finally, the social assessment showed that people's highest priority was access to income-generating activities. This finding led to the introduction of several pilot schemes implemented by the government and financed by the donor com-munity. The project design adopted a labor-inten-sive approach to water supply and sewer-age investments in order to maximize local employ-ment opportunities. Proponents of this approach, however, will still have to battle it out with the external commercial interests who are proposing capital-intensive approaches, but at least there is evidence of support from the affected people.

The social assessment for Uzbekistan pro-vided me—and my colleagues on the project's operational and financial sides—with valuable information, otherwise unavailable, about how much water consumers in rural areas would be prepared to use at various price levels. We also decided that the project would include a pilot demonstration of a water metering system servicing small groups of households organized as water user associations. This will test the benefits of a system that charges consumers for the actual amount of water consumed.

Social Assessments for Emergency and Post-conflict Lending

Since its establishment after the Second World War the World Bank has had the special role of assisting governments with programs to recover from natural and human-caused disasters and civil strife. Project preparation after floods and human-caused disasters (such as oil spills) often has to be telescoped and done under extreme time pressure as emergency interventions. There is a tendency to conclude that there is "no time to consult" with the affected people. In addition, it is suggested that the relief agencies, rather than the World Bank, are the ones that should consult with stakeholders, since choice of relief services will have an immediate effect on stakeholders, in contrast to longer-term reconstruc-tion activities funded by the World Bank.

In reality, however, because of implementation constraints and lack of sufficient money from domestic resources and the donor community, it is common that the reconstruction efforts cannot rebuild completely what has been lost, at least not in the near and medium term. Consequently, consultation of stakeholders about what should be reconstructed, and in what order, is enormously relevant, especially since commercial and political interests often claim that heavy infrastructure recon-struction is more important than social or light infrastruc-ture reconstruction. We have learned that social assessments can be done quickly with results that facilitate decision-making and choices about what needs to be reconstructed and to what standards.

In 1994 the World Bank helped the govern-ment of Tajikistan prepare a prelim-inary pro-gram of reconstruction following severe floods and a pause in the civil strife. The mandate given to the Bank's team emphasized physical and commercial reconstruction, due to the desperate economic situation of the country, rather than other areas such as shelter, for which temporary measures were thought to be adequate. Yet the social assessment—in this case more traditionally ethnographic, without detailed sample surveys—brought to our attention that shelter in Tajik society was more than housing—it was also the nucleus and location for various economic activ-ities of the extended family. Therefore, the recon-struction program we eventually proposed gave more prominence to housing as filling also the functions of a basic eco-nomic unit, much more than it would have had if we consid-ered housing only as shelter.

In 1994 Tajikistan was a new member of the World Bank, and its local institu-tions, including community organizations, were unfamiliar to the international community. The social assess-ment raised the possibility of mobilizing com-munity capital based on what already existed from the communist era or was embedded in traditional structures. When the civil strife less-ened, and it became clear that there would be few external resources available for reconstruc-tion, social assessments were continued in Tajikistan. These surveys revealed what people felt were the highest priorities to be delivered through efficient existing channels such as local and international nongovernmental organiza-tions, in the face of an already overburdened public service.

Social assessments can be especially effective for involving stakeholders in selecting priorities when financial resources are limited. In 1996 the Azerbaijan government requested the World Bank and the United Nations Development Programme to help establish the Azerbaijan Resettlement and Reconstruction Agency to assist internally displaced people returning to demilitarized areas surrounding Nagorno--Karabakh. With lasting peace yet to be estab-lished in Nagorno-Karabakh and in view of the international community's preoccupation with reconstruction in Bosnia, it is unlikely that suffi-cient external resources will be available to Azerbaijan in the near term to restore to former levels the full range of infrastructure, and social and economic services. The government has instituted a process of social assessments, allowing internally displaced people to help decide how the limited financial resources should be used to improve their lives. It remains to be seen whether the social assessment results will have more impact than the central planning mental-ity of many people in this former Soviet Republic.

Emergency lending poses special demands on social assessments because of the need to move quickly. On January 24, 1994, the govern-ment of the Komi Republic, through the govern-ment of the Russian Federation, requested the World Bank and the European Bank for Reconstruction and Development to provide emergency assistance to deal with the oil spill from a major oil pipeline in the Komi Republic near Usinsk. If not contained, the oil spill threat-ened to flow into the Kolva, Usa, and Pechora Rivers, posing a massive threat to the fragile Arctic climate. The spill, estimated at three times that of the Exxon Valdez on the Pacific Coast of North America, had to be dealt with before the spring floods expected in May and June. Moreover, a spill recovery capacity had to be cre-ated in the river systems in the likely event that the oil could not be fully contained. The leaking pipeline had to be replaced over an 84 km stretch under difficult construction conditions before further leaks developed and before the spring and summer floods made it impossible to work in the swampy tundra.

The project preparation effort which began the day after the government request and involved social scientists including representa-tives of a local nongovernmental organization—Save the Pechora Foundation. Using interviews and surveys they assessed the priorities perceived by the 7000 people (10% of the population) living in villages within a 200 km radius of the affected area.

The social assessment revealed that the high-est priorities were preventing the spill from reaching the river systems and protecting against future pipeline ruptures. A long list of local improvements followed, showing a lack of adequate investment in basic social services over many years. At the top of this list, the peo-ple placed funding for children's vacations and emergency food for livestock.

In its implementation the Oil Spill Recovery and Mitigation Project placed highest priority on preventing the spill from spreading. This was successful. Imple-mentation of the social pro-grams received lower priority and was com-pleted at a slower pace than planned. As often happens the "hardware" got more attention than the "software," but in this instance that emphasis reflected the views of the people most directly affected. Also, the social assessment exercise for the Komi Project did not delay pro-ject preparation or implementation, and it was done at low cost.

Social Assessments in the World Bank: The Current Situation

The question inevitably arises: If social assess-ments are as important for World Bank policy work and investment lending as our work has shown, why do we not carry them out system-atically for all projects? And if they are not done very often, what needs to be done to change this?

So far, the Bank's staff members who have championed social assessment—not all of whom are social scientists—have received insuf-ficient support for their efforts.

Some people in the Bank, and in other devel-opment agencies, might contend that social assessments have always been done, have been a part of discussing Bank operations with client countries, and have been included in the work Bank staff did for demon-strating the economic, financial, technical, and environmental justification for projects. This is a retrospective exaggeration, though there has been an improvement in stakeholder consultation in recent years. Such aspects of our social analyses have been done in an ad hoc manner rather than as a result of a systematic, professional approach, as a social assessment should be.

The Participation Sourcebook, published by the World Bank in 1996, states that social assess-ments must be carried out in a project context to do the following:

- Identify key stakeholders and establish an appropriate framework for their participation in the project selection, design, and implementation
- Ensure that project objectives and incentives for change are acceptable to the range of people intended to benefit, and that gender and other social differences are reflected in project design
- Assess the social impact of investment projects and, where adverse impacts are identified, determine how they can be overcome or at least substantially mitigated
- Develop ability at the appropriate level to enable participation, resolve conflict, permit service delivery, and carry out mitigation measures as required.

What this sourcebook recommends about social assessments is what we should have been doing all along—assessing and consulting with those we are trying to help about the best way to help them. It takes humility for the World Bank's management and staff to admit the need to orga-nize differently in order to improve our perfor--mance on consultation. This is what many outside the Bank, and some inside the Bank, have been long saying, and what many more inside the Bank are now admitting.

Good quality, professionally administered social assessments require additional time and financial resources, just when of international donor agencies are being asked to do more with less money and fewer people. The contention that social assessments will save money by improving project performance is probably true. But it is seen by some as a long-term hope better left for tomor-row, especially as Bank staff see their budgets for project preparation being cut. Even fulfilling tra-ditional economic, financial, and technical analy-sis is in doubt. If another unfunded mandate is given, yet allowed somehow to remain voluntary, it can hardly be welcomed by those responsible for project preparation in international develop-ment agencies.

If we add the uneven professional output of the social sciences in general, the sometimes weak technical qualifications of some social science staff, and the frequent lack of quality control over social scientists in development agencies, it will be possible to ignore social assessments and yet not feel as though we are contributing any less to solving problems in developing countries or countries in transition. I contend that the poor quality of some of the social science work in the World Bank has much to do with the prejudices of economists, financial analysts, and technicians toward non-economic "social science." When a non-social specialist staff member says that "surveys have been done," meaning by this that thirty-nine people met on the street over several days were kind of asked about a major sector adjustment operation—it should not pass for social science. Client countries and agencies that have profited from decades of perfecting the way the Bank proceeds in doing economic, financial, and technical analysis, do not have far to look for evidence of the sloppiness of what we have often called "spontaneous" social assess-ments. This situation will not change until the international development institutions intro-duce an exacting *standard of professionalism* for social assess-ments, and quality control by recognized social scientists and other competent professionals that results in acceptable quality.

The quality of social assessments can be enhanced and costs brought down by the use of local country social scientists. The network of social scientists in Central Asian countries, which the World Bank has helped to establish and which has received generous funding from Switzerland (through the Bank) is an important step and support in this direction.

The World Bank has tried to stimulate the use of participatory approaches in general and social assessments in particular through a positive, voluntary series of measures. These mea-sures have ranged from subsidizing the work of social scien-tists to helping budget-starved task managers through a special fund, to describing best practices as examples to follow and to publishing the Bank's *Participation Sourcebook*. This reflects the Bank's early days of environmental work, when it was assumed that attention to environmental concerns would be sufficient to "main-stream" the environment in World Bank policy work and investment operations. Before the recent emphasis in the Bank on what we call "social assessment" as equivalent to the "sociological analysis" or environmental analysis required by the Bank's operational policy on project appraisal, the happenstance initiatives of staff members to discuss with local people did not quite result in the mainstreaming of sound environmental criteria. Often, only when environmental nongovernmental organizations publicized some of the more egregious environmental disasters accom-panying some World Bank loans, did the Bank take a normative or "manda-tory" approach. This change included reissuing operational direc-tives for all staff and the creation of environ-mental organizational units in all Bank regional vice presidencies, both for review and for direct environmental work.

Social assessments and the promotion of participatory approaches seems to be going through the same experience as environmental concerns did earlier. As long as the instructions are only voluntary, and the work unfunded through regular budget allocation, social assessments will often receive the same lip-service that the environment received before structured attention was mandated. Few people will argue that the World Bank is not a better place today due to the seriousness with which it now treats the environment. The same can be said if we treated social assessments with equal seriousness.

The social assessment studies that our division has commissioned were not perfect. But they represent a constructive and useful attempt in some parts of the World Bank to move toward a more professional and relevant process of doing hands-on social analysis and using local social scientists, thus improving the Bank's performance in its new member countries. Social assessments are one of the better means of making the work of international development agencies more effective, more relevant, and genuinely appreciated by the people we are assisting.

Jonathan Brown graduated from Yale in 1966 and the School of Communications at the University of Pennsylvania. After his graduation, he served in the Peace Corps in Chad for 3 years and then returned to the United States to attend the Harvard Business School. He joined the World Bank in 1973. During his 35 year career in the World Bank as a manager of operational units doing lending and policy work he focused geographically on Africa and the countries of the Former Soviet Union, and thematically on energy, infrastructure, health and water supply and sanitation. He reviewed hundreds of projects and sector programs for funding.

Starting as early as in mid-1970s he made sure that people's needs are identified by, and responded to, with the projects of the divisions he headed. He pioneered social assessment and public participation in his work on natural disasters, reconstruction after civil strife, and in policy and project finance. He was involved in assessing the social impacts of numerous projects, particularly in the energy and infrastructure sectors, in preparing mitigation programs dealing with social risks and adverse social impacts, and then in monitoring the implementation of these plans.

After his retirement from the World Bank in 2008, he took on an assignment for 1 year as Director of Operations of the Global Fund against AIDS, TB and Malaria in Geneva to improve the quality of its operations while maintaining high levels of disbursement and to participate in the recruitment of a permanent successor. He helped establish and managed Social Assessment LLC and was the founder of its affiliate, Social Risk Management LLC.

Open Access This chapter is licensed under the terms of the Creative Commons Attribution 4.0 International License (http://creativecommons.org/licenses/by/4.0/), which permits use, sharing, adaptation, distribution and reproduction in any medium or format, as long as you give appropriate credit to the original author(s) and the source, provide a link to the Creative Commons license and indicate if changes were made.

The images or other third party material in this chapter are included in the chapter's Creative Commons license, unless indicated otherwise in a credit line to the material. If material is not included in the chapter's Creative Commons license and your intended use is not permitted by statutory regulation or exceeds the permitted use, you will need to obtain permission directly from the copyright holder.

Social Analysis in Project Lending: Writing New Rules and Changing Old Practices

Susanna Price

Introduction

In 1984 the World Bank placed social analysis formally into the rulebook. For the first time amongst multilateral development banks (MDBs), the Bank's rulebook integrated social analysis into a key operational checkpoint before project approval. This took the form of "sociological aspects" as a policy methodology of the World Bank's investment project appraisal, on a par with economic, financial, institutional, technical, and environmental analyses.

The policies on resettlement and indigenous peoples represented a breakthrough in defining requirements to protect the people adversely affected by Bank projects, but the appraisal rule had a wider scope and intent. However crucial, resettlement and indigenous people's policies were, by definition, applicable only to a proportion of the Bank's investment projects triggering those policies. The new rule was of a different character—applying to the Bank's entire portfolio of investment projects, it provided a proactive strategy to enhance project success and sustainability through social design. It formally launched social, poverty, and gender analysis in operational form, together with participative approaches to project planning and design, recognizing the people as ultimate users for whom loans were intended. Social analysis had formally come of age—but never realized its potential.

Described as an "enabling framework" (Davis 2004) and "conceptually pathbreaking" (Dani 2003: 8) the rule—Operational Manual Statement (OMS) 2.20—was "not systematically implemented" (ibid). The notion of a rule for social analysis in the rulebook, however, gained traction both inside and beyond the Bank, proving that rules can be both ignored in implementation, but also have wider impact by virtue of their existence. This chapter examines this paradox, tracing the story of the

---

S. Price (✉)
College of Asia and the Pacific, Australian National University, Canberra, ACT, Australia
e-mail: susanna.price@anu.edu.au

social analysis component of the appraisal rule, its reason for being, how it came about, and its impact on World Bank operations, and beyond.

Challenging Social Pioneers

Development was bypassing the poor. After decades of lending at the World Bank President MacNamara emphasised:

> ...the critical relationship of social equity to economic growth...the need to design development strategies that would bring greater benefits to the poorest groups in the developing countries—particularly to the approximately 40 per cent of their populations who are neither contributing significantly to economic growth nor sharing equitably in economic progress (MacNamara 1973).

The dominant paradigm was shifting, as rural producers emerged from the mists of their supposedly immutable belief systems to become potential future consumers contributing to economic growth. As pragmatic economic actors they became part of a modernizing economic growth story. Projects that intended to benefit them should, logically, be re-designed to capture that potential also.

MacNamara proposed to lend significantly more money—and to assess the distribution of benefits arising from that expenditure. He proposed several new lending foci to increase the productivity of small agriculturalists: land tenure reform, access to credit, better input supplies, reorganised services, and institutions. The World Bank formed a Rural Development Division to manage these foci and, in 1974, hired its first staff sociologist to work primarily on rural social formations and co-operatives. Other changes included increased financing, new initiatives in evaluation, and in environmental assessment, and more money for social sectors.

Realizing McNamara's vision to reach the lowest 40% of people triggered broader operational questions—how to identify specific groups, engage their support, and to understand the social context that shaped their lives. This chapter explores why it was necessary to write new content into the Bank's policies and procedures, and so into the investment projects.

The absence of social perspectives was not surprising. Multilateral Development Bank (MDB) charters did not mention people or the social context in which lending operations would unfold. For decades, consequently, large sums were spent without knowing how people lived, worked, and networked, what they believed, valued, prioritised, and could access, and whether they had benefitted as intended. National plans abstractedly highlighting improved human well-being rarely specified targets or programs. Borrowers and lenders alike conceptualized "social" or "human factors" at best as residual, of little account, or at worst, as "social constraints" to economic growth transformations. Local institutions were considered impediments, not building blocks, to development. When such investments failed those intractable "social constraints" offered a scapegoat (Apthorpe 1970; Price 2015).

The benefits of economic growth were widely assumed to outweigh any adverse social consequences. Development agencies favoured building urban industrial sectors emulating developed country "progress" from which benefits might trickle downwards. Superimposing external growth-generating inputs, planners ignored pre-existing local socio-economic forms of production and trading (Hart 1970). Iron-clad tradition was thought to stifle individual initiative, despite emerging work showing multiple negotiated reciprocities in complex, and dynamic, agrarian societies (Scott 1976). Intended beneficiaries of urban and rural health, nutrition, and education services, were rarely consulted in planning those services (Rosser 1970; Apthorpe 1970), let alone taking responsibility for setting and implementing their own programs.

Women's role and productivity were routinely ignored. Esther Boserup's work (1970) questioned the widespread assumption that lending was gender neutral, demonstrating that projects could harm women because planners were gender blind to women's roles.

Neither the MDBs nor their borrowers checked before approval for environmental and social costs on differentiated groups of people in the project's zone of impact, nor matched projects to sociological features to improve the prospects for their success. They required no public consultation on investment decisions before approval, nor participation of the intended beneficiaries in project design.

Emerging Social Perspectives

Before 1974, the World Bank had never appointed anthropologists, rural sociologists, and other social researchers to in-house positions. Their skills were not deemed relevant to the core business of planning and managing lending. Gloria Davis, the first anthropologist appointed to the World Bank in 1978, attributed the Bank's social concepts and practices to a "broad spectrum of individuals and institutions both inside and outside the Bank" (Davis 2004: iv). In 1973 Vice president Warren Baum circulated a paper entitled *A Report with Recommendations on the Use of Anthropology in Project Operations of the World Bank Group* (Cochrane and Naronha 1973). The paper recommended increased social input into Bank projects by hiring social specialists. Bank staff supported this idea but did not know how to do it.

The idea that anthropological and sociological knowledge could enhance project impacts was not new. Goodenough's 1963 classic, *Cooperation and Change: An Anthropological approach to Community Development,* in asserting that any development project not founded on a thorough understanding of the client culture was doomed to failure, had earlier provided development workers with a crash course in cultural anthropology. Community development approaches themselves had diverse and longstanding origins which would influence some lenders more than others. Yet anthropologists, emphasizing the importance of understanding the unique characteristics of each society, may have inadvertently reinforced the notion of immutable tradition accompanied by intractable local institutions, in which social scientists served only as translators to the more enlightened shock troops of economic development. Moreover, in studying cultures as unique constructs, anthropologists may have overlooked the broader economic and political transformations occurring in rural societies.

The question of how to translate social concerns into specific planning steps was being addressed during the 1960s, for example, at the Institute of Development Studies in the UK (Apthorpe 1970). Social specialists had been involved in *ex-post* evaluation for some years, providing valuable feedback on project outcomes—but had no clear feedback link into project selection and design to avoid replicating mistakes.

Optimistically assuming that social and cultural factors were irrelevant, planners blindly believed in the transformative value of "progressive" thought, to justify project approval. They assumed successful models were easily replicable anywhere. Albert O. Hirschman, an economist, conversely, opposed such assumptions as deepening the risk of failure. His notion of a "Hiding Hand" might unexpectedly, through human ingenuity, rescue the project from failure.[1] More importantly for subsequent developments, Hirschman found each project, upon close inspection, to "represent a unique combination of experiences and consequences, of direct and indirect effects", resulting from the varied interplay between the "structural characteristics" of projects, and the "social and political environment" in which they were situated (Hirschman 1967: 178). This approach recognized the importance of social and political factors in economic analysis of projects—factors with which he assumed that project planners could work to develop strategies for behavioral change for better projects. Hirschman brought these novel ideas into the World Bank.

The US National Environmental Protection Act (NEPA 1969/70) raised social issues. The first law linking the prediction of environmental impacts to investment planning in a regulatory framework, NEPA required an Environmental Impact Statement (EIS) if proposed investments involved US federal land, laws, or funds. Based upon feasibility study, decision makers could select the design option with least environmental cost, mitigating any remaining impacts. EIS required examination of social and cultural, as well as physical, impacts. NEPA widened investment decision-making to encompass human and cultural factors through what became Social Impact Assessment (SIA). This called for efforts to define social impacts; to predict changes in the distribution of those impacts; to identify the winners and losers of investment decision-making; and, in case of investment approval, to formulate mitigative measures to protect the personal and property rights of the losers (Barrow 2000).

These ideas had barely taken hold in 1973, however, at NEPA, let alone among the World Bank's borrower governments around the globe. The Bank's development investments unfolded in developing country frameworks that had little regulatory

---

[1]Hirschman's Hiding Hand has stimulated a recent debate on whether it is a Benevolent Hiding Hand or a Malevolent Hiding Hand (Flyvbjerg and Sunstein 2016: 1).

recognition of social risks or impacts, with very few social specialists. EIA and SIA parameters were still evolving subject to US court cases (Burdge et al. 2004). A mere subset of EIA, SIA languished in the environmental paradigm. Moreover, as first conceptualized, SIA emphasized the predictive impact of given project alternatives, rather than proactive social design or, even better, project selection.

The United States Congress legislated seminal changes in 1973 and 1975, promoting policy and budgetary efforts to increase employment and more equitable income opportunities for the poor. In an unprecedented step, the law makers required that the poor majority participate in the "decisions that shape their lives" (Hoben 1982). This participatory goal also called for greater attention "to interrelationships among technology, institutions, and economic, social, environmental and cultural factors" (ibid). As a result, USAID required, from September 1975, a Social Soundness Analysis, that aimed to reach beyond statistical data to address the core cultural values and beliefs invoked in many projects seeking to change production, resource use, food supply and social organization—particularly in poor communities (Cochrane 2019). It mandated the participation of those affected in planning projects.

Social soundness analysis had mixed results. Irritating non-social specialists with additional time and expense requirements, it came too late in the project cycle to make an impact for many social specialists (Hoben 1982). It increased exponentially the in-house and contracted anthropologists hired by USAID during the 1970s (ibid). Nonetheless, after only 5 years USAID found that this novel requirement had improved the design of about one quarter of USAID projects processed. Other multilateral agencies such as FAO and WHO were hiring social specialists; as did bilateral agencies, Sweden, Canada and Australia (AusAID 1989).

Social Analysis: Internal Bank Track

The World Bank President had, in 1973, declared that the poorest 40% were missing out on increases in GDP in developing countries, being instead consigned to malnutrition, illiteracy, and squalor—but this farsighted analysis was not accompanied by mandatory requirements on a par with USAID's Social Soundness Analysis. In 1974 the World Bank had reached the paradoxical situation of having a just and farsighted new macro-policy, while its analytical procedures languished, unreformed. In accordance with its official charter, the World Bank's "core business" required only economic, financial, technical, and commercial analysis for preparing new growth projects. The procedural document (1971) governing project preparation envisaged no hint of sociological input, let alone the notion that the people mattered in this process.

Staff faced a challenge: they must identify and reach the poorest 40%, design projects capable of reaching and engaging them, and succeed in reducing poverty tangibly. The Bank's first professional sociologist, Michael Cernea, appointed in 1974, diagnosed retrospectively:

The absence of social analysis from the Bank's arsenal of project crafting tools, was, however, at that time, part of a wider problem. What was missing was not just the "technology" of doing social analysis. The gap was much wider: it was philosophical and cognitive. A theory or social philosophy about the role of people as development actors was missing. In the social sciences, work on "inducing development" was then still an emerging domain. Development sociology and development anthropology themselves were young new fields of research and thinking, rather than disciplines or sub-disciplines with rich research records, codified bodies of knowledge, or mature epistemology.... The Bank would not yet have an articulated overall methodology for inducing social change, except by supplying finance and purchasing technology. Much was still to be invented, tested, articulated on the social dimensions of development investment projects (Cernea 2013).

The obsolete 1971 guideline on project appraisal continued to be used during the entire decade of the 1970s. The guideline provided no way of assessing whether the benefits of the project being appraised would benefit the lowest 40% of the population, nor whether those hard-to-reach people had been consulted.[2]

Cernea in 1977 created a "Bank Sociological Group" (BSG) for the tiny but growing band of in-house staff social specialists, and other staff interested in social and cultural issues. The group's wide ranging, open, intellectual, and practical discussions attracted many, including several Bank staff who had hitherto hidden advanced sociological training. Often, the topics would be one or more Bank projects which had either failed spectacularly or succeeded remarkably. In either case, the presenters were invited to analyze—detached, and with the benefit of hindsight—what led to that success or failure. From there, the discussion of social and cultural circumstances of any development project took flight in the open and 'informal space' of the BSG. Speakers from the Bank's Board of Executive Directors, and most senior management, accepted the BSG invitations to speak to the group; as did talented external social scientists knowledgeable about the Bank's projects.[3]

Since division chiefs responsible for hiring staff had no idea what sociologists or anthropologists could contribute, Cernea organized Bank seminars addressing Vice President Warren Baum's paper defining the typical tasks staff carried out at key points of the project cycle. Promoted as *Model of Entry Points for Sociological Knowledge in the Project Cycle*, an amended document alerted staff, especially middle level managers, to what professional social specialists could contribute at each key step, from the earliest project identification; through to post-project evaluation. Being a purposive intervention for accelerating and targeting development, projects offered scope to involve the intended project beneficiaries. Cernea's additions to Baum's model showed how social science knowledge about the

---

[2]Cernea recounted that in 1974, newly arrived and assigned his first project appraisal mission, he asked what his tasks would be. He was given the 1971 Operations Manual Statement (OMS) on project appraisal, to read and find out. He panicked. Nothing in the OMS required the skills and contributions that he, as a sociologist, could make. That memory stayed with him over the years, reinforced by the conviction that the 1971 document was obsolete and inadequate (Cernea pers. com. January 2019).

[3]See Nuket Kardam's PhD on the BSG's influence on the IBRD (Kardam 1993).

project area, strategy, and objectives could enhance, and enrich, the staff understanding at each project cycle stage, thereby enhancing demand for social specialists on Teams.[4]

It was important to show that social specialists could do more than simply "translate" local culture into non-specialist terms, based on their research among ethnic populations: they could substantially contribute to the planning and design of projects. Cernea's informal guide entitled *Minimal and Optimal Requirements for Social Information in Appraisal Reports* defined the sociological knowledge that was necessary as a basis for project approval (Cernea 1987; 1995).

The emerging discipline of the sociology of development offered the theoretical argument for an alternative model for projects, a model in which the "social actors are the pivotal element, the central core around which all other resources should be marshaled for action" (Cernea 2013; 2015). In 1982 these initiatives paved the way for the formulation of a template for the "sociological aspects" of appraisal of projects. A Bank Task Force which wrote a new "Operational Manual Statement ("OMS")[5] 2.20 on "Project Appraisal" included "Sociological Aspects" of Appraisal. Management approved it in 1984.

Appraising "Sociological Aspects"

In naming "sociological aspects" as an integral element of project appraisal, along with economic, financial, technical, institutional, and environmental analysis (World Bank 1984), OMS 2.20 brought substantive sociological knowledge into the standard for judging whether a project was suitable for Bank financing. Mapping new cognitive and epistemological terrain, OMS 2.20 set projects a standard to meet before their approval. The "Sociological Aspects"—or, as it came to be termed, "social analysis" of OMS 2.20 allowed clearer definition of the project 'target groups' or the 'intended beneficiaries', together with methods designed to ensure that different sub-groups participated in, and benefited from, project interventions.

OMS 2.20 required project staff responsible for processing the project loans—whether they were economic, technical, or financial analysts—to identify the population toward whom a project was directed and to give them an active role in the project itself: *"projects designed to assist specific beneficiaries ... depend* [for their success] *upon participation by the beneficiaries."* Each project required *"the explicit consideration of the social organization patterns, traditions, and values bearing upon the feasibility, implementation, and operation of projects; and the pursuit of objectives such as poverty alleviation"* (World Bank 1984, OMS 2.20, para. 55).

---

[4]The paper was subsequently published in Schwartzweller (ed.). (Cernea 1987).
[5]Operational Manual Statements, subsequently Operational Directives then Operational Policies, were the binding policies approved by management.

In four significant requirements, the scope of sociological analysis at appraisal necessarily included:

a) The socio-cultural and demographic characteristics of local beneficiaries;
b) The social organization of productive activities of the population in the project area;
c) The cultural acceptability of the project, its compatibility with the behavior and needs of the aimed as beneficiaries; and
d) The social strategy for project implementation and post completion operation, able to elicit and sustain beneficiaries' participation (para. 56)

Taking each point in turn, OMS 2.20 first demanded verification that the project design was based upon a sound understanding of the social and gender organization of productive activities—also a basis for analyzing the distribution of project benefits among different social groups (para 57) and thus understanding social equity. Project activities must be demonstrably "culturally acceptable" to the intended beneficiaries, that is: *understandable, agreed to, and capable of being operated and maintained by them* (para 61).

Second, the document formally introduced the principle of people's participation advocated by Cernea, and colleagues such as Gloria Davis and Maritta Koch-Weser. The OMS called for a *"social strategy for eliciting the full commitment to the project of the beneficiaries and their institutions"*—a principle that should operate right through the project cycle and should be supported by capacity building for effective participation.

Third, the OMS required (again for the first time in a Bank normative document) a gender perspective, or analysis of women's possible benefits or risks of negative impacts from a given project. Bank staff and borrowers were asked *to think* in advance about *"the contribution that women could make to achieving the project's goals"* and were also warned against *"changes which the project will introduce that might be disadvantageous to women"* (para 62).

Fourth, the OMS cautioned against imposing social risks on the project's population. If such risks had a high likelihood, a pilot or postponement for adequate counter-risk planning was recommended.

Social soundness data must be researched, collected, and employed by the borrowing country and studied by Bank's staff long before the final appraisal mission, necessitating Divisional staff to request the borrowing agency to engage social specialists to conduct social research, and to assemble the data for use from the start in project preparation. This raised awareness of the importance of social information in borrowing countries and triggered the inclusion of local sociologists and anthropologists in the country preparation teams. Impetus from 1975 onwards from USAID and other bilateral and multilateral agencies, together with modest but growing impact from environmental regulatory frameworks which included SIA all cumulatively helped develop country expertise.[6]

---

[6]For instance, a leading Indian anthropologist, Professor HM Mathur, wrote an article entitled: *"From Onlookers to Participants: How the Role of Social Scientists in India's Development has Changed."*

President McNamara had emphasized the critical relationship of social equity to economic growth and poverty reduction (1973). OMS 2.20 required distributional data to inform an economic analysis—but recognized methodological difficulties. Lack of country consensus might obstruct analysis of the appropriate trade-offs between efficiency, equity, and regional balances. Where reduction of income disparities and poverty were important project objectives, the economic appraisal must include an assessment of the project's contribution to these objectives.

Mostly, qualitative assessment sufficed to demonstrate the worth of projects with marginal economic returns but possibly high-income distribution of benefits. Quantitative assessment required allocation of costs and benefits according to the income status of the affected population—which the OMS 2.20 recognized as difficult, for example in determining poverty "target" income levels of beneficiaries; in allocating costs and benefits; and in achieving consensus on the weights which should be given to costs and benefits at different income levels (OMS 2.20).

The OMS allowed discretion in addressing social equity. Social analysis could inform economic analysis by providing social data, and a means of mobilizing stakeholder engagement for consensus building, but cooperation seems limited on assessing social equity and whether social benefits outweighed social costs.

Disseminating Social Analysis

Once approved, the Bank's social specialist community promoted OMS 2.20 internally and externally among borrowers, incorporating the ideas into influential book publications. The Bank's first sociological book (1985), *Putting People First: Sociological Variables in Development* Projects (Cernea 1985) was based on the central tenet that "people are—and should be—the starting point, the center, and the end goal of each development effort." It advocated a changed approach to planning internationally financed development projects for sectors including irrigation, forestry, cooperatives, livestock, roads, and other rural infrastructure, demonstrating how the principles could be applied in project experience.

Growing internal understanding of social perspectives did not necessarily translate into adoption of the rule, however. Placing social analysis, even into such a crucial point in the rulebook as project appraisal, by no means secured universal attention to it, since "compliance with the new guidelines was far from general and the institutional mechanisms for absorbing them were insufficient. Simply placing new rules on the Bank's internal guidebooks appeared to be not enough for triggering the profound changes in staff work patterns that meeting the new demands implied..." (Cernea and Kudat 1997: 6). As a new dimension in project work, social analysis needed consistent application, knowledgeable bank and borrower practitioners, plus time and resources for field research, and for integrating findings into the project design.

Newly independent former Soviet Union countries began joining the Bank as borrowers without any lending history. Analysis of these social transitions filled critical data gaps essential for loan processing. Gloria Davis wrote how, in 1997, Ayse Kudat led the social assessment thematic team to clarify and deepen the concept of social analysis as "social assessment", making it

> more systematic and rigorous. The objectives of social assessment were formally linked to poverty reduction and to other positive social outcomes such as enhancing social inclusion, strengthening social cohesion, increasing social capital, and reducing adverse social impacts. With increasing rigor, this generation of social assessments had a substantial impact on project design....where quantitative evidence of social impacts and their economic consequences was especially crucial to changing the approaches of policy makers....Through these efforts, and complementary work in the regions, the idea of social assessment was widely disseminated both inside and outside the Bank, and social assessments were increasingly mainstreamed in country programs and in the national procedures of some countries (Davis 2004: 22).

Social assessment in this context facilitated, rather than inhibited, loan processing, easing its acceptance. Even this deepened form of social assessment, however, did not necessarily generate a specific "product" additional to the design—a Resettlement Action Plan, for example. Absence of a visible product made it easier to mainstream the social analysis in OMS 2.20 into other Bank "rules" over time. A 2001 Board-endorsed Gender Strategy and a revised Operational Policy (OP), and Bank Procedure (BP) 4.20, for example, helped client countries address gender disparities that obstruct development. In 2001 OP 4.20 replaced OMS 2.20 for gender, thereby scaling down coverage only to projects in sectors and themes identified by the country strategy. An independent evaluation in 2009 recommended greater attention to accountability, monitoring, and results; and called for gender integration at the project level as had applied with OMS 2.20 (IEG 2009).

A new rule (OD 4.15 on Poverty Reduction, approved in 1991) addressed poverty issues. The Environmental and Social Framework (ESF) that became effective in 2017 now applies to the Bank's investment project financing, passing primary responsibility to borrowers for the necessary social assessments. The ESF identifies a range of potential social risks, including resettlement and indigeneity, particularly those which fall disproportionately on the disadvantaged and vulnerable. Environment and Social Statement (ESS) 10 deals with stakeholder engagement for investment projects and proposes actions to facilitate participation.

A recent view of the World Bank Inspection Reports (World Bank 2017) identified consultation, participation, and disclosure as key issues that had arisen in close to 90% of the 120 inspection requests since 1993. OMS 2.20 was phased out in 2012, leaving no formal "rule" to integrate social analysis into appraisal for investment projects. The next section examines the experience of another MDB in setting social analysis into the rulebook, before drawing lessons for the Conclusion.

Asia Pacific Regional: An Alternative Track

Founded in 1966, the MDB Asian Development Bank (ADB)'s model resembled other development lenders of the time. ADB worked almost exclusively with borrower government agencies, initially on infrastructure loans. In 1973, ADB's President called for development to be brought "directly to the people" (McCawley 2017). Surveys in the mid-1970s revealed that Asia's marginal farmers and landless laborers, particularly those in remote, dryland, and upland areas outside the well-irrigated schemes with their new high yielding varieties, were beset by social problems arising from joblessness, malnutrition, and hunger. Per capita grain production had barely risen given population growth rates, while nutritional levels declined. This situation prompted ADB's Board in 1978 to agree to increase lending for agriculture and rural development by 20% per year until 1982 (ibid).

This marginal group clearly needed attention. As in the World Bank case, however, effective ways had to be found within lending modalities to reach them. ADB staff began working on new approaches to bring project benefits to two groups missing out: women; and poorer, often indigenous small-scale producers. Reaching both groups required new thinking, challenging routine models.

After introducing a policy on women in development (WID) to Australia's bilateral aid agency (1975), ADB staff member Christine Whitlam introduced the concept of ADB Country Briefing Papers on women's role in development. Gender differences in access to and benefits from development reflected in country data from these papers showed women facing major barriers: heavy workloads, restricted access to education and health services, restricted access to planning and loss of status from some projects. Country strategy and programming exercises were envisaged to counter such barriers, and empower women to participate in project design, so as to enhance their opportunities and benefits. Such efforts greatly increased institution-wide awareness and attention to gender issues in ADB's lending operations. A Bank-wide WID policy was proposed to build upon this work and refine gender approaches by sector (Christine Whitlam pers. com. 25 May 2019). The WID Policy, prepared by Yuriko Uehara, and approved by the ADB's Board in 1985, aimed to integrate women into all ADB operations, throughout the project cycle; and to target special strategies for their participation and benefits, through continued WID country assessments. A committee chaired by Christine Whitlam was subsequently established to overcome barriers to women's recruitment and retention on ADB professional staff. Shireen Lateef later advanced the WID policy under a Gender and Development policy (1998) and program. The 1985 original WID policy was the first of its kind among the MDBs.

Cedric Saldanha, a staff member with a background in social justice in India, began piloting new agricultural and fisheries project models for marginal and poor producers, including indigenous peoples—people who regularly missed out on benefits from standard projects working through government outreach. The best way to reach such people was through mobilisation and empowerment methods that directly addressed their needs and priorities, adapting new knowledge, understanding, and practice to local circumstances. Community-based organisations had the skills and experience to work with farmer and irrigator organisations—but engaging them would require changes in loan preparation and lending procedures to allow time and space for these new processes to unfold. The resultant loans challenged some international lending advice. The World Bank, for example, advised against intervening in the financial markets with directed finance. Nonetheless, committed to bringing microfinance to the poor, Saldanha successfully prepared for approval a Microcredit Project, breaking new ground in multilateral lending, by learning from the Grameen Bank model used in Bangladesh. In that project, ADB persuaded the Department of Trade and Industry (DTI) of the Philippines government to on-lend money borrowed from ADB to local microcredit groups for on-lending to small and micro entrepreneurs (Cedric Saldanha, pers. com February 2019).

Country surveys of NGOs followed. The Board's approval of a policy on *The Bank's Cooperation with Nongovernment Organizations,* in 1987 gave higher visibility and priority to the issues, and authority to staff advocating such approaches which they had not had before. Staff also recognized the need for practical guidance on "How to do it" that could take lessons learned more widely across the organization and its borrowers. In another important initiative Bill Staub developed guidelines for project benefit monitoring and evaluation methods that would allow the assessment of project outcomes on intended beneficiaries, and others impacted.

These pioneers also faced barriers. Christine Whitlam recalled the challenges of being one of only 13 professional women on ADB staff in 1981 (Christine Whitlam pers. com 25 May 2019). Cedric Saldanha recalled having to cope with "very substantial resistance from within the organization. ADB was dominated by economists and engineers. Social science and governance experts were given very little recognition or hearing in the early days. This did change substantially by the early 1990s" (Cedric Saldanha pers. com 2017)—when ADB began appointing social development, resettlement, and poverty specialists.

By the end of the 1980s global attention focussed again on poverty. Recognising that, despite some strong country growth, more than half the world's poor lived in Asia, in 1988 ADB established an internal Task Force on Poverty Alleviation to identify ways of prioritizing attention to poverty within its projects. The following year ADB invited five Asian experts, including Amartya Sen, to recommend on ADB's role. Their report recommended, among other suggestions, a balanced approach that included social and environmental goals, and a greater focus on poverty reduction through projects directly benefitting the poor. The concept of poverty reduction itself was broadening to include empowerment of people to benefit from education, health, and gender equity.

ADB's Taskforce on Project Quality in 1994 recommended a major change in focus: more attention to project implementation on the ground and less to achieving higher lending volumes. Board members were also requesting that ADB introduce safeguard policies on environment, involuntary resettlement and indigenous peoples. The donors froze their financial replenishments pending resolution of these issues. The change from the "loan approval culture" to a focus on local needs, capacity building, and changed internal accountability was, however, too radical for the organization (McCawley 2017: 191). The President promised to address these issues through setting strategic objectives and on this basis the donors resumed financing. ADB sought a way to address the new poverty reduction, gender, and social issues, together with safeguards, without compromising its lending volume.

In 1993 Sam Rao, Director of a newly formed Social Development Unit, produced official *Guidelines on Incorporation of Social Dimensions into ADB Operations* (1993)[7] that addressed global concerns for poverty reduction following a decade of structural adjustment. ADB's *Medium Term Strategic Framework* (1992–1995) reaffirmed the economic growth objective, and added poverty reduction, improved status of women, human resource development and environmental management (ibid). Growth quality, sustainability, and equity demanded a stronger focus on 'issues of social significance based on a participatory approach to development, greater gender and social analysis, benefit monitoring and evaluation, and cooperation with...NGOs' (ADB 1992: 47). Social analysis would help realize poverty reduction in lending operations. This approach incorporated the earlier-developed, innovative community-based loan models designed to benefit the poor directly, complementing gender initiatives to reach women.

The *Guidelines* linked the social dimensions to the country operational strategies that formed the basis of the country operational programs. In this way social analysis, integrated into the entire country macro programming and sector analyses, set the basis for subsequent project selection—and then into all stages of the project cycle.

In 1994 the *Handbook for Incorporation of Social Dimensions in Projects* recommended an initial social scoping for all projects to start early in identifying and addressing the social dimensions during project preparation—mandated in the 1995 Board-approved *Policy on Involuntary Resettlement*. The social scoping, which included gender analysis, aimed to ensure that no project went to the Board without integrating social dimensions into its design.

Management approved these rules in the 1997 Operations Manual (OM) Section—the "rulebook" (now updated as OM Section C3 on Bank Policy and Operational Procedures on *Incorporation of Social Dimensions in ADB Operations*). The social "rule", still operational, and subject to compliance review (ADB 2018), encompasses public and private sector investment projects funded by a loans, grants, and other means (equity and guarantees); and program loans. First principles are defined:

> ...social elements such as gender, ethnicity, race, caste, age, and others, influence people's decision making, access to services, resources, opportunities, and ability to cope with risks. These variables affect the character of the institutions (formal and informal rules, norms, and values) that determine the level and nature of people's access and capability... operations can help significantly reduce poverty, inequality, and vulnerability by transforming

---

[7]Drawing upon a publication entitled *Guidelines for the Social Analysis of Development Projects* incorporating community-based methods developed in ADB's pioneering projects (Bysouth and O'Sullivan 1991).

institutions so they promote inclusiveness, equity, empowerment, and social security (ADB 2010: 1).

In early 1997 Management also approved Bank Policies and Operational Procedures on Gender and Development, on Involuntary Resettlement, and on Governance, followed, in 2000, by Indigenous Peoples and Anti-corruption. ADB's then President Chino declared an over-arching Poverty Reduction objective in 1999, in which inclusive social development is one of three pillars. He also raised the proportion of women in senior and professional positions in the Bank.

Comparative Analysis

In both banks, the social "rule", complementing an economic development mandate set in founding charters, situated projects amongst specific groups of stakeholders, and planned for their participation and benefits. In both cases, new work patterns, which were intended to enhance the match between projects and their chosen beneficiaries, challenged standard project lending models, time frames and practices.

OMS 2.20 intended to act at a critical point before loan approval, to ensure the entire project design was socially sound. The World Bank's new, more systematically applied rule for investment projects, the ESF, is primarily a social and environmental safeguard management tool. As a safeguard primarily, the ESF reflects new thinking in identifying and mitigating a range of social risks and impacts; and briefly touches on human rights, including through a ban on forced evictions. Being focused on safeguards, however, it does not require overall project social design to match beneficiary circumstances; nor analysis on a par with economic and financial analysis before loan approval; nor address questions on project benefits distribution and social equity. It does not set a key point before loan approval to question whether the project's long-term benefits will justify its wider environmental and social costs, taking account of the distribution among different social groups. MacNamara's 1973 call to address the critical relationship of social equity to economic growth remains unaddressed.

The lending imperative has only intensified since then, shaping responses. OMS 2.20 was most successful as an enabling framework for social analysis in expanded form to help create the knowledge base needed for effective lending, primarily in the former Soviet Union countries. Subsequent successful loans following Community Driven Development (CDD) principles assign to communities the responsibility for programming and spending significant resources, particularly facilitating expenditure where government programs are weak, and unable to meet spending conditions and targets (Guggenheim and Wong 2018). Both cases facilitated, rather than impeded, lending flows. ADB has faced similar lending pressures throughout also, as evidenced, for example, in 1994 when the Taskforce on Project Quality recommendations were deemed too constraining for a bank. ADB searched for a way to address the new social and poverty agenda without compromising its lending volume.

Writing social rules has necessitated a fine balance between social soundness and the "core business" of lending continuity. Weathering decades of evolving "soft" agendas for poverty reduction, gender, and social development, the lending imperative itself has survived and thrived. Publications, policy documents, and "rules" contend that both social and gender analysis not only make good economic sense, but also foster local support which is necessary for project sustainability. Yet the lending imperative, that "core business" for any bank, has too often prioritized loan approvals above their outcomes, and lending quantity above quality. In Saldanha's words:

> ...whatever the banks' rules and policies, in implementation the crucial factor is—what is the leadership commitment, policies, attitudes, approaches within the borrowing government agencies? The banks have little patience for the hard work required in influencing or changing local attitudes and governance within borrowing governments. They have, I think, failed the greatest challenge of development. They have always been primarily focused on how much they can lend, and to which sectors (Cedric Saldanha, pers. com February 2019).

The underlying Bank charters have not changed. Not all new development lenders, meanwhile, prioritize poverty reduction. Achieving the Sustainable Development Goals, (SDGs) might work best with community-based models as developed in ADB; or along the lines of the World Bank's CDD, in which a menu of options for communities to consider might certainly include infrastructure. Instead, however, the MDBs together present a foregone conclusion, a vision of a vast, and necessary, infrastructure spend which also mobilizes significant private sector financing (World Bank 2018), in which risk analysis focuses more often on risks to project investments rather than risks to people affected by them (ibid).

The views of intended beneficiaries may differ from those of the "borrowers"—the national, sectoral, and provincial level agency staff. Prioritizing choices, strategies, and approaches suggested by sub-groups of people, may be time-consuming—and might lack importance to national officers. Finding the right balance between the skills, timeframes, and perspectives necessary to engage the poor and understand their priorities, compared with those of writing briefs and preparing loans for speedy approval by the head office, presents a continuing challenge (Cochrane 2019). Marginal groups not favored by governments may be particularly at risk of being sidelined, overridden or subjected to human rights violations. Processes that may continue to be viewed in purely technical terms—such as services provision, agricultural intensification or land titling—risk harm without careful social analysis.

Each MDB has its own unique culture. The two MDBs discussed here followed different strategies in formulating social rules. Underlying structural similarities and lending constraints have, nonetheless, built co-operative frameworks upon those early contacts. ADB's Sam Rao visited Michael Cernea in Washington on several occasions, obtaining a copy of OMS 2.20, with its strategic importance as the first MDB formal rule on social—and gender—analysis.

Conclusion

Reducing poverty demanded operational change. This chapter demonstrated how the process of approving new rules triggered discourse in both banks bridging all disciplines, to fill knowledge gaps, move perceptions, and create momentum for organizational change. In both cases the "social" domain was defined broadly, interlinking complementary themes of poverty reduction and gender equity.

Second, lending limits can shift. By addressing objectives of gender equity and poverty reduction, and by operationalizing them in different contexts, the rules helped change the policy mandate for lending—ADB on WID and, later, poverty reduction; World Bank on poverty reduction. These policies changed the underlying conceptualization of "good development" which, in turn, permitted some shifts in lending practices. This meant, thirdly, that rules embodied some flexibility in authorizing resource mobilization to achieve those policy objectives.

Fourth, the codification of new concepts and practices at one moment can, together with a management open to new ideas, become a baseline for change, allowing specialists to take stock, review progress and learn lessons. Rules offer a base for subsequent monitoring and evaluation of outcomes that may deliver important lessons for future projects. For example, ADB's WID country papers formed a baseline for measuring subsequent country change in women's wellbeing.

Fifth, the rules on social analysis could be, and were, later used as a basis for inspection, as both MDBs adopted more sophisticated and adversarial accountability mechanisms.

We began with the paradox of a far-reaching rule that was not systematically implemented. Despite the later risk of non-compliance, rules could be ignored or flouted. Rules are only effective insofar as management continues to support them and to provide enough time and resources to implement them—and the limit here has consistently been the lending imperative, and its underlying conceptualization of what constitutes good development. MDB rules required fine tuning to allow incremental change whilst not impeding "core business" by slowing lending significantly. The scope for change was greatest where those rules expanded the conceptualization of "core business"; and also, where the rules fostered new lending patterns and project models that enabled, rather than impeded, lending flows.

Borrowers set the limits or go elsewhere for financing in a lending environment marked by rapidly diversifying financing sources. The trend in shifting MDB project responsibilities to borrowers raises the question of country standards for SIA where aims, procedures, capacities, and outcomes are uneven. SIA has broadened globally to include a wide range of issues, including human rights, packaged in management plans. In some countries, however, SIA, if mandated and practiced at all, may be defined as a tool to address a narrower range of risks of importance only to project sponsors, financiers or government rather than to people.

There is unfinished business, both for lenders and borrowers. MacNamara in 1973 called for attention to the critical relationship of social equity to economic growth. This call has never been addressed fully. Rules offered, at best, only tentative guidance and significant discretion in addressing the central questions of whether fully calculated benefits outweigh social costs, and how they are distributed among social groups. Beyond that, broader structural shifts and impacts remain unexplored and unaddressed in the context of lending. Sustainability assumes increasing urgency. The challenges of poverty reduction, equality, sustainability, and growth are vast, and perhaps irreconcilable (World Inequality Report 2018). These questions continue as tensions escalate around global and country-specific inequality.

Social pioneers laid the groundwork for questioning pre-existing norms. They made new subjects visible, engaged them in planning projects, and codified these approaches in social "rules". They envisaged continued cooperation among social development specialists, reaching beyond institutional and country borders; and encompassing local partners. Changing global circumstances now heighten new fears about limits to growth, sustainability, and human survival. In such testing times social analysts must brave new frontiers: social and gender equity in interaction with sustainability. The social analysis "rules" have come a long way, but they have some way to go to be realized fully (Fig. 1).

Fig. 1 President James D. Wolfensohn at Michael Cernea's retirement party, together with Michael's wife, the anthropologist Ruth Fredman Cernea

References

Apthorpe, R. (Ed.). (1970). *People, planning and development studies: Some reflections on social planning*. London: Frank Cas.
Asian Development Bank. (1992). *Medium term strategic framework (1992-1995)*. Manila: ADB.
Asian Development Bank. (1993). *ADB guidelines on incorporation of social dimensions into ADB operations*. Manila.
Asian Development Bank. (1995). *Policy on involuntary resettlement*. Manila.
Asian Development Bank. (1999). *Poverty reduction strategy*. Manila.
Asian Development Bank. (2010). Operations manual. OM C3/BP 'Incorporation of social dimensions into ADB operations'. Accessed 25 May 2019. https://www.adb.org/sites/default/files/institutional-document/31483/om-c3.pdf
Asian Development Bank. (2018). ADB *accountability mechanism annual report* 2017. Manila: ADB.
AusAID. (1989). *Social analysis and community participation guidelines*. Canberra: Australian Agency for International Development.
Barrow, C. J. (2000). *Social impact assessment: An introduction*. London: Arnold.
Boserup, E. (1970). *Women's role in economic development*. London: Earthscan.
Burdge, R. J. et al. (2004). *The concepts, process and methods of social impact assessment*. Middleton, WI: The Social Ecology Press.
Bysouth, K., & O'Sullivan, N. (1991) *Guidelines for the social analysis of development projects*. Manila: ADB
Cernea, M. M. (Ed.). (1985) *Putting people first: Sociological variables in rural development* (1st edn). Oxford University Press, World Bank.
Cernea, M. M. (1987). Entrance points for sociological knowledge in planned rural development. In H. Schwartzweller (Ed.). *Research in rural sociology*. Jay Press. http://documents.worldbank.org/curated/en/518211468147833917/pdf/659280WP0Box360entrance0points01987.pdf
Cernea, M. M. (1995) *Social organization and development anthropology: The 1995 Malinowski Award Lecture*. ESSD. Washington, DC: World Bank.
Cernea, M. (2013). Draft. Landmarks in development: The introduction of social analysis. In S. Price & K. Robinson (Eds.), Making a difference (Vol. 2013). Berghahn, NY: Oxford.
Cernea, M. M. (2015). Landmarks in development: The introduction of social analysis. In S. Price & K. Robinson (Eds.), *Making a difference*. Berghahn, NY. 2013 First draft.
Cernea, M. M., & Kudat, A. (Eds.). (1997). *Social assessments for better development: Case studies in Russia and Central Asia*. Washington, DC: World Bank.
Cochrane, G. (2019). *Management by seclusion: A critique of World Bank promises to end global poverty*. Berghahn Books.
Cochrane, G., & Naronha, R. (1973). *Report with recommendations on the use of anthropology in project operations of the World Bank Group*. Washington DC: Report for the World Bank.
Dani, A. (2003, November 24–25). From mitigating impacts to improving outcomes. *Paper to a conference on new directions in impact assessment for development: Methods and practice, Manchester*.
Davis, G. (2004) *A history of the social development network in the World Bank, 1973–2002*. Washington, DC: The World Bank (Social Development Paper No. 56).

Flyvbjerg, B., & Sunstein, C. R. (2016). The principle of the malevolent hiding hand; or, the planning fallacy writ large. In *Social change social research: An international quarterly* (Vol. 83, pp. 979–1004). Johns Hopkins University Press. Winter 2016.

Guggenheim, S., & Wong, S. (2018). *Community driven development: Myths and realities.* Policy Research Working Paper 8435. World Bank Group Social, Urban and Resilience Global Practice.

Hart, K. (1970). Small scale entrepreneurs in Ghana and development planning. In R. Apthorpe (Ed.), *People, planning and development studies: Reflections on social planning.* London: Frank Cass.

Hirschman, A. O. (1967). *Development projects observed.* Washington DC: Brookings.

Hoben, A. (1982). Anthropologists and development. *Annual Review of Anthropology, 11*, 349–375.

Independent Evaluation Group (IEG). World Bank, 2009 Fast Track Brief. *Gender and development: An evaluation of World Bank support, 2002–08.* Accessed 12 May 2019.

Kardam, N. (1993). Development approaches and the role of policy advocacy: The case of the World Bank. *World Development, 21*(11), 1773–1786.

MacNamara. (1973). *Nairobi speech.* Washington DC: World Bank. Accessed August 2019. https://www.worldbank.org/en/about/archives/president-mcnamara-nairobi-speech-1973.

McCawley, P. (2017). *Banking on the future of Asia and the Pacific: 50 years of the Asian Development Bank.* Manila: ADB.

Price, S. (2015). Introduction: Making economic growth socially sustainable? In S. Price & K. Robinson (Eds.), *Making a difference? Social assessment policy and praxis and its emergence in China* (pp. 1–30). New York: Berghahn Books.

Rosser, C. (1970). Action planning in Calcutta: The problem of community participation. In R. Apthorpe (Ed.), *People, planning and development studies: Some reflections on social planning.* London: Frank Cass.

Scott, J. C. (1976). *The moral economy of the peasant: Rebellion and subsistence in Southeast Asia.* New Haven, CT: Yale University Press.

World Bank. (1971). Project appraisal. OMS. Washington, DC.

World Bank. (1984). Project appraisal. OMS 2.20. Washington, DC.

World Bank. (2017). The inspection panel emerging series no. 4, Consultation, participation and disclosure of information. Accessed 2 May 2019. https://inspectionpanel.org/sites/inspectionpanel.org/files/publications/ConsultationParticipationandDisclosureInformation.pdf

World Bank. (2018). *World Bank Group and the 2030 agenda.* Washington DC: World Bank.

World Inequality Laboratory. (2018). *World inequality report.* Accessed 20 May 2019. https://wir2018.wid.world/executive-summary.html

Susanna Price is currently a Lecturer (Hon) in the College of Asia and the Pacific at the Australian National University (ANU) and Council Member, ANU's Burgmann College. She worked in Ausaid; and in Asian Development Bank (ADB), Manila as Senior Social Development Specialist and lead Resettlement staffer. Her PhD is from Kyoto University, Japan. Prizes include the Praxis Prize, Washington Association of Professional Anthropologists (2003); a CIDA Prize (2000); ADB Presidents Prizes and a Australian Public Service Scholarship for overseas study. Recent publications include *Responses to Displacement across Asia–Pacific: Strategies for Development, Disasters and Climate Change* and *Country Frameworks for Development Displacement and Resettlement,* both co-edited volumes for Routledge with Professor Jane Singer. Her latest articles are: "Looking back on development and disaster-related displacement and resettlement, anticipating climate related displacement in the Asia Pacific region" in *Asia Pacific Viewpoint* 2019; and, with Warren van Wicklin III, Dolores Koenig, John Owen, Chris de Wet and Asmita Kabra: "Risk and Value in Benefit Sharing with Displaced People in *Social Change* 50 (3): 447–465 2020. She is currently working on options, if any, for survival on a post-apocalyptic planet.

Open Access This chapter is licensed under the terms of the Creative Commons Attribution 4.0 International License (http://creativecommons.org/licenses/by/4.0/), which permits use, sharing, adaptation, distribution and reproduction in any medium or format, as long as you give appropriate credit to the original author(s) and the source, provide a link to the Creative Commons license and indicate if changes were made.

The images or other third party material in this chapter are included in the chapter's Creative Commons license, unless indicated otherwise in a credit line to the material. If material is not included in the chapter's Creative Commons license and your intended use is not permitted by statutory regulation or exceeds the permitted use, you will need to obtain permission directly from the copyright holder.

Part II
Social Development Work—Live

The 1995 Malinowski Award Lecture: Social Organization and Development Anthropology

Michael M. Cernea

> *In order to be of use, research must be inspired by courage and purpose. It must be briefed by that constructive statesmanship and wise foresight which establishes the relevant issues and have the courage to apply the necessary remedies. Unfortunately, there is still a strong but erroneous opinion in some circles that practical anthropology is fundamentally different from theoretical or academic anthropology. The truth is that science begins with application. What is application in science and when does 'theory' become practical? When it first allows us a definite grip on empirical reality. Bronislaw Malinowski (The Dynamics of Culture Change)*

It is a great honor to receive the Bronislaw Malinowski Award from this scholarly community of development social scientists, and I am deeply grateful for this recognition. Being associated through this Award with the name and legacy of Malinowski, and with the line of distinguished scholars who have preceded me as its recipients, is a moving and stimulating experience.

A World on the Move

When the Society for Applied Anthropology was founded in 1941, few would have anticipated either the current expansion of development anthropology and sociology as applied social science disciplines, or the recognition that social and cultural issues would receive in international and national development.

Consider for a minute the gigantic wave of systemic socio-political changes that during the last decades have restructured the world and transformed beyond recognition the societies anthropologists traditionally studied. Anthropology itself has

---

M. M. Cernea (✉)
Retired, Bethesda, MD, USA

© The Author(s) 2021
M. Koch-Weser, S. Guggenheim (eds.), *Social Development in the World Bank*,
https://doi.org/10.1007/978-3-030-57426-0_9

changed and must further change, largely due to the dynamic of economic and political world changes, and the ascent of many nations to statehood and self-construction.

We live now in a new world system, one that is both integrated and fractured. During the 1980s/1990s, the structures of our contemporary world were changed by the collapse of the former Soviet Union and Eastern European dictatorial regimes, a triple collapse of political, economic, and multinational state models. In turn, ethnicity and religious revivals also are reshaping the planet's social map.

To remain relevant in development, social scientists must learn to think differently about development itself. Development has powerfully changed the individual's everyday life. Since 1960, average life expectancy in the developing countries has increased by about 20 years, a change of incalculable consequences. Adult literacy has risen from about 40% to over 65% by now; average per capita incomes in the poor countries have doubled and in some nations have tripled or quadrupled; a child born today in the developing world is only half as likely to die before the age of five as a child born just a generation ago. The same child is twice as likely to learn to read and can expect a standard of living two or three times higher.

Yet this is only part of the picture. The world still has about 1.3 billion people living in absolute poverty, defined as earnings of less than one dollar a day. More than two billion people still lack access to electricity and are forced to use sticks and dung for their energy needs. Roughly 1.7 billion lack sewage systems, and one billion lack access to clean piped water, resulting in the unnecessary death of some three million infants and children every year from diseases linked to dirty water. The inequality gap continues to widen: during the past 30 years, incomes in the countries with the richest 20% of the world's population grew nearly three times faster than in the countries with the poorest 20%. There are more refugees and displaced persons in today's world than at any time before, even in the aftermath of the World War II. One last, ominous fact: at this very moment, 140 million of the world's adults are unemployed and cannot feed their families.

The Social Development Summit: A Powerful Call to Our Profession

These and other daunting problems prescribe a formidable agenda for curing social ills—an agenda that our soon ending twentieth century will hand over just in a few years to the next.

From the view point of social development, however, we can say that the twenty-first century has already started, Figuratively, I'd say that the new twenty-first century started when the governments of all the world's countries met in Copenhagen in the first ever World Summit for Social Development. This Summit set its sights explicitly beyond *economic growth* alone—toward social goals. I was privileged to be present and I attempted to grasp what might be the Summit's likely consequences for the role and necessary contributions of social sciences in a world that inscribes *social development* on its banners.

The Summit produced a *social charter*—a social contract for the world at large. This is unprecedented. All heads of states signed off on a Program of Action consisting of nine major commitments, each embodying a set of goals and actions regarding: poverty eradication; full employment; fighting social disintegration; human rights; women and equality; enabling legal and institutional frameworks; and other major social objectives. Global social development was spelled out in explicit goals, norms, and tasks. True, there were also major issues omitted, empty rhetoric, agreements not-reached. Yet the historic meaning of this event is inescapable. If there is any link between social research and thinking, on the one hand, and actual social development, on the other, the implications for our duties as engaged social scientists are equally inescapable.

This is an auspicious beginning for the twenty-first century. And this is why I see and hear in it also a powerful call to our profession for knowledge usable for social knowledge.

Anthropology's Debut in an Unexpected Place: The World Bank

The citation for all Malinowski Award recipients states that it is offered in recognition of *"efforts to understand and serve the needs of the world through social science."* This is a tall order indeed. That my work is deemed by this Society to have done so is for me a morally and professionally rewarding judgment, and a strong encouragement for reaching further and deeper.

I feel it incumbent on me today, as it was upon my predecessors, to briefly account for at least part of my intellectual biography, my past and current work, and the ideas that inform it. For some of the structural difficulties and sleep-robbing questions I've faced in bringing social science knowledge into a heavyweight financial fortress, are not fully atypical: many will be confronted by other anthropologists, struggling to accomplish comparable tasks in other bureaucratic and development settings.

The World Bank came rather late, in the early1970s, to recognizing that it needed to bring and incorporate a voice for sociological/anthropological knowledge among the inhabitants of its house, as part of its regular staff. In fact, it wasn't the first international agency to arrive to this recognition. The World Health Organization (WHO), for instance, hired its first anthropologist much earlier, in 1950, i.e., 24 long years *before* the World Bank. Yet that first experience was not a success. In his Malinowski Lecture George Foster noted, tongue in cheek, that in that early encounter between anthropology and an international agency there was "perplexity" on both sides (1982:191): neither part quite understood what the other one could do and needs, to achieve synergy and success.[1]

I can add that such 'perplexity' remains present today within the vast majority of domestic and government organizations that I met during my work on many meridians. One exception, the US Agency for International Development (AID) did attempt to employ anthropologists and sociologists before the World Bank created its first such staff position, to put anthropology on the Bank's skeptical intellectual map.[2] And fortunately, I'm happy to report that since that lone sociological "slot" was allocated in 1974, the World Bank's in-house corps of non-economic social scientists—sociologists, anthropologists, political scientists—has grown steadily in number and also—essentially—in institutional weight. This has been a major leap.

The group of social scientists assembled at the World Bank during these twenty years is today the world's largest group of this kind working in one place—close to 150 professionally trained social scientists who actually practice development anthropology and sociology. In addition, hundreds of social scientists from developing and developed countries are employed each year as short-term consultants, largely due to the demand for social research and analysis legitimized by the Bank's new, pioneering social development policies and by the effectiveness of the initial core in-house group.

Beyond the change in numbers, there has also been change in substance. Regarding cultural substance, the World Bank's original manner of treating its client countries was sarcastically described in a 1952 review of three Bank country studies—for Turkey, Guatemala, and Cuba. The reviewer, C. P. Kindleberger (by the way, he wasn't an anthropologist!) characterized the Bank studies and the experts' fieldwork in this way:

> Essentially,... these [three studies] are essays in comparative statistics. The [field] missions bring to the under-developed country a notion of what a developed country is like. They observe the underdeveloped country. They subtract the latter from the former. The difference is a program (1952:391).

Continuing, the reviewer commented on the Bank work-teams of that time:

---

[1] Commenting on the unsuccessful experience of the first anthropologist who joined the World Health Organization in Geneva in 1950, George Foster wrote: *"She did not plan to recommend specific courses of action. (Her) assignment was plagued by the problem that has affected many subsequent neither she, nor the hiring organization, really knew what she should do. Shortly after joining WHO she left for India and Southeast Asia where, in the regional WHO office her reception was unenthusiastic"* (1982:191). And Foster quoted further the personal description given him by that colleague: *"I was left to make my own plans and schedules and I was more than a little perplexed as to what was expected of me Much the same perplexity about my role obtained when I returned to Geneva"* (Foster 1982:191).

[2] Two years prior to my joining the Bank, two consultants were commissioned to carry out an in-house study to assess whether or not anthropology could contribute—and if yes, how—to Bank activities. After six months they submitted a long—and in my view, good—report with their conclusions and proposals: nonetheless, that report did not convince anybody. Neither of the two consultant authors was retained in the institution.

Most of the members of the missions came from developed countries with highly articulated institutions for achieving social, economic, and political ends. Ethnocentricity leads inevitably to the conclusion that the way to achieve the comparable levels of capital formation, productivity, and consumption is to duplicate these institutions... (1952:392).

This image of the Bank is from a time long past. But please remember it as it helps measure the substantive changes over time in the institution's practices.

Producing Knowledge of Recognized Organizational Utility

When I started work at the Bank in September 1974, I had no way of knowing that it would lead me, twenty-one years later, to this noble rostrum; in fact, I didn't know then many more pressing and vital things, such as what I'd have to do the very next day after my appointment. That "next day" proved to be a field trip to Tanzania to help untangle the agricultural difficulties of a country that had just undergone villagization and "ujamaazation," a forcible grouping of peasants in state-imposed village-cooperatives.

Kigoma, the western region in which we worked on the magnificent shores of Lake Tanganyika, stood out among Tanzania's regions for having carried out *ujamaaization* in a particularly harsh manner. However, the grand lines of this statist approach to agricultural collectivization, and its dire consequences, were known to me from my previous studies on forced collectivization in the 1960s in Romania. Comparing what I knew with what I now observed and learned about patterns of village organization and change greatly facilitated my understanding. Fieldwork in rural communities was what I was comfortable with and what gave me an edge over my other colleagues on the Bank's Kigoma team. This was my first development project test. It opened for me a window into what was needed, from an anthropological perspective, and how my contributions could fit into the patterns of Bank work. It also made clear to me that I would have to pay my way in the Bank in the coin of knowledge of recognizable organizational utility.

I set to work with determination and, I confess, fear. To give you an idea of how it felt then, while trying to bring anthropology's message to a rather agnostic and skeptical professional group, I should recall a story from the Vatican. After Vatican II, Pope Paul decided to do something about spreading the faith in Eastern Bloc countries. He then created a new office in the Vatican, called the *"Secretariat for Non-Believers."* He appointed Cardinal Franz Konig of Austria (who years later told this story to the *Washington Post),* as Secretary to the Non-Believers. The poor Cardinal did not know what he was supposed to do. He went to the Pope and asked: "What shall I do?" The Pope, reportedly, shrugged and said "I don't know." Then he added in Latin *"Usus Docebit":* with God's help, "the use will teach you." And so it was also with me, as I assumed the role of "Secretary to the Non-believers": the use taught me.

That I faced a huge challenge and a tough personal test was intimidatingly obvious. Becoming the first incumbent of a new role within the Bank's organization,

I stepped into an undefined and ambiguous situation. There was no formal status, no structure of expectations, *not* even a stereotype to live up to. My unit was itself new, a special policy experimental division just created by Robert McNamara to pilot the new policy for poverty alleviation that he had launched in Nairobi the previous year.[3] From the outset, I was cast in the role of an "Ambassador of the discipline." I was told in no uncertain terms, that my work was to demonstrate to the institution whether or not the discipline I represented had a legitimate and compatible place in the Bank.

What the Bank only dimly realized at that time was that I had another very strong incentive to succeed—a personal, yet frightening incentive—a win-or-perish option: namely, my children were kept back as "hostages" by the then government of Romania, and were not permitted to join me in my resettlement to the US. The only way to successfully "extract" them was to succeed at my work and hold on to my job, and thereby legitimize my request for their release. It took fifteen long months. I did hold on to my job and I did get them here. I am happy to mention this tonight as my children are in this room with us—now, with their spouses and small children too! Anthropology is about real people, so I thought this well worth mentioning.

My earlier pre-Bank training obviously had little to do with typical World Bank issues or conceptual vocabulary. I can confess now how suspended-in-the-air I felt then hearing the lingo of "credit disbursement curves," "shadow prices," or "economic rate of return calculation." But I was coming from a solid sociological and anthropological tradition of village studies, developed over decades and brought to maturity between the two World Wars by Romania's foremost sociologists and anthropologists, Dimitrie Gusti, Henri H. Stahl, Anton Golopentia. Like Malinowski, Dimitrie Gusti also had studied in Leipzig, with the same professors as Malinowski—the psychologist Wilhelm Wundt and the economist Karl Bucher—and at roughly the same time as Malinowski. Later, Dimitrie Gusti created, conceptually and organizationally, what came to be recognized internationally as the "Bucharest rural sociological school", a thoroughly holistic, anthropological manner of studying village culture, customs, beliefs, natural context, economic activities, and political and social organization. The way rural sociology was conceived, taught, and practiced in Romania was largely akin with social anthropology. Early twentieth century Romanian social researchers such as Gusti and Stahl also advocated an orientation to action, and directed rural research towards social reform activities for bettering the peasants' life—not bad guidance at all for my own later work at the Bank! After WWII, when the teaching and practice of sociology were politically banned in Romania, surreptitiously studying Gusti's, Stahl's, and Golopentia's pre-war writings was, for me and other young researchers, a way of learning about empirical investigation.

---

[3]The special Division for "experimental" poverty projects was headed by Leif Christoffersen, appointed to that new position from his previous assignment as Assistant to the President of the World Bank, Robert McNamara. and was located in the Bank's Central Agriculture and Rural Development, directed by Montague Yudelman.

When the first opportunity appeared in the 1960s, I conducted my own village monographs, restudying communities investigated 35 years before by Gusti's researchers to assess intervening change (Cernea et al. 1970). This is how I gradually gained my dual identity as a sociologist and anthropologist, fieldworker and academic. In that period, rife with a distorting dominant ideology, the top-down prescription for research was to ascribe to reality the image of how it was supposed to be, but wasn't. Genuine fieldwork was ostracized, as it implied a grave threat to the establishment: the threat of deflating the ideological balloon with empirical evidence.

From those years, what I personally cherish most is the contribution I was able to make in the 1960s, with my research team, to resuming and re-legitimizing empirical field work in Romania after an interruption of two decades. What I learned then about the iconoclastic power of facts for toppling falsehoods and inviting action served me then, and serves me now in my current work. That empirical research was also what led, first, to my 1967 work in France, at the Centre d'Etudes Sociologiques, and then, most importantly, to the unforgettable year I spent in 1970–1971 at the Center for Advanced Studies in the Behavioral Sciences at Stanford (CASBS). That intellectually intense year profoundly restructured my thinking and rejuvenated my conviction in the power of social research -power to explain and power to guide action. In short, it changed my life, and I cannot miss this opportunity, a full quarter-century later, to again express my gratitude to the Center.

With my personal brief "pre-historical" account completed, I return to the central issue of employing social science knowledge throughout the range of activities involved in conceiving, preparing and implementing development projects and programs. The anthropological work carried out at the World Bank has helped the institution itself to evolve from its initial ethnocentricity to the deliberate consideration of differences in social variables between and within developing countries and the *"contemporary variations among existing cultures"* (Mead 1976) that are consequential for development processes and programs. My community of practicing anthropologists/sociologists has broken some new grounds not only for the World Bank but, I submit, for our profession as well. I will try further to derive some lessons of broader validity from our group's experiences and propose them for your reflection.

The Rationale for Social Analysis in Financially Induced Development

Several premises underpin my comments. The first is that the type of development I'm referring to is *financially induced development*. This is development that is purposively pursued, accelerated, and programmed, often guided by policies that are based on a mix of technical knowledge, assumptions, and economic doctrines. Financially induced development is significantly different from *spontaneous* development. Thus, while spontaneous development is by and large only observed and passively described in anthropology, a financially induced development interventions (e.g, "projects") is one which trained social specialists can influence if they participate in their crafting and implementation.

The second premise is that anthropologists do possess a body of professional knowledge about social organization and cultural systems that is sorely needed for inducing development deliberately, with larger gains and fewer pains.

The third premise is that the key ontological and methodological principles for using social knowledge are common to applied anthropologists working either in international programs or in domestic programs. So, much of what I am saying about the former applies also to the latter. The cross-cultural nature of some development programs has spawned much misguided writing about the anthropologist's role as "intercultural broker." This is a concept that was developed in dignity (Wolf 1956; Wiedman 1973) but ended up frequently trivialized by practices that marginalized the utility of anthropologists, miscast as mere guides or translators of the local vernacular to their team co-members.[4] In both domestic and international programs, anthropologists can and must be more than "inter-cultural brokers."

My fourth premise is that development anthropology and development sociology have essential commonalities that prevail over their differences.[5] Therefore, it is beneficial to both professional communities *to bridge their traditional disciplinary divide* and mutually empower their bodies of knowledge and methods, as our Bank group of sociologists and anthropologists has done harmoniously. In what follows, I will refer to both anthropology and sociology and will often use one or the other term interchangeably.

Shifting Social Analysis from Projects' Tail-end to Upfront

The main work bench for anthropological endeavor in the World Bank is the development project. Projects come in all forms, sites, and sectors: from health care systems in Asia to urban infrastructure in Latin America, from irrigation in the Maghreb to reforestation in Pakistan, from education in Africa to reducing environmental pollution in Thailand, to combating AIDS in Uganda, to structural adjustment reforms, and to projects for building hydropower dams, curing cataract

---

[4] In a broad sense, what anthropologists typically do is try to understand and explain culture. In this perspecgive, "cultural brokerage" is non- controversial as concept and role. What is objectionable— and I witnessed numerous instances of this practice—is the limitation of anthropologists' roles to the minor aspects of language intermediation or other mechanics of "development tourism," to use Robert Chambers' expression, while their competence on essential issues of social organization, stratification, ethnicity, and local institutions is not treated as indispensable to the job at hand.

[5] I note, as a testimony to the intimate relationship between these two disciplines, that Malinowski himself did not hesitate to term his analyses of the Trobriands "sociological," not just "anthropological" (Malinowski 1922).

blindness, or improving family planning and nutrition. More than 1800 Bank assisted projects are proceeding today, with Bank financing $150 billion and total investment costs of some $500 billion. Despite this enormous diversity, some common features exist. Every "project" is a social process, not just a commercial investment, and brings into play an array of different *social actors*. Yet, for a long time, the conventional approach was to treat projects as only economic or technical interventions. How to craft projects as units of purposive and organized change intervention was not, and still is not for the most part, a science taught in the Academy. We had to invent and learn, in parallel with similar efforts of other colleagues elsewhere.

Noteworthy in this learning process are several shifts and trends over the years. The key shifts we accomplished are: (I) moving away from ghettoizing social scientists in tail-end project evaluations of limited consequence by placing them up front in project design and decision-making; and (2) moving from working on projects only, to crafting policies as well. We have forcefully asserted that at issue is not the task entrusted to an individual sociologist but the overall input made by the body of knowledge encapsulated by the discipline. An individual social expert can usefully perform a segmented role, such as an expost evaluation, but the non-economic social sciences should not be pigeonholed into one segment of the project cycle and excluded from others; nor should they be dispatched to work exclusively on projects, while being ostracized from policy for mulation. I have developed a matrix of "entrance points for social knowledge" tailored along all the key stages of the entire project cycle and including policy work as well (Cem (Cernea 1979, 1985/1991). The main lesson of our entire experience is that the key contribution of anthropologists is not to be only data collectors or make static "assessments," but to actively *design* the content of induced change and chart the social action path toward accomplishing it.

Does this work make a difference to the countries where we are working and to their people? Affirmative evidence is accumulating. Quantified proof was provided, for instance, by an independent secondary analysis carried out by Conrad Kottak (1985) on a set of 57 Bank-financed projects. Kottak hypothesized that if the projects' sociocultural fit at appraisal is higher, these projects will be associated on average with a higher rate of return at completion. Conversely, initial sociocultural misfit will be associated on average with lower rates of return.[6] The overall findings showed that enhanced sociocultural fit was associated with economic payoff: the average rate of return at audit time was 18.3% for projects found socio-culturally compatible, while for projects that were incompatible socio-culturally the returns were less than half that at only 8.6%. These findings are averages, and not every

---

[6]Kottak's secondary analysis was "blind," in that the coding of sociocultural and socioeconomic variables (including variables of social organization. stratification. ethnicity, gender-based divisions of labor, and others) was completed without knowledge of the project's economic performance: only after the social coding had been done were the rates of return introduced in the analysis.

single project matched the overall trend. Better proof may be forthcoming about more recent projects.

However, it is also fair and responsible to say that social analysts have not been mistake-free. Some made erroneous judgments or validated misguided projects. Others have mis-assessed and mis-predicted the behavior of the populations involved. The tools for our analyses, and the methods for translating social knowledge into prescriptions for action, are only developing. Judgments often need to be made with far from perfect social data, and error has not graciously bypassed us. Yet what is novel, despite such errors, is that new variables are taken into account, variables about social and cultural organization. These variables are factored in precisely because social specialists have started to "inhabit" the project-crafting process at its core, not just its periphery.

Two observations are in order: the first is about the nature of knowledge needed in applied work, the second about the institutional rules of using it. Applied and development anthropologists need two categories of knowledge: "knowledge for understanding" and "knowledge for action" (Scott and Shore 1979), to explain and to prescribe. My experience confirms that knowledge for action is indeed a distinct body of knowledge, but one that taken alone can be utterly pedestrian and deceptive. Knowledge for action is valid only if it is incremental to, and relies on, knowledge for understanding, because otherwise, precious as it may be, it is rarely self-sustaining in the long haul. These two distinct categories of knowledge, both indispensable, result from different cognitive itineraries, and only segments of these itineraries pass through university halls. It is part and parcel of applied anthropologists' jobs not just to apply knowledge, but *to create and recreate both types of knowledge* in each of their assignments. This makes the applied job no less demanding than teaching or academic research. The second observation, also from my Bank home ground, is that inserting social knowledge in projects cannot occur on a significant scale just by simple accretion of in-house individual anthropologists. Knowledge organizations also have formal bureaucratic rules. To create systemic room for new social knowledge, we had to militate for changing these rules. In other words for institutional change to mandate the use for this kind of knowledge. Modifying rules is an arduous effort in itself. In anthropology we call this "change in the organization's culture." Although advances have been made, there still is a way to go for mainstreaming and generalizing social analysis in the World Bank.

Important as formal rules are, the actors behind some of the new rules—those who caused rule-changes to happen—are even more important. May I take therefore a minute to give special public credit to my colleagues, the anthropologists and sociologists of the World Bank, without whom the progress I am talking about would not have happened. I want to call your attention to the theoretical-cum-applied work of Gordon Appleby, Michael Bamberger, Doug Barnes, Lynn Bennett, the late David Butcher, Maria Clark, Michael Cohen, Cynthia Cook, Gloria Davis, Sandy Davis, Ashraf Ghani, Dan Gross, Scott Guggenheim, Steve Heyneman, Maritta Koch-Weser, Ayse Kudat, Marlaine Lockheed, Alice Morton, Shem Migot-Adholla, Raymond Noronha, William Partridge, Ellen Schaengold, and many others. The lives of uncounted people across meridians have been significantly improved due to their committed and creative work, which exceeds by far the published record.[7]

Social analysis for development investment decisions is under exacting demands at the Bank, being expected to meet, in the words of a Bank Manager, "three explicit characteristics: it must be based on a coherent analytical framework, must be predictive, and it must be prescriptive as well" (Serageldin 1994:vi). My colleagues—responding to these challenges through social theorization or fieldwork, through analytical studies, designing tangible project components or even through earmarking budgetary provisions for social components in many programs—have stimulated and contributed to a more sophisticated treatment by the Bank and many governments of development tasks. They have helped to produce better solutions to human problems.

There is a more general lesson in this: as year after year more social specialists have joined the Bank's staff, we have gained critical mass in-house. This has enhanced our impact, creating room for professional self-organization, networking, more refined strategies, and informal and formal alliances in intellectual battles (see Kardam 1993). The absence of a "critical mass" in many organizations also explains why the handful of social specialists are hampered and confined in their influence. External factors have also converged in influencing this in- house institutional process. First, the outside applied community has supported our work inside the Bank in multiple ways. Eminent scholars and development anthropologists—may I highlight especially among them Thayer Scudder, Theodore Downing, Norman Uphoff, Michael Horowitz, Robert Chambers, Conrad Kottak—have contributed so regularly throughout the years that they virtually are part of our in-house community. Second, and equally important, external criticism by NGOs and public interest groups has increasingly emphasized social issues in recent years. Significantly, the criticism from the environmental community (a lobby infinitely more vocal than the social science community) now concentrates not only on physical issues but on sociocultural ones as well. Without taking into account the convergence of these (and other) factors, we could not understand what I described as a major progress of theoretical applied anthropology and sociology in World Bank-assisted activities.

---

[7]The written record of their published work is described in our an-notated bibliographic volume: *Sociology, Anthropology and Development. An Annotated Bibliography of World Bank Publications 1975–1993*. ESD Studies and Monograph Series No. 3.

Fighting Econo-centric, Techno-centric, and Commodo-centric Development Models

The kind of knowledge brought into the Bank by development anthropologists did not land in a vacuum of knowledge. It landed on territory long colonized by economic or technical thinking, both with entrenched tenure. I know that this is the case in many other institutions. In large-scale organizations, different bodies of knowledge compete for jurisdiction over tasks and over policy formulation. The interlocking of theories and practice in inducing development creates "battlefields of knowledge". Therefore, how to carry out intellectual clashes with opposed conceptual paradigms is a pragmatic, tactical question that many of us must face. In our case., intellectual combat has been part of the history of anthropological work in the Bank, and it continues to be so—a creative struggle of ideas, interpretations, and models.

Several different approaches to inducing development display a similar and profoundly damaging conceptual bias. They underestimate the sociocultural structures in the development process. This distortion is often and painfully visible in the design of development projects. Most widespread among these biased perspectives are what I term the *econocentric* model of projects, the *technocentric* model, and the *commodocentric* model. (Comparable biases appear in other institutional contexts).

By the *econocentric model* I have in mind approaches *that* one-sidedly focus on influencing the economic and financial variables, regarding them as the only ones that matter. Their presumption is that if you can "get the prices right," everything else will fall into place. This widespread econo-mythical belief remains a mutilated representation of reality. It simply wishes away the noneconomic variables from theory, but does not remove them from reality. But we have seen that when the social determinants of development are left out by econocentric mindsets, projects display an unrepressed and not at all funny propensity—they fail.

By the *technocentric model,* I have in mind the approach that caters to the technological variables of development more or less "in vitro," dis-embedded and disembodied from their contextual social fabric. "Technology transfer" was once described as the ultimate development paradigm. Although this rage has been muted, there is still considerable disregard of the necessary proportionality between developing new physical infrastructure and creating the social scaffolding for it simultaneously. Technocentric models under-design and underfinance the social scaffolding. My point is that it is not enough to "get the technology right" for the missing social infrastructures to spring up automatically overnight, by God's "*Fiat lux.*" Overcoming techno-centrism requires careful social engineering for institution building, to induce and nurture the cultural arrangements in which the physical infrastructure is necessarily enveloped.

By the *commodocentric model* I have in mind scores of programs that focus on the commodity, the "thing," more than on the social actors that produce it. They focus on coffee production but less on coffee-growers, on "livestock development" but not enough on herders, on water conveyance *but* not on water users. *"Putting people first"* is not a familiar idea in these approaches.

Development anthropology and sociology must militantly reject such fallacious models or exaggerations and provide integrated, convincing, and actionable alternatives. Development is not about commodities. It is not even about new technologies or information highways. It is about people, their institutions. their knowledge, their forms of social organization. This is why I think that non-economic social scientists must be present and work hand-in-hand with economists and technical experts in the core teams that formulate development paradigms, policies, and the content of specific programs.

My personal conviction is that shying away from engaging in intellectual battles about the paradigms of development results not in more "friendly acceptance" of applied anthropological or sociological work, but in less. By now, you have heard my answer about strategy in conceptual clashes on the battlefields of knowledge. We must assert our conceptual differences, because they make a difference. We must take firm positions without posturing, must be earnest without an offensively earnest tone, and must be opinionated while being free of fixed opinions. For applied social scientists, quibbling only for improving practical fixes is never enough. Winning requires intellectual wrestling and theoretical engagement.[8]

Where Do Biases Originate?

A question is inescapable at this point: Where do these distorting conceptual models originate? What should be done, and where should we do it, to correct or prevent them?

My answer is a brief story. Not long ago, I was invited to give a seminar for the social science faculty of an Ivy League university. During the discussions, some highly respected academic anthropologists expressed their well-worn hopelessness and skepticism about the legitimacy and effectiveness of development anthropology or applied sociology, and in general about development dominated by biased models.

My response was, in turn, a question: "Where do you see the roots, I asked, of these biases? Why do they persist and reproduce themselves?"There was silence, or circuitous explanations.

I gave my own answer to these questions. Yes, there is a definite place where these models originate. "My Bank colleagues with econocentric or technocentric

---

[8]Of enormous impact in this—not-always-smooth—in-house theoretical engagement has been our long and tenacious program of sociological seminars and training courses, delivered by Bank sociologists and anthropologists to the rest of our colleagues—hundreds and hundreds of such seminars over the years (see also Kardam 1993). Many outside social scientists have joined us in this intellectual reconstruction process. There is a lesson in this respect as well—about shaping and carrying out strategies of gradual cultural and institutional change over time.

biases, I said, came from this place, from among your own best and brightest graduates. From your university, or from other universities of similar excellence. They are the former *magna cum laude* students in finance, economics, or technical specialties, who spent eight to ten years here next to your anthropology or sociology department doors, but never entered, and were not touched intellectually by your scholarship." Indeed, I explained to my academic colleagues, "I work at the receiving end of your university's 'line of products.' Many of the former students of your university bring to the Bank, or to governments and the private sector, biased, one-sided conceptual models. The models I am fighting reflect nothing else, unfortunately, than the training received in your university's economics department, training that inculcated models that ignore social variables." Can we correct afterwards what the university has not done at the right time?

As the seminar's chairman volunteered, there was "blood on the floor" after that seminar, but it was a discussion useful for all of us.

This is a huge issue. I submit that the way social sciences are taught in most universities in the US, and across the developing world, goes sadly against, rather than in support of, the role social science knowledge must exercise in modern societies. Trends and practices are at work, by commission or omission, that undermine the proactive role of noneconomic social sciences.

In my view, there are two major strategic errors in academia in this respect.

The first common strategic error is the small dose, or the "zero dose," of social science taught to the vast majority of students majoring in non-social fields. Quite often, what they are told about social sciences does not greatly help either when they are taught generalities instead of being taught the parts of anthropology or sociology that are directly relevant to their own specialization and future work.

The second strategic error is the scarce or often nonexistent curriculum emphasis on the teaching of social science for practice, as opposed to teaching for general understanding or for, so to say, just *weltanshauung*. The results of these anachronistic attitudes, to return to my Vatican metaphor, are that the armies of "non-believers" expand with every new cohort of undergraduates, while the "Secretaries to the Non-believers"—you and, I, my colleagues face a harder uphill battle.

The first battlefield of knowledge for the minds of tomorrow's developers and policymakers is in our universities

- And this is where the battle should not be lost. I leave it to my academic colleagues to draw the sober conclusions about the major restructurings indispensable, indeed imperative in the teaching of social sciences, for they prepare the terrain—fertile or infertile—for society's practical use of social science.

The Rationale for Development Anthropology

My next question at this point is: if we propose to put the biased models of development interventions on trial, how do we make the prosecution's case for anthropology?[9] How do we argue anthropology's "can do" claim to relevance?

The constructive argument is far more crucial than the critique, for several reasons, not least because the way we legitimize to others or to ourselves the need for social analysis in development interventions creates a structure of expectations that becomes compelling. Eventually, this turns out to be the way we end up practicing social analysis. In other words, if we argue just the pragmatic, short-term operational benefits' side of using anthropology, we will end up playing a mundane fix-it- here and fix-it-there role. If, however, we convincingly construct the argument for a theoretical applied anthropology, we lay claim to having voice over the substance of development paradigm and policies.

The rigid dichotomy between applied and theoretical anthropology is a simplistic representation that must be rejected. The "practice" of anthropology can generate value-added for society only if it is practiced *as theoretical-applied anthropology.* What has to be "applied" through applied anthropology is our theoretically generalized knowledge about societies and cultures. What else would anthropologists have to apply? They use the research methods. What they apply is the storehouse of knowledge (van Willigen 1993; Angrosino 1976). Anthropologists bring to their work the knowledge about what is general in individual local societies ("cross cultural commonalities") and proceed to uncover what is unique in that individual society. I can- not imagine applied anthropology without this "theoretical understanding" lodged and carried along in the mental back-pack of practicing anthropologists.

Upon scrutinizing much of the literature, I can see several types of arguments—models of rationalizing, or ways of "making the case"—for development anthropology. I'll refer to three of them. (Another, the "cultural brokerage" model, was mentioned earlier.) Not all the models in circulation are correct or equally powerful. I submit that some of them would result only in a peripheral and diminished, even if real, role for anthropologists. Our discipline can do better than that.

---

[9]This is a deliberate reversal of Polly Hill's title to her 1986 book "Development Economics on Trial: The Anthropological Case for a Prosecution." Unfortunately, despite many valid observations about statistics, surveys, and so on, this book, in my view, did not fulfill the promise of its provocative title. Nor did it construct the *positive* case for anthropology.

The widest spread but weakest model is what I'd call the *add-on* model (or argument) for anthropology sociology's case. This is the time-honored route of vaguely claiming that there are "some" cultural-social implications to all environmental issues (or to health, or to that whatever else may be the issue of the moment) and, therefore, one needs anthropology too, in addition to... and on, and on. You know the litany.

This way of making our case inherently begs for a marginal role, a glorified place at the periphery, a stereotypical add-on: "me too." Such an add-on is not even our sacred holism, because if holism is pleaded as an additive list of traits it becomes un-holy, a messy eclectic mix. Consequently, the "add-on" model is neither compelling nor apt to change opposed mind sets. In our vernacular, one could also call it the "hodgepodge model," because it sees reality syncretically as an amalgam of aspects, without grasping structures, priorities, and causalities within the belly of the social beast.

The core point, as I will stress further, is that the social-cultural variables are not just another "aspect," a minor side of a mainly technical issue. These variables are essential to the structure of most major problems we encounter.

Another model is the *behavioral model,* so named because it focuses on the need for individuals to understand and amend their detrimental behaviors *vis-a-vis* the environment. This model is not invalid, because education and attitudes are significant for shaping individuals' behavior. It is merely insufficient. Indeed, it gives little weight to group structures and vested interests. It also places the anthropological endeavor in the province of environmental education—a relevant but not central position either. The logic of this argument pushes anthropologists toward an educational approach undully limited to the individual's misconstrued attitudes, but leaves out the structural economic and societal dimensions.

An alternative model—in my view, the strongest way of arguing the case for practicing applied anthropological and sociological analysis—is to focus on the patterns of *social organization* within which social actors act. Predicating the value-added of anthropological analysis primarily on revealing the models of social organization that underpin social processes and link their social actors will best position applied research on the strongest theoretical ground. This "locks" the laser of applied inquiry onto structural issues, giving it centrality and maximizing its contribution. This is the natural position that anthropological/sociological analysis should occupy, not because social scientists subjectively so desire it, but because of two indisputable facts. First is the centrality of social actors in development; second is the knowledge about patterns of social organization and their actors' motivations. This is the very core of the anthropological and sociological enterprise, the comparative advantage and special competence of our disciplines.

The Focus on Social Organization in Applied Research

To some, suggesting social organization as the underpinning conceptual matrix in applied anthropology may appear, at first sight, as impractical or remote. We all know that applied anthropologists are expected to be "pragmatic," "operational," quick on their problem-solving feet. Yet, in my own fieldwork, taking social organization as the starting point for conceptualizing, thinking through, and analyzing specific practical problems in very diverse cultural contexts turned out every time to provide precisely the unexpected and original frame of reference absent in my economists' or technical colleagues' perspectives. This was true in my work on pastoralists in Senegal, on reforestation constraints in Azad Kashmir, and on irrigation and water-user societies in Thailand, Mexico, and India. Social organization provides a context and a launching pad for analysis, points out to linkages and dependencies, reveals encoded knowledge and meanings,[10] and helps identify all possible social actors, local and distant, with a stake in the problem under analysis.

Furthermore, "bringing social organization in" does not send applied analysts always and necessarily to the *macro-societal* level. It gives applied researchers, working at whatever social level, the theoretical impetus to identify patterns of social organization in large social bodies, in remote rural communities, in inner city quarters, in service processes and sub-systems, or even in small "street corner societies." This is true also regardless of whether the problem at hand concerns environmental pollution, health services, crime in the neighborhood, resettlement of displaced people, or irrigation water supply systems.The analyst should not be surprised—indeed, is rewarded

- when such conceptualization redefines both the problem at hand and the conventional solutions. Robert Merton pointed out (1973:94) that "perhaps the most striking role of conceptualization in applied social research is its transformation of practical problems by introducing concepts which refer to variables overlooked ... [and which may] lead to a statement of the problem that is dramatically opposed to that of the policymaker" or of whoever else is the user of applied research.

Environmental management is a domain that compellingly illustrates, first, the centrality of anthropological analysis, and second, the analytical superiority of the "social organization of actors" model over the "add-on model" or the "behavioral" model. Anthropological knowledge—from Malinowski to Radcliffe-Brown, from Raymond Firth to Fredrik Barth—is traditionally grounded in the study of the forms and patterns of social organization within which societies use the natural resources

---

[10]What accounts for the forcefulness and path-breaking quality of Malinowski's selective analysis of one of the Trobrianders' activities economic exchange? The answer is the context: social and cultural. As Malinowski wrote, in this monograph the reader "will clearly see that. though its main theme is economic—for it deals with commercial enterprise. exchange and trade—constant reference has to be made to social organization, the power of magic, to mythology and folklore".

on which they depend. This storehouse of knowledge and research methods is a major thesaurus for framing environmental policies and resource management programs in both developing and developed countries.

Yet the centrality of social organization issues to environmental problems and programs, however familiar it is to us, is *not* a self-evident truth. This is sadly proven by the abundance of one-sided technological eco-speak, or one-sided econo-mythical "solutions," and by the dearth of in-depth social understanding of these issues. Indeed, the intellectual debate about resource domains is overwhelmed by the enormous diversity of the technical issues intrinsic to each resource. The overall picture becomes fragmented into technical resource-specific approaches, while the common social underpinnings of all these domains remains clouded, less visible.

The intellectual argument that I regard as the main entry point for social scientists into the environmental debate is that an improved and sustainable use of natural resources depends decisively on improving the patterns of social organization for their management by the users themselves. Who are these users? Primarily the world's enormous mass of small farmers. My basic proposition is that *effective environmental policy must promote and rest on appropriate social organization.* Neither technology unembedded in social organizational structures, nor free-market fundamentalism unable to control externalities, can alone tackle runaway resource abuses.

Anthropologists as social architects must help build practical models for collective action in resource management. And we have to recognize that we must also revisit some of our own models, lovingly advocated in the anthropological literature but ineffective—for instance, the rather romantic model of community-based tree-lot planting. Communities are generally heterogeneous social entities and, thus, are seldom able to be the social agents of collective (unified) social actions. A case in point is the costly failure of most "village woodlot" and "community woodlot" schemes financed through hundreds of millions of wasted dollars. Although long praised uncritically by many social scientists, they have failed—and failed for social design reasons. Inadequate social models have misled many investment strategies into financing approaches which, on social grounds alone, could not—and did not—succeed, thus wasting both goodwill and money (Cernea 1992a, 1992b).

The focus on social organization compels development analysis to be actor-oriented. This is germane to both the explanatory and prescriptive functions of applied research. We did not claim that people were totally out of sight in conventional approaches. But we showed that the characteristics of a given social organization were stripped of the flesh and blood of real life in what I termed econocentric or commodocentric models. We demonstrated that key social actors of development were dealt with as an afterthought, mostly as passive, nonparticipating recipients. Our argument was, and is, this: putting people first in projects is not a goodwill appeal or a mere ethical advocacy .... It is a theoretically grounded request to policy makers, planners, and technical experts to explicitly recognize the centrality of what *is* the primary factor in development processes. It calls for changing the approach to planning. The requirement to admit *the centrality of people in projects* is tantamount to asking for *reversal of the conventional approach to project making. The model adopted in projects that do not put people first clashes with the model intrinsic to the real social process of development,* at the core of which are—simply—its actors (Cernea 1985/1991:7–8).

Relying on theoretical and empirical knowledge about models of social organization provides development anthropologists with tested analytical tools and social techniques. It is important not only to define social organization theoretically but also to "deconstruct" social organization into its building blocks, such as: the social actors at the local level; the social contract governing relations (including conflicts) between users and stakeholders (local and distant); prevailing symbolic and cultural systems; rules of entitlements, e.g. usufruct, ownership or custodianship rules; authority systems and enforcement mechanisms; an infinite range of producers' organizations (from family based units to large corporate enterprises); macro- social factors that undermine or solidify local social organization; etc. In turn, this facilitates creative social engineering work. For instance, the social expert must be able to figure out which available building blocks can make up more adequate social arrangements and culturally-sound action strategies in given circumstances.

As social architects, anthropologists are called to define the needs for associational infrastructure, social capital, grassroots organizations or higher order institutions, and help design them. In her Malinowski lecture, Elizabeth Colson pointed out that our Society for Applied Anthropology was created to promote the use of "skills of social engineering" (1985:192), and Raymond Firth, in his Malinowski address, emphasized the complexity of "analyzing the strength of relations in human engineering" (1981:196). Social engineering skills are indispensable for designing better social arrangements, improving institutions, enabling legal frameworks, and constructing adequate incentive systems. What for policymakers and development managers may seem "elusive" sociological elements can be translated, with help from the social scientist, into policy prescriptions and pragmatic action-oriented strategies.

When they work as social architects, anthropologists regularly face economic variables. What they have to propose bears directly upon the economy. Yet applied anthropologists often skate rather lightly over the economic determinants of social organization and their implications. We have very much to learn (not just criticize) from our colleagues the economists about economic analysis and measurement methods. When anthropologists bypass economic variables—and I have witnessed many such instances—the resulting recommendations are embarrassingly naive or directly erroneous. Conversely, when they consider the relevant economic dimensions, the results are powerful. Take, for instance, the path-breaking research and policy prescriptions developed by the Institute for Development Anthropology (IDA) in their Senegal River Basin studies. That study, as Michael Horowitz wrote, "was persuasive in large part because it provided hard field data on economic decision-making at the level of the rural production unit" (1994: 11), and considered variables absent in earlier economic analyses, such as yields per unit capital, per unit labor, and per unit land.

We must remind ourselves of Gunnar Myrdal's words, when he received the Malinowski Award, about how he lost his "inhibitions about transgressing the boundaries of separate social sciences," to delve into anthropology and sociology. He invited anthropologists to reverse the journey. "In dealing with a problem," Myrdal said, "it could never be a legitimate excuse that certain facts or causal relations between facts lay outside one's own field of knowledge" (1975:327).

Living daily inside an economic tribal culture, I can confirm that anthropology as practice can—indeed must—be enriched and strengthened by learning more from economic concepts and by internalizing quantifying methodologies. This is not a ritualstic tribute to powerful neighbors: economic knowledge is intrinsically indispensable for understanding social organization patterns anywhere. Anthropologists cannot relegate the study of economic variables to the subdiscipline called "economic anthropology." The understanding and manipulation of economic variables through applied social engineering is essential for *all* development anthropologists who take the concept of social organization as their basic guide.

Can Theory be Derived from Applied Research?

Applied anthropology is often deprecated by unfriendly voices and accused of being intrinsically incapable of benefiting theory. Long ago, Malinowski firmly advocated a "practical anthropology" (1929) concerned with answering the issues of the day. He rejected the "erroneous opinion ... that practical anthropology is fundamentally different from theoretical or academic anthropology. The truth is that science begins with application. What is application in science, and when does 'theory' become practical? When it first allows us a definite grip on empirical reality" (Malinowski 1961:5).

Applied anthropology facilitates such a "grip" on empirical reality. Even more, it is able to help change social reality.

The view that applied research is atheoretical—either does not use theory, or does not lead to theory—disempowers the discipline of anthropology. For some in the academic community, this opinion justifies disengagement and less concern with the public issues of the day. But this view has also induced some resigned defensiveness among a segment of the practicing anthropological community.

This charge is not only misplaced it is epistemologically unwarranted. First, the research objects of applied anthropology generally have no less intrinsic potential to generate theory than the research objects of academic anthropology. Development programs are complex social processes no less theory- worthy than kinship systems, or reciprocal gift-giving, or funerary rituals. Second, the methods of data generation are not necessarily different—many are similar—in applied and academic research. The overall research designs are different, but neither holds the monopoly on method. Individual researchers can choose either to distill from their data a course for future action, or to pursue theoretical proposition building. Both are valid endeavors.

Sol Tax was correct when, in his Malinowski lecture, he expressed the conviction that:

we deal not with a distinction between pure and applied anthropology but rather an amalgam or continuum of the two, a differing mixture of models in all of us who are anthropologists. At different times one of us can be doing much that is theoretical and general; at other times much more than is particular and applied, and at still other times engage in activities that are inextricably intertwined (Tax 1977:277).

Whatever our personal inclinations, the general state of our art—which ultimately is more than the sum of each individual's work—does reveal difficulties of growth and unresolved problems. Although work in applying anthropology has expanded significantly during the last decade, progress appears mostly as a vertical accumulation of primary case accounts—with too little horizontal cross-synthesis of comparable cases. Fragmentation results also from the sheer mass of what is published. Methodologically, the overestimation of "rapid appraisal methods" has resulted in all-too-ready excuses for sloppy assessments, for weakening longitudinal research, and for neglecting the collection of long time-series data. Comparative research is little practiced. It seems that most practitioners are so driven by their case-focused pursuits that little time is left for the essential task of looking back and around—for comparison, thinking, synthesis, and generalization. These weaknesses should be of concern to all of us.

I submit, however, that the task of generalizing empirical data resulting from applied research is not the charge only of those who define themselves as applied anthropologists. It is equally a task of those working in academic and theoretical anthropology and sociology. A vast volume of factual material is laid out in countless applied development reports and studies and is readily available to those interested in extracting theory from empirical findings. No tribal taboo forbids access to these empirical treasures to non-applied academic anthropologists. An outstanding example of what can be done for theory with data from applied research and case studies was given by Goodenough (1963). Spicer termed Goodenough's approach to using applied findings for theory building as an "exciting discovery in anthropology" (1976: 134).[11] Yet it is rather sad to realize how little this promising breakthrough has been replicated. I urge all colleagues in anthropology—academic as well as applied—to join in the effort of distilling theoretical propositions and methodological lessons from good applied research findings and experiences. "All human behavior," noted George Foster in his Malinowski lecture. "is grist for our mill, and all good research data—whatever the context in which they are gathered—have theoretical potential" (Foster 1982:194).

To sum up: first, data from good applied research do have theoretical potential; second. exploiting that potential is a collective (professional community) task, rather than a segregated subgroup task; third. a broad spectrum of "theoretical products"

---

[11]Praising Goodenough's *Cooperation in Change* for its success in developing "pure theory" by interpreting descriptive case studies of administrative action, Edward Spicer wrote: "In a sense [Goodenough's book]represented a swing back full circle form anthropologists' 'discovery' that the processes of administration can be brought into the context of pure theory in anthropolohy".

can be extracted from applied work—concepts, propositions, methodologies for purposive action, hypotheses, models, etc.

The "Third Leg" of the Dichotomy: Policy Development

The part of development anthropology that perhaps best demonstrates the infertility of a dichotomy between applied and theoretical anthropology is the work in policy formulation. Such work can be neither claimed nor performed by an atheoretical applied anthropology. To combine and convert knowledge and field findings into predictive and prescriptive policy propositions is intrinsically a theorizing operation.

Tom Weaver has written a passionate argument in support of anthropology's potential as a policy science, showing how it engages "the very basis of this field, its goals, its subject matter, research techniques, theory, methodology, its very future" (Weaver 1985a, 1985b:203). In this vein, our experiences in practicing anthropology at the World Bank have taught us a crucial lesson: however effective our anthropological inputs have been in various individual development projects, the most important successes, those with the farthest reaching impact, have been in policy formulation.

Several categories of World Bank policies have incorporated substantive anthropological/sociological contributions, yet such contributions are little known. My point is to show not just what we have done, but what can be done along policy lines.

Cross Sectoral Social Policies Among the essential policies of this kind, written virtually in full by social scientists., are the World Bank's policy on involuntary population resettlement entailed by development programs (World Bank 1980, 1986, 1991c, 1994; see also Cernea 1988, 1993; Partridge 1989), the policy on indigenous peoples affected by development projects (World Bank 1982, 1990; Davis and Wali 1993), and the policy regarding non-governmental organizations in Bank-supported activities (World Bank 1989; Cernea 1989).

Sectoral Social Policies Non-economic social scientists have made very substantial contributions in the formulations of several of the Bank's major sector development policy statements in co- operation with technical specialties, such as the urban growth policy (World Bank 1991a), the policy on investments in primary education (World Bank 1990); the forestry and reforestation policy (World Bank 1991b; Cernea 1992a), and the water resources policy (World Bank 1993).

Socioeconomic and Environmental Policies The poverty alleviation policy, the environmental policy guidelines, and others have benefited significantly from similar inputs. Vast efforts are being invested now in codifying participatory approaches and preparing policy guidelines for other social policy domains.

For all these domains, the multiplier effect from investing the knowledge and efforts of social scientists in policy formulations is enormous. Consider the case of involuntary population resettlement. I have written too much on resettlement lately to repeat this here, so I call your attention to one fact only: At least ten million people each year are subjected to forced displacement by the construction of dams and urban infrastructure. And resettlement policies are, perhaps, the most telling case of breaking the isolation and disinterest in which much good anthropology used to be held. As you know, a valuable body of knowledge was generated in the 1960s and 1970s on the disasters of forced displacement, yet to no avail. That research was gathering dust on library shelves, ignored by planners and policy makers. In the late 1970s, we took that knowledge as an empirical and theoretical basis for writing a policy on resettlement for the Bank. But rather than repeat descriptions of development's disasters, we proposed policy and operational solutions to solve them. The Bank then adopted the policy in 1980.

What happened next? This is most significant: over these last fifteen years, a "cascade" of policy advances occurred in this area, all with the participation of social scientists.

The Bank's resettlement policy itself was improved in four subsequent rounds (1986, 1988, 1991, 1994).

Promoting the resettlement policy beyond the Bank itself, we helped to draft a policy statement on resettlement (essentially identical with the Bank's policy) for all 25 OECD countries, to be applied by the bilateral donor agencies of OECD countries in their aid programs. Formal adoption of this policy by OECD ministers took place in 1991 (see OECD 1992).

The multilateral development Banks for Asia, Africa, and Latin America have adopted or are now vetting their resettlement policy.

Some countries (Brazil, China, Colombia, and others) have developed domestic social policies and legal frameworks on resettlement, borrowing more than a page from the policy written by social scientists for the World Bank.

Further, and unexpectedly, some anthropologists in the United States have proposed that the US Government adopt the World Bank's resettlement policy for resolving the Navajo-Hopi dispute (Brugge 1993).

- a long shot, though, we all agree

And at the Social Summit in Copenhagen in March 1995, as a result of an explicit initiative of Bank social scientists supported by other anthropologists (particularly Downing), and backed by several governments (Uganda, Canada, Switzerland) and by NGOs, involuntary resettlement issues have been incorporated in the Summit's Program of Action (see Cemea 1995).

So this is an indisputable fact: we are today a long, long way from the point when anthropological studies on resettlement were languishing forgotten on library shelves and no resettlement policy whatsoever existed, neither in the Bank nor anywhere else in the developing world.

For our "state-of-the-art housekeeping," we should also note that these policies are not the whole story. During the past fif-teen years the body of social science knowledge on resettlement itself has been greatly expanded, enriched, tested, corrected and recreated due primarily to operational applied research. A series of seminal papers on the anthropology of displacement and resettlement have resulted from on-the-ground association with resettlement operations, and have stimulated creative contributions in legal thinking and other related fields (Bartolome 1993; Cook 1993; Davis and Garrison 1988; Downing 1995; Guggenheim 1990, 1993; Partridge 1989; Partridge and Painter 1989; Cernea 1988, 1990a, 1990b, 1993, 1995; Scudder 1991; McMillan et al. 1992; Mathur 1994). This knowledge accumulation is bound to yield further progress in the years ahead.

Most important is that the social science contribution has resulted in major changes in the practice of involuntary resettlement throughout the world—changes in resettlers' entitlements, in planning, in financing, even in turning around insensitive bureaucracies. The overarching meaning of all these changes is that the lives and fates of many people worldwide are improved through better protection and added opportunities. We know that resettlement remains painful, and much does not yet happen along ideal policy lines. But, in improving this development process, we are now farther ahead than any development anthropologist would have dared to dream just a decade ago.

For me personally, this kind of progress is the most gratifying reward. I feel privileged, indeed, to have had the chance to be part of this process, to be a development applied social scientist, and am excited to practice this vocation. My message tonight is that our profession is consequential. It makes a difference. I would want this message to reach the students who engage in the study of anthropology and sociology, and who consider dedicating their life and work to applying this knowledge. It is not an easy profession, but it is a generous and useful one. On this very point, it is appropriate to conclude. In its great wisdom, the Talmud teaches that "One who saves a single life is as one who saves an entire world." From this view we can derive courage and motivation for each single one of our projects, big or small, be it a major policy or a small inner-city health project. Each of you has probably experienced being the local "Secretary to the Non-believers" in one place or another. But we are gaining converts. We "win" when we make lasting professional contributions that benefit many people. Let us broaden our knowledge, refine our tools, and embolden our moral commitment to do this beautiful work better and better.

Acknowledgments This is a fitting time to express gratitude to my family for the strength and motivation they impart to my endeavors—in particular, thanks to my children and to my wife Ruth, a fellow anthropologist, for her support of my work, including her counsel in preparing this lecture. My profound appreciation and tribute to my many close colleagues, in the World Bank and outside, who are committed to the kind of social science work discussed in this paper—and in particular to Cynthia Cook, Gloria Davis, Sandy Davis, Ted Downing, Ashraf Ghani, Scott Guggenheim, Steven Heyneman, Maritta Koch-Weser, Ayse Kudat, William Partridge, Ted Scudder, Ismail Serageldin, and Andrew Steer.

References

Angrosino, M. V. (Ed.) (1976). *Do applied anthropologists apply anthropology?* (SAS Proceedings No. 10). Athens: University of Georgia Press.

Bartolome, L. J. (1993). The Yacyreta experience with urban resettlement: Some lessons and insights. In M. M. Cernea & S. E. Guggenheim (Eds.), *Anthropological approaches to involuntary resettlement: Policy, practice, and theory*. Boulder, CO: Westview Press.

Brugge, D. M. (1993). The relocation of Navajos from the Hopi partitioned lands in relation to the world bank standards for involuntary resettlement. In J.-e. Piper (Ed.), *Papers from the third, fourth and sixth Navajo studies conferences*. Window Rock, AZ: Navajo Nation Historic Preservation Department.

Cernea, M. M. (1988). *Involuntary resettlement in development projects: Policy guidelines in world bank-financed projects*. Washington, DC: The World Bank.

Cernea, M. M. (1989). *Nongovernmental organizations and local development*. Washington, DC: The World Bank.

Cernea, M. M. (1990a). *Social science knowledge for development projects* (World Bank Discussion Paper No. 114). Washington, DC.

Cernea, M. M. (1990b). *Poverty risks from population displacement in waler resources development* (Harvard University/HIID, DDP No. 355). Cambridge, MA.

Cernea, M. M. (1992a). In N. Scrimshaw & G. R. Gleason (Eds.), *Re-tooling in applied social investigation for development planning. Some methodological issues. Rapid assessment procedures (RAP): Qualitative methodologies for planning and evaluation of health related programs*. Boston, MA: INFOS.

Cernea, M. M. (1992b). A sociological framework: Policy, environment, and the social actors for tree planting. In N. Sharma (Ed.), *Managing the world's forests: Looking for balance between conservation and development* (pp. 301–335). Iowa: Kendall/Hunt Publishing.

Cernea, M. M. (1993). Anthropological and sociological research for policy development on population resettlement. In M. M. Cernea & S. E. Guggenheim (Eds.), *Anthropological approaches to involuntary resettlement: Policy, practice and theory*. Boulder, CO: Westview Press.

Cernea, M. M. (1995). Understanding and preventing impoverishment from development-induced displacement. reflections on the state of knowledge. *Keynote address to the international conference on development-induced displacement and impoverishment*. Oxford: University of Oxford.

Cernea, M. M. (1979) *Entry points for sociological knowledge in the project cycle* (Seminar paper). Manuscript.

Cernea, M. M. (Ed.). (1985/1991). *Putting people first: Sociological variables in development*. New York: Oxford University Press.

Cernea, M., Kepes, G., Larionescu, M., et al. (1970). *Doua Sate: Structuri Sociale si Progres Technic*. Bucuresti: Edit. Pol.

Colson, E. (1985). Using anthropology in a world on the move. *Human Organization, 44*(3), 1–15.

Cook, C. (1993). *Involuntary resettlement in Africa* (World Bank Technical Paper No. 227). Washington, DC.

Davis, G., & Garrison, H. (1988). *Indonesia: The transmigration program in perspective. A World Bank Country Study*. Washington, DC: World Bank.

Davis, S., & Wali, A. (1993). *Indigenous territories and tropical forest management in Latin America* (World Bank Environment Department Policy Research Working Paper). Washington, DC: Environmental Assessment and Programs.

Downing, T. E. (1995). *Mitigating social impoverishment when people are involuntarily displaced*. Paper presented at the Oxford conference on development-induced displacement and impoverishment.

Firth, R. (1981). Engagement and detachment: Reflections on applying social anthropology to social affairs. *Human Organization, 40*(3), I93–20I.

Foster, G. M. (1982). Applied anthropology and international health: Retrospect and prospect. *Human Organization, 3*(3), 189–197.
Goodenough, W. (1963). *Cooperation in change. An anthropological approach to community development.* New York: Russell Sage Foundation.
Guggenheim, S. E. (1990). Resettlement in Colombia: The case of El Guavio. *Practicing Anthropology, 12*(3), 14–20.
Guggenheim, S. E. (1993). Peasants. Planners, and participation: Resettlement in Mexico. In M. M. Cernea & S. E. Guggenheim (Eds.), *Anthropological approaches to involuntary resettlement: Policy, practice, and theory.* Boulder, CO: Westview Press.
Horowitz, M. M. (1994). Development for anthropology in the Mid-1990s. *Development Anthropology Network, 12,* 1/2.
Kardam, N. (1993). Development approaches and the role of policy advocacy: The case of the World Bank. *World Development, 21*(11), 1773–1786.
Kindelberger, C. P. (1952). *Review of the economy of Turkey: The economic development of Guatemala: Report on Cuba: Review of Economics and Statistics* (Vol. 34, pp. 391–392).
Kottak, C. P. (1985). When people don't come first: Some sociological lessons from completed projects. In M. M. Cernea (Ed.), *Putting people first. Sociological variables in development.* London: Oxford University Press.
Malinowski, B. (1922). *Argonauts of the Western Pacific. Prospect heights.* Reprinted in 1984 by Waveland Press, Illinois.
Malinowski, B. (1929). Practical anthropology. *Africa, 2,* 22–38.
Malinowski, B. (1961). *The dynamics of culture change.* New Heaven, CT: Yale University Press. Reprinted in 1976 by Greenwood Press Inc., Westport, Connecticut.
Mathur, H. M. (Ed.). (1994). *Development, displacement and resettlement. Focus on Asian experiences.* Delhi: Vikas Publishing House.
McMillan, D. E., Thomas Painter, and Thayer Scudder. (1992). *Settlement and development in the river blindness control zone* (World Bank Technical Paper No. 192). Washington, DC
Mead, M. (1976). Applied anthropology: The state of the art. In *Perspectives on anthropology Mead, Margaret 1976. (A special publication of the American Anthropological Association No. 10).* Washington, DC: Anthony F.C. Wallace.
Merton, R. K. (1973). Technical and moral dimensions of policy research (originally published in 1949). In R. K. Merton (Ed.), *The sociology of science* (pp. 70–80). Chicago, IL: The University of Chicago Press.
Myrdal, G. (1975). The unity of the social sciences, Malinowski award address. *Human Organization, 34*(4), 327–332.
OECD (Organization for Economic Corporation and Development). (1992). *Development Assistance Committee. Guidelines for Aid agencies on involuntary displacement and resettlement in development projects.* Paris: OECD.
Partridge, W. L. (1989). Involuntary resettlement in development projects. *Journal of Refugee Studies, 2*(3), 373–384.
Partridge, W. L., & Painter, M. (1989). Lowland settlement in San Julian, Bolivia—Project success and regional underdevelopment. In D. Schumann & W. L. Partridge (Eds.), *The human ecology of tropical land settlement in Latin America.* Boulder, CO: Westview Press.
Scott, R. A., & Shore, A. R. (1979). *Why sociology does not apply: Sociology in public policy.* New York: Elsevier.
Scudder, T. (1991). A sociological framework for the analysis of new land settlements. In M. M. Cernea (Ed.), *Putting people first: Sociological variables in rural development.* New York: Oxford University Press.
Serageldin, I. (1994). Foreword. In *Sociology, anthropology and development. An Annotated Bibliography of World Bank Publications 1975–1993.* Michael M. Cernea with assistance of April Adams. ESD Studies and Monograph Series No. 3.
Spicer, E. H. (1976). Early applications of anthropology in North America. In A. F. C. Wallace (Ed.), *Perspectives on anthropology.* Washington, DC: American Anthropological Association.

Tax, S. (1977). Anthropology for the world of the future: Thirteen Professions and three proposals, Malinowski award address. *Human Organization, 36*(3), 225–234.
van Willigen, J. (1993). *Applied anthropology: An introduction*. Westport, CT: Bergin & Garvey.
Weaver, T. (1985a). Anthropology as a policy science: Part I, a critique. *Human Organization, 44* (2), 97–105.
Weaver, T. (1985b). Anthropology as a policy science: Part II, development and training. *Human Organization, 44*(3), 197–205.
Wiedman, H. H. (1973). In praise of the double inherent in anthropological applications. In M. V. Angrosino (Ed.), *Do applied anthropologists apply anthropology?* Athens: University of Georgia Press.
Wolf, E. R. (1956). Aspects of group relations in a complex society: Mexico. *American Anthropologist, 58*, 1065–1078.
World Bank. (1980). *Operational manual statement no. 2.33: Social issues associated with involuntary resettlement in bank financed projects*. Washington, DC: World Bank.
World Bank. (1982). *Operational manual statement no. 2.34: Tribal people in bank financed development projects*. Washington, DC: World Bank.
World Bank. (1986). *Operational Manual Statement No. 10.08: Operations policy issues in the treatment of involuntary resettlement*. Washington, DC: World Bank.
World Bank. (1989). *Operational directive 14.70: Involving nongovernmental organizations in bank-supported activities*. Washington, DC: World Bank.
World Bank. (1990). *Primary education: A World Bank policy paper*. Washington, DC: World Bank.
World Bank. (1991a). *Urban policy and economic development: An AGENDA for the 1990s. A World Bank Policy Paper*. Washington, DC: World Bank.
World Bank. (1991b). *The forest sector: A World Bank policy paper*. Washington, DC: World Bank.
World Bank. (1991c). *Operational directives 4.30, involuntary resettlement*. Washington, DC: World Bank.
World Bank. (1993). *Poverty reduction handbook*. Washington, DC: World Bank.
World Bank. (1994). *Resettlement and development: The bank-wide review of projects involving involuntary resettlement 1986–1993*. Washington, DC: World Bank.

Michael M. Cernea is the 1995 recipient of the Malinowski Award, presented at the 1995 Annual Meeting of the Society for Applied Anthropology, Albuquerque, New Mexico. This annual award is given to a senior colleague "in recognition of efforts to understand and serve the needs of the world through social science." Michael M. Cernea is the Senior Adviser for Social Policy and Sociology of The World Bank (1818 H Street, NW, Washington, DC 20433, USA).

Open Access This chapter is licensed under the terms of the Creative Commons Attribution 4.0 International License (http://creativecommons.org/licenses/by/4.0/), which permits use, sharing, adaptation, distribution and reproduction in any medium or format, as long as you give appropriate credit to the original author(s) and the source, provide a link to the Creative Commons license and indicate if changes were made.

The images or other third party material in this chapter are included in the chapter's Creative Commons license, unless indicated otherwise in a credit line to the material. If material is not included in the chapter's Creative Commons license and your intended use is not permitted by statutory regulation or exceeds the permitted use, you will need to obtain permission directly from the copyright holder.

Anthropology at Work

My 20 Years as World Bank Development Anthropologist

Maritta Koch-Weser

This is a personal record. I describe my work at the World Bank for over 20 years, telling you how we began a new and continuously evolving professional practice four decades ago, and to what effect. I hope to transmit to students of a next generation the causes that *development anthropology* stands for, and to pass on my passionate conviction that it must remain a mainstream discipline in the twenty-first century.

Beginnings

In the 1970s, development anthropologists began to work on economic development issues in the world's poorest corners and among indigenous populations. For me, as one of them, development anthropology became a lifelong passion, a way to contribute meaningfully towards the larger social and environmental challenges of our times.

The term *Development Anthropology* had come up in the early 1970s as a variant of sociology, designating the operationally oriented transition from theory to applied analytical and design work. My own interest had been triggered early-on during my 1970–1972 doctoral fieldwork on "Yoruba Religion in Brazil". Two experiences, two planning failures, had sharpened my sense for the fundamental value of social and cultural understanding in local development work—and for the rather simple opportunities that were being missed:

> The first experience was the rough, poorly conceived involuntary resettlement of Favela Catacumba in Rio de Janeiro to the distant fringes of the city. Some of the followers of the

---

M. Koch-Weser (✉)
Earth3000, Bieberstein, Germany
e-mail: mkochweser@earth3000.org

Macumba and Umbanda rituals I was studying were forcefully resettled. In their previous favela location in central Rio de Janeiro, they had kept live animals behind their shacks—sacrificial animals to be offered to the *Orixas*, typically a goat, or some chicken or doves—a firm element of their Afro-Brazilian rituals. Now, in their new social housing flats, I found animal husbandry—smelly goats—on the third floor, in peoples' new bathrooms—an absolutely disgusting, unhygienic mess. Why, I asked, had nobody looked into peoples' lives, religion, and special needs beforehand? Better design—simply a place outside for the goat—could probably have been provided at no additional cost.

The second experience was a visit to the early-stage construction of the grandiosely planned, first east-west Transamazon Highway in 1971. We witnessed the intrusion of gigantic forest clearing equipment, the horrific screeching of huge, falling trees, and the conversion of landscapes as entire forest tracts were removed. This destruction of nature's grand rainforest, scars left alongside visibly failing human resettlements, left a deep impression. These settlements, mechanically planned by land surveyors and engineers, were social and economic failures. Close to Altamira in the State of Para, semi-cleared forest lands had been distributed to landless peasant families from far away, drought-stricken areas in Brazil's arid Northeast. These people had no familiarity with the plants, soils, insects, and snakes surrounding them in Amazonia. Some also suffered from malaria. Whatever they had known about agricultural cycles in their native arid Sertão environment had become irrelevant. Surely the unfortunate settler families could have at least have fared better with appropriate induction and socio-cultural designs.

As a student, I had already become convinced that participant observation—the art of listening to people, observing interrelationships in communities, and gaining knowledge about the local web of history and religion, must all inform any effective tailoring of aid. Michael Cernea's later, seminal 1985 book was rightly called "Putting People First".

Practice

When I refer to Development Anthropology, I think of practice rather than theory. In development planning and project implementation we seek to make useful contributions through field work, careful participant observation, interviewing, walking into houses, kitchens and storage rooms, and by observing gender roles, power relationships, power struggles, and the interplay and differences across communities.

As development anthropologists, we participate in endeavors which seek the best ways to improve local livelihoods, health, nutrition, incomes, land rights, women's rights, access to credit, and more. Our analysis can give voice and promote inclusion—through community participation, attention to the social roles of men, women, and minorities, and indigenous safeguards.

Development anthropologists must bring to the task an appetite for field work,—for listening, observing, interviewing with compassion—and yet with a cool head, systematizing what they learn in the course of open, interactive interviews and participant observation. They must measure success in terms of development outcomes on the ground.

Participant Observation

Participant observation means going to the end of the line. As a development anthropologist, you should travel endless rural roads, where most government official will have never set foot. The objective is to look and to observe, to ask people—and to put yourself into the place of your interviewees to the greatest extent possible, across cultural barriers, finding your very own, pragmatic shortcuts to get at least some sense of what development looks like "from within".

A plain, positive example always stuck in my mind: We had asked Larry Salmen, a fellow anthropologist, to analyze the appropriateness of a World Bank financed social housing project in Guayaquil/Ecuador. Larry decided that participant observation meant not just interviewing new residents, but spending a few nights sleeping on the floor of one of the already finished housing units. This way he discovered a world beyond what the building engineers had previously registered—the world of noises and lack of privacy, the terrible heat and lack of ventilation, and more. Obviously, it does not take a social science PhD to check these, but the fact remains that in this case, just-in-time "participant observation" field work helped improve the design for these poor people's new houses—improvements that would not have happened otherwise.

Another example along those lines was my own discovery during a field visit in Karnataka, India. Here, houses lacked toilets, and this had caused problems, especially for women who feared going down to the snake infested river at night. Their problem had been addressed in the World Bank financed project I had come to supervise. To provide more safety, a village female toilet facility had been built close by at the edge of the village. As a woman, I could interview local women—expecting, but not getting, nods of approval. Something seemed strange. I insisted—earning endless giggles—to personally visit the site of supposed improvement, the female toilet facility. I walked into a walled rectangle, followed only up to the entrance by a sizable crowd from the village. Inside there was absolutely nothing—no toilets, no water, no pipes—only clean, dry sand. Visibly, nobody had ever used this fraud as a toilet. I invited the hesitant Chief Minister of the State to come inside to inspect the place. I hope the crooks who had failed to deliver a true toilet facility were punished.

Courage to Experiment

Projects are social laboratories. At the outset, the acceptance of new designs is uncertain, and must be checked over the years. Will midwives stop using rusty knives or dusty concoctions on the umbilical cords they cut? Will expecting mothers take advantage of pre-natal care? Will community decisions to manage forests sustainably on Nepalese hillsides be respected or enforced?

Interdisciplinary cooperation and team work are key. In field situations anthropologists will work alongside colleagues specialized as engineers, agronomists, health or education experts, or economists. When innovations are contemplated, doubts often center on attitudinal or cultural uncertainties. Will land purchase credit work—will it be used by sharecroppers, and will borrowers indeed pay their dues? When vaccinations are offered, will mothers bring their children? When water user associations or cooperatives are established, will the members make them work, and stick to common rules? In cases such as these, development anthropologists take on their share of project risks.

In most cases, taking the risks turned out to have been worthwhile. Some of the very best development innovations of the 1980s came from organizations outside the public sector. For want of precedent, they had to be imagined. In Bangladesh, Mohammed Yunus successfully experimented with at least three major innovations in parallel: the principal one being a reliance on promoting a leading developmental role for women (as he saw it); group micro-credit; and the introduction of the Grameen Phone—a technical innovation for connecting largely illiterate communities to the market. Fathom how courageous he was. No previous studies could have proven him right, only close follow-up with women's and community groups could provide proof of concept over time. Grameen phone became a national success. It will take more such imagination, and more and larger experimentation to attain the United Nations Social Development Goals (SDGs) in the coming years.

Tasks then and Now

The war on poverty is still with us—now in a world which has doubled its population since 1970. We live in a predominantly urban world now, rather than a mostly rural one then. Yet the tasks we faced 4–5 decades ago are still with us, especially in sub-Saharan Africa and so many more remaining poverty niches on earth. Average national statistics have often improved significantly, hiding the fact that severe poverty niches have been left behind nevertheless. Today the challenge is to focus "surgically" on those niches.

The record of development achievements over the past 50 years is not bad. Many battles have been won: agricultural productivity is up, and statistics on child mortality, life expectancy, literacy rates have improved significantly. Biodiversity, climate and ocean protection have all made enormous strides. Now the achievements of yesteryear must be upheld or completed way beyond the lifetime of past development loans—among them the protection of most vulnerable minorities and indigenous people, the education of girls and women, the just compensation and resettlement of people affected by infrastructure works, and the integrity of protected nature areas and World Heritage Sites around the world.

Priorities have shifted. Fields to which development anthropologists must now especially contribute include:

- the urgent task of **salvaging and preserving indigenous knowledge,** before it vanishes forever;
- the task of helping societies **overcome outdated labels, stereotypes and assumptions**—uncovering socio-cultural undercurrents in governance, religion, drug trade, and internet-based community formation;
- tasks related to **migration**: the integration of migrants, patterns of remittances, and intercultural integration; and
- the task of fostering **global cooperation in preserving this earth. The** task is global, but much of the needed action remains a local, behavioral and cultural challenge.

Downsides

In an international development agency, development anthropologists work at an intermediary level. The development agency work routine with its short field visits rarely allows for well calibrated "own" field research. Therefore, a fleeting visit by a World Bank anthropologist can never substitute for much needed in-depth studies, which need to be commissioned and carried out by professionals fluent in local dialect and culture.

In my work experience I regularly depended on local experts. But our own short visits were useful starting blocks. They served to let us scan for priority socio-cultural issues, and they allowed us to develop terms of reference for appropriate in-depth analysis, commissioned with local universities and experts for the life-span of a project—for advice in project design and monitoring, and for independent evaluation.

Development projects involve dynamic, multi-year social processes, some foreseeable, others not. No project I know of—if it involved people at all and not just a single physical construction site—has ever been implemented successfully without intelligent adjustments over the course of time. Social design assumptions must always be tested "on the ground", within different communities, and in complex not entirely foreseeable institutional, political or market contexts.

In our group of colleagues we experienced, painfully, that the impact of our work also very much depended on proper timing. It is frustrating when social expertise is brought in too late, in a trouble-shooting mode, or in the perfunctory manner of ticking off a list of formal requirements, without any real care for the results. Once things get off track, they will be far more difficult to turn around.

I experienced such situations in several of my early field assignments. One was a Honduran afforestation project supported by the Organization of American States in the late 1970s, where we found local farmers pulling out "project" tree seedlings that had been planted for erosion control on steep hillsides. It was an untenable project design: hungry peasants replaced tree seedlings with the corn that they needed to eat. Afforestation could not succeed without mitigation of extreme hunger and landlessness. Far more positive examples for "social forestry" were developed later in India and Nepal, where from the start the emphasis was on social consensus to implement communal strategies for re-growth and highly controlled use, such as the gathering of firewood.

Another example was the World Bank's first-ever Nutrition Improvement Project in the state of Sergipe in Northeast Brazil in the early 1980ies. This project was testing and comparing four design experiments to improve child nutrition. At mid-term we found that all experiments were failing for one reason or another. Even worse, simple routines of driving small children on trucks to weighing stations had met with immense fear and anger of the left behind parents. Had social expertise been employed earlier, at least such culturally unacceptable design features might have been avoided.

Around the same time, a further early example was a USAID funded settlement project in San Julian, which I reviewed at the request of the World Bank. In a tropical forest region in Bolivia, north of Santa Cruz de la Sierra, the project attempted to settle land-starved Indios from the Bolivian Altiplano 3000 m above. Much like the failing resettlements I had seen as a student in the Brazilian Amazon, the Aymara in their woolen garb, estranged from their intricate social and agricultural highland rules of life, and afraid of snakes and insects would not succeed in this sweltering environment. The basic design of the settlement project was fraught, and belated social expertise could point out, but not correct failure.

Upsides

Projects are experiments—searches for the most effective development opportunities. Cases, like the ones just mentioned, where the original project design turned out to be fatally flawed, were fortunately very few over the years—and in Latin America they all belonged to the late 1970s and early 1980s. Later, as greater attention had been paid in project design to social factors, timely monitoring and evaluation became key so that emergent problems could be caught, reviewed, and used for mid-course corrections. Refinements of social (but also of technical) designs continued throughout the multi-year life of a project—taking account of unforeseen events or attitudes on project performance.

My list of monitoring and evaluation "successes," where good monitoring alerted early on to problems and the need to correct course could fill a book. Let me give you three examples:

> I recall unwanted outcomes of the land distribution schemes run by INCRA, the Brazilian Agrarian Reform Agency in the Brazilian Amazon, in the new frontier state of Rondonia in the early 1980ies. Breaking a tradition of sharecropper exploitation, peasants had been assigned their own plots of land. For the first time in their lives they had become proud and independent land owners. What happened? Soon enough they repeated the only economic model they had ever experienced, now turning other rural laborers into "their" sharecroppers.
>
> In Mexico, the PIDER program—Programa Integrado de Desarrollo Rural—as well as other rural development projects cosponsored by IFAD (for example, in the Oaxaca

highlands) had at its core the work with communities, which could opt for rural development measures that the villages wished to prioritize. "Listening to the people", the question of power and voice in community meetings, turned out to be a challenging task. For example, I witnessed that men wanted soccer fields, instead of asking for a better well to free their women from hauling water bucket-by-bucket from more than 100 m depth in dry southern Yucatan. In one village which had opted for and received a "cattle unit", I remember the local way of "benefit-sharing" aligned with local power structures. The project financed "cattle unit" consisted of the animals, establishment of new pastures, and fences to protect them. On supervision we found that the richer half of the village had appropriated the cattle (and already quickly sold them for money to improve their houses). This left the poorer, less powerful people stranded with useless fences and pastures—and without cattle. As a result, economic progress was nil, except for the better roofs that the cattle sellers had put on their houses. Monitoring and Evaluation provided fast learning on how to more carefully conduct community work, benefitting subsequent village planning under this nation-wide rural development program.

As a third example, let me mention rural development in Kigoma, at the western edge of Tanzania, bordering Rwanda. A project designed to improve rural productivity was in its third year of implementation, when we came to carry out a mid-term evaluation. Already, the project was seen by government officials as a failure, because the project-financed public storage facilities had remained largely empty. Nevertheless, during our field visit agricultural production under this project seemed to be successful and thriving. Interviews with peasants did not provide any plausible answers on why the marketing component was failing, and why the warehouses remained empty. Soon enough we could see what was happening: long lines of people, wares on their backs, were winding up the path towards the border. On foot the production was carried up the mountain into adjacent Rwanda, where prices several times higher than in Tanzania level could be caught in those days.

Fields of Danger

The job of a development anthropologist can be dangerous. Going to "the end of the line"—especially in frontier areas where the rule of law is fragile—or to isolated groups who do not understand the purpose of your visit, can be tough.

I helped design and worked on the first Amerindian Protection Projects in Northwest Brazil, and also in the wider area of influence of the Carajas Iron Ore project in Brazil. To fly in one-engine planes in order to visit recently contacted tribal groups like the Urueuwauwau, in Rondonia—leads to unpredictable situations.

My colleague Daniel Gross once called from Rondonia where he had wanted to see close up whether the health post at the Cinta Larga indigenous reserve had been duly constructed. He was attacked and never managed to even get off the FUNAI government plane. As it turned out, the Indios had been befriended and bribed by illegal diamond and gold "garimpeiros", who regularly brought them gifts (e.g. much appreciated frozen chicken). The Cinta Larga did not wish to see this relationship interrupted by Government authorities, with whom Daniel Gross, a World Bank anthropologist, had arrived. Dan just about escaped with his life.

Also related to the protection of indigenous lands under a World Bank project, I once arrived in the Brazilian State of Bahia at the Kiriri de Mirandela indigenous reserve. Before we reached the Reserve, we were "greeted" by a most aggressive group of local farmers, their sharp hoes high in the air, who saw the government Jeep and objected to a program that was advancing competing indigenous land rights (as required under Brazilian law). I was 7 months pregnant and doubly worried. Praise the day when you arrive home safely after facing armed conflict over indigenous lands.

Or worse, in a forestry project in southern Colombia, a guerrilla zone in the 1980ies, you ride and walk to reach a group of farmers attending a cocoa treatment workshop. No telephones can announce your visit. As you surprise the group, each of them grabs the gun that they hold between their legs, ready to fire on the unexpected visitors. Here a World Bank project was taking place in a war zone. Every anthropologist working in those far-off places where development is most needed will have stories like these.

Authenticity

I found it impossible to always remain as neutral and respectful of local culture as I thought outside "objective" observers should be. A scene from highland Bolivia: A small child fell, was badly wounded, and cried desperately. Nobody acted and I picked it up—although bystanders thought this inappropriate and ridiculous.

Among the Nambikwara Indios in Brazil twins were born, and this was considered a bad omen. Traditionally one had to be killed (a custom probably rooted in age old survival methods—reflecting the excessive challenge of feeding and carrying two infants instead of one). The medical project staff tried to salvage both children, explaining there would be enough food.

Equally, how could you hold back when you hear of female circumcision, child marriages, or harmful techniques applied by midwives? Development Anthropologists come with their own cultural baggage.

My World Bank Years: In Retrospect

In the late 1970s sociologist and development anthropologist positions were not advertised, simply because they did not exist. My first "foot in the door" was a brief consultant assignment in Bolivia, where a rural poverty alleviation project had met with unexpected opposition from the local population. As it turned out, the rural roads had been widened, in some cases touching on the edges of fields where here and there ancestors had been buried. It was literally an unspeakable problem, but one local anthropologists would readily point out to me when I visited. Similarly, intricate age-old local labor exchange systems had not been taken into account in this project—and hence the Dutch cooperative specialist ended up having a hard time. With findings like these I and the first handful of social scientists began to conquer new places at the World Bank, case by case.

Robert S. McNamara, World Bank President since 1968, had brought a healthy measure of impatience and moral compassion to the development task, dissatisfied with the snail pace of poverty eradication globally. In his 1973 Nairobi Speech he framed the challenge: "... This is absolute poverty: a condition of life so limited as to prevent realization of the potential of the genes with which one is born; a condition of life so degrading as to insult human dignity- and yet a condition of life so common as to be the lot of some 40% of the peoples of the developing countries."

Convinced that economic development could not be reached in the poorest corners of the world by infrastructure projects alone, McNamara set up the Agriculture and Rural Development Department as a hub for piloting innovations. Back then, poverty was still concentrated in the rural world: 70% of people in developing nations lived in rural areas (in contrast, today 70% are urban). In addition, the World Bank commissioned its first analyses and programs for health, nutrition, education, population control, and environment. McNamara pressed for measurable outcomes, and the monitoring and evaluation of project results became standard. An ultimately truly transformative path had been established, but even with steep growth in lending and a multi-sectoral broadening of the development agenda, reality rarely matched the speed of change McNamara that would have liked to see.

A Foot in the Door

Here's how I got started. Equipped with my German doctoral degree, I started teaching courses in Latin American and Development Anthropology at George Washington University in Washington DC in 1975. In parallel I began in 1977 to work occasionally as a consultant for international organizations in our university's immediate Washington DC neighborhood—first for the Organization of American States, then The American Association for the Advancement of Science, and then for the World Bank, which I joined on a full-time basis in 1980.

My first 3 years as a World Bank consultant (1977–1980) were both fascinating and frustrating. I worked on the outer fringes of what was then a singularly economics- and engineering-oriented organization. Consultants were able to observe and recommend, but they had to leave operational decisions entirely to the staff members who had hired them. As a junior consultant working alongside my teaching jobs, I had no leverage in decision making, and remained stuck in the smallest, windowless office.

Nevertheless, getting my foot in the World Bank door turned out to be the best direction my professional life could have taken. It was my good fortune that I was eventually hired into the hub of innovation, the Agriculture and Rural Development Department under the great leadership of Montague Yudelman and Leif Christoffersen, and in the direct neighborhood of Michael Cernea, the World Bank's first ever rural sociologist. Twenty fascinating years filled with challenging field work lay ahead, eventually landing me with more than my share of responsibilities out there in Latin America, North Africa, Sub-Saharan Africa, South and East Asia, and some countries of the former Soviet Union.

I became a full-time staff member in 1980, I believe as the third professional social scientist that the organization had ever hired. When I left in 1998, there must have been close to 200 social scientists; tremendous change had taken place. With Michael Cernea's arrival in the 1970s, social disciplines had gained their intellectual champion, and, under Michael's leadership, more and more social scientists were hired—first as consultants, and later as staff. We came together in an intense learning-by doing process in the 1980s and throughout the 1990s. An informal internal platform—the World Bank's Sociological Working Group—interconnected us. To avoid the usual problems of too many bureaucratic silos and not enough time to interact as a community, we regularly got together over brown-bag lunches, sharing experiences and getting inspired by outside speakers.

We all shared a steep and sometimes arduous learning curve. With hindsight, major blind spots remained in the early 1980ies. To name a few, micro-credit, cultural heritage, disaster preparedness, fighting corruption, and analyzing local governance—all were as yet not on the screen. Governance constraints were suppressed—to the detriment of longer-term structural change: To shape projects into efficient spearheads, the management of World Bank projects often established temporary institutional enclaves where good people were hired for decent salaries. Once projects ended, the previous advantage turned into a drawback, because of a lack of insertion into the overall national patterns of governance and payrolls. This led to some discontinuities and setbacks.

Another blind spot was the consideration of ethnic minorities and indigenous people—a thorny issue as World Bank projects began to reach into far-away frontier lands in Indonesia and Brazil, and into ethnically complex regions in Africa.

Environment may have been the biggest blind spot of them all: resettlement programs like Transmigration in Indonesia and POLONOROESTE in Brazil, programs which transformed vast and pristine rainforest areas into agricultural settlements, would be unthinkable today. Environmental lending was equally unthinkable in the early 1980s. Direct investments into environmental protection and institution building only came on line years later, when economic tools to value returns on national investments into environmental management were developed in the run-up to the 1992 Earth Summit. The new economic thinking and recognition of biodiversity and climate protection as core global concerns were consolidated under the leadership of Andrew Steer in the World Development Report on "Environment and Development." To his credit, McNamara had at least begun to institutionalize environmental work at the World Bank, creating a first, tiny specialized unit already in the early 1970s.

Uphill Battles

Things were not easy to begin with. Finance Ministry officials from World Bank borrower countries balked at demands for environmental and indigenous safeguards. And our supposedly "soft science" was hardly appreciated by our World Bank peers and managers.

My own tough experience in this regard was the negotiation of indigenous and environmental safeguards and monitoring and evaluation obligations under the POLONOROESTE loans for Brazil—the very first program in Latin America dealing with settlements in Amazonian frontier rainforest areas. Our Brazilian Borrowers gave assurances most reluctantly. Top management at the World Bank remained convinced that the financing of an orderly land occupation process could bring lasting benefits to poor settlers in this malaria-ridden frontier region. Once the program got underway, Evaluation reports soon pointed out massive problems, which are well described in Robert Wade's contribution to this book.

But in this uphill battle there was also growing appreciation of our role—especially among agronomists and irrigation experts leading project work at the field level. Among social science colleagues we took strength from the practical usefulness of our inputs, which seemed to matter for people on the ground—the intended "beneficiaries" of World Bank projects.

I found my work meaningful and exciting at a very personal level. At the University, I had earlier taught students about the lousy Indigenous Protection Service of Brazil in the 1960s; but then, under a series of World Bank financed projects, I had become able to bring about programs for indigenous land demarcation in Brazil, or to channel social and health programs to indigenous communities in Mexico. It was a marvelous opportunity "to walk the talk". I have among my best memories the village level work under the Mexican PIDER program which had started in the late 1970s, and the integrated, multi-sectoral rural development work in Northeast Brazil in the early 1980s. In both cases, findings during field visits translated clearly into project design and implementation.

We found ourselves on an inspiring, yet perilous "uphill" path. We had to fight and take risks—all along aware of our fragile knowledge base: World Bank missions were extremely short, with little time to scratch more than the surface. In the early years we fought our way, case by case, theme by theme, confronting many issues for the first time. We matured conceptual frameworks and "case-law", but there were, as yet, no binding guidelines. Michael Cernea, Gloria Davis, and Robert Goodland became the foremost promoters of the subsequent development of social and environmental ground rules. Shelton Davis added the fight for rules relating to indigenous peoples.

Looking Back

So what did we achieve? Looking back at our two decades as World Bank development anthropologists or sociologists, to which products and to which innovations could we contribute?

We started with project work, and built sets of guidance and institutional norms based on lessons learned and cases lived. Key products to which my colleagues and I specifically contributed can be characterized in two groups: systemic improvements and innovations within the World Bank system, and project-cases.

In their days, many amounted to battlefronts, with their successes and setbacks. Based on my early experiences which had taken me beyond Latin America also to Burkina Faso, Benin, Cameron, Tanzania, Algeria and even Portugal (which at the time was still a World Bank Borrower), I joined the drive for new, systemic instruments.

Innovations

To negotiate with Borrowers and Co-financiers, clear and binding codes of conduct for social and environmental safeguards became indispensable. Especially in lending operations which involved large works—dams and roads—we needed firm directives that could be easily understood by our counterparts. Project-based rules-development spanned a broad thematic spectrum—indigenous peoples, water user associations, involuntary resettlement, cultural heritage and, above all, routine social and environmental impact assessment requirements. Sociologists and environmentalists joined hands, developing detailed guidance. In parallel, transparency and accountability were fostered by an independent Operations Evaluation Department, and later also an Ombudsman Function. In addition, public access to environmental impact assessments was instituted.

We also initiated institutional innovations. For example, I wrote some of the first proposals for what was to become the Global Environment Facility. We launched studies on the need to eliminate perverse fiscal incentives (Binswanger & Mahar) which were undercutting environmental protection programs. We looked into debt-for-nature swaps and other imaginative new forms of environmental finance. I had oversight of several innovative World Bank programs, among them a first renewable energy unit, that served all regions. I established the first disaster preparedness facility supporting projects for more resilience in earthquakes, floods, or high storms; we hoped to prevent loss of life in future catastrophic events among the poorest populations living in unsafe housing on hillsides, or in low-lying flood plains. We not only listened carefully to criticisms from NGOs, but we also hired some of their environmental experts. We promoted and got Board approval for performance-based lending instruments—Adaptable Lending, and in particular

Learning & Innovation loans. It would take another book to write up these and more stories.

A Record of Project Cases

What kind of projects did I work on the most? Let me highlight some categories:

Rural Development. It was my good fortune, my "foot in the door" that when I started work at the World Bank, I was able to carry out useful field work—interviewing farmers and working with local counterparts in their native language all over Latin America. To begin with, I worked on programs in Bolivia, Northeast Brazil, Mexico, and later also in Colombia. When a staff member or consultant fell ill, I readily substituted, also in Monitoring and Evaluation training courses for counterparts in Brazil or in Costa Rica.

Land tenure improvement. Landlessness and pathways to ownership are thematic areas relevant in much of Latin America to this day—not easy, complex in technical and social terms, but worth every effort. My list of hard tasks also included responsibility for a "Land Tenure Improvement" Project for Northeast Brazil. I was designated as project officer half way through this complex but most interesting process designed to recover land occupied illegally by larger owners. Cadastral maps identified such parcels, with the objective to redistribute them to landless peasants and, in turn, to provide these with technical and credit support.

Frontier Development. In 1980, as soon as I had joined the regular World Bank staff, I was immediately put to work last minute on the appraisal of the World Bank's first lending program in Amazonia—the POLONOROESTE Program, combining road, integrated rural development, and Amerindian and environmental protection in frontier areas in Mato Grosso and Rondonia. I highlighted this program above already, as hard to negotiate and a milestone in Monitoring and Evaluation.

This was a first attempt of the World Bank to bring order into a most disorderly frontier occupation process in Mato Grosso and the just established State of Rondonia. It had all started with the BR 364 trunk road built by the military. The rationale for World Bank involvement was that settlers and regional development would be better off with agro-ecological zoning, decent health, education, and extension services, and environmental and indigenous safeguards. I was given responsibility for the last-minute development of two components: Monitoring and Evaluation and Amerindian Protection. Already, in the first two years of this program, the multi-disciplinary Independent Evaluation contracted out to the University of Sao Paulo had begun to document numerous violations of the Loan Agreements—gross violations of the environmental and Amerindian safeguard agreements that the Brazilian Government and the World Bank had signed. This became an uncontrollable frontier settlement. Satellite images show how POLONOROESTE, along with the "Transmigration" program in Indonesia, literally changed the face of the earth. Today, the scars of fishbone-like deforestation can be seen from outer space. It was an ugly story involving poor settlers, rich speculators (not funded by the World Bank), lenient government officials who allowed invasions of unsuitable lands and titled them after a small waiting period, and it became a story of impotent, underfunded environmental and indigenous protection agencies at the federal and state levels. A small consolation: the large indigenous reserved and nature protection areas demarcated under the World Bank program remain largely intact to this day—positive exceptions in an ecological disaster area.

Mining. The early 1980s were a time of mega-projects. The Brazilian Carajas Iron Ore project financed by World Bank, Japan and the European Union was one of them. It developed the then largest iron ore mine on our planet, and, in addition, an 800 km railroad from the inland mine site to the shipping harbor of Sao Luis do Maranhão in Northeast Brazil. Here my task was again the design of an Amerindian Protection Project, in a radius of 100 km of the mine and the railroad. Together with Companhia Vale do Rio Doce we identified 13 Reserves which needed to be properly protected and demarcated by FUNAI, the Indian Protection Agency. Later, as the project was implemented, additional tiny groups of hitherto uncontacted Indios were detected by aerial photography.

The larger project region included one of the most contentious areas of land struggle in Brazil, the "Bico do Papagaio" south of Marabá, and Serra Pelada—a wild cat goldmine with thousands of gold seekers (a place close to hell which the photography of Sebastiao Salgado has engraved in history). To make matters worse, environmental and Amerindian protection, painstakingly designed under the World Bank project, were soon undercut by a parallel central Government Program, the so-called Greater Carajas Program. It promoted land settlements and charcoal production, a driver of deforestation, for local production of pig iron. Nevertheless, at least the Amerindian Protection Program continued to be implemented, much to the credit of one highly committed professional, Maria de Lourdes Davies Freitas, at Companhia Vale do Rio Doce.

Resettlement was associated with mega infrastructure projects for hydropower and irrigation. Because resettlement became such a major social challenge in many projects, it is addressed in a special section here in our book. Difficult as it will always be, resettlement remains indeed one of the most daunting tasks, as the world modernizes and changes. Today, with more wind, gas, and solar renewable energy options, we hope to see fewer displacements of people by large hydro-power and irrigation dams. But just think of the many roads that wait to be widened in high density India and elsewhere in Asia. Guidelines for as fair as possible resettlement schemes must be upheld and adjusted to new situations—always with the objective to not only substitute for losses, but also to seize positive opportunities to improve livelihoods of affected people.

My own encounters with resettlement issues included in Brazil the development of a Social and Environmental Master Plan for the Brazilian Power Sector and, in that context, the development of the Itaparica resettlement plan. They also included Yacireta in Argentina and Paraguay, irrigation and power projects in Karnataka, India, the Xiaolangdi Hydropower and Flood control dam in China, and the Nam Theun Dam in Laos. Working on resettlement is tough: Social design can only attempt to produce mitigation plans, but can never eliminate the basic pain of involuntary resettlement.

New Products. Shaping first-ever *National Environmental Programs* counts among my best, most positive memories. The Brazilian National Environmental Program led the way, funding the build-up of a National Environment System with specialized Government agencies, Protected Areas, and Coastal Zone Management, and social and environmental impact assessment routines. Later Mexico, Venezuela, Philippines, and more followed. National Environmental Programs came up around the time of the first Rio Earth Summit, when environmental management and protection got due recognition around the world as a government sector in need of institution building.

Governance and Accountability

The work of our generation of development anthropologists has been challenging and fulfilling. Yet, looking back, so many things could have turned out better. Over the years, it is hard not to become cynical with hindsight: How many good Government Commitments have my colleagues and I seen signed in World Bank Loan Agreements—initially signed and upheld by the government in power at loan signing, but subsequently not honored after the next election.

Too often attitudes of irresponsibility have undermined project outcomes. Too often we have seen successor governments feeling less and less bound by their predecessors' commitments. The lack of long-term responsibility structures is clearly one most important, unresolved problem. Looking ahead, a key question is how long-term responsibility systems might be locked-in more reliably, for example by setting aside long-term finance in escrow accounts for the completion of 10–20 year resettlement consolidation processes.

Above all, unkept promises have to be addressed more squarely. Lending should be suspended more often, more swiftly and more rigorously when agreements are broken, even if this might include leveraging the full weight of an overall country lending program. One loan must condition another—cross-referencing of compliance is needed.

How to Get Better?

I left the World Bank after some 20 years, looking ahead—convinced that development finance needed to make a greater difference. In so many respects we had done well, but not well enough.

I remain convinced that international assistance programs often need to (1) start smaller, and faster—to make them more responsive to local community needs, (2) that environmental and social impact assessments need to become more central early-on in any project preparation process, and (3) that we need stronger enforcement and long-term responsibility systems.

(1) *Start smaller, and faster—responsive to local community needs*: Elephantine, slow bureaucratic processes—dishing out of large loans at low cost-per-$ invested is often misrepresented as being "efficient". However, if efficiency is instead defined in terms of results-per-$ on the ground smaller packages, smaller yet faster starts, turn out to be far more effective. In many cases, it is wise to first experiment with social strategies (e.g. in water user associations or communal social forestry). This is why Learning and Innovation loans were introduced in the 1990s, which allowed for quick loans in amounts smaller than 5 million$ without formal Board approval.

> *Adaptable Program Loans* and *Learning and Innovation Loans (LILs)* were approved by the Bank's Board of Directors on September 4, 1997, especially as a tool for working in poorly understood social contexts, with programs needing experimentation and constant adjustments in "…. the kind of poverty-oriented project where the learning was occurring during this particular (project implementation) period", as Gloria Davis put it in her oral history recorded in June 2004.
>
> Special credit for supporting the Learning and Innovation Loans goes to Robert Picciotto. In his oral history recorded November 1, 2000, he states …"the adaptable lending products (Learning and Innovation Loans and Adaptable Program Loans) were the result of work I personally did in my spare time in cooperation with Maritta Koch-Weser. The new products reflected the experience I had gained in two decades of project work. The new learning and innovation cycle involves listening, piloting, demonstrating and mainstreaming. I think the LIL is a very promising instrument. The basic difference between the adaptable loans and the blueprints kind of project loans is a sense of constant adaptation and learning. Wolfensohn right away understood the value of the product when we made a presentation to him. The Board liked it. And I think the majority of the staff liked it. So now we have to evaluate how well it's working. My guess is that there are problems because people use the new instruments while still having a blueprint mentality…. So, I think the evolution of the new project cycle is not yet complete".

(2) *Environmental and social impact assessments need to be started earlier in project preparation.* They have become mandatory, and this is an achievement that we wanted. However, at closer look, this has often also turned them into last-minute perfunctory exercises, carried out when all else has been planned. Opportunities for better design can be lost in this way: When the design of a dam has been decided, alternatives in terms their environmental and social impacts are beyond the point.

In projects which may require major resettlements (I remember Jamuna Bridge in Bangladesh as a case in point) the social assessment should in fact start from the very beginning, to register before all else who actually would be affected, and as such be entitled for resettlement benefits under a potential later project. Provisions for legal recourse of affected people, and minorities in particular, need to be built into project design.

Downstream risks need to be understood early on as well. Some not-so-large projects are wolves in sheep's skin: first, a low impact project, only to be followed some years later by larger, much higher impact phases (the Belo Monte hydropower project in Brazil is a recent example).

And, finally, in development assistance organizations we must carry out self-assessments, recognizing limits to our own implementation and supervision capacity. For example, at the World Bank we were fortunate not to finance the Three Gorges Dam in China, which came with resettlement of about 2 million people. This order of magnitude would surely have surpassed the loan supervision capabilities of international development agencies.

(3) *Stronger responsibility and enforcement systems.* Our multi-year responsibility systems are intrinsically weak. Over five and more years of project implementation, the cast of characters at both the World Bank and in the Borrower Government can be expected to change. Institutional memory and the political will to adhere to challenging demands of yesteryear tend to fade on both sides. The local population and social and environmental safeguards bear the brunt.

For me, a most frustrating example was the Itaparica Dam Resettlement program, where—once the reservoir had been filled and Government had changed, commitments to complete the irrigation districts for resettled communities were not honored. If, instead of written commitments only, a resettlement escrow fund had been established, funds for completion-as-promised might have remained available.

I am convinced that to assure systems of compensation over what we already know will be a 10–20 year resettlement consolidation period requires setting aside and locking-up corresponding funds from the start, way beyond a project's limited financing period proper.

Formalistic reliance on local law (which often is not in keeping with international standards) should not be acceptable, but clear "own" rules of development agencies are needed to take their place.

20 Years: In Stages

From 1977–1990, I worked as a "sociologist"—initially as a team member in rural development programs in Latin America and Africa, and then also as a member of that Department's Monitoring and Evaluation unit. Soon I also worked on social and environmental assignments in Latin America outside the agriculture sector—in the forestry, mining, and energy sectors. My responsibilities grew. I became a full-fledged project officer, responsible for multidisciplinary projects and programs, first in Brazil, and then all over Latin America. And before long, I joined the advance team, alongside other colleagues, who promoted the establishment of the first-ever social and environmental safeguard rules at the World Bank.

Since the late 1980s I worked as a Division and then Department manager in the field of environmentally and socially sustainable development. For several years, I headed the "Environmental Assessments and Programs" Division of the newly established Environment Department within the World Bank's central policy vice-presidency. Later yet, I returned to the operational side of the World Bank, working for several years as Head of the Asia Environment Division on the entire South and East Asia portfolio. Finally, following yet another overall reorganization of the World Bank—I became Director of the Latin America & Caribbean Department for Environmentally and Socially Sustainable Development, a position I held until the end of 1998.

Beyond World Bank Days

When I left the World Bank, I joined the World of NGOs, continuing the very same social and environmental quest as head of IUCN (The International Union for the Conservation of Nature), and then Earth3000, an organization I founded in 2001 in support of innovations in governance for environment and development. For many years since, I have continued to support development anthropology and environmental causes, among them the Global Exchange for Social Investment, World Heritage Watch, and as leader of a program on modern Amazonia at University of Sao Paulo, in Brazil. As Board Member I have over many years shared responsibilities with organizations, businesses, and academic institutions engaged in nature conservation, social banking and impact investment, climate, and academic programs.

Always, inside the World Bank and in the international world of NGOs I have enjoyed playing my part in a larger orchestra—working alongside and being inspired by like-minded colleagues.

20 Years Well Spent

My career at the World Bank allowed me to care for causes that had stayed with me since student days. As a student, Brazil had been my learning ground. I had seen extreme poverty—starvation in the face of drought, child mortality so frequent in a hospital without medicines in Penedo, Alagoas/Brazil that there were not enough cardboard boxes to carry the dead babies to the cemetery. A German nurse worked there, desperately trying her best. Now, working at the World Bank, I could engage in rural development in some of those very same regions, helping to design and run integrated rural development programs that sought to increase incomes, access to credit, basic health care and primary education.

At the University I had written an article about the fate of Brazil's declining remnant indigenous population—and the ways in which they had fared so badly under the Indigenous Protection Service during the years of Brazil's military regime. Now, I could help convince the Brazilian Government of the 1980s to demarcate land and to implement indigenous legislation under the country's new Constitution.

I had first seen environmental destruction in the Amazon as a student. Now I had a chance to design and supervise first environmental Protection Programs in Rondonia, Mato Grosso, and the Carajas Regions in Para and Maranhão, and later to lead preparation of first National Environmental Programs in Brazil and Mexico. As satellite pictures show, at least indigenous and environmental reserves have so far been mostly spared from the onslaught of forest destruction.

Next?

To a next generation of development students I recommend to move beyond academic desk work soon, and to experience field assignments early on. Find out how it feels—may be applied Development Anthropology is for you. Our world is replete with technology and finance—help make them work for the neediest people and for a livable future on our blue planet.

Maritta Koch-Weser was one of the very first social scientists at the World Bank. Since 1977, she spent over two decades as a leader in the growing social and environmental practice at the World Bank, working in Latin America, Asia, Africa, and Eastern Europe. In this contribution to Michael Cernea's Festschrift, she recalls challenges that she and her colleagues saw as development anthropologists, and contemplates today's needs. Above all, the author hopes to stimulate professional interest in Development Anthropology among a next generation of students and practitioners.

Open Access This chapter is licensed under the terms of the Creative Commons Attribution 4.0 International License (http://creativecommons.org/licenses/by/4.0/), which permits use, sharing, adaptation, distribution and reproduction in any medium or format, as long as you give appropriate credit to the original author(s) and the source, provide a link to the Creative Commons license and indicate if changes were made.

The images or other third party material in this chapter are included in the chapter's Creative Commons license, unless indicated otherwise in a credit line to the material. If material is not included in the chapter's Creative Commons license and your intended use is not permitted by statutory regulation or exceeds the permitted use, you will need to obtain permission directly from the copyright holder.

Social Development (Excerpts from Her 2004 Oral History)

Gloria Davis

I did my anthropological research in Indonesia between 1972 and 1974. I happened to work on the movement of Balinese to central Sulawesi, a part of the Indonesian transmigration program, which, in fact, after a few years is what led directly to my being hired by the Bank. I taught at Yale for three years. While I was teaching, a person came up after my lecture, and said, "The World Bank wants you."

I have to admit I didn't even know what the World Bank was. I had a general notion, but nothing specific. To make a long story short, World Bank President Robert McNamara had been to Indonesia and had committed a billion dollars to the Indonesians to expand the Indonesian transmigration program, which he regarded as a very important mechanism for poverty alleviation.

So, in 1978, I agreed to go for six months. I took six months of leave from Yale and went to the Bank to work with a newly-established group under Robert Sadov, which was called Transmigration and Land Settlement. It was focused on Indonesia. And that's the way I got to the Bank.

My first mission in Indonesia was for ten weeks. For the team, it was very helpful to have an anthropologist who knew a lot about the sending areas, Java and Bali. I knew those areas very well, understood a little of both local languages and also spoke Indonesian, so I could tell them a lot about what the farmers were saying about what they could and couldn't expect. When you're using a translator, you always get the official version, like being told that everybody got 1.2 tons of rice. But when you actually ask them how long they could feed their families for and things like that, you get very different answers.

My agriculture colleagues were enormously supportive of me because they wanted to know what I knew. They also wanted to teach me a lot about what they

---

Gloria Davis was the first Director of Social Development in the World Bank.
This essay is derived from Gloria Davis's 2004 oral history interview. There are no changes of substance, but the editors have made editorial changes (such as sentence breaks, re-sequencing etc.) to conform to written copy. The full interview can be found at https://oralhistory.worldbank.org/person/davis-gloria

knew about agriculture. We'd go out with the world's most famous rubber processing specialist or bull specialist or things like that. So I was also learning a lot about technology and what could be introduced and what couldn't be introduced and so forth.

Gradually, I became a mission leader. I want to stress that I had a long and very profitable apprenticeship. For three years people were teaching me how to work in the Bank. They were teaching me the importance of the economic analysis. I learned how to do economic analysis.

My career wouldn't have been the same if I hadn't had that experience. So two things that I felt, and I continued to feel during my period as a manager is that social scientists needed to be integrated into teams, and that they needed to have a very broad knowledge of the objectives that the Bank teams had in order to be helpful to them Later on, when I was the Director of Social Development, I tried every six months to have instruction courses on the Bank project cycle because I felt that they were being isolated from the real activity of the Bank, which was making loans for agricultural activities which were benefiting, we hoped, the smallholders.

In July 1987, Dr. Davis was promoted to unit chief, and then became division chief of the Environment and Social Division in the Asia Technical Department.

During that period, the Bank's regional environmental units all added social scientists. And by the end of that time, there was the expectation that in projects with significant environmental impact those impacts would be addressed, and that social issues needed to be handled. So we had moved quite a way. The next stage of that would be the time when the macro issues become the predominant issues.

We began to see in the Cold War period an alignment between U.S. interests in keeping leaders of countries in my area—[Ferdinand] Marcos, Suharto—in power because they were pro-development, because they were pro-Western, and because they could be counted on as allies. But they would also become these nucleuses of patronage and corruption and so forth. So there was a sort of a whole new constellation of issues that were emerging that were bigger than what the social scientists were used to but also not being addressed at all by the economists.

And another shift that happened at that time (which is just an organizational one, but it accounts for this anomaly of having the social development people in the Environment Department) was that Michael Cernea was debating about whether he could be more effective in agriculture and rural development, which did not give him an overview of other sectors, or whether he should move to the Environment Department. And he decided at that point that he would move and he would become an adviser to the environment director—as I mentioned, it changed—on social issues.

I actually moved first, with a mandate to deal with social issues in an environmental context. We focused on land tenure, social forestry, the impacts of irrigation, agricultural revolution, all of these environmentally-related social issues. We did not yet have a mandate to deal with social issues in general. To give another example, Shelton Davis eventually moved into the division which I headed to bring the indigenous people's agenda, which had been mostly in the Latin America Region at that time, to a more central level to see what could be done with people who had traditional ways and traditional cultures in other regions.

I later moved to the Central Environment Department. Initially, I was dealing with natural resources management issues. We agreed, under Andrew Steer, on a reorganization where there would be one unit that explicitly dealt with pollution, one on natural resources, and then one on social.

About this time, Ismail Serageldin came into the picture, with a passion for social issues. I can't overemphasize how influential he was in also shaping and influencing the direction of the Bank during this sort of transition period in how we approached social issues.

I think Narmada was a critical watershed. The Bank had commissioned its first independent report, which was the [Bradford] Morse Report. And the 1992 Morse Report was very critical of the Bank. In particular, it criticized the Bank for failing to fully plan for the resettlement of people.

The Morse Report is important for two reasons. First, it led to the 1994 Bankwide resettlement report by Michael Cernea, which had a lasting impact on the Bank. But the second is that it led directly to the Inspection Panel. The Inspection Panel has had a very profound effect on the Bank in terms of keeping it honest and, in fact, in some cases terrorizing staff about the variety of issues which might be encountered in a particular project.

The resettlement report, which was orchestrated by Michael Cernea, reviewed all of the resettlement projects that the Bank had been involved in and found that we had been associated with the resettlement of 2 million people. It was quite an extraordinary revelation to most people. As a result of this report, the Bank then required that any project that had poor resettlement implementation develop an action plan to address those issues. So this resettlement report was not only a critique of a Bank set of projects, but something that built into it after it came out a mechanism for resolution. Those action plans considerably improved the quality of resettlement implementation. Again, this was at the urging and with the advocacy of Michael Cernea, and that was very important.

It's fair to say that resettlement was sort of the flagship or keystone policy for the entire social work at that time. And it was an important entry point for other kinds of social impact assessment. Although Michael and people who assisted him who have since become very senior social scientists in the Bank (Scott Guggenheim, Bill Partridge), a number of these people concluded that the Bank's policies had had an important impact that significantly improved resettlement, which had been a very informal activity in the past.

The reason this is important is because this is the only place where we had a formal policy. So it reinforced for those people, who, as I say, became the nucleus of the social development family, the importance of having a policy, having it on the books, and having a mechanism for external scrutiny that could say whether or not the policy was being appropriately applied.

By this time—this is probably in 1992 to 1994—there was for the first time a critical mass of social scientists in the Bank who were working in the different regions and at the center. Those of us who had kind of come up through the environment channel, so to speak, and also observing the weight of the resettlement policy, we wanted a broader social impact. Assessment policy, for projects, the emphasis was initially on identifying adverse impacts and avoiding, minimizing or mitigating them. But by 1992–1994, we also realized that there was a very important positive role to play in ensuring that social impact assessment was linked to participation, that it involved participatory processes, that we talk directly to affected people, and that we were able to introduce elements into projects that would improve their effectiveness in terms of the people who were intended to benefit.

Now, we weren't alone. If we look around, the Bank was one of many institutions trying to formalize policies that dealt with social impact assessment. We were about a decade behind. The approach to environmental impact assessment had been formalized in the early to mid-1980s. The approach to social impact assessment was being formalized, whether we got a policy or not, in the early to mid-1990s. During this period, although the policy itself was not on the books, actually every region in the Bank began formal social impact assessment, sometimes in parallel with environmental impact assessment. But there was a lot of resistance to formalizing this policy at the level of the Bank. People were concerned that it was too broad, it was too specific, and that it would be too onerous to actually apply.

James Wolfensohn' as arrival in 1995 became the watershed for the way in which we approach social issues. I don't think any of us could have anticipated the impact it would have. What happened is that when Jim Wolfensohn came to the Bank, Michael Cernea approached him very early in his tenure and told him that he was a sociologist. I remember Michael saying that Wolfensohn said he didn't know there were sociologists in the Bank. Michael urged Mr. Wolfensohn to consider much more broadly how social factors were taken into account in the work of the Bank. And Wolfensohn agreed. He came in with an emphasis on sort of human impacts, human values and so on, and he felt that these needed to be much more mainstreamed within the Bank. Michael Cernea had written a book called *Putting People First*, but I think it was the social development report that brought that home in the Bank as a part of Bank policy or a part of Bank mainstream thinking.

Wolfensohn passed his wish for a broader agenda along to his senior management. It was agreed that there would be a task force would prepare a report on social development in the Bank. Somewhat unexpectedly, it would be half economists and half social scientists. It was chaired, not (as we might have originally thought) by Michael Cernea, but by Javed Burki, who was a senior vice president in the Bank at the time but also one who had very humanistic values and a very broad view. Although an economist himself, his view of economics certainly embraced the kind of social and equity concerns that the rest of us shared. So he was, in my view, a very good choice to lead this.

The emphasis of the group—which was not fully achieved, I have to tell you—was to bring economists and social scientists together and to get them to decide how social factors should be incorporated. Not just social impacts, but also broad social factors, political factors, issues related to equity and so forth. The mandate was to get these two sometimes polarized groups, the macro economists and some of the micro economists, to speak to the social scientists.

To be perfectly honest, the social scientists had everything to gain from this initiative and the economists who were involved in the group were willing participants but also felt they had a lot to lose. They felt they were already dealing with social issues and social impacts. Joanne Salop, who eventually had the thankless job of writing the final report in conjunction with a senior economist and myself, said that we often talked past one another, and that was true. The economists felt that the social scientists were too particularistic, too interested in differences to be able to recommend universal laws or approaches. The social scientists felt the economists were too universal, too generalized, to appreciate the particulars of what was going on in countries and to adapt and tailor projects and programs to the realities of what was happening on the ground.

The one thing that I think gradually brought some consensus was that there was a grudging acceptance of participation as a test for both groups. We had been promoting participation through the NGO group and the social group in the Environment Department, but people recognized that it was a test of economic policy. If people were not satisfied, if the impacts of economic policies were not positive in a relatively short amount of time on poor people, there would not be political support for these kinds of activities.

There was a sub-group on conflict. People already working on conflict were able to show that 16 of the poorest 20 countries in the world were in conflict; that this was no longer an isolated phenomenon; that it wasn't post-war reconstruction of the sort we'd had at the end of World War II; that these were civil conflicts, often conflicts between governments and their people; and that dealing with conflict was going to be an important element of poverty. There were a number of substantive issues—social capital, conflict, culture—that were addressed by the subcommittees, as well as the overall concern that, as we said at the beginning of the report, the success of development is measured by its impact on people.

The report came out. It was an extreme compromise. There was an original report to which the social team subscribed and a kind of a compromise report written, as I said, between the three of us, based on the input of all of the others. It was a middle-of-the-road report. Its importance was that even this kind of discussion and dissent led everybody to recognize—no, or at least some people, and certainly Ismail—to conclude that there needed to be a formal structure that recognized the importance of social development. We also had some important advocates in very high places in the Bank, so that when the Strategic Compact was prepared there was money included for advancing social development.

I was the social scientist who had provided the major input into the Presidential Report, though not necessarily the workings of the committee. Among the others there was a major advocate for the creation of a network particularly to advance the social development agenda. As a matter of fact, if it hadn't been for Ismail Serageldin and his strong views on that, I think there wouldn't have been a social development network. But having created one, when management went looking for a leader who was relatively senior and had been involved for a time, I was fortunate to have been selected.

From the outset, I was mainly interested in setting up the network and handing it over to others, and this is in fact what we did over the next sort of three to five years. We tried to develop a structure, an institutional structure, and leaders that could take over from some of we old hands that had been doing it at that point for about 20 years.

Like other networks, our social development board consisted of a representative from each of the regions, someone who normally headed a social development division or at least a unit in that particular region. Collectively, the board was interested initially in determining what were the areas of work to which we should devote our limited resources and then building a record of results on the ground Since each region had somewhat different social problems, it was often very difficult to get agreement on what should be the emphasis within a newly-emerging agenda.

But in the end, and after a lot of sort of trial and error, we could see that there were several issues that really characterized what we did. Within about five years of the founding of the network—it seems long, but it involved a lot of work—there was a document issued on poverty and social impact assessment. I think it was important for a couple of reasons. One is that the economists in the Poverty Reduction and Economic Management Network, worked closely with the social development team to develop that document. It basically that gives pointers on tools and perspectives for evaluating whether economy-wide policies are having the desired impacts on the poor.

The other area that was already pretty far along when the network was formed is the subject of participation. That had an interesting evolution. In the earliest stages, participation really meant consultation; that is to say that if you were trying to figure out what was going on, you would ask people. Now, they didn't get a say in the outcome, but they could provide important feedback. This type of consultation was institutionalized both in the social impact assessment process and also in the environmental impact assessment process, which became much more "participatory" over time. But with the publication of the participation report, which was a very participatory process led by Aubrey Williams—20 different groups and so forth—the people who were advocating participation came to see this more and more as control over decisions and resources on the part of people who might be affected by them. This changed perspective played into a lot of things that we did later on—social capital, understanding the institutions of the poor and so on.

The culmination of that within the 1997 to 2002, was Deepa Narayan's work on voices of the poor. This was a kind of listening to something like 60,000 people in different countries. It was done in preparation for the poverty report in the year 2000–2001. It was criticized by some for its lack of empirical rigor, but it was absolutely overpowering in terms of what poor people were saying about themselves.

It was a very, very important document. It had a big influence on Wolfensohn. It had a big influence, I think, on the poverty people who were working on the poverty report. So this was one place where interests really came together, this very strong thrust toward participation and the sort of change over time to being more empowering and getting people more involved in decisions.

This emphasis on participation, empowerment and community-driven development, which is a derivative of that, also gave both socially-oriented economists and social scientists an opportunity to actually be involved in the design and implementation of projects. With the advent of a whole series of projects related to empowerment, civic engagement and so on, there was much more latitude for people who were sympathetic to these objectives to be involved in the design and implementation of projects.

Another sort of thrust of our work was also coming together. I was very, very interested in local-level institutions—in fact, it's sort of what I had done my dissertation on, and I had been waiting to get back to it—because it had seemed evident to me even 20 years before that communities with strong institutions were more likely to be resilient and they could move forward faster than communities within cultures or even the same culture that didn't have strong institutions. In about 1995 we once again got some funds from our friends in Norway for a study of local-level institutions that eventually became the work on which social capital and community-driven development was based.

We had originally hoped to get six countries but only three of them were completed. There were some surprising findings. NGOs in terms of advocacy groups and social service groups and so on, were not well represented at the village level in any of these studies. Religious groups were often more important than we anticipated, particularly in societies that weren't particularly religious. Obviously, every society has its own religious beliefs and constructs and so on, but even where we didn't see religion as a major motivating force, religious organizations often provided a sort of a network for both protecting vulnerable groups and also for reaching out to local-level groups.

But village organization was really important. All villages were organized; they all had headmen. Where those people were positive and proactive and where their objectives were linked to the objectives of the community, there was a lot more sense of trust and confidence and people working together than where the head men were corrupt and taking, you know—as you can imagine. It seems self-evident. But it did lead to a series of hypotheses about how we might try to reach communities more directly and how we might try to circumvent elites that had been co-opting resources in the past and, you know, set up organizations at the community level that could actually pay attention to the community interests.

There are many, many good examples of social capital initiatives, some of which emerged from this, some of which had independent origins. And in my paper I have cited the ones that Scott Guggenheim has done. I think he has done the most to develop the idea about how you can circumvent elites, how you can reduce corruption at the community level by making things very transparent, by making people accountable for how resources are being spent. He even has components in all of his projects for NGOs and newspapermen to go to villages and discuss with villagers whether the money is being used appropriately, to cut through this kind of tradition of elite co-option, let's say, of all of these resources. So he has done a lot of both substantive and research-related work on that, and that moved very effectively.

Now, it was interesting—because as we moved more and more toward economy-wide lending, we also were arguing that there needed to be a component of the Bank's lending program that went directly to people and didn't go into the sort of national coffers and never saw the bottom. And Hans Binswanger was instrumental in bringing that view. It wasn't his view initially, but he brought that view to Wolfensohn's attention, and Wolfensohn agreed that a significant portion of Bank lending should be directed to the community level. This led to, as it often does a lot of renaming of projects that weren't exactly community-driven, but it also was a tremendous impetus to having a certain number of projects that were community-driven. And the aggregate total of community-based projects is now very large, something around 6 billion dollars. A lot of Bank resources now go to the community level.

There was also another thrust of the participation agenda that I think has promise and is beginning to show it, which is on social accountability. There are a number of countries now where the team has worked with the government—or perhaps in NGOs in some cases where that's acceptable—to put in place mechanisms for the public to assess public institutions.

The Philippine report card is one of them. Two thousand or five thousand people are surveyed about their attitudes toward, let's say, the education department, the postal department, the health resources. The institutions are then graded publicly, in the newspaper. This has had a tremendous impact. Institutions that are getting Ds, Cs even, are publicly exposed in these sort of report card activities, and we have seen some change.

I've seen other examples of social accountability, even, for example, in education projects where parents are now encouraged to give an assessment of the schools, and then those are aggregated to see which schools appear to be doing better and which are doing worse in the subjective impression of the people. Now, those seem like commonplace things, opinion polling and so forth, in the United States, but here we're trying to formalize them for use in developing countries.

In speaking about local-level institutions, we also felt that we needed to move local-level institutions from the local level to the state level because it was clear that state institutions were the glue that held countries together. If we were going to do program lending, understanding accountability, transparency and the relationship to the functioning of the institutions of the state was really important.

This class of work was also directly relevant to our interest in conflict. When states fail, what you have is conflict, and often civil conflict. And unlike the earlier wars which had been between countries and were ideologically-driven, what the Bank was seeing in these very poor countries it was dealing with was civil war within countries, often based around ethnicity. States had been ineffective in sharing the wealth, in giving disenfranchised groups reason to think that they should be confident that the state would be acting in their interests and so on.

So, the conflict program also became part of the social agenda. We took the same series of steps that we had in a number of other areas to try to institutionalize and give a higher profile to that agenda. First, we wrote a paper showing how important conflict was in the poverty agenda. When there was agreement that conflict was a high-priority area, we were able to assemble a group, first at the regional vice president level but then at the level of operations officers when it became more routinized. They met on a regular basis to decide what should be done about the conflict agenda, what DEC [Development Economics] would be doing.

Then, finally, there was one part of the social agenda that I actually was quite sympathetic to and thought had promise, but our group was very divided. This was on poverty and culture. In the end, that agenda has been very dispersed. The tensions were around the definition of culture.

The social development group had been given the responsibility for follow-up on culture, but it contributed to the problem by defining it a little bit differently and wanting to work more with the cultural assets of the poor. One program worked with radio and local languages because radio stations in many countries were only in the national language and not accessible to poor people. Another example might be about traditional artisanal activities and crafts and how they might be strengthened. But it was a much more kind of locally-based interest in culture.

The social development team as a whole felt that culture was a universal and ought to be integrated into everything that we were doing. It wasn't about historical monuments or even about artisanal activities. If you would talk to the people in the Eastern Europe region, culture, you know, underpinned conflict, economic reform, all—there were a whole series of things. They were the ones that were most interested in cultural monuments and cultural heritage in the sort of traditional sense because it was so closely linked to identity and the dissolution of the Russian Federation. But if you went to Latin America, there was a different definition of culture that was smaller, more locally-based, probably reflected traditional practices, for example, indigenous people, where the issue was how the way of life of an entire group could be to some extent preserved and not simply exterminated in the process of development. So there were these sort of contending views on the nature of an agenda that was focused on culture.

And, finally, the Board made it very clear that certainly the Bank needed to be culturally sensitive in all aspects of its work and anything that we were doing or that others were doing that would make staff more sensitive or managers more sensitive was appropriate; that, of course, if work actually had economic benefits for the poor, that using cultural, artisanal activities (to refer to the one we just talked about) were appropriate; but the Bank really had no role, unless it had very clear economic benefits—and there were other institutions much better able to do this, in the UN, for example—in protecting and preserving cultural monuments.

And I have to say this was a very confusing activity. I mean, it's pretty easy to clarify what was going on, but nobody gave up on their own position. And eventually when resources became more and more constrained, the diversity of opinion around this meant that this program was being supported largely with external resources, mainly from the Italians, and became more and more constrained within the Bank context. But I do expect culture to re-emerge as an important issue.

One thing that surprised me was that it was much easier to promote social impact assessment than environmental impact assessment. And that's true because countries could immediately see—not that they were dying to do this as a requirement of the World Bank—but that they could see the logic of the fact that they couldn't alienate the people that were going to have to support them politically in carrying out projects. So whether or not they had a sort of poverty objective, they could understand that it was important to figure out whether people were going to be harmed, what could be done about that, whether there are opportunities for improving their welfare and so forth.

If I look at myself and think of a person who came in with the idea that they would be going to Indonesia and speaking Indonesian to farmers and trying to improve projects who became someone who has had to deal with issues as large as economic equity, or large-scale conflict, for example, there's obviously a lot of room in the Bank for a social person to grow and evolve. And I think that there's no question among the applied social scientists that hardly any of us would ever return to an academic environment. Virtually all of the people who are in the social development community want to have an impact on the ground.

As I mentioned at the outset, I taught at Yale, which is a wonderful experience. The students are all unbelievably bright, but you realize that, over time, they are the ones that are going to have an impact. You're having an impact on them, and they should have an impact on others, but it's very indirect. Development is not like that. You're working with poor people, and if what you're doing makes a difference, the life of those specific poor people could actually be improved. And that is very, very, very rewarding.

Gloria Davis was the first anthropologist hired by the World Bank. She specialized in Southeast Asia, receiving her Ph.D. from Stanford University in 1975 with a dissertation on Parigi: A Social History of the Balinese Movement to Central Sulawesi, 1907–1934. She then taught anthropology for three years at Yale University. In 1978 Davis joined the World Bank's Indonesia Transmigration and Land Settlement Program, where she became part of the team assessing the Bank's support for transmigration projects in Indonesia. This led to the publication of the major report, Indonesia Transmigration Program Review, in 1981. In 1984 Davis became the senior operations office in the agriculture division of the East Asia and Pacific Region. She participated in various missions, often to Indonesia but also to Fiji in 1984. During this period she lead the review of the entire Indonesia transmigration sector, culminating in a major report, Indonesia Transmigration Sector Review, in 1986. Following the general reorganization of the World Bank in 1987, Davis became the chief of the Environment Division of the Asia Technical Department. In 1990 she wrote another major study, Indonesia: Sustainable Development of Forests, Land and Water. She became chief of the Social Policy and Resettlement Division in the Environment Department in 1993 and director of the Social Development Department from 1997 until 2000. Davis retired from the Bank in 2000 but continued to serve as a consultant until 2004. Gloria Davis was born in 1943 in Minneapolis, Minnesota.

Open Access This chapter is licensed under the terms of the Creative Commons Attribution 4.0 International License (http://creativecommons.org/licenses/by/4.0/), which permits use, sharing, adaptation, distribution and reproduction in any medium or format, as long as you give appropriate credit to the original author(s) and the source, provide a link to the Creative Commons license and indicate if changes were made.

The images or other third party material in this chapter are included in the chapter's Creative Commons license, unless indicated otherwise in a credit line to the material. If material is not included in the chapter's Creative Commons license and your intended use is not permitted by statutory regulation or exceeds the permitted use, you will need to obtain permission directly from the copyright holder.

Putting People First in Practice: Indonesia and the Kecamatan Development Program

Scott Guggenheim

Michael Cernea's key insight was that the core concepts of sociology and anthropology—social organization, culture, participation, and symbolic construction—could improve the quality and effectiveness of development. His key achievement was in the fact that he and the people he inspired were able to bridge the gap between analyst and practitioner to show that these anthropological and sociological concepts really could make a difference in how development affected the poor. In this article, I'll do my best to use describe my own journey from naïve graduate student to World Bank team leader for the Kecamatan Development Program, one of the world's earliest and largest community development programs.

Discovering Development

I came to know Michael Cernea after finishing a graduate program that had been heavily focused on Latin American anthropology. In fact, I ended up doing my Ph.D. on the political economy of agrarian change in the northern Philippines because I'd planned to return to Mexico and this would be my last chance to get a US funding organization to finance comparative research. During the course of my fieldwork, I now and then found myself spending several days accompanying wedding parties that were bringing *Ibanag* brides from the lowland villages where I was working on long hikes up to the communities of the Kalinga highlands. Several of these Kalinga groups lived alongside the Chico River. There, the Marcos government, supported by World Bank financing and a German engineering firm hired to handle the technical design, was just starting on the construction of the first of four large hydroelectric dams. The Kalinga villages had already rejected the fairly paltry

---

S. Guggenheim (✉)
Edmund Walsh School, Georgetown University, Washington, DC, USA

compensation they were being offered. They argued that both that these lands were historically and culturally sacred. And, contradicting the national modernizers who were accusing them and their NGO allies of wanting to stay preserved in an outdoor museum, their leaders often said that while they had no objection to joining "modern" society, they had no plans to join it at the bottom.

The government's reaction was ferocious. Aside from the Philippine Constabulary forces already assigned to the province, the 60th Philippine Constabulary Brigade, the 51st Philippine Constabulary Brigade, and the 44th Philippine Army Brigade were brought in to suppress opposition to the dam project. Villages were bombed and then burned. This achieved little. The largely urban originated New People's Army began making its presence known, fortified by a rising level of local support, which of course then brought more military to the north. As the conflict worsened, I visited the World Bank's office in Manila to see what they knew about the unfolding mayhem, but they had no records and it seemed that nobody from their team had ever visited the highland communities to check for himself or herself what was going on. But I had a thesis to write, so I returned to Tuguegarao, saddened, disgusted, and angry, but also pretty irked by my powerlessness. Years later, though, the entire scheme was cancelled.[1]

Like most graduate students, I had sufficient funding to do my fieldwork, barely, but when the time came to turn the notebooks into a dissertation, my choices were pretty grim. After spending a painful year scraping by doing adjunct teaching in a place where I spent more money getting to the college than the college was paying me for the course, I called pretty much everyone I knew to see if they could find a job that would at least fund my write-up.

My third call was to a very smart classmate who had been working at the World Bank, and was obviously fed up with the place. "You want it?" she asked, "Be my guest!" She arranged for an interview with her boss, a disheveled and slightly scary Romanian sociologist who grilled me about Robert Chambers, the Anand dairy cooperative in India, and my views on the potential of social forestry, none of which I had ever heard of before. Fortunately, we also managed to chat a bit about Eric Wolf and Sidney Mintz, both of whom I knew because they were my thesis advisers. Over a wrap-up lunch in the lush World Bank cafeteria, he asked about my views on whether Henry Kissinger and the Nixon administration might have had a point given what ensued. Realizing that I'd completely blown the interview, I figured why not just say what I really thought, temple of expansive capitalism though this was.

After Michael hired me, we began a small project together to see if the Chico River projects that I'd seen in the Philippines were an aberrant case of a military dictator bypassing development's ground rules, or whether there were more examples of Bank-financed projects ignoring the Bank's own social and environmental policy requirements. Just 2 years earlier, Michael had somehow recently managed to

---

[1]Though, proving Michael's dictum that there is no such thing as a dead project, in 2019 it was again revived, and as of this writing in 2020, it has again been suspended for again lacking the informed consent of the indigenous population.

turn into compulsory if frequently ignored planning requirements for all large projects. Well, needless to say, wherever there was information—and in most cases there wasn't—we did not find a very complimentary story. In fact, the main factor governing whether the Bank even raised a peep over poor people's forced displacement and subsequent misery seemed to be whether the individual project officer was a nice guy or, in a few cases, a nice woman. Most simply thought this wasn't the Bank's business, and some, unwittingly but openly repeating Josef Stalin, would say in that hard-eyed, flinty, willing-to-make-the-tough calls sort of self-confident, dismissive way, "well, you can't make an omelet without breaking some eggs."

Having by then scraped together enough money to finish my thesis, I happily left the World Bank to take up a post-doc with the International Fertilizer Development Centre in Cali, Colombia, South America, where I spent the next 3 years doing farming systems research across the northern Andes, still planning to return to Mexico.

Fate had a different plan for me. One day, I picked up the phone. It was someone from the World Bank, asking whether I could join them on an environmental assessment of the impacts that a large dam on Somalia's Baardhere River would have on the population of endangered Nile crocodiles. The problem was not the impact that a large dam would have on the endangered Nile crocodiles, but that turned out that while the Nile crocodile population was probably not all that threatened, there were no plans for resettling the 140,000 local farmers and refugees settled along the river banks who hadn't been counted in the feasibility assessments. Soon after, civil war broke out and that Baardheere River dam was never built.

But I was hooked.

Rejoining Michael back in Washington DC, my first job was mostly helping Michael finish the editing for the chapters that eventually became *Putting People First, 2nd edition*. But that was just the platform for the much more exciting job of helping Michael work through a strategy for getting the World Bank's resettlement policy turned into actual actions, not just largely ignored lip service. One day, Michael casually asked me to join a supervision mission to a large project in western India, one that he said was the touchstone for the seriousness of the human issues at stake and the high-stakes that were involved when so much power and money were in play. I vaguely remembered reading the Narmada River Sardar Sarovar Dam and Irrigation Project report from my time doing that first resettlement review with Michael, but since then, Narmada had become an international *cause celebre*.

The first big surprise after I got to western India was how little of what had sounded like very precise planning in the Bank's documents was anywhere to be found in the actual project. However, what was actually there was a mass civic mobilization opposed to the project, a dug-in government and Bank project team, and a whole range of international environmental and activist groups who saw Narmada as a test case for attacking World Bank style big development.

Philippines, Somalia, India......there was a trend developing. We dived, headfirst, into a global effort to find out what was happening to the people being displaced by some 200 World Bank projects that were causing resettlement. The Bank's guidelines, we thought, were clear enough. But were they being followed? And what happened to those people? Did anyone know?

Four years later, in late 1994, Michael and I were finishing off the Bankwide Review of Involuntary Resettlement. We were exhausted. Retrospectively, it's hard to convey how emotionally difficult it was to carry out a review that needed to translate some pretty horrific violations of the basic rights of very poor people into a language that could be heard by and convince powerful, articulate people who were intellectually vested in the basic "big push" development framework. Many of them were also ensnared in strong institutional and even personal interests, such as lending pipelines to a big borrower, and individual career promotions. Sparks flew in almost every meeting. While after finishing that report I just wanted to get out of Washington and possibly even the Bank, the controversy seemed to energize Michael even more, and the high-level follow-up that ensued is entirely to his credit.

Indonesia was the first World Bank country office that asked Michael for help in cleaning up their resettlement portfolio. Faced with an increasingly uncomfortable public image, the Bank program in Indonesia had recently formed a special unit to handle social and environmental issues. But one project, the Kedung Ombo Dam and Irrigation project, was just too complex to be handled locally. Singled out by the global activists as one of the five World Bank "global disasters," Kedung Ombo was yet another large Bank-financed irrigation dam that had closed its gates to start filling the reservoir before the resettlement was done. In fact, a fairly large fraction of its 35,000 villagers was still living in the flood zone. Many were people who had accepted the government's "transmigration" offer but had returned when they found that the transmigration sites were unlivable, lacking virtually all of the promised amenities and often surrounded by sullen and hostile people whose lands had been taken away by force. Nearly all of them were poor people whose livelihood problems were exacerbated by the government's belief that many of them had been supporters of the Indonesian communist party at the time when the 1965 coup and massacres of as many as a million people took place, 30 years previously. They were still being punished by the New Order administration, the quasi-military government led by general Suharto that had taken place after the coup. Official lies and cover-ups were everywhere.

In the end, we achieved very little by way of remedial action, despite a few pilots and a lot of pressure, both from the Bank itself and from the international activist community. What we tried was just too late, and as the East Asia financial crisis began spreading across Indonesia, the entire New Order administration's development apparatus had started to crumble, which pretty much ended anyone's interest in pursuing the problem. But that experience gave me a very painful crash course in Michael's first lesson: that the challenge for a development anthropologist is not just to understand local social structure, social organization, or culture. That is, as always, key. But the other half of that story is to learn to use the language of the Bank, to know how its rules, tools, and ways to frame the world in a way that lets the Bank act on it. It really didn't take more than one trip to Kedung Ombo to see what a mess the resettlement was. By that point, only a few holdouts claimed otherwise. But now that everyone agreed that it was awful and something must be done, what was that "something" and who should be doing it? I quickly found out that other than bleating about how horrible it all was, I was not really able to translate that knowledge into the concepts, vocabulary, and instruments that states and development agencies use to think with. My real education was just starting.

Ethnography for Development: The Local Institutions Studies

Before leaving Washington for Jakarta, I'd spent some time working with Gloria Davis (see chapter by Gloria Davis), an anthropologist who not only had become the Bank's first Director for Social Development but had also done her Ph.D. and professional work in Indonesia. Gloria had put together a global study team guided by the Harvard political scientist Robert Putnam, whose task was to assess whether we could measure and perhaps one day use Putnam's concept of social capital for development.[2] The unique feature of the study was not so much the idea that communities can act collectively, but that we could contrast the way that communities naturally carry out collective action with what happens when Bank financed development projects rely on government staff to control local development decisions.

The answers were not quite as simple as "community good/government bad". I've described elsewhere the results from those local institutions' studies,[3] but I can summarize them briefly here. First, they *did* show that indigenous community institutions covered as diverse a range of activities as development agency created user groups did; they were in general more participatory and more inclusive; and they operated under both formal and informal rules that gave mechanisms for addressing problems and resolving complaints. They were also multi-functional and were sustained over time, much like the "corporate" community structures that my adviser Eric Wolf had described 40 years earlier. But unlike Wolf's closed corporate peasant communities, Indonesian villages were well networked with the external world, particularly, in many places, through market centers and traditional small principalities that under the Dutch had been given the juridical status of "*kecamatans*," subdistricts composed of anywhere from 6 to 40 or more villages. However, our potted ethnographies also showed that many communities lacked

---

[2]Robert D. Putnam, *Making Democracy Work*, Princeton, New Jersey: 1993.
[3]See Scott Guggenheim, "Crisis and Contradictions" in M. Woolcock, A. Bebbington, and S. Guggenheim, Eds, *Understanding Social Capital Debates at The World Bank*. Washington, DC.; also Kamala Chandrakirana et. al, *The Local Institutions Study*, unpublished World Bank report, 1999, but summarized in http://siteresources.worldbank.org/INTSOCIALCAPITAL/Resources/Local-Level-Institutions-Working-Paper-Series/LLI-WPS-2.pdf

technical skills, that many of them were experiencing a leadership crisis, and that they were often defrauded by urban or market players.

But the most interesting aspect of all this wasn't necessarily these findings about social capital in Indonesian villages. It was what was going on in the national government and how that was about to transform the relationship that these communities had with the state.

Indonesia's development model had been very textbook development. Large-scale technocratic service delivery ministries that built thousands of roads, schools, clinics, and so on complemented good macro-economic management and lots of foreign investment. Development was still largely low skilled, and most people lived from farming, But an economy traditionally dependent on hydrocarbons and forestry exports was already diversifying into light manufacturing and services. Poverty rates, though still dire, were nothing like they were when the Dutch left Indonesia in 1949.

The Bank was very vested in this model. Some people grumbled about the lack of political liberty and we, who spent a lot of time in the field, were often appalled by the levels of corruption and authoritarianism that were not so visible in official reports. Even so, most people were expecting that the next 20 years would be more or less like the previous two decades, with the economy continuing to grow, poverty rates slowly declining, and President Suharto anointing a successor from his inner circle.

Boy, were we wrong.

Indonesia's Kecamatan Development Program When Indonesia's economic and then its political crisis first broke in 1997, we were just putting the finishing touches on a small pilot program that tried to build on the social capital studies by seeing if we could switch from development project created community groups to just letting communities use the groups they already had. This was turning out to be harder to do than I had anticipated. It was great to argue that villagers should be allowed to plan and manage their own development projects, but you can't just hand out bags of public money to villagers and say "go for it," or at least you couldn't legally do that back then. Issues of who gets the money, what can it be spent on, who is liable for it, how is it accounted for, and what happens when things go wrong were just the opening round of questions.

I actually never could figure out the answers to most of these questions. But I didn't have to, either. Once we had the evidence to show that community organizations could carry out small-scale projects if we could shed much of the typical project superstructure, which had too many steps and was too complicated for managing community level programs, it turned out that the Bank and also the Indonesian government had a whole tier of specialists who were just dying to help make an experiment like this work. We spent the next 5 months working through the ethnographic data on how people organize, the government's legal and financial structure for how to move money down to whatever community organizations would end up doing the work, and what kind of reporting flows government auditors and others would require to prove that the money had been well spent.

Our pilot was just getting underway when, on May 21, 1998, President Suharto resigned. The economic crisis had already started, but after Suharto's fall, the extent to which the New Order officials had looted the banking system was revealed. That year, GDP shrank by 13.5%, taking much of the middle class and all of Indonesia's development apparatus with it. Desperate for ways to get money to the communities that were being directly and indirectly hit by the crisis, both the government and the Bank turned to our little 6 *kecamatan* (subdistrict) pilot and asked whether we could scale it up, no matter how unprepared we thought we might be. I generally believe that the value of a development pilot is from the analytical and practical work that goes into its design rather than the analysis of the results, which usually takes too long to be useful. So, we assembled a small task force that would work on the design, carry out some fast and dirty surveys to monitor the unfolding crisis,[4] and help the government begin recruiting field staff so that they could launch the emergency program.

The basic architecture of the KDP (*Kecamatan Development Project*) project that emerged from all of this mix consisted of block grants provided directly by the central government to *kecamatan* (subdistrict) councils. They could use the grants to fund development plans that had been prepared through a 4–6 month long participatory planning process. Planning began in hamlets. Community plans were then consolidated, presented, and reviewed in village-wide decision meetings before being submitted to the *kecamatan* council, where the proposals from a number of villages were presented for a public discussion. KDP rules required that any village group submitting a proposal must send a delegation of at least six community representatives, including the village head and at least three women, to the *kecamatan* meetings where villagers would collectively decide which proposals would be funded. Each village could submit up to two proposals to the *kecamatan* council. This always led to proposals for more projects than could be funded with the available resources, so the villagers had to negotiate among themselves which proposals were the most worthy. Once the *kecamatan* forum agreed on which proposals merited funding, nobody further up the system could modify them. Funds were released from the provincial branch of the national treasury directly to a bank account held in the name of all of the villagers. Villagers then ran the show.

In many senses, much of KDP's architecture was built out of spare parts: the funding system was swiped from one of Suharto's top-down transfer programs for "left behind" communities; the engineering came from another World Bank village roads program; and some of the planning ideas came from the UNICEF inspired participatory water and sanitation projects that were popular at the time (and which let villages plan for whatever they wanted as long as it was water).

But other parts came from the sociological fieldwork that the local institutions team had carried out. Whereas most of the operational bits that we borrowed from other projects were concerned with how to adapt development rules to community

---

[4]Sudarno Sumarto, Anna Wetterberg, Lant Pritchett, "The Social Impact of the Crisis in Indonesia: Results from a Nationwide Kecamatan Survey," World Bank, 1999.

level work, what the studies were really concerned with was how to build in better processes for providing voice, agency, and representation in the ways that communities engaged with development projects. From a development project standpoint, some of KDP's most innovative ideas involved things like dramatically simplifying contract formats, or disbursing against village plans rather than requiring paid receipts for bags of cement or contractor's reports. From an anthropological perspective, the most innovative parts were actions such as locating planning within the hamlet (*dusun*) but decision-making in the sub-district (*kecamatan*), the historical and symbolic meeting point. Similarly, while traditional culture in most of Indonesia had defined public roles for women, in pretty much no part of Indonesia was there a decision-making role for women outside of the official "homemaker's" organization ("PKK") when it came to deciding on government projects or spending development funds. How malleable was local culture going to be on giving women a voice in how KDP funds would get spent and accounted for?

More elaborately, our fieldwork had uncovered the ways in which the transactional structures of government projects provided both monopoly control over information flows as well as too much official discretion over community decision-making, big parts of what was needed to explain why there was so much corruption and distrust in so many of the current projects. As the team unpicked the ethnographic data, we worked hard to turn it into design steps that would start to break the monopolies and eliminate most of the discretion, producing the kinds of sociologically informed designs that Michael was recommending to Bank operations as a whole.

KDP then and Now From its operational launch in 48 villages in 1998, KDP went through a continual scale-up, reaching some 2000 villages by 2002; and then 6000 by 2006, when it was renamed as Indonesia's National Program for Community Empowerment. From there, it scaled up very rapidly, reaching 60,000 villages by 2011, and all of Indonesia's 75,000 villages by 2017, by which time the government had enshrined it in a national village law that embedded the program in the national budget. By 2019, the program was disbursing some US$8.8 billion/year, nearly 6% of Indonesia's GDP, a sum far beyond anything a development agency like the World Bank could ever have supported by itself.

But KDPs influence was not just through the 20-year scale-up. Once the dam had been broken, the government realized that shifting from a project delivery mode to community partnerships gave them a new template for a wide range of activities. The government's globally noteworthy program for its recovery from the devastating 2004 Aceh/Nias tsunami was built on this same community development platform, one of whose foundational features was to get displaced people out of the camps and back working on their community's reconstruction within weeks of the disaster. The government has now made this model of community-based recovery a mainstay of its disaster-handling program. Colleagues from education and health also began looking at ways to use the community partnership model to increase coverage and move past some of the highly centralized models of the New Order era. And other countries, such as the Philippines, Myanmar, Afghanistan and even Liberia claim to have borrowed and adapted elements of the program—including the admonitions that they needed to do their own social analysis, experimentation, and adaptation, not just replicate Indonesia.

Not all has been rosy, however. Social analysis could help map out the institutional landscape and some basic negotiating procedures that could make the state and its development projects accessible to villagers, but communities have their own patterns of inequality, conflict, and social exclusion. KDP always faced a tension between its principles of local decision-making and the fact that elite capture and rules that exclude women were always going to require some forms of outside intervention.

As KDP got larger, the schizophrenia that was already present in its early architecture returned to the forefront of problems. Was the goal of the program to increase the state's ability to deliver development services to villages, or was it to help villagers organize and engage with Indonesia's newly democratic state and its representative institutions? While the overarching law that embedded KDP into the budget kept the core principles intact, much of KDP's scale-up and appropriation by mainstream government ministries concentrated on restoring official's roles in the planning process, largely at the expense of KDP's bottom-up, more participatory and transparent approach. However, the battle continues to rage. KDP did not operate in isolation from the rest of Indonesia, and as Indonesian democracy continues to consolidate and popular expectations for responsive government continue to rise, there is pushback against the re-assertion of New Order-style bureaucratic control.

Michael Cernea's Living Lessons

KDP today, in its latest incarnation as the Indonesian Village Law, is the largest community development project in the world. It's scope crosses three time zones, from Aceh in the far northwest of Indonesia to Papua in the far east, adapting and adjusting to local social structures in a country known globally for its cultural, linguistic, and economic diversity. If the test of an applied development anthropology is whether it can produce projects that go beyond a single village, KDP has passed it. By 2018, the World Bank alone was financing over 190 large-scale community development projects in 79 developing countries.[5]

It is hard not to reflect on Michael's development contribution without noting here the extent to which the KDP story recapitulates the larger question of whether development should be a technocratic application of administrative and economic models for enabling a country's modernization, or whether it should be a more humanistic, values-driven enterprise that gives ordinary people more of a voice in

---

[5]Susan Wong and Scott Guggenheim, *Community-Driven Development: Myths and Realities*, Policy Research Paper 8435, Washington, DC; The World Bank, 2018.

governance and development. KDP and its successors tried to do both, but the balancing act has not been without tensions.

Tania Li, in her often insightful and widely cited book, "The Will to Improve,[6]" has critiqued KDP as a project that uses technocratic language to turn questions of political economy, local autonomy, and community culture into projects that reflect a development bureaucrat's vision of a better life. While I think Dr. Li misunderstands where the line between prescription and choice sits within KDP, she is right that project documents are written in the language of the World Bank, not in the language of the community. But this was Michael's genius. If anthropologists wanted to do more than provide critique after the fact, or stay confined to writing detailed community ethnographies and social assessments that would be read and set aside, they needed to learn the language and culture not just of the villages, but also of the agencies that had the resources and power. If KDP were to ever give villagers a fighting chance to build the roads or water sources that they actually wanted rather than what a government or a donor agency wanted them to do, then the puzzle of how to provide agency to villagers needed to be solved when somebody else held the money. That meant becoming fluent in two languages, not one. As Gloria Davis also somewhat facetiously advised me shortly before I left Washington for Indonesia, "if you can't write a contract for it, it isn't going to happen."

Much of Michael Cernea's message for development reflects a belief that it's not just incentives, but also institutions that matter. Sociology and anthropology offer a powerful set of empirical tools for uncovering how community and local institutions mediate and organize social action. Programs that work with and through local organizations will be more effective and more long-lasting than programs that just sweep them aside. KDP and the Indonesia community program became a laboratory for putting this idea to the test in a broad range of different areas: anti-corruption, social protection targeting, conflict recovery, and poor people's education, to name just a few examples.[7]

However, while much of Michael's early work was about how to get international development to open its doors to social science, by the time of KDP the most important questions were already what should social scientists be doing once they've been invited to walk through them. Because KDP was built around the tension between international and state development institutions on the one hand and

---

[6]Tania Li, *The Will to Improve: Governmentality, Development, and the Practice of Politics*, Durjam, North Carolina; Duke University Press, 2007, *Governing Indonesia: convergence on the project system*, Critical Policy Studies 10, 2015.

[7]Ben Olken, "*Monitoring Corruption: Evidence from a Field Experiment in Indonesia*" Journal of Political Economy 11(5): 200–249; V. Alatas, A. Banerjee, R. Hanna, B. Olken, and J. Tobias, "*Targeting the Poor: Evidence from a Field Experiment in Indonesia*", M. Woolcock, P. Barron, and R. Diprose, *Contesting Development: Participatory Projects and Local Conflict Dynamics in Indonesia*. New Haven, Yale University Press 2011; and M. Pradhan, D. Suryadarma, A. Beatty, M. Wong, A. Gaduh, A. Aliisjabana, and R. Artha, "*Improving Educational Quality Through Enhancing Community Participation: Results from a Randomized Field Experiment in Indonesia*." American Economic Journal 6(2): 105–126, 2014.

community-owned planning on the other, the social team working on it had to move beyond design and come up with a long term program for sociological monitoring, evaluation, research, and adaptation as both government and community became more adept at using the program's rules to further their own interests. I still laugh when I recall how one subdistrict head in Aceh province got so frustrated by village women demanding that he account for KDP's reconstruction funds that he issued an official decree banning the public discussion of government budgets, a decree that he was quickly forced to revoke. But the point of the story is not that officials would try to undo KDPs transparency. That was entirely predictable. It was that there was something about KDPs transparency that was changing villagers' willingness to challenge traditional ways that local officials were exerting power. Had we stuck to monitoring disbursement and checking the government's compliance with key performance indicators from our home base in Jakarta, we never could have used the Aceh example to set up village-based women's monitoring groups across the entire program.

Michael was always too much the outsider trying to penetrate the technocracy to openly state how his political beliefs and his own personal history as an outsider permeated his approach to development. Nevertheless, they are present throughout his work. For all of the arguments about making development more efficient, ultimately the arguments for programs like KDP that try to empower poor communities are moral ones. Why was it important that women attend village planning meetings? Will that do the villages, or even the women, any good? Why should local governments bypass their own bureaucracies to provide funds to village community groups? What should the role of the bureaucracy be, if not to manage funds for the public good? Why do community groups need to be provided with facilitators to carry out tasks that could be performed by experienced, professional bureaucrats? Why do community groups build better, cheaper village infrastructure than government agencies?

In his seminal book, *Development as Freedom*,[8] the economic philosopher Amartya Sen defined development as a quest for *the freedom of individuals to live lives that are valued.* Development, therefore, must include the freedom to choose among opportunities for realizing one's human potential. Sen argued that not only is the *goal* of development the achievement of this freedom, it is also the *means* by which it is achieved. Sen outlines five specific types of freedoms: political freedoms, economic facilities, social opportunities, transparency guarantees, and protective security. Political freedoms refer to the ability of the people to have a voice in government and to be able to scrutinize the authorities. Economic facilities concern both the resources within the market and the market mechanism itself. Income and wealth in the country should serve to increase the economic facilities for the people. Social opportunities deal with benefits like healthcare or education for the populace, allowing individuals to live better lives. Transparency guarantees allow individuals to interact with some degree of trust and knowledge of the interaction. Protective

---

[8] Amartya Sen, *Development as Freedom*, New York, Random House, 1999.

security is the system of social safety nets that prevent a group affected by poverty being crushed and constrained by terrible misery.[9]

Before Sen's work, these had been viewed as only the ends of development; luxuries afforded to countries that needed to focus on increasing income. Sen argues, however, that the increase in real freedoms should be both the ends and the means of development. While Sen strenuously defends the proposition that the development of these institutions will increase economic prosperity rather than being a burden upon it, he also insists that these represent significant goals *in and of themselves*, and not merely as a *means to an end*. In this context, political freedoms in particular have not just an instrumental and constructive role, but a constitutive role as well. Sen argues that "our conceptualization of economic needs depends crucially on open public debates and discussions, the guaranteeing of which requires insistence on basic political liberty and civil rights." Without such rights, the validity of a dominant political and economic agenda is not susceptible to alternative interpretation by those whose interests are at variance with those who control that agenda.

The large number of people who worked on KDP understood from the beginning that changing the way that Indonesia approached development was a small part of a much bigger social change. Indonesia's democratic transition is still being written, and even now we don't know for sure whether it will succeed or whether the authoritarian elitism of the past will return. Social analysis as advocated by Michael Cernea provided a way for development to engage people not just as individual beneficiaries, but as social and political beings whose institutions, priorities, values, and voice mattered. In today's world, when trust in government, in institutions, and in democracy itself are at record lows amidst the record high standards of wealth and consumption that unfettered markets had always promised, these lessons are not just historical relics to be studied in graduate classrooms, but guides for the development ideas of the future.

Scott Guggenheim is an anthropologist with a Ph.D. from Johns Hopkins University. After several years working on involuntary resettlement with Michael Cernea that included both policy work and operations in Colombia, Mexico, Somalia, India, Cote d'Ivoire, Cameroon and elsewhere, Mr. Guggenheim moved to Indonesia, where he became a global leader in community-driven development. He was team leader for the East Timor National Community Employment Project in 1999, the 2002 National Emergency Solidarity and Employment Project in Afghanistan, and was the World Bank's field coordinator for the 2004 Aceh tsunami recovery program. Between 2014 and 2018, Scott returned to Afghanistan, serving as senior development adviser to President Ashraf Ghani. Scott's publications include: *Power and Protest in the Countryside* (with Robert Weller); *Anthropological Approaches to Involuntary Resettlement* (w/Michael Cernea), *The Search for Empowerment* (with Michael Woolcock and Anthony Bebbington); and *Community-Driven Development: Myths and Realities* (with Susan Wong). Scott is currently an adjunct professor in Georgetown University's School of Foreign Service.

---

[9]https://en.wikipedia.org/wiki/Amartya_Sen

Open Access This chapter is licensed under the terms of the Creative Commons Attribution 4.0 International License (http://creativecommons.org/licenses/by/4.0/), which permits use, sharing, adaptation, distribution and reproduction in any medium or format, as long as you give appropriate credit to the original author(s) and the source, provide a link to the Creative Commons license and indicate if changes were made.

The images or other third party material in this chapter are included in the chapter's Creative Commons license, unless indicated otherwise in a credit line to the material. If material is not included in the chapter's Creative Commons license and your intended use is not permitted by statutory regulation or exceeds the permitted use, you will need to obtain permission directly from the copyright holder.

The World Bank and Indigenous Peoples

Shelton H. Davis

Introduction

In 1982, the World Bank issued a brief operational policy statement which outlined procedures for protecting the rights of so-called "tribal people" in Bank-financed development projects.[1] Experience has shown, the World Bank directive stated, "that, unless special measures are adopted, tribal people are more likely to be harmed than helped by development projects that are intended for beneficiaries other than themselves. Therefore, whenever tribal peoples may be affected, the design of projects should include measures or components necessary to safeguard their interests, and, whenever feasible, to enhance their well-being." The directive further stated that, "As a general policy, the Bank will not assist development projects that knowingly involve encroachment on traditional territories being used or occupied by tribal people, unless adequate safeguards are provided.[2] In those cases where environmental and/or social changes promoted through development projects may create undesired effects for tribal people, the project should be designed so as to prevent or mitigate such effects."

While the World Bank has been criticized by non-governmental organizations for the adverse impacts upon indigenous or tribal populations of some of the projects that it finances, there is little doubt, as one source put it, that the World Bank "has become the first international development agency to recognize that economic

---

The following chapter was prepared for a panel discussion on Indigenous Peoples and Ethnic Minorities at the Denver Initiative Conference on Human Rights, University of Denver Law School, Denver Colorado, April 16 & 17, 1993. The interpretations contained in the chapter are solely those of the author and should not be attributed to the World Bank, its Executive Directors or its Member Countries.

---

[1] "Tribal Peoples in Bank-Financed Projects," Operational Manual Statement 2.34, February 1982, para. 4.

[2] OMS 2.34, para 5.

development places in jeopardy the survival of tribal people."[3] The same source wrote that the World Bank's proposed policy, "if fully implemented, will support their rights to their lands, resources, ethnic identities and cultural autonomy."

Some sources estimate that there are over 250 million tribal or indigenous peoples worldwide living in more than seventy countries.[4] Over the past decade, the World Bank has financed numerous projects which contain special programs or components for the protection of the lands and other resources of these peoples. As a result of this experience, the World Bank has revised its original policy toward indigenous peoples, bringing it more in line with current thinking on the role of these peoples as active participants in and beneficiaries of development projects.[5]

All of this activity has taken place in an international context of increasing organization and voice of indigenous peoples and the drafting of new international standards for the treatment of these peoples by agencies such as the International Labor Organization and UN Human Rights Commission.[6] It has also occurred during a period when there is growing awareness, among policy makers and scientists, of the important role which indigenous peoples can play in the conservation of biodiversity and protection of fragile and threatened ecosystems.

The following article describes the policies and experience of the World Bank in relationship to indigenous peoples. The article opens with a discussion of the Bank's 1982 policy statement. It then describes the findings of a 5-year implementation review of Bank-financed projects with tribal programs. Lastly, it discusses the Bank's new policy toward indigenous peoples, and places within the larger framework of the Bank's increasing concern for social and economic rights.

One of the themes of the article is that there has been a fundamental change in the World Bank's thinking about indigenous peoples, from an early concern with protecting small, isolated tribal societies (many of them forest-dwelling tribes in the lowlands of South America) from the negative impacts of development, to the promotion of conditions among its Borrowers for the active participation of indigenous peoples in the development process itself. This new approach is reflected in the Bank's current policy directive, as well as several recent projects being prepared and financed by the Bank. It is also reflected in the Bank's growing emphasis upon participatory forms of development and the increasing incorporation of social and cultural analysis into its investment program and other development work.

---

[3]Guardian, London, 12 August 1981.

[4]Julian Burger, *The Gaia Atlas of First Peoples,* New York, Anchor Books. 1990, p.18.

See, Russel Lawrence Barsh, "Indigenous Peoples' Role in Achieving Sustainability," in Helge Tie Bergesen.

[5]Magnar Norderhaug, and Georg Parmann (editors), *Green Globe Yearbook* 1992. Oxford University Press. 1992, pp 25–34.

[6][...] for a broader discussion of the limits and challenges which the World Bank faces in dealing with human rights [.........] see: Ibrahim L Shihata. "The World Bank and Human Rights: An Analysis of the Legal Issues and the [..........] of Achievements," *Denver Journal of International Law and Policy,* Vol. 17, No. 1, 1988, pp. 39, 1966. Introduced in Ibrahim F.I. Sihata, *The World Bank in a Changing World,* Dordrecht, Martinus Nijhoff Publishers, chapter 3, pp. 97–134.

Tribal People in Bank-Financed Projects

The first policy directive of the World Bank concerning indigenous peoples (Operational Manual Statement (OMS) 2.34) was issued in February 1982 under the title "Tribal People in Bank- financed Projects." Even previous to the release of this directive, the Bank's office of Environmental and Scientific Affairs, which was then responsible for the Bank's environmental assessment work, had initiated a study of the effects of economic development on the lands and cultures of tribal peoples. Released soon after the issuing of OMS 2.34, the study contained some interesting insights on the traditional land use practices of indigenous peoples and their potential role as natural resource managers. However, a major emphasis of the report was that there was an historical continuum or range of types of tribal societies from those which are geographically and culturally isolated from national societies (so-called "un-contacted" tribes, of which there are relatively few remaining in the world) to those which have been fully integrated into the wider political economies and rural societies of the country's which they form part (the so-called "indigenous peasant populations"). In between, the report noted, there is a continuum of societies from "semi-isolated tribal groups" to those in "permanent contact" but still not "fully integrated" with their respective national societies.[7]

Using this notion of a "continuum of acculturation," or the integration of tribal societies, came from two sources. One path was from the experience of the Bank in financing frontier development and colonization programs in the lowland tropical forest areas of Brazil and other countries of South America where, at the time, there were still a number of un-contacted or only recently contacted forest-dwelling tribal groups. A second path stemmed from the notion, then prevalent among some government indigenist agencies in Latin America, that it was inevitable that these relatively remote tribal societies would, if adequately protected during a transition period, forsake their traditional cultures and tribal identities and eventually integrate into wider society. Much of this second viewpoint was based upon the "protectionist" provisions of International Labor Organization Convention No. 107, which was drafted in the 1950s and ratified by several Latin American countries in the 1960s and early 1970s.[8]

Ironically, the Bank published the report on Tribal Peoples and Economic Development and issued its operational policy statement just at a time when many Latin American indigenous organizations and anthropologists were criticizing the "integrationist" theory for not adequately recognizing the historical persistence of indigenous ethnic identities and cultures. It also occurred at a time when the ILO was considering revising its convention on the subject of tribal and indigenous peoples

---

[7]See, Robert Goodland, *Tribal Peoples and Economic Development: Human Ecologic considerations*, Washington, World Bank, 1962.

[8]For background on the role of ILO Convention No. 107 in Latin American indigenist policies, see: Lee Swepston, "Latin American Approaches to the Indian Problem." *International Labour Review*, Vol. 117, No. 2, March-April 1978, pp. 179–196.

and when the UN Human Rights Commission had established a special working Group on Indigenous Populations to develop new international standards on the treatment of indigenous peoples.[9]

If one analyses the 1982 directive, it is clear that some of the protectionist and integrationist premises of the early ILO Convention found their way into the Bank's policy statement. Although more limited in scope than the ILO definition, the term "tribal" peoples in the Bank's policy directive referred to those ethnic groups that have "stable, low-energy, sustained-yield economic systems," and exhibit in varying degrees the following characteristics:

1. Geographically isolated or semi-isolated;
2. Unacculturated or only partially acculturated into the societal norms of the dominant society;
3. Nonmonetized, or only partially monetized; production largely for subsistence, and independent of the national economic system;
4. Ethnically distinct from the national society;
5. Nonliterate and without a written language;
6. Linguistically distinct from the-wider society;
7. Identifying closely with one particular territory;
8. Having an economic lifestyle largely dependent on the specific natural environment
9. Possessing indigenous leadership, but little or no national representation, and few, if any, political rights as individuals or collectively, partly because they do not participate in the political process; and,
10. Having loose tenure over their traditional lands, which for the most part is not accepted by the dominant society nor accommodated by its courts; and, having weak enforcement capabilities against encroachers, even when tribal areas have been delineated.[10]

The directive also contained an important footnote indicating that the Bank's policy was "not concerned with projects designed specifically for tribal people as the direct beneficiaries, but rather with other types of projects that impact on (emphasis mine) tribal people." Tribal peoples, because of their isolation and acculturation status, were seen as being more 'vulnerable' in the development process. Therefore,

---

[9] For a description of the rethinking which took place in the ILO prior to the revision of Convention No. 107 (1957), see, Lee Swepston and Roger Plant, "International Standards and the Protection of the Land Rights of Indigenous and Tribal Populations." 11 *International Labour Review*, Vol. 124, *No. I*. January-February 1985, pp. 91–106. The key attributes of the revised Convention No. 169 (1989) are described in Lee Swepston, "A New Step in the International Law on Indigenous and Tribal Peoples: ILO Convention No. 169 of 1989," 11 *Oklahoma City University Law Review*, Vol. 15, No. 3, Fall 1990, pp. 677–714. See, also, Russel Lawrence Barsh. "An Advocate's Guide to the Convention on Indigenous and Tribal Peoples." *Oklahoma City University Law Review*, Vol. 15. No. 1, Spring 1990, pp. 209–23.

[10] OMS 2.34, para. 2.

it was necessary to design projects in such a way to increase their "capacity for change and adaptation to new circumstances".[11]

While the Bank policy recognized that it was the responsibility of governments to implement measures that will "effectively safeguard the integrity and well-being of the tribal people," it also stated that it would not support policies at either extreme: "either those that perpetuate isolation from the national society and needed social services; or, those promoting forced, accelerated acculturation unsuited to the future well-being of the affected tribal people." For example, the Bank "would not be prepared to assist with a project if it appears that the project sponsors had forcibly 'cleared' the area of tribal people beforehand."[12]

The guiding principle behind the Bank's policy was that development projects that affect tribal people should provide "adequate time and conditions for acculturation."[13] To be successful, the operational directive stated, such acculturation needed to be "slow and gradual."[14] Furthermore, projects should contain special tribal components or parallel programs which would mitigate the adverse effects of the wider development project and provide tribal peoples with adequate conditions and time to adapt to the national society at their own pace. "Sound project planning and design," the directive stated, "reduce the risk that tribal people will suffer from the project's consequences or disrupt its implementation. More positively, tribal people may offer opportunities to the wider society, especially by increasing the national society's knowledge of proven adaptation to and utilization of fragile and marginal environments."[15]

The design of tribal components or parallel programs, which formed the essence of the Bank's operational response to the adverse effects of development projects on tribal peoples, should be "based upon detailed, contemporary knowledge of the peoples to be affected,"[16] and contain four elements:

1. The recognition, demarcation and protection of tribal areas containing those resources required to sustain the tribal people's traditional means of livelihood;
2. Appropriate social services that are consonant with the tribe's acculturation status, including, especially, protection against diseases and the maintaining of health;
3. The maintenance, to the extent desired by the tribe, of its cultural integrity and embodiments thereof; [and,]
4. A forum for the participation of the tribal people in decisions affecting them and providing for adjudication and redress of grievances.[17]

---

[11] OMS 2.34, footnote 2 and para. 3.
[12] OMS 2.34, para. 5.
[13] OMS 2.34, para. 6.
[14] OMS 2.34, para. 7.
[15] OMS 2.34, para. 4.
[16] OMS 2.34, para. 8.
[17] OMS 2.34, para. 7.

The remainder of the policy directive indicated ways in which Bank project officers and Borrowers could incorporate tribal components and parallel programs into the Bank's project cycle. During project identification, for example, the directive stated, the "approximate numbers, location, and degree of acculturation of tribal people in the general region of the project should be ascertained." At this stage, assessments should be made of relevant government agencies and their policies, the status of indigenous lands, and the enforcement capabilities of the government.

The directive also stated that "pre-investment funds could be used for studies to inform the tribal people about the proposed project and obtain their views."[18]

The actual tribal component or parallel program was to be designed before or during project preparation, the second stage of the Bank's project cycle. This should include the incorporation of information provided by pre-feasibility anthropological studies and site visits, ways of institutionally strengthening government agencies responsible for indigenous affairs, and the design of special programs for the demarcation of tribal lands and protection of the health of tribal populations. "Land tenure and water rights," the directive stated, "may need special attention" during the project preparation stage.[19]

At project appraisal, the third stage in the project cycle, project officers were responsible for assessing the "adequacy and appropriateness of the tribal component, the need for legislation concerning the relevant government agency and other aspects, and the capability of the designated agency to implement the component."[20]

Finally, during project implementation and the Bank supervision stage, specialist input (mainly by anthropologists and "indigenists") would again need to be called upon to evaluate the performance of the tribal component. If necessary, the tribal component should be "updated and reassessed" based upon unforeseen changes which had taken place during project implementation. Because of the special needs of tribal peoples and the need to monitor the performance of government agencies, the supervision of the tribal component might need to extend over a longer period of time than other components of the project. Furthermore, a specific monitoring and evaluation system might be needed to ensure the progress and performance of the tribal component.[21]

In general, OMS 2.34 provided a set of guidelines for assuring that tribal people's needs (as defined by the directive) were met in Bank-financed projects. Without such guidelines, past experience had demonstrated that development projects would often have negative, and sometimes permanently damaging, effects on the lands, subsistence resources, health and cultures of tribal populations. By introducing the guidelines, the Bank hoped to avoid or mitigate these effects while at the same time, suggesting to its Borrowers that there are indigenous cultural and ecological models for utilizing the fragile environments where most tribal peoples live.

---

[18] OMS 2.34, para. 10.
[19] OMS 2.34, para. 11.
[20] OMS 2.34, para. 12.
[21] OMS 2.34, para. 13.

The 5-Year Implementation Review

In 1989, the office of Environmental and Scientific Affairs conducted a desk review of the experience in implementing the policy directives contained in OMS 2.34. The implementation review surveyed 33 Bank-financed projects that were identified, appraised and implemented between 1982 and 1986 and that were known to have demonstrable effects on the lands, resources and cultures of tribal or indigenous peoples. Of these 33 projects, 15 projects (11 from Latin America and the Caribbean region, 2 from Africa, and 2 from Asia and the Pacific region) were selected for more in-depth analysis, because they contained special components or parallel programs for protecting or improving the welfare of tribal or indigenous populations. The results of this analysis were shared with each of the five regional offices of the Bank, and a set of recommendations for improving Bank policies and performance were developed based upon staff comments and interviews.[22]

One of the major findings of the review was that the issuing of OMS 2.34 had significantly increased the identification by Bank staff of tribal or indigenous peoples affected by Bank- financed projects. Until the late 1970s, it was standard Bank practice to assume that all rural populations in developing countries were essentially alike (i.e., economically underdeveloped and poor) and that there was no need to make special provisions in project design for ethnically or culturally distinct populations. The effects of OMS 2.34 in changing this practice were reflected in the increasing number of Bank-financed projects that were indicated as having consequences for the general health, cultural integrity and economic well-being of tribal or indigenous groups. In 1983, for example, only 15 Bank-financed projects were identified as having tribal peoples in their areas of influence and hence coming under the purview of the new Bank guidelines. This number increased to 36 projects in 1984, and to 53 projects by 1986. The number of projects with special tribal components or parallel programs also increased from a project in 1983 to 15 projects in 1986. The majority of the latter projects, as already noted, were in the lowland tropical forest areas of South America where the Bank was increasingly financing road construction and land settlement programs.

The implementation review also indicated that Bank staff generally assumed (justifiably, given the definition contained in the original operational statement) that the Bank's policy mainly applied to relatively small, isolated and unacculturated tribal societies (what were euphemistically termed "vulnerable ethnic minorities"), such as the rainforest Indians of South America or the pygmies or bushmen of Central and South Africa; and, not to larger and more heterogeneous tribal populations, such as the nomadic pastoral societies of the Sahel region or of Eastern and Western Africa or the "tribal" peoples of India and Southeast Asia. These latter groups, which sometimes number in the hundreds of thousands or millions of

---

[22]Office of Environmental and Scientific Affairs, *A Five-Year Implementation Review of OMS 2.34 (1982–1986)*. World Bank, Projects Policy Development, June 1987.

peoples, are integrated into national and regional political economics but still maintain a strong sense of ethnic identity and cultural separateness.

This staff perception of the limited applicability of OMS 2.34 was noted in earlier implementation reviews as well as the 1987 review. A 1983 review, for example, stated that "the idea that certain tribal peoples (e.g., in Asia and Africa) are outside the scope of OMS 2.34 because they are "acculturated" appears in several documents. In some of these cases, such judgements are not supported by data or-analysis." Similarly, a 1984 review, noted that "principles contained in OMS 2.34 can be applied to projects where the tribal populations are dominant and heterogeneous, rather than vulnerable ethnic minorities targeted by the OMS."[23]

The 1987 review indicated that several Bank-financed projects experienced unnecessary delays and conflicts because inadequate attention was being given to the unique ethnic and cultural characteristics of affected populations. While special protective measures were necessary for the most vulnerable or unacculturated populations, there was also a need to extend the focus of the Bank's concern to larger and more heterogeneous populations, some of them (as already mentioned) numbering in the hundreds of thousands or millions of people. The real issue, the 1987 review noted, was less one of defining tribal or indigenous peoples by their isolation and acculturation than it was of recognizing that these peoples possess socio-cultural system, modes of production and forms of ecological adaptation which are often distinct from national societies and which need to be taken into account in project preparation and design.

The implementation review also indicated that while the Bank had some success in convincing its Borrowers to include special tribal components or parallel programs in its projects, many of these components were being designed on an *ad hoc* basis and not with the rigor assumed in the policy directive. For example, of the 15 projects containing tribal components analyzed in the review, only two contained all of the four protective measures (land demarcation and protection, adequate health and social services, measures for protecting tribal cultural integrity, and tribal participation and adjudication mechanisms) outlined in OMS 2.34. Furthermore, land demarcation and protection, which are so vital to the integrity and survival of tribal or indigenous populations, only occurred in six of the 15 projects and, even in these cases, they were severely delayed or out of pace with the progress of the overall projects.[24]

The Bank was successful in convincing Borrowers to provide social, health and other services to tribal populations (program-of this nature existed in 13 of the 15 Bank-financed projects). However, even in these cases, the social services and

---

[23] Cited in Office of Environmental and scientific Affairs, *Five-Year Implementation Review*, pp 15 and 16.

[24] For detailed analysis of Bank-financed indigenous land regulation programs introduces under OMS 2.34, see, Alaka Wali and Shelton Davis, *Protecting American Lands: A Review of World Bank Experience with Indigenous Land Regularization Programs in Lowland South America*, Latin America and Caribbean Region, Technical Department, Regional Studies Program Series, Report 19 (Washington, World Bank, 1992).

health programs were not designed in terms of the cultural needs and preferences of the tribal population, nor did these peoples participate in their preparation or implementation. In fact, participation by the tribal peoples only occurred in three of the 15 projects, and what programs existed resulted from the presence of strong regional or tribal federations which pressured their governments and the Bank to take into account their needs and wishes.

The implementation reviews also found that many of the government agencies responsible for designing and implementing tribal components were institutionally weak, under-funded and lacked adequate anthropological personnel. While non-governmental organizations (NGOs), such as missionary groups and grassroots development organizations, were providing-needed social services and legal support to some tribal and indigenous groups, government agencies often saw themselves in conflict with these organizations and seldom invited them to participate in the planning process.

Furthermore, the Bank itself was unprepared for the new tasks assumed under its tribal peoples policy. At the time of the introduction of OMS 2.34, there were relatively few anthropologists employed by the Bank, and almost none employed in the regional and country departments where all of the operational work relating to project design and appraisal took place. Nor was the Bank's Legal Department prepared for the myriad and complex issues relating to domestic indigenist and agrarian law regimes which so affected the situation and prospects of tribal and indigenous peoples, as well as other traditional ethnic groups.[25]

The implementation review was carried out just prior to a major reorganization of the Bank, which saw the establishment of a new central Environment Department and four regional environmental units, three of which were staffed with anthropological personnel. The pending reorganization, the review argued, provided an excellent opportunity to continue to focus institutional attention on the policy goals and measures outlined in OMS 2.34. In terms of general policy, it recommended a revision of OMS 2.34, based upon a broader definition of tribal and indigenous peoples more in keeping with the experience of the Bank and the diverse social, cultural and legal situations of its Borrower countries.

Lastly, the implementation review recommended that the Bank assist in the strengthening of government agencies responsible for tribal or indigenous affairs, promote more consultation with national and international NGOs about development projects which affect tribal and indigenous peoples, and increase the direct participation of tribal and indigenous peoples in the planning of development projects. "In the end," the review stated, "the most effective way of strengthening Bank-financed tribal components is by convincing Governments to include tribal and indigenous peoples in project design and execution." Without such participation, it went on to state, "there are several dangers that development projects will not only fail to satisfy

---

[25] Some of the legal issues which the Bank faced in implementing OMS 2.34 are described in an unpublished paper by Antonia Macedo, *Land Rights of Indigenous and Tribal Peoples: Role of the World Bank*, November 1990.

the manifest needs of indigenous peoples, but may also be initiated and developed at their expense."[26]

The Revised Policy Directive

With the institutional reorganization of 1987, the Bank began to focus more systematic attention on improving the performance of its projects which affected tribal and indigenous peoples. Not only were anthropologists now available (albeit still in limited numbers) in the African, Asian and Latin America and Caribbean environment units to review the Bank's portfolio, but the country departments and sector divisions began to contract specialists to assist in the design and supervision of these projects. Furthermore, the Legal Department began to take a more active role in the design of Bank-financed projects which contained both tribal populations and resettlement, and to assist in finding ways of legally dealing with what were considered by the Bank as a series of problem projects.[27] One of the outcomes of this experience was the decision to revise the operational directives dealing with tribal peoples and involuntary resettlement, based upon the Bank's experience with these issues and what was then taking place in the wider international discussion of the social aspects of resettlement and indigenous peoples rights.

After 2 years of discussion within the Bank, and some consultation with outside organizations and experts, in 1991, the Bank issued a revised Operational Directive (OD 4.20) on "Indigenous Peoples." The new directive is much more detailed than the first and contains several changes and shifts in emphasis which are important to note.

First, the definitional criteria used to identify indigenous peoples in the revised directive are much broader than those in OMS 2.34. The revised directive notes that for purposes of Bank work, the term "indigenous peoples" (or other equivalent terms such as "indigenous ethnic minorities", "tribal groups", and "scheduled tribes") refers to "social groups with a social and cultural identity distinct from the dominant society that makes them vulnerable to being disadvantaged in the development process."[28] It also notes that there are varying national legal contexts and sociocultural criteria for identifying "indigenous peoples," and that "no single definition can capture their diversity." Some people are truly isolated from mainstream culture and society, while others are integrated into the wage labor force and national

---

[26]Office of Environmental and Scientific Affairs, *Five-Year Implementation Review*, p. 70. The reference to the UN assessment was to the report by Jose R. Martinez Cabo, Study of the Problem of *Discrimination Against Indigenous Populations*, United Nations, Geneva. 1986.

[27]The most serious of these problem projects were the Northwest Regional Development (Polonoroeste) Projects in Brazil and the Sardar Sarovar Projects in India, both of which were prepared under the policy guidelines of OMS 2.34 and considered in the 1987 implementation review.

[28]"**Indigenous Peoples**," Operational Directive 4.20 , September 1991, para. 3.

markets. In particular geographical areas, indigenous peoples can be identified by some characteristics, such as:

1. A close attachment to ancestral territories and to the natural resources in these areas;
2. Self-identification and identification by others as members of distinct cultural groups;
3. An indigenous language, often different from the national language;
4. Presence of customary social and political institutions; and,
5. Primarily subsistence-oriented production.[29]

Second, Bank policy recognizes the need to both protect indigenous peoples against the potential harm or damage caused by development projects, as well as to provide them (if they so wish) with new opportunities to participate in the benefits of the development process. The revised policy states:

> The Bank's broad objective towards indigenous peoples, as for all the people in its member countries, is to ensure that the development process fosters full respect for their dignity, human rights, and cultural uniqueness. More specifically, the objective at the center of this directive is to ensure that indigenous peoples do not suffer adverse effects during the development process, particularly from Bank- financed projects, and that they receive culturally compatible social and economic benefits.[30]

The directive notes that there is great controversy about how to approach indigenous peoples within the development process, with some advocating their total insulation from the forces of modernization and others promoting their rapid acculturation into the dominant society's values and economic activities. Rather than taking a position on this issue, which in many cases is only of theoretical or historical interest, the Bank's policy calls for the informed participation and recognition of the preferences of indigenous peoples.

> The Bank's policy is that the strategy for addressing the issues pertaining to indigenous peoples must be based on the informed participation (emphasis in original) of the indigenous peoples themselves. Thus, identifying local preferences through direct consultation, incorporation of indigenous knowledge into project approaches, and appropriate use of experienced specialists are core activities for any project that affects indigenous peoples and their rights to natural and economic resources.[31]

A third innovation of the Bank's revised policy is the incorporation of indigenous people's concerns into several other aspects of Bank work besides that of investment projects. For example, the revised directive notes that issues concerning indigenous peoples, including threats to their environments and natural resources, should be identified through environmental assessments, which since 1989 have been mandated for all Bank projects which have a significant impact on the

---

[29] OD 4.20, para. 5.
[30] OD 4.20, para. 6.
[31] OD 4.20, para 8.

environment.[32] Bank Country Departments are also mandated, under the new directive, to "maintain information on trends in government policies and institutions that deal with indigenous peoples," and to address issues relating to indigenous peoples in country economic and sector work and in the Bank's country dialogue with its Borrowers.[33]

Another area where the revised directive breaks new ground is in indicating the willingness of the Bank to provide funds for technical assistance to improve Borrower abilities to respond to the needs of indigenous peoples. "Technical assistance", the revised directive states, "is normally given within the context of project preparation, but technical assistance may also be needed to strengthen the relevant government institutions or to support development initiatives taken by indigenous peoples themselves." [34]

Finally, the revised directive devotes its major attention to ways of incorporating indigenous people's concerns into Bank-financed investment projects. The main innovation here is the requirement that special Indigenous Peoples Development Plans (IPDPs) be prepared, consistent with Bank policies, for all Bank funded projects which affect the lands, resources and cultures of indigenous peoples. These IPDP's can either form the basis of special components or provisions within broader Bank-funded development projects, or in certain cases be the entire project, when the main beneficiaries are indigenous peoples. Numerous paragraphs in the new directive outline the prerequisites, contents and technical, institutional and financial arrangements for designing these IPDPs.[35]

While it is beyond the scope of this chapter to discuss all of the elements of IPDP design and preparation as outlined in the operational directive, some critical aspects of the Bank's thinking on these matters are noteworthy. One is that the IPDP is prepared under Bank-financed projects should take adequate account of the legal frameworks which affect indigenous peoples. "The plan", according to OD 4.20:

> should contain an assessment of (i) the legal status of the groups covered by this OD, as reflected in the country's constitution, legislation, and subsidiary legislation (regulations, administrative orders, etc.); and (ii) the ability of such groups to obtain access to and effectively use the legal system to defend their rights. Particular attention should be given to the rights of indigenous peoples to use and develop the lands that they occupy, to be protected against illegal intruders, and to have access to natural resources (such as forests, wildlife and water) vital to the subsistence and reproduction.[36]

---

[32] Operational Directive 4. 01 ("Environmental Assessment", 1991; originally issued as Operational Directive 4.00, Annex A, 1989) makes specific reference to the need to consult local populations, including indigenous peoples, when environmental assessments are being conducted for projects on or in the areas of influence of their comunities and lands.

[33] OD 4.20, para. 10.

[34] OD 4.20, para. 12.

[35] OD 4.20, paras. 14 and 15. Footnote 3 of the OD notes that "regionally specific technical guidelines for preparing indigenous peoples components, and case studies of best practice, are available from the Regional environment divisions." The Africa region has initiated a process of drafting such technical guidelines, the purpose of which is to adapt the OD to the specific political and cultural conditions of the African continent.

[36] OD 4.20, para. 15 (a).

Another important aspect of IPDP preparation is the need for adequate baseline geographical and socio-cultural data. OD 4.20 indicates that plans should include:

- Accurate, up-to-date maps and aerial photographs of the area of project influence and the areas inhabited by indigenous peoples;
- Of the social structure and income sources of the population;
- Inventories of the resources that indigenous people use and technical data on their production systems; and,
- The relationship of indigenous peoples to other local and national groups.[37]

The issue of indigenous peoples participation, which is fundamental to the philosophy behind the entire policy directive, is also raised in the section of the OD concerning the contents of IPDPs. In fact, the directive states that all IPDP's should contain explicit strategies for ensuring such participation.

> Mechanisms should be devised and maintained for participation by indigenous people in decision making throughout project planning, implementation, and evaluation. Many of the larger groups of indigenous people have their own organizations that provide effective channels for communicating local preferences. Traditional leaders occupy pivotal positions for mobilizing people and should be brought into the planning process, with due concern for ensuring genuine representation of the indigenous population.[38]

Other paragraphs of the OD mention that IPDPs should give adequate attention to the recognition of customary or traditional land tenure systems,[39] to indigenous knowledge such as that possessed by traditional health providers,[40] and to the monitoring of projects by representatives of indigenous peoples' own organizations.[41]

Since the issuing of OD 4.20, the Bank has prepared and appraised several projects which contain IPDPs and are based on the active participation of the affected tribal or indigenous populations. These include, among others, a special plan for the incorporation of tribal peoples (many of them tribal women) in a rubber cultivation project in India, an agricultural and rangelands management project with Bedouin tribes in the western desert of Egypt, and a natural resource management and forestry project with indigenous and Afro-American communities in the Choco region of Colombia. The Bank is also involved in a number of sector studies relating to indigenous peoples, including a statistical survey of poverty and indigenous peoples in Latin America, a study of tribal health and nutrition programs in India, and several country-level forestry sector reviews which discuss indigenous peoples land rights.[42]

---

[37] OD 4.20, para. 15 (b).
[38] OD 4.20, para. 15 (d).
[39] OD 4.20, para. 15 (c).
[40] OD 4.20, para. 15 (e).
[41] OD 4.20, para. 15 (h).
[42] In March 1993, the Bank issued a new Forestry Policy which makes specific reference to the need to incorporate local people (including "forest dwellers") in environmentally sound forestry conservation and development plans. See, Operational Policy 4.3 6. para 1 (d) (ii).

Conclusion

This article has argued that there has been a fundamental shift in the way in which the Bank is conceptualizing and approaching the concerns of indigenous peoples in its policy and project work. Rather than focusing solely on attempting to mitigate the adverse impacts of its projects on relatively small and isolated tribal groups, it has broadened the definition of the subject population to include a much more diverse assemblage of peoples and to seek ways in which these peoples might both participate in and benefit from the development process itself. This policy is more in keeping with current international thinking on the rights of indigenous peoples, as well as with the general trend to recognizing the social and economic rights of poor and marginalized peoples throughout the world.

At the current time, it is difficult to tell whether this new approach will be any more successful than the Bank's earlier policy concerning tribal peoples in Bank-financed projects. There are some indications, however, that the Bank has learned from the experience of the past decade and has a much stronger institutional commitment and capacity to ensure the implementation of its current policy framework than it did in the past.

Shelton H. Davis was a cultural anthropologist who for many years led the World Bank's work on indigenous people. Already well-known globally for his leadership of the Anthropology Resource Center and his path breaking book Victims of the Miracle, which described the social and economic costs of development in the Amazon, Dr. Davis became the World Bank's lead sociologist and the sector manager for social development in Latin America and the Caribbean. His contributions included helping to develop the Bank's policy on indigenous people affected by Bank investments, some of the first development work anywhere intended to help Afro-Latinos, and some of the earliest efforts to introduce a human rights perspective into World Bank development policy and practice.

Dr. Davis's many books and articles include Land Rights and Indigenous Peoples: The Role of the Inter-American Commission on Human Rights (Cultural Survival, 1988); of Indigenous Views of Land and Environment (ed., The World Bank, 1993) and Traditional Knowledge and Sustainable Development (The World Bank, 1995). Dr. Davis passed away on May 27, 2010.

Open Access This chapter is licensed under the terms of the Creative Commons Attribution 4.0 International License (http://creativecommons.org/licenses/by/4.0/), which permits use, sharing, adaptation, distribution and reproduction in any medium or format, as long as you give appropriate credit to the original author(s) and the source, provide a link to the Creative Commons license and indicate if changes were made.

The images or other third party material in this chapter are included in the chapter's Creative Commons license, unless indicated otherwise in a credit line to the material. If material is not included in the chapter's Creative Commons license and your intended use is not permitted by statutory regulation or exceeds the permitted use, you will need to obtain permission directly from the copyright holder.

The Need for Social Research and the Broadening of CGIAR's Paradigm

Amir Kassam

Anthony Bebbington's essay profiling the development thinking and contributions of Michael Cernea in the anthology dedicated to *Fifty Key Thinkers on Development* (Simon 2006) described how Cernea explains to his students both the attractions and the challenges of practicing development anthropology and sociology, by using a metaphor from athletics. "*Practicing development anthropology*—Michael is warning them—*is a contact sport*" (Bebbington 2006).

Really?! How could this elegant and reflexive academic discipline be seen and compared to a "contact sport" ? Therefore, when I myself also heard Michael Cernea using the same metaphor, I asked him, point blank, to be more explicit. He answered: "*Practicing development social science needs people who not only have brains, but also are ready to stand and fight for their convictions; people who not only have knowledge, but also do have action-oriented minds; and people whose social science knowledge is doubled by a fair and moral compass. In sum, development anthropology demands sharp insight and character.*"

I had the privilege of working closely for nearly one decade with Michael Cernea and saw first-hand how the work of a militant "contact anthropologist" is unfolding. This article will share my reflections on our joint work in the CGIAR, during which we battled for getting CG's Centers to employ sociological and anthropological research on agriculture's central actor: the farmers, their production systems, households, communities, and institutions, not only research on the, biophysical, genetic and technical variables of the agricultural process.

The CGIAR (Consultative Group on International Agriculture Research) was established in 1971 as a global consortium of pre-existing agricultural research centers.[1] Each center had a different specialization, but they shared a common

---

[1] The financing of CGIAR's network of scientific centers is provided by the Governments of developing and industrialized countries, foundations, the World Bank, the FAO (Food and

A. Kassam (✉)
University of Reading, London, UK

goal: to enable the world's agriculture to feed the world and eradicate hunger. However, their common characteristic was that all were limiting themselves to carry out *only technological research* on plants, animals, soil, and water.

What was missing, both conceptually and in terms of staffing, was the deliberate orientation and a robust professional capacity to research agriculture's most important component: its *human actor*, the farmers themselves, their production systems, and farmers' behavior as producers. Those disparate centers[2] were staffed only with technical specialists—e.g., geneticists, plant breeders, agronomists, biologists, crop physiologists, water specialists and other technical experts, each outstanding in his or her specialty; however, paradoxically, they were totally lacking social researchers such as anthropologists or rural sociologists. In sum, CGIAR's initial paradigm for improving the developing countries' agriculture was narrow, in that it was conceived to do research only on agriculture's *natural* and *technical* variables.

Consistent with the general theme of the present volume, this chapter attempts to reconstruct in broad lines the gradual process through which the CG consortium of research institutions and scientists has evolved—I must say, rather slow, and with fits and starts—towards the recognition that CG's narrow paradigm of technical research must necessarily be broadened to encompass also the social, economic, and cultural/behavioral variables of agricultural development. That process included the recognition that CGIAR must also rely on knowledge available from social sciences, and also that CGIAR as a comprehensive system must itself *produce* such social knowledge, to complement its biophysical and technological research. In other words, CGIAR had to complement its staff with scholars in social sciences and with professional social researchers, in order to gain additional 'lenses' *trained upon the farmer* as agriculture's central actor, his production systems, family, and the knowledge farmers have—or lack—about how to self-organize and carry out their hard and incessant work.

Agriculture Organization), the UNDP (United Nations Development Program) and a series of other international and regional organizations. The consortium consists now of 15 International Agricultural Research Centers, which collaborate with hundreds of partner organizations, including national and regional research institutes, civil society organizations, academia, and the private sector (See also footnote 2).

[2]The organism that advises on and guides CGIAR's policies and scientific research work has been initially its TAC (Technical Advisory Committee), then renamed as its Science Council (SC) and recently as its Independent Science and Partnership Council (ISPC); it consists of 10–12 scholars of high international reputation specialized in sciences crucial for CGIAR's mission. The multidisciplinary research staff of each Center is also multinational. The Centres include: CIMMYT—Centro Internacional de Mejoramiento de Maiz y Trigo; CIP—Centro Internacional de la Papa; ICARDA—International Center for Agricultural Research in the Dry Areas; ICRISAT—International Crops Research Institute for the Semi-Arid Tropics; IFPRI—International Food Policy Research Institute; IITA—International Institute of Tropical Agriculture; ILRI—International Livestock Research Institute; IRRI—International Rice Research Institute; CIAT—Centro Internacional de Agricultura Tropical. The new wheat varieties from CIMMYT and rice varieties from IRRI, created after years of extraordinarily painstaking genetic research have triggered the Green Revolution, making possible gigantic increases in agricultural production and productivity.

A Brief Comparative Look at CGIAR and the World Bank

Both the World Bank and the CGIAR are major global institutions which have influenced and contributed—in different ways and proportions—to the fundamental international shift from the initial narrow pursuit of economic development (the WB) and, respectively, the narrow pursuit of technological development (the CG), to today's broader paradigm of *social* development.

Some of these ways have been partly interdependent and converging, and, over time, the World Bank as a major institution and its community of its social specialists have tenaciously 'nudged' the CG to also move in the same direction.

An eminent anthropologist, Scott E. Guggenheim, who has worked for years in both the CG and in the World Bank, observed that *"the two institutions may be usefully compared"*. He outlined this comparison retrospectively, in 2006, writing:

> Both institutions have global mandates. Both have gone through far-reaching reorganizations and introspective examinations of their role, whose objective has been to align institutional mandates and procedures to the global objective of poverty reduction. Both institutions first began experimenting with using social scientists in mid-1970s (World Bank on its own decision, and CGIAR due to some pump-priming support offered by the Rockefeller Foundation which financed a post-doctoral programme that would, in principle, later to be taken up by CGIAR core budgets).

> However, the trajectory of social scientists in the two institutions has diverged. In the World Bank the leading social scientists have moved from only supporting operational projects towards playing a growing role in formulating social policies and development strategies, so much so that even IMF-World Bank macro-level adjustment programs increasingly incorporated social science team members. Social scientists have also come to play a bigger role in rural development programs.... By contrast, CGIAR doesn't appear to have capitalized well on the splashy start enabled by its generous Rockefeller support... In addition, while the World Bank has funded a Social Development Department and Network at the World Bank's center to offer guidance across the Bank's system, CGIAR has nothing of this kind at its headquarters (see more on this comparison in Guggenheim 2006, pp. 425–426).

Given that a comprehensive history of the CGIAR, regretfully, has not yet been written, this rich history is far less known than it fully deserves, due to CG's immense contribution to increasing our world's capacity to feed itself. Therefore, this essay attempts also to reconstruct several key pages from CG's overall history. These pages are capturing and describing with their factual evidence significant events and moments of the gradual shift of CG from its initial technical research model oriented exclusively on biophysical and genetic components of the agricultural production process toward embracing and practicing a more encompassing research paradigm—one that took account and included also the study of the determinant social and cultural drivers of agricultural development.

The "Rocky-Docs" and the Fight to Overcome the Absence of Social Research in CGIAR

Soon after CGIAR was created in the early 1970s, discussions started among donors regarding the need to complement CG's agro-technical research with anthropological and sociological research on farmers, their needs and productive behavior. Nonetheless, the Centers weren't quite acting in this direction.

Therefore, in 1974 the Rockefeller Foundation (RF), in consensus with the World Bank and the UNDP, launched a strategically tailored initiative: it conceived and funded a *Social Science Fellowship Program* that aimed to create inside the CGIAR the professional capacity able and indispensable for carrying out social research focused on farmer's work, practices, needs and knowledge. This critical RF external initiative created a range of slots across the CG Centers to be staffed by specially recruited young and promising PhDs in social sciences. They became the first cohort of professionally trained social specialists working in the CG Centers: sociologists, anthropologists, economists, social geographers and cultural ecologists. They brought along a body of new knowledge: *social* knowledge and social methodologies, that is, capabilities previously missing in the CG's Centers. By joining the traditional pattern of multidisciplinary teams of eminent scholars and researchers specialized in other disciplines. Overall, as an evaluation paper authored by RF experts assessed after a number of years, the substantial contributions of this cohort of social specialists has broadened and enhanced CGIAR's capacities to understand and address the human-behavioral complexities of agricultural improvement (see Conway et al. 2006).

Over the next 22 years this program placed 114 young 'Rocky-Docs' in CGIAR and its associate centers. Some of these social researchers were retained in the core staff by the Centers themselves. Yet, considering that the CGIAR had 15–16 Centers, and that most of the social researchers stayed on their RF fellowship slots only between 1 and 3 years, their spread inside the CG was still pretty thin and insufficient. On an annual basis, the average number of social researchers working at the same time each year in the entire CGIAR amounted to about 30–35, which still was by far less than reaching the needed "critical mass". The RF initiative also helped the CG Centers to extend their outreach to some national agricultural research systems and incorporate farmers into problem identification. The RF program also had the distinction of long being the single major source for channeling female scientists, some 43 of them, into the CGIAR centers.

Nonetheless, the newly recruited Rocky-Docs, social anthropologists and sociologists, didn't have it easy in their first years. One substantive difficulty was comparable with the difficulty that, at the World Bank, was encountered by its first sociologists and anthropologists. That difficulty was properly described by Scott Guggenheim, an anthropologist who worked alternatively in both institutions (World Bank and CGIAR) and coined the concept of "*trained inattentiveness*" of many excellent economists to the social variables of projects and, respectively, many excellent biophysical scholars and researchers. Guggenheim wrote:

> If keeping an eye on the technological ball was a key virtue of CIAT's excellent biophysical scientists, their trained inattention to the sociological and organizational determinants of what makes technology useful to poor farmers was an eye-opening experience... (Guggenheim 2006, p. 426).

Moreover, in most CG Centers the Rocky-Docs were long still prejudged and seen as "imported", rather than *intrinsic* and *essentially relevant* to the processes to be dealt with.

A consequence inside the CGIAR of this kind of second rank, 'late comer' and 'secondary status', the social sciences did not have a "voice" in CGIAR's top forum and the CG's central brain-trust, the Technical Advisory Committee. By "voice" I mean a member of that top guidance body, a scholar in sociology or anthropology who would knowingly speak for the potential and the role of the social scientists in the research programs and working plans of each CG Center. This, of course, did not help their work and roles, and limited their influence in the CG's research projects.

The first large, collectively prepared, and widely noticed affirmation of the research "products" of the Rocky Docs was the conference they organized at end of the 1970s with UNDP support titled "*Exploratory Workshop on the Role of Anthropologists and Other Social Scientists in Interdisciplinary Teams Developing Improved Food Production Technology*", held at IRRI, reflected also in a publication (IRRI 1981). The workshop was attended, among others, by some of the standard bearers of social research in the CGIAR and by some outside scholars: Susan Almy, Jacqueline Ashby, Benjamin Bagadion, Gelia Castillo, Grace Goodell, Robert Herdt, Romana de los Reyes, Robert Rhoades, Richard Sawyer and Robert Werge.

Besides the fieldwork research findings reported in the workshop's papers, participants together with some of the CG managers agreed upon a set of policy recommendations to address fundamental questions related to the role of anthropologists in interdisciplinary teams developing improved food production technology. In this way, the event marked a step forward in the status of social scientists in CGIAR, defining the area of CG's social problems and pointing out specific social methodologies beneficial for CGIAR:

> Specific research topics in agricultural development, which directly or indirectly involve human beings in their physical, social, or cultural nature, are as numerous as the concerns of the research institutions as a whole. Anthropologists and other social scientists must contribute to the definition and solution of these problems at all stages. They must work jointly with the institution's scientists of other disciplines....The social anthropologist has a role to play in an organization developing improved food production technology by increasing efficiency through process-oriented rather than product-oriented activities. (IRRI 1981)

Following that very good workshop, research by CG's social specialists gained a lift and diversified during the 1980s. Examples of such research are described in detail by their authors in the volume edited by Cernea and Kassam (2006), such as CIP's incorporating a new path—'from farmer back to farmer'—into the center's research strategies; CIAT's research experiments on farmers' fields, that expanded afterwards to farmer-managed experiments and to farmer-led participatory plant breeding; the pioneering sociological research done by Murray and Vermillion (IWMI) on farmers' organizations proven potential for managing irrigation systems;

the methodological contribution to the research methods of CGIAR, produced by the sociologists working at CIAT, led by Ashby (see Ashby 1986) who dealt with the participation of small farmers; the research at IFPRI, led by Meinzen-Dick, who dealt with collective action and property rights issues, and research that continued for many years (see Meinzen-Dick 2006).

However, as will be seen later, the flowering of interest in social research in the CGIAR system generated by the 'Rocky-Doc' initiative did not take permanent and deep roots in the system. When the RF funding ended, several CG Centers did not take over the costs of the Rocky-Docs positions, as was the premise of the RF's early support strategy. Many had to leave. As a result, the CGIAR system remained weaker than it could be today through organically integrating social research, and ecological research, into the mainstream CGIAR agenda. For this, as will be evident from this chapter's end section, it is regarded quite critically in the outside academic community of social scientists specialized in agriculture, who are university based.

The World Bank's Influence on CG's Research

It was for the first time in the history of the CGIAR, after 27 years of existence, when an eminent sociologist, Michael Cernea, was appointed to its top scientific council: the TAC (Technical Advisory Committee), later renamed as CGIAR's Scientific Council (SC). Cernea's appointment to the TAC was recommended in 1997 by the three international organizations sponsoring the CGIAR: the UNDP, the FAO, and the World Bank. At that time I was the senior staff specialist in the Secretariat of CGIAR's TAC, located at FAO in Rome, and interacted with Cernea since his joining the TAC.

Even before joining the World Bank Michael Cernea already had a prominent national and international status as a sociology scholar specialized in rural societies. Europe's rural sociologists had elected Cernea in 1973 as Vice-President of the European Society for Rural Sociology.[3] In fact, his rural research-focus and specialization—'the economic thinking and rationality of peasants'—had weighed heavily in his hiring in 1974 by the World Bank's central agricultural department. Thus, Michael came to CGIAR after a long and brilliant career of nearly a quarter century in the World Bank, which earned him the high responsibility of Senior Advisor for

---

[3] In his country of origin as well, Romania, Cernea had pioneered in the mid-1960s the resumption of empirical field-based rural sociology, helping revive the long and rich tradition of rural sociology in Romania, a discipline that had been for years denied as a "bourgeois science" under the then socialist regime in Romania; his pioneering role in that revival was recognized domestically and internationally. Among other initiatives, Cernea also organized a comparative monographic research on two villages, one of which had been researched and monographed by Romanian sociologists during the 1930s. The book became a landmark: it was the first such comparative research done in Romania and one of the few of this kind produced in the world at large (Cernea et al. 1970).

Social Policies and Sociology to the World Bank's management; he also had the principal role in building and leading the Bank's large community of social specialists; (at his retirement in 1996 there were already 160 regular staff social specialists; "As of 2020, social development could count on more than 300 professional staff throughout the World Bank Group" (pers. comm. Louise Cord, Director, Social Development, World Bank, October 2020). He had been known in CGIAR long before he joined it, too, because during his decade of work in the Bank's central AGR Department he interacted with CG's social researchers and did involve some in Bank projects and joint social studies (see Meinzen-Dick and Cernea 1984).

The natural basis of CG-World Bank continuous collaboration was the commonality of their central objectives of improving agriculture and reducing rural poverty. Over the years, the Bank became the institution which supported and influenced intellectually and supported financially the CGIAR more than any other organization in many respects, including also in broadening its social research on farmers' needs and capacities. What CG's social specialists placed by RF in CGIAR were advocating—a broader and more intense focus on farmers—was what the Bank was already doing; and this became an impetus for CG too.

On the Bank's side, the main engine driving this Bank-intended influence was the Bank's central agricultural department, led by Montague Yudelman, himself a highly reputed South-African agricultural researcher of small farmers' productivity; AGR's deputy directors, Leif Christoffersen and Don Pickering, as well as its senior advisers on crops and research, John Russell and John Coulter, and later another senior adviser, Jock Anderson, were largely focused on the Bank's numerous projects in Asia and Africa that financed the creation of state managed social systems for the organized extension to farmers of science-based recommendations for their practices. In this context, Michael was tasked to study on-the-ground in India how India's extension projects were implemented and performing, and to design a system for monitoring the extension apparatus and its impact of the farmers' knowledge; monitoring was still an innovation at that time. Written jointly with a statistician, the study that outlined a comprehensive monitoring system became Cernea's first Bank publication (Cernea and Tepping 1977). Shortly thereafter, Michael initiated two collective books on *"knowledge from research to farmers"* (Cernea et al. 1983), which were sent by the Bank to all the countries with Bank-financed extension projects, and to all CG's research centers. Encouraged after these three publications Michael started working on what was to become in the following years the classic, landmark book *"Putting People First. Sociological Variables in Rural Development"* (Cernea 1985/1991), with wide international impact.

To conclude this too rapid overview on how the World Bank's worked with, nudged and influenced CG's gradual paradigm shift and broadening, I'd like to mention another most potent Bank lever for influencing CG's research orientation. CG's founders agreed from the outset, in 1971, that the Chairman of the CGIAR should always be a Vice-President (VP) of the Bank, namely the VP in charge of the Bank's lending for agriculture. Certainly, not everyone of the successive Bank VPs/CG Chairmen personally pushed the social envelope. The big exception was Ismail Serageldin, who became CG's Chairman in 1993; from his very start, he regularly directed all CG Centers to conduct their work along the principle that "CGIAR's main clients are people" (Serageldin 1996) (see also Serageldin's chapter "Social Sciences at the World Bank and the Broadening of the Development Paradigm" in this book).

Once entering in CGIAR, and in an influential position, Michael took a pro-active, militant stand in championing the social science disciplines, sociology and anthropology, searching in every adequate occasion to resource better and expand its assignments of social research projects.

The changes that had occurred even earlier in the CGIAR due to its interaction with the World Bank were also helped by the fact that Cernea and other supporters, mentioned further below, were located in the Bank's central agricultural department (AGR) which was the part of the World Bank most directly connected to the CGIAR Centers. Thus, this point of departure became the turning point at the CGIAR towards the same direction in which agriculture and general lending of the World Bank were going. A comprehensive reflection of what had happened (Cernea 2016) suggests that efforts and changes in various parts of the development aid process amounted to a "broadening of the economic development paradigm" that reigned in the 1960s and beginning of 1970s at the World Bank and elsewhere towards a more encompassing "social development paradigm". The impact of this achievement has continued globally ever since, as captured by Cernea (2016).

However, as will be seen in the last section, the flowering of interest in social research in the CGIAR system resulting from the 'Rocky-Doc' initiative did not take permanent roots in the entire system. As a result, the CGIAR system remains weak not only in the integration of social research into the mainstream CGIAR work but also in ecological research and knowledge which can only function effectively at the practice level with farmers in the presence of social research on farmer innovation, social organizations, and farmer-driven stewardship initiatives for natural resource management and rural development.

He thus became the first-ever sociologist to receive membership in it in the 20-year existence of CGIAR. Further, from 2000 onwards, Michael became also an active member in TAC's Standing Panel on Priorities and Strategies (SPPS) led by Alain de Janvry, of which I was the Coordinating Secretary. I worked closely with Michael Cernea throughout his CGIAR tenure on numerous sessions of the TAC and of the SC, and we much intensified our collaboration in 2001–2002 when Michael and I were in charge of preparing and organizing a system-wide conference of the social scientists (non-economists) working in the CGIAR. Michael had initiated that conference by proposing repeatedly its organization until TAC finally agreed. The Conference on Social Research took place at CIAT, in Cali, in 2002, the largest in CGIAR history. Subsequently, I worked with Michael for editing a substantial volume on the status, accomplishments, weaknesses, and future perspectives of social research in the CGIAR (Cernea and Kassam 2006). It remains to date the most comprehensive volume about the history and contribution of sociological and anthropological research to the CGIAR system.

It was not difficult for me to feel sympathetic and in-tune with what Michael Cernea was concerned about in TAC because, despite my different scientific background, his arguments always made eminent sense from an agro-ecological viewpoint. Michael acted on his belief that social researchers' mission was to produce knowledge usable as an international public good, by, and for, farming communities. I do not believe that TAC had ever experienced anyone like Michael before. He conceived his role in CGIAR as being the lead militant for promoting non-economic social science knowledge as an indispensable component of the broader body of knowledge that had to be generated for the farmers' world, as the Centre's scientific products and recommendations. As a consequence, Cernea was deeply concerned about the relevance and effectiveness of CGIAR research in real life, particularly because often CGIAR's social research, with some exceptions, received little support from cost Centers' managers, and was often marginalized and chronically underfunded. This was happening despite the fact that the social research that had been carried out in prior years in CGIAR had proven many times its value and indispensability, beyond any doubt. A good number of truly excellent social scientists had joined in earlier years the CGIAR ranks through the "post doc" program financed by the Rockefeller Foundation, and many of them proved their mettle brilliantly by producing insightful research and findings highly relevant to CGIAR objectives. The names of stalwart social anthropologists and sociologists such as Robert Rhoades, Jacqueline Ashby, Ruth Meinzen-Dick, Joachim Voss, Carol Colfer, Pablo Eyzaguirre, Douglas Merrey and some others had written important pages in the annals of CGIAR research. One of them, Joachim Voss, acceded even to the position of Director General for the major CIAT Center, but altogether, despite successes and demonstrated usefulness and usability, social research had been constantly under pressure and gradually squeezed in terms of its institutional position. When the "Rocky-Doc" program stopped, the CGIAR defaulted on its prior commitment to continue expanding and funding more social researchers from its own resources.

From the outset, Cernea developed close links with these and other social researchers, and relied on them and his advocacy and organizational initiatives taken as a member of the TAC or Science Council. This collaboration helped reinforce the cause of social research but the high days of the "Rocky-Doc" program were over, and competition for resources inside the CGIAR was acerbic and the "climate" was not favoring social research expression by any measure. The struggle continued to be an uphill struggle. A key argument was that social research findings should not be seen as just an add-on, but rather as a quality-enhancing intrinsic part of any research and any resulting strategy. We also co-authored a paper on 'Guarding the Relevance and Quality of Science in the CGIAR' (Kassam et al. 2004). In it, among others, Cernea argued that CGIAR must put in place a vastly more "biting" and effective *ex-ante* peer review process of all research proposals to ensure that from the very start of a research project, the social dimensions are incorporated in the research plan and that every new research project is justified by its social and economic relevance to farming communities.

Our typical work pattern in TAC's 2–3 annual sessions included the analysis of the comprehensive external evaluation reports on scientific research by one or another of the CGIAR Centers. It was quite frequent for Michael to challenge the

Director General or Board-Chair of the analyzed Center, for marginalizing social research and underestimating its value. Since certain weaknesses were almost chronic rather than temporary or contextual, sparks were flying quite often. It was difficult to imagine a better-crafted argument in favor of social research than Cernea was able to provide based deeply on his familiarity with agricultural development projects in different countries in which he had worked over the years on behalf of the World Bank. The dominant feature was the constructiveness of his discussion, which invariably offered substance for including in the meetings' decision recommendations and commitments to expand the scope of social research and the resources allocated to the Center's social scientists.

His analyses revealed not just passing weaknesses but structural ones in the way research was designed or on the tenure and management over natural resources— water, trees, soil—that were studied by CGIAR's physical scientists. Michael would often argue that high-yielding varieties cannot succeed if we do not create for them "high-yielding patterns of social organization" through which farmers would get the adequate means required for cultivating them.

The allocation of social researchers to the Center's key themes was also an object of frequent controversy. Often, Center Directors tended to assign the social scientists excessively to the tail-end of the research process, simply to measure impact, while Michael would argue that their contribution should be incorporated from the very start of the research process so as to factor in farmers' needs, constraints, and factors like access to credit and markets. Only ex-ante factoring in knowledge on such social values, argued Cernea, could the biological and physical research become germane to the potentials and capabilities of local farming systems and communities.

The Resonance of the CGIAR's Social Research Conference. An Illuminating Public Discussion

The brief description above, however, elaborates on the structural parameters of Michael Cernea's work in the CGIAR. However, the most interesting question is: what did he actually do and accomplish? What were Cernea's views about the status, vocation, the successes and the failures, and mostly the challenges of doing social research within a set of scientific institutions dominated by biological and natural resource scientists as well as economists who claimed to do research on crops, animals, fish, trees, etc. and on natural resource and ecosystem management etc. all in the name of poverty alleviation, food and nutrition security?

The answer is not simple. Summarizing in just a few pages the content of some 8–9 years of work that Michael Cernea invested in CGIAR and in the valedictorian volume he left behind is a hard test. To confront this challenge, I will not follow the chronological path but rather go straight to that interval's end, when Cernea wrote his summing-up valedictorian assessment of social research in CGIAR. And I take permission to not put forward here only my personal opinions on Cernea's contributions, but instead rely on a public discussion and assessment by other academics, from outside CGIAR, of Cernea's leading role and ideas-impact. I can do this because *Culture & Agriculture*, a specialized journal of the American Anthropological Association, published in its pages the lead chapter that Michael wrote for our jointly-edited volume on social research in CGIAR (Cernea and Kassam 2006) and invited its readership to participate in a public debate of its content.

The "Call to Open Discussion" was signed by the journal's Chief Editor, Prof. James McDonald (McDonald, 2005). About a dozen scholars sent articles and Culture & Agriculture published them in three issues spanning three years (Fall 2005, vol. 27 no. 2; Spring 2006, vol. 28 no. 1; and Spring 2007, vol. 29, no. 1). A lot of scholars responded promptly: Murray Leaf (Leaf, 2006), Stephen Brush (Brush, 2006), William Loker (Loker, 2006), Ben Wallace (Wallace, 2006), Donald Cleveland (Cleveland, 2006), Jude Fernando (Fernando, 2007), Kendall Thu (Thu, 2006), Lois Stanford (Stanford, 2006), Mina Swaminathan (Swaminathan, 2007). Their comments are particularly relevant also because their authors are prominent social scientists who are independent of CGIAR, as full professors and scholars in various U.S. universities, who observe CGIAR as part of the academic community.

Michael's study ignited the public discussion because it was an expression of the personal creed of a well-known scholar a true "manifesto" on behalf of social science's entitlement to solid "citizenship" in the CGIAR. Without mincing words, he protested the fact that social research, despite its indispensability, was nonetheless "*a domain that still today has to keep fighting hard for asserting itself against institutional barriers, against scholarly biases from other researchers or some centers' managers and against virtually constant underfunding.*" He documented the innovative contributions of social research to improving farmers' livelihoods, while also blasting the "*major obstacles and institutionalized weaknesses in how social research is being carried out.*"

Cernea also postulated another important idea that critiqued the dominant practice in most CGIAR Centers: namely, that social research should not be exclusively a "component" immersed in the vaunted inter-disciplinary research in the CGIAR but must be empowered to also do full-scale stand-alone studies on certain independent social variables of agricultural production and development. He had no hesitation to denounce the "*shrinkage of human and financial resources allocated to social research in various centers*" on the grounds that "*behavioral and social cultural variables of resource management are no less important for sustainability than physical parameters.*" "*The actual human capacity for social research in the CGIAR system at large and in some centers in particular*" he wrote, "*is either long-stagnant or has been severely depleted.*" He hailed the function of social researchers as "*human knowledge conveyer-belts*" between the CGIAR and outside scientific research and practice. He also constantly argued for bringing into the CGIAR some of the "*important developments taking place in outside research in sociology, anthropology and social geography.*" To Michael, CGIAR's goal of germplasm enhancement, production intensification and natural resources management would not be complete without intensified socio-cultural research that would keep

CGIAR's research programs and strategies relevant to pro-poor development and impact oriented.

Throughout his tenure in the TAC and in the Science Council, Michael Cernea was consistent in taking an exacting analytical position to evaluating the contribution provided by social research to the objectives of each international research center, while at the same time incisively examining the usually scarce support provided by the respective center to social researchers and to integrating the social findings with the finding of biological and natural scientists.

Cernea's valedictorian study submitted for public discussion was, as usual, provocatively titled, critiquing closed "entrance gates" and claiming the right to recognized status for sociological research: *"Rites of Entrances and Rights of Citizenship: The Uphill Battle for Social Research in CGIAR"* (*Culture & Agriculture*, 73–87). He critiqued the obstacles to a broader "entrance" of social research in CGIAR, arguing that the nature of the agricultural process, performed by the widest profession in human history—the profession of farmer—gives social sciences a preeminent and legitimate "right of citizenship" inside CGIAR Centers.

The discussants liked Cernea's key ideas and conclusions, and embraced the entire book, which in the words of Mina Swaminathan from India,

> gives rich and comprehensive image of the heroic contributions of social scientists in the CGIAR over three decades, accomplished against many odds and obstacles. But the book and [Cernea's] article also paint a dismal picture of the structured institutional constraints and deep-seated intellectual biases against social research in many centers belonging to the international agricultural research system (Mina Swaminathan, 1).

It was no surprise that others joined, in their own words. The breath of fresh air coming out from Cernea's sharp and candid study was received very well by the scholars outside of the CGIAR, no less than by those inside of it, expressing extraordinary support from CGIAR scholars to his critique and recommendations:

> "...Cernea has done the readers of Culture & Agriculture a great service by publishing this piece in our journal"—wrote William Locker, Professor of Anthropology and Dean at the California State University—"And the editors deserve congratulations for inviting debate and discussion on the important topics raised [...] in Cernea's article. Most of us...retain a belief in the power of methodologically sound empirical research as a public good: when deployed intelligently, it has the potential to ameliorate social problems. [This]...bears out the need to focus our intellectual energies on understanding and resolving the social and environmental crises affecting broad swaths of the globe" (William Loker, 17–19).

To this another discussant, Kendall Thu from Northern Illinois University, added:

> ...The challenges posed by Michael Cernea's thought-provoking article on social research in CGIAR reflect a broader ongoing challenge in anthropology to make our efforts resonate more widely with a greater impact on policy...My primary theme takes a cue from Michael Cernea's ontological point that culture has a reality in the everyday lives of agricultural practitioners. My view is that we would do well to turn this around and not just reintegrate culture into agriculture but also integrate agriculture and food systems into broader cultural research, theory, and practice (Kendall Thu, 25–27).

The participants in the public discussion appreciated Cernea's role in CGIAR in promoting social research, emphasizing the intellectual continuity between what

Michael as social scientist militated for and achieved previously at the World Bank and what he undertook to do to change CGIAR patterns as well. Murray J. Leaf, professor of anthropology and political economy at the University of Texas, noted that,

> Cernea has been central to the effort of urging the Bank to incorporate more noneconomic social science expertise in the design of projects. He also had a central role in organizing external scholars around themes that the Bank leadership could find intelligible. These primarily revolved around the problem of letting the Bank staff see the projects from the prospective of the intended [...] beneficiaries.
>
> Cernea's article raises concern about the use of social scientists across the entire development spectrum and entails fundamental issues of social theory. Note that Cernea is not calling for just any kind of social theory, but theory that will provide: better understanding of the decision-making process of individuals and groups; identifying the characteristics and needs of the ultimate beneficiaries, poor farmers and poor urban food consumers; the institutional arrangements needed to foster social capital creation; and improved property rights and custodianship regimes and their management and distributional implications. It also should be theory that 'puts people first' and facilitates the design of development projects which do so ... [We know] what CGIAR could do. What could anthropology do? (Murray Leaf, 11, 14)

Cernea's robust argument obviously prompted CGIAR's outsiders to do their own self-questioning about the future of their own research.

Murray Leaf's "What could anthropologists do?" was further echoed by Kendall Thu:

> Cernea's insights from his experiences in CGIAR raise fundamental questions about the future of agricultural research in anthropology. The challenge Cernea poses transcends agriculture and resonates within our field as a whole. As such, the issue should not be what we can do to increase the viability of social research in agriculture. Rather, I believe our research, methods, and findings will lead the way, but what are the overarching questions and issues we are tackling?
>
> I agree wholeheartedly with poverty reduction as a research goal of CGIAR and anthropologists in general. However, the fact that we face obstacles in becoming systemically effective in policy matters raises the question: why is this and what do we do about it? (Kendall Thu, 25–27)

Ben Wallace, a professor at Southern Methodist University, added to this strand of the debate a mobilizing comment addressed to the world's anthropological community at large about the overriding responsibility of social scientists to their ultimate "clients"—the people. In a remarkably strong statement, he said:

> ...In conclusion, the call here is for those of us who work in the field of rural development to remind ourselves occasionally, and others, that while we may work as an anthropologist, a plant pathologist, or an entomologist, and although we are paid by a particular institution, we are fundamentally responsible to the people of the world. If we fail them, we have failed not only ourselves but also those who are most dependent on us for help. Those of us who have chosen to work in the applied environmental sciences have a client—the people of the world. The only way to ensure that our clients are served is to ensure that people remain the central focus of our research and development endeavors (Ben Wallace, 31).

To which Murray Leaf memorably concluded his powerful article with:

> To change the place of anthropology in development and in development policy, we have to change anthropology [itself] (Murray Leaf, 16).

Other participants extended the debate to another very relevant area: the insufficient attention to social research in the National Agricultural Research Systems (NARS). Despite the abundance of rural sociologists in developing countries, the NARS did not use their skills within the national research centers. The strongest critique of this situation was formulated by Mina Swaminathan, an advisor of India's major M. S. Swaminathan Research Foundation, who wrote that that situation would be "laughable if it were not so tragic."

> ...Ignoring the content and methods of social science research has been damaging enough for national research systems, damage many times multiplied in the case of international systems. Just imagine dozens of highly trained and well-equipped scientists, arriving with all sincerity, zeal, and commitment in various parts of the developing world, and attempting to solve their agricultural problems without any understanding of those societies, their structures, and systems! It would be laughable if it weren't so tragic (Mina Swaminathan, 3).

The above excerpts are only a partial image of the intellectual richness of C&A's public discussion. This debate showed that Cernea's analyses resonated with the anthropological profession at large. It also offers a robust platform to the CG management for follow up.

The book 'Researching the Culture in Agri-*Culture*' did not embrace the official rhetoric pretending that all is well with social sciences research in the CGIAR. The CGIAR system would do well to recognize the gaps that persist in its current performance in social science research and take the necessary measures to overcome them. Moreover, many of the substantive issues raised by the above mentioned outside scholars, who are specialists in their topics, and most powerfully by Cernea, are still valid and unaddressed.

His own interest in continuing to write and publish academically the lessons and generalizations he was deriving from his operational development work and field research in many countries had strengthened also his scholarly status.

Concluding Remarks

Today, we have more reasons than ever to drive further the needed paradigm change in agriculture, for both social and ecologically reasons. This applies to the developing world as well as to the industrialized world. Social and ecological research for sustainable production intensification and for environmental stewardship is a reality and must be made to become a greater force for good for all mankind.

Many of us have learned from Michael Cernea that in any human development activity, including those related to agricultural research, the object and the subject must merge and remain united to ensure 'positive-sum outcomes' as much as possible. There is indeed much to rethink, learn and teach about the future multi-functional role of agricultural land use which must respect and use the resources of the socio-cultural environment as much as the ecological and economic environment, and to reflect upon past short-comings and achievements. The combat is far from over! For example, for the alternate agro-ecological paradigm involving

Conservation Agriculture to spread and replace the old intrusive and narrow out of date Green Revolution paradigm will require, as Cernea has urged, "people who have not only brains but who can fight, people who have not only knowledge but also have conviction, and people whose anthropological knowledge is accompanied by a moral dimension".

This is Cernea's challenge to us all—to carry on our work with readiness to engage scientifically and proactively, in the spirit of "militant social scientists", with farmers and their communities.

References

Ashby, J. (1986). Methodology for participation of small farmers in design of on-farm research. *Agricultural Administration, 22*(1), 1–19.

Bebbington, A. (2006). On Michael Cernea. In D. Simon (Ed.), *Fifty key thinkers on development* (p. 67). Abingdon, UK: Routledge, Tyler and Francis.

Brush, S. B. (2006). Cernea comment. *Culture & Agriculture, 28*(1), 1–3.

Cernea, M. M. (1985/1991). *Putting people first. Sociological variables in rural development*. New York: Oxford University Press.

Cernea, M. M. (2005). Rites of entrance and rights of citizenship: The uphill battle for social research in the CGIAR. *Culture & Agriculture, 27*(2), 73–87.

Cernea, M. (2016). The state and involuntary resettlement: Reflections on comparing legislation on development-displacement in China and India. In E. Padovani (Ed.), *Development-induced displacement in India and China: A comparative look at the burdens of growth*. Lanham: Lexington Books.

Cernea, M. M., & Kassam, A. H. (Eds.). (2006). *Researching the culture in agriculture: Social research for international development* (p. 497). Wallingford: CABI.

Cernea, M. M., & Tepping, B. J. (1977). *A system for monitoring and evaluating agricultural extension projects in India*. Washington, DC: World Bank.

Cernea, M., Kepes, G., Larionescu, M., et al. (1970). *Două Sate: Structuri Sociale si Progres Tehnic* [Two villages: Social structures and technical progress] (Under the editorship of H. S. Henri, M. M. Cernea, & G. Kepes). Bucuresti: Editura Politica.

Cernea, M. M., Coulter, J. K., & Russell, J. F. A. (Eds.). (1983). *Agricultural extension by training and visit: The Asian experience*. Washington, DC: World Bank.

Cleveland, D. A. (2006). What kind of social science does the CGIAR, and the world, need? *Culture & Agriculture, 28*(1), 4–9.

Conway, G., Adesina, A., Lynam, J., & Mook, J. (2006). The Rockefeller Foundation and social research in agriculture. In M. Cernea & A. Kassam (Eds.), *Researching the culture in agriculture: Social research for international development* (pp. 373–381). Wallingford: CABI.

Fernando, J, L. (2007). Culture in agriculture vs. capital in agriculture: CGIAR's challenges to social scientists in culture, *Culture in Agriculture, 29*(2)

Guggenheim, S. (2006). Roots: Reflections of a "Rocky Doc" on social science in CGIAR. In M. Cernea & A. Kassam (Eds.), *Researching the culture in agriculture: Social research for international development* (pp. 421–430). Wallingford: CABI.

IRRI. (1981). *The role of anthropologists and other social scientists in interdisciplinary teams developing improved food production technology*. Los Banos, Philippines: International Rice Research Institute.

Kassam, A., Gregersen, H. M., Fereres, E., Javier, J. Q., Harwood, R. R., de Janvry, A., & Cernea, M. M. (2004). A framework for enhancing and guarding the relevance and quality of science: the case of the CGIAR. *Experimental Agriculture, 40*, 1–21.

Leaf, M. J. (2006). Michael Cernea's excerpt: What it means for us. *Culture & Agriculture, 28*(1), 10–16.

Loker, W. (2006). Comments on Cernea: 'Keeping agriculture in anthropology'. *Culture & Agriculture, 28*(1), 17–19.

McDonald, J. H. (2005). Keeping culture in agriculture. *Culture & Agriculture, 27*(2), 71–72.

Meinzen-Dick, R. (2006). Studying property rights and collective action: A systemwide programme. In M. Cernea & A. Kassam (Eds.), *Researching the culture in agriculture: Social research for international development* (pp. 285–298). Wallingford: CABI.

Meinzen-Dick, R., & Cernea, M. (1984). *Design for water users associations: Organizational characteristics. Environment department.* Washington DC: World Bank.

Serageldin, I. (1996, July 22). The challenge for rural sociology in an urbanizing world. Keynote address delivered at the 9th world congress of rural sociology on rural potentials for the global future held in Bucharest, Romania.

Simon, D. (2006). *Fifty key thinkers on development.* New York: Routledge.

Stanford, L. (2006). Response to Michael Cernea. *Culture & Agriculture, 28*(1), 20–24.

Swaminathan, M. (2007). Cernea's thesis: A perspective from the South. *Culture & Agriculture, 29* (1), 1–5.

Thu, K. (2006). Agriculture in culture. *Culture & Agriculture, 28*(1), 25–27.

Wallace, B. J. (2006). Keeping people in culture and agriculture. *Culture & Agriculture, 28*(1), 31–34.

Prof. Amir Kassam OBE, FRSB, PhD. Dr. Kassam is a Fellow of the Royal Society of Biology (FRSB), UK. Born in Zanzibar, Tanzania, Kassam received his BSc (Hons) in Agriculture and his PhD in Agro-ecology from the University of Reading, and MSc in Irrigation from the University of California-Davis. During his career, Dr. Kassam has worked with several national agricultural research and development institutions in the fields of sustainable agriculture, land resources evaluation, crop and suitability assessments, research management and education and extension training. His positions have included: Deputy Director General at WARDA (the AfricaRice Centre, CGIAR); FAO; Senior Agricultural Research Officer at the CGIAR Technical Advisory Committee (TAC) Secretariat, and at the CGIAR Science Council Secretariat, FAO; Chairman of: the Aga Khan Foundation (UK); Chairman of the Focus Humanitarian Assistance Europe Foundation; and Chairman of the Tropical Agriculture Association (TAA), UK.

Dr. Kassam's is currently a Visiting Professor in the School of Agriculture, Policy and Development, University of Reading, UK, where he teaches Conservation Agriculture as an alternative paradigm of agriculture. He is also the Moderator of the Global Platform for the Conservation Agriculture Community of Practice (Global CA-CoP) hosted by FAO. His current research, education and development work is focused on globalizing and mainstreaming the application of Conservation Agriculture for sustainable agricultural and land management to address national and global development needs and challenges. In 2005, Dr. Kassam was awarded an OBE in the Queen's Honours List for services to tropical agriculture and to rural development.

Open Access This chapter is licensed under the terms of the Creative Commons Attribution 4.0 International License (http://creativecommons.org/licenses/by/4.0/), which permits use, sharing, adaptation, distribution and reproduction in any medium or format, as long as you give appropriate credit to the original author(s) and the source, provide a link to the Creative Commons license and indicate if changes were made.

The images or other third party material in this chapter are included in the chapter's Creative Commons license, unless indicated otherwise in a credit line to the material. If material is not included in the chapter's Creative Commons license and your intended use is not permitted by statutory regulation or exceeds the permitted use, you will need to obtain permission directly from the copyright holder.

Fighting Poverty, Combatting Social Exclusion

William L. Partridge

The Chinese have a saying: through a drop of water you can see the whole ocean. This chapter analyzes the process of integrating social development policy and practice into the operations of the World Bank through the lens of my own personal experience, a drop of water through which we will see how sociologists and anthropologists transformed the larger organizational culture of the institution.

My work in the World Bank grew out of my research on the social and cultural impacts of involuntary resettlement. The filling of the reservoir of Mexico's Aleman Dam, constructed on the Papaloapan River in the mid-1950s, forced some 20,000 Mazatec indigenous people to abandon their homes and farms. They were provided new homes and farmlands in five different resettlement sites by the Government of Mexico. When I visited them in the mid-1970s four out of the five new settlements were complete failures. One was successful.

Prior to their resettlement, the Mazatec had been independent small-scale peasant farmers, marketing coffee, maize, sesame, and other cash crops to urban markets. But the inhabitants of the four failed settlements had been impoverished: they no longer farmed the replacement land that had been allocated to them, education and health conditions were dismal, and they had been reduced to wage labor on neighboring plantations and cattle estates. In contrast, the Mazatec in the successful settlement were producing surplus maize, plantain, mango, citrus, sugar cane, and other crops sufficient to permit investments/savings in the form of livestock. They enjoyed levels of income, education, and health significantly higher than those of neighboring communities that had not been resettled.

How can one explain the dramatically different outcomes? With support from the National Science Foundation (USA), this was the focus of my field research which continued through 1977–1978. Without my being aware of it, the published research results were read by staff of the World Bank, Inter-American Development Bank,

---

W. L. Partridge (✉)
Vanderbilt University, Nashville, Tennessee, USA

World Health Organization, Organization of American States and others.[1] Those staff were aware that involuntary resettlement operations caused by hydroelectricity, irrigation, water supply, transport corridor, and other large-scale infrastructure projects were almost always failures, leaving the displaced people impoverished.

This was the opposite of what was supposed to be the purpose of a development investment in the first place. I began to receive requests to consult on resettlement operations in projects underway, to speak at seminars and training courses at headquarter offices, and to participate in the preparation of new projects. Throughout 1983, 1984, and 1985 my time was increasingly absorbed by consultancies for these multilateral government organizations, and I increasingly postponed academic pursuits to concentrate on practicing anthropology.

Critic and Gadfly

Two examples will illustrate what that work was like.

- In India the Maharashtra Composite Irrigation III project was underway, displacing and presumably resettling over 18,000 people from land flooded by the storage reservoir. The World Bank had received protests claiming that displaced farmers had not been resettled to new lands, but the Government of India claimed 90% had been provided land to replace the farms that had been flooded. I was sent to investigate. Not speaking Hindi or Marahrati, I recruited Professor L. K. Mahapatra (University of Orissa) who had studied resettlement disasters elsewhere in India and he agreed to assist me in a field survey of the affected villages. I paid his fees and expenses from my consulting earnings. We surveyed 13 of the 20 affected villages. We found that only 5% of farmers had received compensation sufficient to buy replacement land; fully 95% were made landless and impoverished. Back in Washington my report resulted in disciplinary measures for the team leader responsible for the preparation, appraisal, and supervision of the project. The World Bank department responsible requested that the Government of India take corrective measures to help the victims in regaining their lost lands, to which the Government of India responded by ignoring the request. By then the loan had been entirely disbursed and the World Bank staff

---

[1]Partridge, W. L., A. Brown, and J. Nugent (1982) The Papaloapan Dam and Resettlement Project: Human Ecology and Health Impacts. In *Involuntary Migration and Resettlement*. A. Hansen and A. Oliver-Smith (eds). pp. 245–263. Boulder, Colorado: Westview Press; Partridge, W. L. and A. Brown (1982). Agricultural Development Among the Mazatec: Lessons from Resettlement, *Culture and Agriculture* 16, pp. 1–9; Partridge, W. L. (1983) Desarrollo Agrícola Entre Los Mazatecos Reacomodados, *American Indígena* XLIII, 2, pp. 343–362; Partridge, W. L. (1984) "Relocalización en las Distintas Etapas de Desarrollo de los Emprendimientos Hidroeléctricos" en *Efectos Sociales de las Grandes Represas en América Latina*. F. Suárez, R. Franco, E. Cohen (eds). Buenos Aires: Organización de los Estados Americanos y Naciones Unidas. pp. 151–182.

felt they had little leverage left to force the issue. The affected people were left impoverished.[2]

- The Inter-American Development Bank (IDB) contracted a comparative analysis of a successful resettlement project, the Arenal Hydroelectric Project resettlement in Costa Rica, and what they considered to be a failed resettlement operation, the Chixoy Hydroelectric Project in Guatemala, for the purpose of advising on establishing an IDB resettlement policy. After presenting my findings at an IDB seminar in Washington I was asked by the World Bank, which together with IDB had co-financed the Guatemala project, to present the analysis of the Chixoy experience to the staff of the department responsible for Guatemala. The presentation reported the human disaster that was resettlement at Chixoy: two years after the reservoir filled I found 3700 Maya huddled in temporary shacks just above the reservoir margin, their corn fields, fruit trees, and pastures under water, surviving by selling off their livestock, with no schools, no potable water, no roads. The World Bank team responsible had not once visited the resettlement operation, and the unfolding disaster was never mentioned in the team's supervision reports to management over the previous 4 years. The World Bank project team in attendance was incensed; they angrily defended themselves and attacked me. At that point a man stood up in the rear of the room, who turned out to be the Vice President for the Latin America and the Caribbean Region, and said: "What we have here is a fuck up, and I want it fixed." He then left the room. The fix turned out to be holding up a new loan to the Government of Guatemala until they signed a legal agreement incorporating a resettlement plan designed to restore the lands, production systems, and livelihoods of the affected Maya. I was asked to help prepare and appraise the new plan in the following months.[3]

These and other consultancies convinced me that one could practice anthropology in the World Bank, that there was need and scope for making positive contributions, and that there were managers and staff willing to use empirical findings to make better decisions. In 1986 I was invited to work as a full-time consultant by the World Bank's Social Policy Adviser, Michael M. Cernea, a sociologist from Romania and the first non-economist social scientist hired by the World Bank. It was a one- year contract, but I accepted without hesitation, resigned as Chair of the Anthropology Department at Georgia State University, and with my family's support moved to Washington DC.

---

[2]Professor Mahapatra and other social scientists in India with support from colleagues in the multilateral governmental organizations continued working to influence governments at the national, state, and local level to assist these displaced people and others in other similar projects to regain their lost livelihoods.

[3]While the Guatemalan Electricity Institute that owned the Chixoy project agreed to the new plan at the time of appraisal, the lawyer for the government succeeded in excluding any mention of it in the legal agreement for the new loan. The Government of Guatemala consequently ignored the agreement entirely. See Partridge, W.L. (2006). "The Guatemala Chixoy Project Resettlement Disaster," presented to the American Association for the Advancement of Science workshop on *Reparations and Resettlement*. American School of Social Research, Santa Fe, New Mexico.

The following year when the World Bank created its first Environment Divisions in each of its Regional Vice Presidencies I was offered and accepted a permanent staff position as Anthropologist in the newly-formed Environment Division for the Asia and Pacific Region. I learned soon that working within the institution would be unlike what I had experienced as an external consultant.

Staff Member

My anthropological training had been in Latin American, I was fluent in Spanish, and had 15 years of research experience in Latin America. So it may seem a bit odd that I would be hired by the World Bank initially in the Asia and Pacific Region. What that tells you is that the Bank hired me not because I was a cultural or regional expert but because I could help them solve a problem. That problem was most pressing in the Asia and Pacific Region, where there were many ongoing resettlement operations, all of them failing, and many more in the pipeline. World Bank management could care less if I was an anthropologist or a Martian—what they wanted was someone who could help member governments come up with workable resettlement plans.

My role had changed from being a gadfly and critic of World Bank management and staff actions or omissions, independent and not responsible for decision making, to a member of the staff responsible for making decisions. Now I was to work directly with the engineers, lawyers, and other civil servants of member governments—Ministries of Public Works, Secretariats of Agriculture, Electricity Corporations, Departments of Irrigation—to correct past errors and avoid future ones. In that role I was to confront opposition from my government counterparts ranging from polite indifference to undisguised hostility. Many viewed forced resettlement as a kind of "collateral damage" that was an unavoidable cost of development and, moreover, the exclusive provenience of government. And opposition from government counterparts translated into opposition from some World Bank staff, many of whom resented having to share scarce Bank budgets historically monopolized by economists, engineers, financial analysts, etc. with anthropologists, environmental scientists, and other "new guys on the block."

To be viable, an involuntary resettlement operation must fit a country's legal, regulatory, and policy framework, specifically, the statues governing land acquisition, compensation, and resettlement. My anthropological training had not prepared me for legal research. Some of my greatest allies were found in the World Bank's legal department. They guided me to the relevant statutes in India, Indonesia, Nepal, Philippines, China, etc. Reading them became my nightly homework.

I quickly learned that the majority of countries legal frameworks for land acquisition, the major cause of involuntary resettlement, are entirely silent on the resettlement and re-establishment of displaced people.[4] Yet member countries and the World Bank staff must comply with the World Bank's operations policy on involuntary resettlement issued by its Board of Executive Directors, representing all member countries.[5] That operations policy explicitly requires (1) avoidance or minimization of resettlement where possible and (2) where resettlement cannot be avoided, the formulation and implementation of a resettlement plan designed to improve, or at least restore to pre-project levels, the livelihoods and standards of living of people displaced by the project. Thus major portions of my work became helping draft and negotiate resettlement policy frameworks and plans—their designs, staffing, and financing—to socioeconomically re-establish affected people.

Opportunities Discovered

Much of my work was shuttling between projects, sometimes alone but usually as part of a World Bank team, to supervise, prepare, appraise, and monitor and evaluate resettlement operations. I was in the field about 200 days a year. Most countries in which I worked had well-developed faculties of anthropology, and I made it a priority to recruit in-country colleagues to work with me. Typically I would disappear for a week or two into the villages affected by a project, accompanied by my in-country anthropological colleagues, while my fellow team members remained in the capital city conversing with government officials. Consequently, my findings from the field often did not match the information conveyed to my colleagues by our government counterparts. And this usually meant rather tense meetings in the capital city and back at headquarters. With the support of World Bank management, and sometimes despite resistance from Bank staff, the result was the first generation of solid resettlement and re-establishment plans incorporated into projects and, most importantly, into legal agreements between the Bank and its borrowers.[6]

---

[4]Shihata, Ibrahim F. I. (2000). "Involuntary Resettlement in World Bank Financed Projects." In *The World Bank in a Changing World: Selected Essays by I.F.I Shihata, Vice President and General Counsel, The World Bank*. Dordrecht/Boston/London: Martinus Nijhoff Publishers.

[5]World Bank (1980). *Operational Manual Statement 4.30: Involuntary Resettlement*. Washington DC; World Bank (1990) *Operational Directive 4.30: Involuntary Resettlement*. Washington DC; World Bank (2001) *Operations Policy 4.12: Involuntary Resettlement*. Washington DC.

[6]Forced resettlement is always perceived as a disaster by displaced people. But human communities are not homogeneous and neither are their responses to disaster. Generally the elite take their compensation money and leave, rather than be subjects of a government resettlement program. At the other end of the spectrum, some of the most vulnerable will fail for lack of capacity to take advantage of the investments in resettlement programs. Most others, however, often discover a silver lining in the disaster. The effect of the exit of corrupt elites—large landowners, commercial middlemen, shopkeepers, money lenders—is like taking the lid off a boiling pot. The capable, hardworking majority are liberated to make the most of new opportunities represented by the resettlement investments, opportunities that previously would have been captured entirely by the corrupt elite. See Partridge, W. L. (1989) "Involuntary Resettlement in Development Projects: Text

Equally important was contributing to the operationalization of the World Bank's resettlement policy. Michael Cernea was the principal author of the Bank's operations policy on involuntary resettlement issued by the Board of Executive Directors.[7] While the policy was explicit regarding the risks of impoverishment and the overarching objective of involuntary resettlement operations to restore lost production systems, housing, infrastructure, etc. to avoid impoverishment, it was less explicit regarding how to achieve those objectives. One of my first assignments, therefore, was to design and write up guidelines of what steps World Bank staff and governments should take to comply with the policy, what were the component elements of a workable resettlement plan, and what actions were required to achieve the policy objectives. That guideline was included as an Annex to Cernea's landmark *Involuntary Resettlement in Development Projects: Policy Guidelines in World Bank-Financed Projects*.[8] Its basic message was: because forced resettlement destroys a previous way of life, all resettlement operations must be designed and appraised as development projects. This and other technical materials we produced became the basis for a series of training seminars and workshops for Bank staff, managers, and consultants in the coming years. The feedback from staff and consultants regarding accumulating experience was an ongoing learning process that contributed to our refinement of the policy and its reissuance by the Board in 1990 and again in 2001.

An additional responsibility was identifying and recruiting anthropologists from the member countries of the World Bank who could strengthen our capacity. When I was appointed Environmental Assessment Manager and later Chief of the Environment and Social Development Unit of the Latin America and Caribbean Region most of my staff were Greek, British, and US nationals. Few spoke Spanish or Portuguese and most knew little of the societies where they were working. There existed in the World Bank the belief that staff should not work in their own countries or region in order to remain "objective." I believed the opposite—to be effective one had to know the society, its language, and system of governance. So I began to hire high caliber Latin American professionals, eventually assembling a team of 23 sociologists, anthropologists, environmental engineers, biologists, ecologists, and economists from Brazil, Colombia, Ecuador, Costa Rica, Chile, and so forth.

Finally, a fourth area of activity was reviewing proposed World Bank loans to ensure that they were in compliance with the institution's involuntary resettlement, environmental assessment, and indigenous peoples policies. When the Board of Directors created the environment and social development units in each Regional Vice Presidency, it also instituted a process of mandatory screening and technical

---

of the First Annual Elizabeth Colson Lecture, Oxford University, 8th of March 1989." *Journal of Refugee Studies* 2:3:373–384.

[7]Cernea was assisted by anthropologists Thayer Scudder (California Institute of Technology) who had studied the disastrous Kariba Dam resettlement and David Butcher (Edinburgh University) who had documented the equally tragic Akosombo Dam resettlement in drafting the policy statement.

[8]Cernea, Michael (1988). *Involuntary Resettlement in Development Projects: Policy Guidelines in World Bank-Financed Projects*. World Bank Technical Paper Number 80. Washington, DC: World Bank.

review by environmental and social specialists of future lending operations. This gave our small Environment and Social Development Unit unprecedented influence in decision making. More than once we found project preparation to be incomplete—institutional capacities weak, technical designs questionable or absent, social impacts denied or ignored, financial management systems nonexistent—or even in violation of World Bank social and environmental policies. More than once World Bank management backed us up and sent the project back to the drawing boards. Such review responsibility also represented a tremendous work load for the few environmental and social specialists then employed, and fueled our recruitment of more. In the space of 5 years the number of environmental and social scientists in the Bank grew from a handful to more than 200 professionals.

New Challenges

The Environment and Social Development Unit's responsibilities extended considerably beyond involuntary resettlement. We provided the experience and expertise to ensure that a formal Environmental Assessment (EA) was carried out for all projects that entailed significant social and/or environmental impacts.[9] A core element of the EA process is prior and informed consultation with and participation of stakeholders likely to be affected and, especially, local communities that would suffer direct or indirect negative impacts.[10]

In that regard a particularly difficult and sensitive challenge was prior and informed consultation with indigenous populations of the Americas, who were structurally excluded from the dominant societies due to ubiquitous language, culture, and race discrimination. Consultation with indigenous peoples, much less their participation in EA's, or participation in development projects of any kind, was unprecedented in Latin America and the Caribbean. Only Canada and Mexico had evolved mechanisms, instruments, and processes, albeit, incomplete and flawed, for including to any extent indigenous peoples in the development process. Throughout the rest of the Americas indigenous peoples remained voiceless, invisible, isolated, and impoverished.

While we began by insisting on consultation and participation in the EA process our larger agenda quickly moved to involving indigenous communities in the design, staffing, implementation, and monitoring and evaluation of all development projects affecting their territories, natural resources, and cultures. The pushback was strong and immediate. World Bank staff were well aware that borrower governments of the region almost always represented only the dominant and profoundly racist segments

---

[9]World Bank (1991). *Operational Directive 4.01 Environmental Assessment.* Washington, DC.

[10]Partridge, W.L. (1994). "People's Participation in Environmental Assessment in Latin America: Best Practices," *LATEN Dissemination Note Number 11,* Latin America and Caribbean Technical Department. Washington, DC: World Bank.

of their societies, and they did not relish attempts to redress this deeply rooted inequity.

We had three powerful allies in the struggle to direct Bank investment towards indigenous communities. First, in the 1990s the indigenous communities themselves were rising up to demand their right to "development with identity."[11] In some cases they achieved voice and representation peacefully (Ecuador), in others their efforts were violently repressed (Guatemala). But the tide could not be turned back.

Second, the international community, including the United Nations and human rights non-governmental organizations mobilized in support of the indigenous movements. We were able to secure a major grant from the Swedish International Development Agency to conduct consultations with indigenous organizations. We used it to finance a series of workshops with indigenous communities (costs of travel, lodging, meals for indigenous leaders and in-country anthropologists) in eleven countries of the region. In these workshops we invited them to propose development projects for their communities and we promised to put those proposals on the table with their governments. We followed up with further visits by international and in-country anthropologists to help them formulate their proposals in forms and formats the World Bank could act upon.

Finally, our indigenous development initiative was strongly endorsed by the Regional Vice President for Latin America and the Caribbean, Shahid Javed Burki of Pakistan, and his Chief Operations Adviser, Myrna Alexander of Canada. Without this high-level support and the efforts of in-country anthropologists we would not have been able to overcome the resistance both within the World Bank and in member governments. Within two years we shepherded through the first generation of World Bank loans to indigenous organizations in Ecuador, Mexico, Argentina, Guatemala, and Peru. Recognizing the significance of this initiative, the Vice President then made the decision to hire a sociologist or anthropologist in each of the resident offices of the World Bank throughout the region to help target World Bank investments to benefit the structurally excluded: the afro-descendants, the indigenous, ethnic minorities, and other communities trapped in the informal sector of a country's economy.

---

[11]Partridge, W. L. (1990). "The Fate of Indigenous People: Consultation and Coordination Can Avoid Conflict", *The Environmental Forum* 7:5: pp. 29–30. Partridge, W.L. and S. H. Davis (1994). Promoting Indigenous Peoples Development in Latin America, *Finance and Development*, March, pp. 38–41. Partridge, W. L., J. Uquillas Rodas and K. Johns (1998). "Including the Excluded—Ethnodevelopment in Latin America". *Poverty and Inequality: Proceedings of the Annual World Bank Conference on Development in Latin America and the Caribbean 1996*, Bogotá Colombia. pp. 229–250. Washington, DC: World Bank.

Final Reflections

Practicing anthropologists bring to multilateral government organizations like the World Bank the capacity to analyze the myriad stakeholders, countervailing forces and vested interests of society which perpetuate the structural obstacles that exclude the poor and vulnerable. But analysis is merely the first step. Overcoming such obstacles always entails going beyond the normal functioning of government institutions. It is not that government institutions do not function well, but that they do so only for their clients. The excluded are not and have never been their clients. Reaching the poor and those at risk of impoverishment entails designing innovative mechanisms, processes, and instruments that permit the flow of services, goods, and works to those who have never had access to development resources. It means going beyond business as usual to challenge and correct the institutionalized social exclusion that perpetuates persistent poverty.

Practicing anthropologists in multilateral government organizations like the World Bank depend upon empirical field investigation. It is only through *in vivo* field investigation that the institutionalized structural obstacles that perpetuate poverty in any given society can be recognized and addressed. While anthropologists on the staff of such organizations do not conduct lengthy ethnographic research, they identify, recruit, and commission in-country anthropologists who have conducted in-depth investigation, who are familiar with the languages and cultures of their societies, and who manifest an ethical commitment to people's participation in the development decisions that will affect their lives. The latter have the requisite knowledge and skills to tailor development interventions to defeat structural social exclusion, and the former have the job of involving them and making it stick.

William Partridge recently retired from Vanderbilt University where he was Professor of Anthropology and Professor of Human and Organizational Development. From 1986 to 2001 he worked for the World Bank in Washington, DC and Buenos Aires, Argentina. He is author of *Guidance Note for Socio-Cultural Analysis* (with M. C. Mejia), Washington, DC: Inter-American Development Bank (2012); *Social Analysis Sourcebook* (with A. Dani, T. Dichter, K. Kuehnast, A. Kudat, B. Bulent Ozbilgin, M. Mejía), Washington, DC: World Bank (2002); *Reasentamiento en Colombia* (edited). Bogota and Washington DC: United Nations High Commissioner for Refugees, World Bank, Corporacion Antioquia Presente, and Office of the President, Government of Colombia (2000); "Successful Involuntary Resettlement: Lessons from the Costa Rica Arenal Project". In M. Cernea and S. Guggenheim (editors). *Anthropological Approaches to Resettlement*. Boulder, Colorado: Westview Press, pp. 351–374 (1993); *The Human Ecology of Tropical Land Settlement in Latin America* (edited with D. Schumann). Boulder, Colorado: Westview Press (1989); and *Applied Anthropology in America: Revised Second Edition* (edited with E. Eddy), New York: Columbia University Press (1987). Partridge received his PhD in Anthropology from the University of Florida.

Open Access This chapter is licensed under the terms of the Creative Commons Attribution 4.0 International License (http://creativecommons.org/licenses/by/4.0/), which permits use, sharing, adaptation, distribution and reproduction in any medium or format, as long as you give appropriate credit to the original author(s) and the source, provide a link to the Creative Commons license and indicate if changes were made.

The images or other third party material in this chapter are included in the chapter's Creative Commons license, unless indicated otherwise in a credit line to the material. If material is not included in the chapter's Creative Commons license and your intended use is not permitted by statutory regulation or exceeds the permitted use, you will need to obtain permission directly from the copyright holder.

Part III
Involuntary Resettlement

The Risks and Reconstruction Model for Resettling Displaced Populations

Michael M. Cernea

Introduction

Impoverishment of displaced people is the fundamental risk in development-caused involuntary population resettlement. To counter this central risk, protecting and reconstructing displaced peoples' livelihoods is the central requirement for equitable resettlement programs.

Empirical evidence shows that, more often than not, the risks of impoverishment and social disruption turn into a grim reality. In India, for instance, researchers found that the country's development programs have caused the displacement and involuntary resettlement of approximately 20 million people over roughly four decades, but that as many as 75% of these people have not been "rehabilitated" (Fernandes 1991; Fernandes et al. 1989). Their incomes and livelihoods have not been restored. In other words, the vast majority of development resettlers in India have been impoverished.

Similar findings about impoverishment and the *de facto* lack of equity in involuntary resettlement processes come from many other countries. The material loss in each case is vast. No less serious a consequence is the political tension that surrounds forced relocation. The cultural and psychological stress experienced by people who are forcibly uprooted lingers, affecting their subsequent individual and group behavior.

What is the appropriate response to this major pathology of development?

M. M. Cernea (✉)
Bethesda, MD, USA

Social Justice and Planning with an Equity Compass

Development programs that provide irrigation for thirsty lands, energy for growing industries, hospitals and schools within residential areas, and wider roads in clogged downtowns are indisputably necessary. They improve many people's lives and develop both the national and local economies. Nonetheless, these developments can also cause the forced displacement of segments of the local population. The forcibly displaced populations, often already poor, end up worse off, and poorer for a very long time, an impoverishment that sometimes even extends across generations. The overall result is that some people enjoy the gains, while others share only in the pains of development. Even though some degree of population relocation is at times unavoid-able, this inequitable distribution of gains and pains, benefits and losses, is neither inevitable nor justified. It is, in fact, profoundly contrary to the very goals of development. Spatial rearrangements and their pernicious consequences should not be accepted as a God-given tragedy, worthy of little more than a compassionate shrug of the shoulders.

The magnitude and frequency of development-related displacements makes involuntary resettlement a problem of worldwide relevance. Based on World Bank and other data, we have calculated the global magnitude of development caused forced displacements.[1] During the last decade of the 20th century, about 10,000,000 people each year were displaced worldwide by infrastructural development programs (dam construction, urban development, highways, roads). This amounts to some 90–100 million people displaced during the decade, which—surprisingly to many—is much greater than the total number of refugees from wars and natural disasters. The impoverishment of such large numbers of people constantly adds to the problem of worldwide poverty. Therefore, understanding the processes that cause impoverishment under development programs and ways to prevent them is crucial for mitigating the hazards intrinsic to displacement.

"Social justice" and "social injustice" are notions not frequently used in the development discourse, yet they are essential. Recently, these concepts have been brought to the public forum in authoritative statements. "We must act" stated the President of the World Bank "so that poverty will be alleviated, our environment protected, social justice extended, hu-man rights strengthened... Social injustice can destroy economic and political advances" (Wolfensohn 1995). Undoubtedly, involuntary resettlement is one domain in which the call for social justice and equitable distribution of development's benefits resounds loudly. This was also the reason for which the World Summit on Social Development (Copenhagen, March 1995) incorporated the call for reestablishing resettlers' livelihoods into its Program of Action (United Nations 1995).

---

[1] See World Bank (1994/96). This large-scale study, carried out by a World Bank Task Force, reviewed all 1986–93 World Bank-financed projects that involved involuntary population displacement. The study was written by M. Cernea and S. Guggenheim. The calculation of worldwide displacement magnitudes estimates was part of that study.

Studies that I have carried out over 40 years identified and reconfirmed the main "impoverishment risks" inherent in forced resettlements (Cernea 1986, 1990, 1995b; World Bank 1994/96). Based on the evidence, however, I argued that impoverishment is not inevitable. It is not an "unavoidable" cost of necessary development. For this reason, impoverishment caused by development should not be tolerated with passive resignation. It is the outcome of choices. Displacement is a socially caused disruption, not a natural disaster, and its perverse effects must and can be counterbalanced. Redressing the inequities caused by displacement and enabling affected people to share in the benefits of growth is not only possible but is also necessary, on both economic and moral grounds.

Although as a class of processes relocations are unavoidable, not every individual case of displacement proposed by planners is either inevitable or justified. There are pragmatic ways to avoid, or at least reduce, specific instances of forced displacement. There are ways to reduce their hazards and socioeconomic adverse impacts. Socially responsible resettlement—that is resettlement guided by an equity "compass"—can counteract lasting impoverishment and generate benefits for both the regional and for the local economy. Yet much too often, those who approve and design programs causing displacement are deprived of a compass that can guide them in how to allocate financial resources equitably and to prevent (or mitigate) the risks of impoverishment (Cernea 1986, 1988, 1996b; Mahapatra 1991). Indeed, the planning approach which causes many to be displaced but only a few to be "rehabilitated" has proven itself a big failure, unable to prevent impoverishment.[2] The repeated instances of resettlement without rehabilitation point to even deeper congenital defects in the current policies of many countries, not only in planning approaches. These policies, and the resulting planning methodologies, must be changed.

Functions of the Risks and Reconstruction Model

How does impoverishment through displacement occur? How can it be prevented and how can the livelihood of displaced people be reconstructed?

These are both theoretical and practical questions. For decades, these basic questions have confronted social researchers, policy makers, plan-ners, and—more than anyone—resettlers. A vast social science and policy literature exists on them (Guggenheim 1994), offering many answers, some more and others less convincing. We still have much that we need to learn.

---

[2] The Indian sociologist Victor D'Souza, in an insightful analysis of development planning in India, wrote: "Gigantic social problems... cast serious doubt on the suitability of the current mode of planning.... They call for a drastic change in the method of setting the goals of planning; it is not the rate of growth of the economy per se, but the degree of fulfillment of human needs and the elimination of glaring inequalities in society which should be the yardstick of success in planning" (D'Souza 1990).

Relying on much of the worldwide displacement research and on my field experiences in many countries with multiple national policies, planning practices and development projects, I'm proposing below a conceptual model for analyzing the socioeconomic content of displacement. The model anticipates displacement's major risks, explains the behavioral responses of displaced people, and can guide the reconstruction of resettlers' livelihoods. This conceptual framework could be named "the risks and reconstruction model" for resettling displaced populations.

Like any other conceptual template, this one is a tool—first a tool for generating and organizing knowledge, but also a tool for guiding action by generating proposals that are usable for policy and planning. This model can serve various social actors of resettlement processes—namely policy makers, project designers, social researchers and of course the resettlers. In addition it should be possible to extend this model, with appropriate adjustments, to the analysis of comparable processes affecting other displaced populations such as refugees (Kibreab 1996) deprived of their habitat and assets not by development but by civil war, ethnic persecution, or natural disasters (Hansen 1990; Cernea 1996a). Further explorations about the utility of the model could benefit its conceptual and operational applications.

The four distinct but interrelated functions which the risks and reconstruction model can perform are best described as:

- A diagnostic—explanatory and cognitive—function;
- A predictive—warning and planning—function;
- A problem-resolution function for guiding and measuring resettler's reestablishment; and
- A research function for forming hypotheses and conducting theory-led field investigations.

The ease of using this model results from its simplicity. It is built around a core concept: the multisided risk of impoverishment. Impoverishment risks are embedded in all displacements. In this context, the sociological concept of risk[3] is understood as the potential that a certain course of action will trigger future injurious effects—losses and destruction (Giddens 1990). It is widely held that the concept of risk is a counter-concept to security (Luhman 1993). The social actors of this course of action are involved in risk differentially—a few, as decision makers, many others as at-risk populations.

---

[3]The literature on the conceptual definition of "risk" is vast, and the modern society itself is more and more defined as the "risk society" (Beck 1990). Frequently the terms "risk" and "danger," or "hazard" and "danger", or "hazard" and "risk" are used as interchangeable and overlapping. Some sociologists (e.g., Giddens 1990) explicitly reject the distinction between risk and danger. Other researchers, however, argue that in some situations a difference exists, and define risk as the probability of an injurious effect resulting from a hazard (Kaplan and Garrick 1981). Consonant with most of the current risk literature, risk may be defined as the possibility embedded in a certain course of social action to trigger adverse effects (losses; destructions; functionally counterproductive impacts; deprivation of future generations, etc.)

There have been several other conceptual frame-works for resettlement, proposed in the past by various scholars, which circulate in the literature (e.g., Nelson 1973; Chambers 1969; Chambers and Morris 1973; Scutter and Colson 1982). Some of these frameworks have emphasized the institutional variables; others were centered around the concept of identifying sequentially the main stages of settlement processes; and others have highlighted "stress" or alternative variables. These valuable frameworks helped generate results in various research projects, but they also appeared unsatisfactory in others. Some proved more and others less effective as tools for action. Over the last 30 years, however. social research on development-caused resettlement, as well as on refugees displaced by other events. has increased exponentially (Guggenheim 1994; Cernea 1995b, 1996a). expanding our knowledge and changing the "state of the art." This surge in knowledge makes possible—in fact, demands—new theorizing.

Building upon lessons and awareness of the inadequacies from the use of previous frameworks, the risks and reconstruction model carries the modeling effort further in three essential ways: (a) it captures the core economic and social substance and consequences of displacement and relocation which is impoverishment and reconstruction, (b) it points to the imperative of preventing and overcoming the risks through the very policy decisions that create them; and (c) it informs about the kind of socioeconomic processes that must he initiated for problem-solving.

The risks and reconstruction model benefits from the new state of the art in resettlement research and responds to it by offering a more comprehensive theoretical framework for diagnosis and advance warnings, a framework that is usable operationally; it explains the response of displaced populations to economic and social deprivation; suggests novel areas for conducting field inquiry; and most crucially, it outlines the constitutive elements of a strategy for problem-solving and planning. It is also a conceptual template within which further knowledge will he built to improve the understanding and measurement of resettlement.

A brief characterization of each function of this model is in order, before proceeding to a more detailed discussion.

(a) *The diagnostic*—explanatory and cognitive—capacity of the model rests on a mountain of analytical evidence gathered through research and past resettlements. As a cognitive and explanatory tool, the model diagnoses the recurrent pathologies of forced displacement. These consist of eight major economic and social impoverishment hazards. The practical utility of this diagnostic function is that it reveals—to policy officials, who decide on triggering displacements, and to the affected populations who incur the consequences—the nature, the risks, and the possible outcomes of impending forced displacements.

(b) The model's *predictive* capacity rests on converting the diagnosis into a prognosis for better planning. It provides early warnings about adverse effects long before the decision to displace is made. It equips the planners with better understanding and anticipation power. The practical utility of this function is that it enables planners, as well as would-be displacees, to recognize the

impoverishment risks in advance, to search for alternatives to avoid displacement, and/or to respond with effective mitigatory and coping strategies.
(c) The *problem-resolution* capacity rests on the model's reach beyond just explanation to its orientation toward action. To achieve this, the part of the model that identifies pauperization risks is fully reversed, as will be shown below. As a result, the model points out ways to overcome the problems that displacement causes. Thus, the practical utility of the model increases greatly by moving from diagnosis and prediction to prescription for action. In the end, the model becomes a compass for strategies to reconstruct resettlers' livelihoods, going beyond mitigatory mechanisms and advancing a development orientation.
(d) The *research guiding* capacity rests on the conceptual scaffolding it provides to social researchers for formulating hypotheses on both displacement and relocation, and for conducting theory-led fieldwork. The practical utility of this function is that it guides the field collection and aggregation of empirical data in a coherent manner along content variables. It also simplifies the comparison of specific findings regarding the same variables across cultures, countries and time periods.

Diagnostic and Analysis: Ten Impoverishment Risks

The core content of unmitigated forced displacement is always economic and social uprooting. Capturing and conceptualizing this core content is the first call upon the conceptual framework. Therefore, to identify the basic socioeconomic mechanisms set in motion when people are involuntarily displaced by development-related programs, I examined an extensive body of empirical data and compared the field findings of numerous researchers.

Beyond the enormous diversity in individual country and project-specific situations, the comparison revealed a number of basic regularities. Thus, I found a pattern of ten subprocesses whose convergent and cumulative effect is the rapid onset of impoverishment (Cernea 1990; Cernea 1995b). Before the displacement operation actually begins, these processes are only imminent economic and social hazards. But if adequate counteraction is not initiated, these hazards become actual components of a multifaceted impoverishment disaster. Relying on the worldwide empirical evidence about such disasters, I constructed a general "risk-pattern" apt to inform decision makers and project designers long before the project starts. These risks threaten not only the people displaced: they are risks incurred by the local (regional) economy as well, to which they may inflict major losses and disruptions.

The following ten impoverishment hazards are not the only ones that result in processes of economic and social deprivation, but are the most important ones. Depending on local conditions, these risks have variable intensities. They are:

Landlessness

Expropriation of land removes the main foundation upon which people's productive systems, commercial activities, and livelihoods are built. The loss of land is the principal form of decapitalization and pauperization of displaced rural people, as they lose both natural and man-made capital.

Selected empirical evidence.[4] Unless the land basis of people's productive systems is reestablished elsewhere or replaced with steady income-generating employment, landlessness sets in and the affected families become impoverished. In the Kiambere Hydropower project in Kenya, a sociological study (Mburugu 1993) found that farmers' average land holdings after relocating dropped from 13 to 6 hectares; their livestock was reduced by more than a third; yields per hectare decreased by 68% for maize and 75% for beans. Family income dropped from Ksh. 10,968 to Ksh. 1976—a loss of 82%. In India's Rengali project, the percentage of landless families after relocation more than doubled—from 4.6 to 10.9% (Ota 1996), while in the coal mining displacements around Singrauli the proportion of landless people skyrocketed from 20% before displacement to 72% after (Reddy 1997). In Africa, Lassailly-Jacob's (1994, 1996) studies on the Kossou Dam and other major reservoirs have empirically quantified and documented resettlers' loss of land and the insufficiency of the land-replacement remedies adopted. In Indonesia, a survey by the Institute of Ecology of Padjadjaran University (1989) around the Saguling reservoir found that resettled families' land ownership decreased by 47% and their income was halved. Similar evidence is available from Brazil (Mougeot 1989). Findings from sociological and anthropological field studies show that for farm families, loss of land generally has far more severe consequences than the loss of a dwelling.

Joblessness

Loss of wage employment occurs both in urban and rural displacements. Those losing jobs include landless laborers, enterprise or service workers, artisans, or small businessmen. Yet creating new jobs is difficult and requires substantial investments. Unemployment or underemployment among resettlers often endures long after physical relocation has been completed.

Selected empirical evidence: For several categories of rural people whose livelihoods depend on jobs—including landless laborers; employees of local services, or other small enterprises; shopkeepers and small businessmen—job loss due to

---

[4]The empirical evidence for each of the model's variables is enormous, and is available in many of the studies listed in the references, and in other works. For each variable of the model, I will refer only to selected significant field findings.

displacement causes lasting painful economic and psychological effects. The previously employed may lose out in three ways: in urban areas, they lose jobs in industry and services, or other job opportunities; in rural areas, they lose access to work on land owned by others (leased or share-cropped); and they also lose the use of assets under common property regimes. In the Madagascar Tana Plain project, for example, private small enterprises displaced in 1993—workshops, food-stalls, artisan units—were not entitled to compensation, and lost their place of trade and their customers.[5] A survey carried out among tribal households in five villages at Talcher, Orissa found an increase in unemployment from 9 to 43.6%, accompanied by a large shift from primary to tertiary occupations (when available); reported reductions in levels of earnings were between 50 and 80% among tribes and scheduled castes. Vocational retraining, offered to some resettlers, can provide skills but not necessarily jobs. Similar findings come from developed countries: in the Churchill-Nelson Hydro project in Manitoba, Canada, the economic activities of resettled indigenous people—fisheries, waterfowl capture, fur processing—were curtailed; field studies found a significant increase in non-productive time in the community. Joblessness among resettlers often surfaces after a time delay, rather than immediately, because in the short run they may receive employment in project-related jobs. This employment, however, is not sustainable. Evidence compiled from several dam projects[6] shows that the "employment boom" created by new construction temporarily absorbs some resettlers, but severely drops toward the end of the project. This compounds the incidence of chronic or temporary joblessness among the displaced.

Homelessness

Loss of housing and shelter may be only temporary for many displacees, but for some homelessness remains a chronic condition. In a broader cultural sense, loss of a family's individual home is linked with the loss of a group's cultural space, resulting in alienation and deprivation, as argued by students of "place attachment" (Low and Altman 1992). Families subjected to compulsory villagization schemes, as argued by de Wet (1995), also experience a lasting sense of "placelessness."

Selected empirical data: If resettlement policies do not explicitly provide improvement in housing conditions, or if compensation for demolished shelters is paid at assessed value rather than replacement value, the risk of homelessness increases. A 1990 World Bank report on the Cameroon-Douala Urban resettlement (which was completed in 1989) found that over 2000 displaced families were hindered in their efforts to set up new permanent houses; less than 5% received loans to help

---

[5]Personal observation, Madagascar 1993.

[6]E.g., the China-Gezhouba dam, Brazil-Tucurui dam, Turkey-Ataturk dam, Togo-Benin Nangbeto Hydropower dam, and Korea-Chungju dam.

pay for assigned houseplots. From the Danjiangkou reservoir China has reported that about 20% of the relocatees became homeless and destitute.[7] To speed up evictions, violent destruction of houses belonging to people labeled squatters still occurs in some places (e.g., in Uganda in the Kibale park area). When resettlers cannot meet the time, labor and financial costs involved in rebuilding a house, they are compelled to move into "temporary" shelters. The "emergency housing centers" and temporary "relocation camps" used as fall-back solution in poorly planned resettlement tend to make homelessness chronic rather than temporary. At the Foum-Gleita irrigation project in Mauritania, only 200 out of the 881 displaced families successfully reconstructed their housing; the rest lived precariously for 2 years or longer in tents or under tarpaulins. In the Kukadi-Krishna irrigation subprojects in Maharashtra, India, 59% of the displaced families were found living in temporary/semi-permanent houses 10–15 years after their relocation (Joseph 1997). Yet the risks of homelessness—like joblessness, marginalization, morbidity—can definitely be avoided through timely pre-project preparation and adequate financing instead of the routinely undercalculated compensation.

Marginalization

Marginalization occurs when families lose economic power and slide on a "downward mobility" path: middle-income farm households do not become landless, they become small landholders; small shopkeepers and craftsmen downsize and slip below poverty thresholds. Many individuals cannot use their previously acquired skills at the new location and human capital is lost or rendered inactive, useless. The coerciveness of displacement also depreciates the image of self. Marginalization materializes also in a drop in social status and in a psychological downward slide of resettlers' confidence in society and self, a sense of injustice, a premise of anomic behavior. Moreover, we know that relative economic marginalization begins long before the actual displacement, because of disinvestments or no investment in infrastructure and services in condemned areas.

Selected empirical data: Resettled families seldom restore lost social status and economic capacity fully. For farm families, partial but significant loss of farming land to roads or canals may make their farm economically nonviable. High-productivity farmers on fertile valley-bottom land tend to become marginalized when moved uphill to inferior, infertile soils. In the Nepal Kulekhani Hydroelectric project, an independent study found that the majority of displaced people were worse off socially and economically, due to lower productivity of their new

---

[7]The sad experiences of Danjiangkou and Sanmenxia Dam displacements led to the adoption of new and better resettlement policies in China, policies that attempt to transform resettlement into an opportunity for development.

land, and less diversified production. Marginalization also occurs through the loss of off-farm income sources. In Sri Lanka's Kotmale project a field study reported that marginalization occurred because opportunities for non-farm income generation were lost or limited through displacement, increasing the economic differentiation between evacuees and hosts (Soeftestad 1990). Psychological marginalization and behavioral impairments, anxiety and decline in self-esteem, have been widely reported from many areas (Appell 1985; Appell 1986). For urban resettlers, marginalization is sometimes gradual and may occur after relocation, as when resettlers received jobs (instead of land) that are temporary, unsustainable income sources in the long run. Governments and project agencies also tacitly accept lasting marginalization of resettlers when they consider it "a matter of course" that the displaced cannot regain their prior social standard of living.

Increased Morbidity and Mortality

Serious declines in health result from displacement-caused social stress, insecurity, psychological trauma, and the outbreak of relocation-related illnesses, particularly parasitic and vector-borne diseases, such as malaria and schistosomiasis. Unsafe water supply and poor sewerage systems increase vulnerability to epidemics and chronic diarrhea, dysentery, etc. The weakest segments of the demographic spectrum—infants, children, and the elderly—are affected most strongly.

Selected empirical data: People forced to relocate increase their exposure and vulnerability to illness, and to comparatively more severe diseases, than those who are not. In Sri Lanka an outbreak of gastroenteritis occurred along the Victoria dam reservoir (Rew and Driver 1986) and in Mahaweli's System C resettlement site the incidence of malaria rose from 8.9 to 15.6% (Jayewardene 1995). At Akosombo in Ghana, the prevalence of schistosomiasis around the reservoir rose from 1.8% prior to resettlement to 75% among adult lake-side dwellers and close to 100% among their children, within a few years after the dam's impoundment in the 1960s. The Foum-Gleita irrigation project in Mauritania exceeded its anticipated increase of schistosomiasis, reaching 70% among school children; farmers' health also worsened from contaminated drinking water and agrochemical intoxication. At Nam Pong reservoir in Thailand, monitoring confirmed that local rates of morbidity—from liver fluke and hookworm infection—were higher among resettlers than the provincial levels, the result of deteriorated living conditions and poor waste- disposal practices. Exposure to "social stress" was highlighted as having differential consequences on mental health across age, gender, marital and occupational status (Scudder and Colson 1982; Scudder 1991; Turner et al. 1995), but empirical measurements related to displacement-induced social stress are not readily available (see Appell 1986 for an interesting discussion on measuring social stress). Overall, direct and secondary effects of compulsory dislocation in the absence of preventive health measures include psychosomatic diseases, diseases of poor hygiene (such as diarrhea and dysentery), and outbreaks of parasitic and vector-borne diseases (such as malaria and schistosomiasis) caused by unsafe and insufficient water supplies and inadequate sanitary waste systems. Increased mortality rates are also reported as a result of either accidents associated with new reservoirs or epidemic malaria outbreaks around new bodies of water. Lack of proper information and precautionary measures resulted in 106 deaths by drowning at Saguling Lake (Indonesia) during the first 14 months of operation; at Cirata reservoir (Indonesia) 10 people drowned in the first 10 months after impounding (Padjadjaran University 1989).

Food Insecurity

Forced uprooting increases the risk that people will fall into chronic undernourishment, defined as calorie-protein intake levels below the minimum necessary for normal growth and work, and food insecurity.

Selected empirical data: Undernourishment is both a symptom and result of inadequate resettlement. Sudden drops in food crop availability and/or incomes are predictable during physical relocation, and hunger or undernourishment tend to become lingering long-term effects. Forced up- rooting increases the risk that people will fall into chronic food insecurity, as rebuilding regular food production capacity at the relocation site may take years. At the Foum-Gleita irrigation project, Mauritania, paddy-rice monocropping replaced multiple cropping and animal husbandry, and diets and cash-crop income deteriorated (Ngaide 1986). At Sri Lanka's Victoria dam project, some 55% of resettled families were receiving food stamps even after a long period (Rew and Driver 1986). Because the area of cultivated land per capita in the Bailiambe reservoir in China decreased from 1.3 mu to only 0.4 mu after relocation, local food production became insufficient and 75,000 tons of annual food relief had to be provided for several years.

Loss of Access to Common Property

For poor people, particularly for the landless, and assetless, loss of access to common (non-individual) property assets that belonged to relocated communities (forested lands, water bodies, grazing lands, burial grounds, etc.) results in significant deterioration in income and livelihood. Typically, loss of common property assets are not compensated by government relocation schemes. Losses of access to various basic public services, as pointed out by an Indian anthropologist (Mathur 1997), also occur rather often and should be linked to this class of risks.

Selected empirical data: Empirical evidence shows that fruit and other forest products—firewood and deadwood, common grazing areas, and public quarries—account for a significant share of poor households' income. For example, in semi-arid regions of India, 91–100% of firewood, 66–89% of domestic fuel, and 69–80% of poor households' grazing needs are supplied by lands held under common property regime (Sequeira 1994; Gopal 1992). A study of seven projects causing displacements during 1950–94 in Orissa, India has found that no compensation has been paid for common properties by any of these projects (Pandey et al. 1997). In the Rengali dam area in India, while prior to displacement all families had access to common grazing lands and burial grounds, after relocation only 23.7% and 17.5% respectively had such access. After losing the use of natural resources under common property, displaced people tend either to encroach on reserved forests or to increase the pressure on common property resources of the host area population. This is a source of both social tension and increased environmental deterioration. Secondary adverse effects of resettlement on the environment also occur when oustees who do not receive cultivatable land move uphill into the reservoir watershed. This migration intensifies deforestation and cultivation of poor soils, accelerating erosion and reservoir siltation.

Social Disarticulation

Forced displacement tears apart the existing social fabric: it disperses and fragments communities, dismantles patterns of social organization and interpersonal ties; kinship groups become scattered as well. Life-sustaining informal networks of reciprocal help, local voluntary associations, and self-organized mutual service arrangements are dismantled. The destabilization of community life is apt to generate a typical state of anomie, crisis- laden insecurity, and loss of sense of cultural identity, tending to transform displacement zones into what has been termed as "anomic regions" or "anomie-ridden areas" (Atteslander 1995a, b). The unraveling of spatially-based patterns of self-organization, interaction and reciprocity is a net loss of valuable "social capital," that compounds the loss of natural and man-made capital (discussed previously). The social capital lost through social disarticulation remains unperceived and uncompensated by planners, and this real loss will reverberate long and detrimentally during subsequent periods. "The people may physically persist, but the community that was—is no more" (Downing 1996a), because its spatial, temporal, and cultural determinants are gone.

Selected empirical data: Dismantled social networks that once mobilized people to act around common interests and to meet their most pressing needs are difficult to rebuild. This losses are bigger in projects that relocate families in a dispersed manner, severing their prior ties with neighbors, rather than relocating them in groups and social units. A detailed sociological study by Nayak (1986) on a dam project in India found various manifestations of social disarticulation within the kinship system, such as the loosening of intimate bonds, growing alienation and anomie, the weakening of control on interpersonal behavior, and lower cohesion in family structures. Marriages were deferred because dowry, feasts, and gifts became unaffordable. Resettlers' obligations towards and relationships with non-displaced kinsmen were eroded and interaction between individual families was reduced. As a result, participation in group activities decreased; leaders became conspicuously absent from settlements; post-harvest communal feasts and pilgrimages were discontinued; and common burial grounds became shapeless and disordered. A monograph on the Hirakud dam in India found that displaced households whose "economic status had been completely shattered as a result of displacement" did not become "properly integrated" in host villages for many years after relocation (Babboo 1992). On a larger social scale, studies by historians of migration have also concluded that the costs of population relocation go, in general, much beyond "simply the financial costs": among the "heaviest costs of all are the severing of personal ties in familiar surroundings, to face new economic and social uncertainties in a strange land" (Sowell 1996). Overall, if poverty is not only an absence of material means—such as land, shelter, work, food—but also powerlessness, dependency, and vulnerability, than the disarticulation of communities and the loss of reciprocity networks are significant factors in aggravating poverty.

Differential Impacts: Specific Risks to Women and Children

These eight basic impoverishment risks discussed above affect various categories of vulnerable people differentially. The evidence suggests that, depending on the sector in which displacement occurs, or on local circumstances, resettlers at different locations may experience some or all of the eight basic risks. Moreover, certain population groups are hurt more than others. For instance, recent research revealed that women suffer more severe impacts (Feeney 1995; Koenig 1995). Agnihotri (1996) signals clear- cut discrimination against women in compensation criteria—e.g., entitlement to land compensation for unmarried individuals is set in Orissa at age 18 for men, but only at age 30 for women! In turn, tribal groups are more vulnerable than the general population to the impoverishment hazards discussed above; in India, a vast research literature empirically documents this statement (Fernandes 1991; Mahapatra 1994).

Differential Impacts: Specific risks for Children, as an age category, are subjected to particularly perverse consequences. Elaborating on the risks and reconstruction model in light of evidence from India, Mahapatra (1996) suggests that "to the impoverishment risk model one may add the specific educational loss affecting children." Indeed, relocation often interrupts schooling and some children never return to school after displacement, as a result of drops in family income, many children are drafted into the labor market earlier than what would have otherwise been the case. Often, the new relocation sites are not yet equipped with school buildings from the outset, causing children to miss critical years of education that have negative impacts on the rest of their lives. Differences between particularly vulnerable groups clearly call for targeted responses.

We have seen that as a conceptual construct, the analytical impoverishment framework captures not only the economic hazards but also the social and cultural ones. Since it shows that during displacement people lose natural capital, man-made (physical) capital, human capital, and social capital, this analysis concludes that strategies to assist displaced people must help them restore their capital in all its forms. This points to the need for fairly complex preventive and reconstruction programs, to which our conceptual model can, in turn, serve as guide.

Prediction and Planning: The Chance of a Self-Destroying Prophecy

The predictive-*cum*-planning capacity of the risks and reconstruction model results from the forewarning virtue of the knowledge packaged in it. By incorporating information about the outcomes of many prior displacements, the model predicts future outcomes certain to occur if its warnings are ignored. Without counteraction, these potential impoverishment risks will turn into real and hard deprivations.

Ideally, as Robert K. Merton has convincingly demonstrated, the prediction of an undesirable outcome may act as a "self-destroying prophecy" (Merton 1979). It follows that a risk prediction model becomes maximally useful not when it is confirmed by disastrous events but rather when, as a result of its warnings being absorbed and acted upon, the risks are prevented from becoming reality, or are minimized, and the consequences predicted by the model do not occur. This is how the predictive model acts as a self-destroying prophecy.

In this sense, risk recognition and analysis are a crucial prerequisites for the practice of sound planning. Indeed, more than offering just general warnings, the set of risk variables identified in the model provides a matrix directly convertible into planning provisions and substantive activities. Attempts to use this model as a tool for actual planning and resettlement preparation have started in India (described by Thangaraj 1996) and in the Philippines (Spiegel 1997). Other resettlement specialists have used this model in field supervision of resettlement operations (Downing 1996a, b). Furthermore, an all-India workshop was organized in New Delhi in 1996, with resettlement planners and practitioners from many states, to explore the model's research-cum-planning potential for projects entailing resettlement (Mathur and Marsden 1997).

For achieving the preventive potential inherent in the risks and reconstruction model, four steps are essential:

– A risk assessment in the field, tailored to the situation at hand;

- Adequate response of the decision makers and planners to predicted risks;
- The proactive response of the population directly at known risks; and
- Transparent information and communication between decision makers/planners and populations at risk.

The optimal response to anticipated risks is when planners and decision makers start searching for technical alternatives that altogether will obviate the need for displacing people, or at least will reduce the number of displacees. Such alternatives are some- times technically feasible, for instance, by modifying the routing of a planned highway to circumvent existing settlements, by changing the location of a dam, or by reducing the dam's height. When it is not possible to avoid displacement, however, the warned planners and managers are informed by the model to conceive special measures targeted against each one of the predicted impoverishment risks, rather than being general and vague in their "planning." Such measures could be of an economic, financial, technical, legal, and cultural nature.

The generic risks described above will of course each take on a different weight, varying from one location to another. An experienced planner will use the model as a guide and will identify which risks loom larger in each case, how they interact, and which to counteract first. In the ongoing Philippines Batangas Port Development project, for instance, a social planner is applying the impoverishment risks and reconstruction model in attempting to move away from "traditional planning" and to sharpen the project's reconstruction strategy. He used a simple five-point Lickert scale to hypothesize the risk intensity for Batangas relocatees (i.e., low risk potential, moderately low. medium, moderately high. high) for each one of the eight risk variables: landlessness, joblessness, homelessness, etc. The strategy he pursued was to tailor a comprehensive risk-response package which is not only more complete, but also allocates differential resources commensurate to each risk-intensity, in ways better tuned to specific circumstances in that location.

In tum, for resettlers themselves, the predictive- *cum*-warning utility of the model is that it enables them, and their organizations, to develop coping and resource-mobilization strategies with some lead- time. For this, resettlers must be informed transpar-ently, understand well the impending displacement, and overcome disbelief or the tendency to denial. Yet this "telling to resettlers" is a process that happens much too seldom or late, for reasons I will mention below. The model's utility to resettlers is that it enables them to explore alternatives, to resist unjustified or inadequately prepared displacement before it occurs, and to pursue their rights and entitlements when displacement is unavoidable.

Communication between planners and resettlers is instrumental for effective early warning and for making possible joint preventive activities. I use here the term "communications" in its broad sociological sense, encompassing: transparent information (regarding the causes of displacement and its likely impacts); consultation between planners and affected groups of resettlers, hosts, and their organizations; and genuine participation in finding acceptable solutions. Drawing from research on natural disasters, we emphasize that displacement warnings must be seen as a social process "involving multiple actors, phases and feedback" (Quarantelli 1980, 1981; see also Drabek 1987). Yet, in development practice this still happens rather rarely.

Dysfunctional relationships between planners and groups affected by displacement are one of the roots of resettlement failure. It should not be surprising that absence of, or breakdowns in, communication processes tend to result in "reversed participation." i.e., in active opposition movements against development programs. as analyzed pertinently by Oliver-Smith (1994). In fact, such resistance is often almost guaranteed by the ill-advised position taken by some agencies, which try to maintain an information embargo about likely displacements and about resettlers' entitlements. Withholding information is sometimes "justified" by officials as intended to prevent panic and stress, but in fact it is deceptive and self-defeating because it deprives the program of the vast contribution which the energy of displacees (and their nongovernmental organizations), if mobilized early on, could provide to reconstructing their own livelihoods. This energy can be an exceptionally important factor, which so far the resettlement literature has seldom studied in depth.

To reinforce the argument that good communication is indispensable for actualizing the preventive potential of our risk and reconstruction model, I will use a representation of warning communication, adapted with modifications from a study on early warning mechanisms by Galtung (1994). The opportunity for counteraction and mitigation is much larger in the case of social risks than in natural disasters and the benefits from advance warning can be vast.

Galtung's key point is that situations that require "early warnings" and "preventive therapies" are basically similar for different categories of disorders. They imply interaction between four elements: "the situations" (which in our case is the project), "the warners," "the warning," and "the warned." Further, the warning process should function rapidly, moving as fast as possible the information about the "situation pathology" from the warners to the "early warned," which are the bulk of the population at risk.

In our case, a displacement risk situation, the loop is more complex but also requires quick and full warning and communication. The warners (in our case, the displacement planners), must not only issue warnings, but also prepare actual risk-offsetting reconstructive programs. In turn, in our adjusted scheme, the population at risk has two strategy loops: (a) one to "negotiate" with the source of risks, and simultaneously (b) a parallel one to develop its own actual "coping responses".

The crucial point that I want to emphasize, using the analogy with Galtung's argument, is the enormous importance of early systematic warning through transparent communication: only such warning gives full advance time to resettlers, both to negotiate with the project, and to initiate their own coping activities. If this information is not communicated from the outset to the population at risk (of course, with all the caveats that the planning stage may require) a great resource for reconstruction activities is not being mobilized early enough.

To sum up, the model's predictive capacity to warn early, trigger action, and inform the adoption of targeted counter-risk measures is exceptionally important and can greatly influence the final outcome of resettling displaced populations.

Flawed Approaches to Social Risks: The Ill-Logic of Cost-Benefit Analysis

Our next question is: if our model can diagnose, analyze, and predict the social risks of displacement, can it also guide problem resolution?

The answer is affirmative. The Impoverishment Risks and Reconstruction (IRR) conceptual framework contains, in a nutshell, the model for the socioeconomic reestablishment of those displaced. Thus, it is not just a model of inescapable pauperization, but one that is also a guide toward counteracting the risks and resolving the problems displacement creates. Turning the risks matrix on its head results in an action-matrix for reconstructing the livelihoods and incomes of those displaced. For instance, the risk of landlessness is prevented through land-based relocation strategies; joblessness—through sustainable reemployment; homelessness—through a house reconstruction program; and so on, as will be discussed in detail in the next section.

Before that, however, we need to examine the traditional risk-response pattern in programs that entail displacement, a pattern that has allowed impoverishment risks to run rampant in so many cases, but nevertheless continues to be practiced widely.

The currently predominant conventional response to the adverse impacts of displacement is methodologically inadequate. It has failed to achieve equity in resettlement and it has failed to prevent impoverishment. This approach has been traditionally based on aggregate cost-benefit analysis (CBA). But however adequate CBA may be for many purposes, it nonetheless is insufficient and ill-applied in this case.

Using CBA, economists and technical planners justify counter developmental impacts by claiming that the sum of a project's benefits outweighs the sum of project "costs," and they include some adverse effects in these costs. Superficially, a quantified "justification" of this kind may at first appear sufficient. Closer examination reveals, how- ever, that this answer is neither legitimate nor equitable, for two main reasons.

First, the costs of displacement are typically not included and accounted *fully* in projects' CBA. The first part of this chapter documented many of the social costs that are routinely overlooked under the current procedures. Yet a large share of the real costs are seen as "externalities" in current costing practice. They are externalized out of the projects' budgets and are left to be borne by those who suffer the displacement.

Second, the argument that harm caused to the displaced individuals is compensated by the aggregate benefits of development, *independent of the allocation of these benefits,* is grossly flawed. When one cannot predict and channel the allocation of a program's future benefits with reasonable certainty, this wholesale accounting of costs and benefits is morally and practically fallacious. This fallacy becomes physically obvious on the ground, when, by some "wheel of fortune"—as in the case of downstream development *vis-a-vis* upstream destruction—the program generates benefits for certain population segments (who, fortunately for them, reside downstream) while it inflicts adversity upon other population groups (unlucky enough to live upstream) that are victimized. Thus, this methodology legitimizes—and helps perpetuate—situations where some people share the gains, while others share the pains.

The logically crude "justification" of individualized costs through aggregate cost-benefit accounting glosses over the real impoverishment risks and impacts. The devaluation of individuals' losses becomes the premise for giving priority to civil works, while people are put last; neither detailed social planning nor allocation of sufficient financial resources is typically required; and misguided implementation further allows many negative socio-economic effects to go unaddressed. This scenario understandably raises the fundamental question asked by a respected Indian resettlement scholar: "Development for Whom?" (Mahapatra 1991).

The fact that planned programs often produce long-term gains for those defined as "project beneficiaries" does not make the hardship of being uprooted any lighter for those displaced. In real life, personalized costs are neither fully subtracted from the aggregate benefits not paid for by the project's beneficiaries. These costs are only in part covered by the state and are borne in large part by the population that is victimized in the name of the "greater good for the greater numbers." This kind of spurious rationality conflicts with social justice, vitiating development philosophy and planning practice. This inadequate methodology of economic analysis also diverts planners from seeking alternative approaches and solutions. It is responsible for tolerating unnecessary risks, and even magnifying the ill effects of projects. which otherwise could be counteracted—by prevention or mitigation.

In contrast with this conventional approach, so deeply entrenched in the current practice of many developing countries, the correct principle for adequate resettlement is not simply to justify and "compensate" property losses, but to pursue the actual restoration and enhancement of the income- generating capacity and livelihoods of the displaced people. This principle is embedded in the fundamental policy adopted by the World Bank for involuntary resettlement operations occurring under Bank-financed projects (World Bank 1990; Cernea 1986, 1988, 1995a). This policy prescribes avoidance or reduction of involuntary resettlement, reconstruction of resettlers' livelihood and their sharing in project benefits, and allocation of project resources adequate to achieve these major objectives.[8] The comprehensive resettlement study carried out by a Bank Task Force (World Bank 1994/96) to assess the consistency of project practice with policy made a very strong case, derived from its critical findings, against externalizing displacement project costs on the resettlers themselves and for mobilizing the resources necessary to reestablish them equitably.

---

[8]The social content of the World Bank's policy on resettlement has been in recent years the subject of much analysis and discussion, and several other major agencies (aid agencies of OECD countries, the Asian Development Bank, and others) have adopted the same policy principles (see references). But many difficulties and deficiencies appear in sticking to policy standards during implementation, particularly because implementation performance depends primarily on the institutional capacity and political will of the borrowing governments.

The risks and reconstruction framework described in this chapter serves explicitly the principle of reconstructing resettlers' livelihoods. It goes far beyond "compensation of loss" and helps chart the spectrum of reconstruction activities.

The challenge to resettlement practice worldwide, today, is to adopt a new concept of resettlement goals, a new approach, and new methodologies. What we have had until recently, and in fact still have in many developing countries, are typically "minimalist, residualist, or welfarist approaches" (Marsden 1997), predicated on paying the least compensation possible, on externalizing a large part of real costs, and on abandoning the displaced people to fend for themselves with little follow-up assistance after the project uprooting them is completed. What is needed instead, as the record of many tragic failures in resettlement demonstrates, is a change in concept and method predicated on treating resettlement operations as opportunities for development, as development projects in their own right, benefiting the resettlers. This includes risk mitigation but goes on to construct a new socioeconomic basis on which resettlers' livelihoods can first be restored and then lastingly improved, so that their "income curve" could exceed predisplacement levels (Cernea 1995b; Shi and Hu 1994). The risks and reconstruction model expresses this concept and offers a framework for strategies aimed at such resettlement with development.

One essential implication of this approach must be spelled out clearly: the cost of reestablishing a family and a community is generally bound to exceed the strict market value of the physical losses imposed on that family or community. Compensation alone, by definition, is therefore never sufficient for reestablishing a sustainable socioeconomic basis for resettlers.[9]

> The key to development-oriented resettlement is to adopt a people-centered approach, not a property- compensation approach.

This is why resettlers' sharing in the stream of benefits from the development they make possible is not only an equitable way of financing the true costs of reconstruction but also a necessity, given the limitations of other available resources.

The survival of improper methodologies for costing resettlement is due in many countries to the absence of national policy and legal frameworks that define the rights and entitlements of people affected by state-imposed displacements. Within such policy vacuums arbitrariness easily sets in. The powerless are victimized, rather than being enabled to share in the benefits of the development project for which they incur sacrifices. Normally, policies and legal frameworks for resettlement must embody principles of equity and social justice. But in reality,

> in many countries the national legal framework of resettlement operations is incomplete... Resettlement legal issues [are treated] as a subset of property and expropriation law. For various reasons, these national laws do not provide a fully adequate framework for

---

[9]This, of course, has profound implications for the methodology of economic and financial analysis of the costs of displacement and reestablishment, which need to be addressed separately. In at least some organizations, however, it is already accepted that new methods of doing that assessment, financing, and budgeting of the full costs of displacement and reestablishment are indispensable (World Bank 1994/96).

development-oriented resettlement.... New legislation often must be introduced, or existing laws must be modified, in order to plan and carry out involuntary resettlement adequately (Shihata 1991).

Reconstructing Livelihoods and Reversing the Risks

The risks and reconstruction model for resettling displaced population derives its strength from complementing risk diagnosis with the approaches and concepts for the reconstruction of the displaced peoples' dwellings and livelihoods.

The policy message embodied in the model is clear: the general socioeconomic impoverishment risks intrinsic to displacement can be controlled by an integrated problem-resolution strategy, but not by piecemeal palliatives; and by allocating adequate financial resources. The adverse effects cannot be tamed simply through cash compensation for lost assets. Only concerted multifaceted cooperation and action by all the social actors involved can pursue development, rather than pursue just risk mitigation. Resettlement is apt to generate opportunities to improve lives, not only disrupt them.

The Components of Reconstruction Reversing the impoverishment risks and the reconstruction of livelihoods require convergence between the actions and resources of both the agent that triggers displacement—the state or private enterprises—and the population that is displaced. While it is incumbent upon the state to pursue a policy of reestablishment and allocate needed resources—financial, organizational, technical, etc.—it would be unrealistic to conceive of reconstruction only as a top-down, paternalistic effort, without the participation and initiatives of the displaced people. The strategy charted through the risk model is not a one-actor strategy, for the state alone; rather, it is an all-actors strategy. Despite the polarized situation to be expected in many displacement contexts, the participation of the relevant actors—including resettlers, local leaders, nongovernment organizations (NGOs) and other organizations, host populations, etc.—in reconstruction is necessary.

In examining the components of reconstruction, I will follow a slightly different order than in discussing risks. First, I will address the basic economic variables—land and employment then, those referring to community reconstruction and social integration.

Unfortunately, there is less empirical research on reconstructive aspects than on impoverishment processes, and considerably more efforts are needed to identify, analyze, and disseminate positive experiences in reconstructing livelihoods. Sociologists and anthropologists have been more concerned with describing and deploring displacement's pathologies than resettlements successes. Even though success is still far less frequent than failure, developing knowledge on the former remains nonetheless essential for policy and practical purposes.

(a) *From landlessness to land-based reestablishment*
(b) *From joblessness to reemployment.*

Settling displaced people back on cultivatable land or in income-generating employment is the heart of the matter in reconstructing livelihoods. Successful approaches often involve identifying equivalent lands, or bringing new lands into production through land recovery, crop intensification or a shift to more valuable crops, diversification of on- farm/off-farm activities, use of project-created resources such as reservoirs, irrigated areas downstream, new employment, etc.

Selected empirical evidence. Land scarcity around the Shuikou dam (China) led project officials to make a bold effort to convert unproductive hillsides and uplands around the reservoir into regular terraces for horticulture or forested areas. Project-paid mechanical equipment was used for land recovery on a massive scale, and orchards were planted several years in advance of resettlers' relocation, so that trees were close to fruit- bearing at relocation time (personal observations). The approach resulted in some 53,000 mu of fruit trees, 10,000 mu of tea plantations, 26,000 mu of bamboo trees, and over 200,000 of forest trees.

This intensified agriculture and change in cropping patterns provided new land, work and livelihood to about 19,700 resettlers (World Bank 1996), and their average income from the new crops is actually higher than the level anticipated in the project's original resettlement plans. Significantly, this improvement in the resettlers' economic situation occurred even though on a per capita basis farmland was reduced from 0.98 to 0.32 mu. Complementary strategies and diversification benefited the remainder of Shuikou's resettlers: animal husbandry, including duck raising and reservoir fishing (6% of resettlers), jobs in the service sector and transportation (13.4%), jobs in new enterprises (19.3%), etc. Resettlers' initiative in Saguling (Indonesia) saved the fertile topsoil about to be lost in the reservoir area, moving it to upland plots and increasing their fertility (Costa-Pierce 1996). Project support combined with resettlers' initiative and resources, succeeded in turning many new reservoirs into an income source through aquaculture. In Mexico's Aquamilpa reservoir area fishing represented in 1989 a mere 4.1% of productive activities among those to be affected by the reservoir, but by 1995 about 60.8% of that population was engaged in fishing activities. In the Cirata reservoir area (Indonesia) cage aquaculture workers earned about Rp. 56,000 more a month than rice field workers in the same area before the dam construction (Costa-Pierce 1996). Training reset- tiers in new skills, when accompanied by actual employment, is effective: in Dudichua Coal Project in India, 225 of 378 fanners displaced by the new mine were retrained and employed (one job per family), reaching earnings about eight times the average rural wage (World Bank 1995b).

Resettling displaced reservoir farmers on land newly irrigated downstream is an excellent option for resettlement, but is nonetheless rarely used. Some states in India (Madhya Pradesh, Gujarat, and others) try to relocate oustees into command areas by enacting land-ceiling laws for new irrigated land, an administrative measure that should be reinforced by gaining the cooperation of command area farmers.

(c) *From homelessness to house reconstruction*

Improving shelter conditions is one of the relatively easier achievable improvements in reconstructing resettlers' livelihoods, even though it is still far from occurring widely. The improvements take one or more of the following forms: more square footage per capita; better quality housing materials; connection to services (electricity, water) and safer sanitation facilities; space for house gardens; and others.

Typical constraints are longer average commuting distances and transportation costs in urban areas; affordability issues and long-term mortgage burdens; and differential entitlements for the housing of former squatters. Best results are obtained when project compensation for housing (at replacement value) is supplemented by resettlers' resources (labor, cash, etc.)

Selected empirical evidence: Real gains through improved housing conditions, rather than just restoration, have been obtained by the initial cohorts of resettlers from Yacyreta dam (Argentina), by those from Shuikou—a total of additional 600,000 square meters, i.e., about 25 additional square meters per family (World Bank 1996) and from other urban resettlements in China, and by the resettlers from Kenya export development projects (World Bank 1995a), among others. In Shanghai, families displaced by a Sewerage Project can choose between state apartments supplied on rental basis, or private apartments available at one-third of the construction cost. Field studies have reported innovative approaches in reconstruction—house vouchers in Korea, daily transportation of resettlers by project vehicles to new sites in Togo's Nangbeto project enabling them to construct the core house-unit for each family, to which additional rooms can be added later (personal observation). Many displaced people show strong interest in improved housing and voluntarily use personal savings to supplement compensation. Evidence worldwide confirms the enormous potential for reconstructing shelter at improved levels.

(d) *From social disarticulation to community reconstruction;*
(e) *From marginalization to social inclusion;*
(f) *From expropriation to restoration of community assets.*

The above three facets of a social reconstruction process are the least addressed in current approaches. Planners tend to overlook these socio-cultural and psychological (not just economic) dimensions, and are rarely concerned to facilitate reintegration within host populations, or to compensate community-owned assets. Addressing all of these three—partly distinct but partly overlapping—dimensions of reconstructing livelihoods can achieve synergistic effects. Community reconstruction refers to group structures, including informal and formal institutions, while overcoming marginalization refers primarily to the individual family/household level. Strategies may differ when villages or neighborhoods are created as new social units, or when fill-in operations insert scattered resettlers within preexisting communities.

Selected empirical evidence: The most interesting experience in purposively maintaining communities or assisting new community formation comes from China. By law, project authorities in China must negotiate with prospective displacees simultaneously as individuals and as community groups. The state-allocated resources for financing resettlement are divided between individual households and community bodies (township committees) for some group-purposes. Community-owned assets lost in dis- placement are valued and financially compensated by the state, to enable the reconstruction of the same, or of comparable, community assets, which contribute to the livelihoods of resettlers (Shi and Hu 1994). Thus, by design, some patterns of the social organization of the displaced village are empowered to have a function in resettlement, and thus to continue their existence and role (personal observation). Furthermore, the Chinese approach is unique also in that it fosters community solidarity in sharing some of the losses (particularly land) and requires some amount of redistribution of non-affected village lands between the non-displaced farmers and their community neighbors who are displaced. Evidence regarding community assets is also reported from Mexico's Aquamilpa resettlement program, which both restored prior community services and built several new community facilities (Johns 1996). In Thailand's Khao Laem project a group of better-off farmers avoided marginalization by negotiating with the project a land exchange, which allowed them to develop business activities (OED 1993). The overwhelming evidence, however, indicates that restoration of access to common property assets occurs much less frequently than replacement of private property lands, causing adverse sociocultural effects that undermine both livelihood restoration and the formation of new working communities, while fostering conflicts between resettlers and hosts. Overall, in light of our conceptual model these three reconstruction processes appear complex because they require institution-building and response from all actors involved. Yet to date they are least understood by practitioners, are least addressed, and tend to lag behind other reconstructive processes.

(g) *From food insecurity to adequate nutrition;*
(h) *From increased morbidity to better health care.*

Nutrition levels and health will depend in the long term on progress in resettler's economic recovery (land and/or employment). But in the short run, the strategy that our reconstruction model calls for requires that sudden disruption in food supply and adverse effects on health are arrested through immediate counteraction, even before full economic reconstruction. This is necessary to lower morbidity and prevent increases in mortality rates. Displacement-triggered difficulties are compounded by suddenness of change and, sometimes, by resettlers' behavior and culture. Borrowing from successful experiences with assistance to refugees (emergency relief) can be highly effective for offsetting immediate nutrition and health risks to resettlers, with focus particularly on most vulnerable groups (children, elderly, pregnant women, etc.). Sustainable reconstruction, however, requires long-term planning as well, beyond rapid relief measures, together with information and education, to foster resettlers' behavioral change and their learning to cope with the circumstances of the new habitat.

Selected empirical evidence: Existing evidence indicates that the risks of immediate food scarcity are more readily recognized by resettlement agencies than the health risks incurred by resettlers. Problem-resolution tends to gravitate around temporary food aid and allowances for a limited "transition" time. Long-term planning is seldom done. Resettlers' coping response tends also to address first the more easily perceivable food needs. Education campaigns among resettlers do little to stimulate adaptive behavioral changes in time, particularly regarding sanitation practices, which in the medium-term increases hazards to health. Thus, overall evidence confirms that the strategic directions indicated by the risk and reconstruction framework are indeed essential, yet not regularly incorporated into problem- resolution strategies in resettlement operations.

While I discussed above the constitutive elements of livelihood reconstruction one by one, or in subclusters, it is important to repeat that the risks and reconstruction framework emphasizes their interdependence and synergy. Therefore, every reconstruction strategy should ideally pursue these directions in an integrated manner. In turn, empirical research should attempt to identify the presence or absence of all of them in the same process or project cycle—something I have not usually found in current studies. Finding evidence that predisplacement levels have been restored (or even exceeded) in only one of these dimensions is an indicator that at least one sequence of pauperization has been broken and stopped. But it will take effective action on all or most to succeed in restoring livelihoods fully.

The Model as a Research Tool

The risks and reconstruction model can serve, last but not least, as a conceptual tool for guiding further research on resettlement. For researchers who may apply and test this model, there is a lot to do in terms of constructing new research strategies on resettlement, formulating hypotheses on risk correlation, testing the model in particular settings (Pandey et al. 1997), comparing with longitudinal studies (Scudder 1991) or measuring variables and outcomes. Despite all the recent expansion in research, there is much that we still do not know about resettlement, especially about the behavioral responses of various populations and subgroups, and about their own initiatives for coping and reconstructing.

As a conceptual codification of already accumulated knowledge, the model generalizes and theorizes about resettlement in a way that further invites, and hopefully may inspire, creative new research to be carried out. It presents in a nutshell an entire program for further, and systematic, studies on resettlement. This refers both to operational and basic research.

For operational research, the preparation of any project that involves resettlement should include analysis of the issues *in situ,* carrying out first a local risks assessment. That means finding out how the risks identified in the generalized model manifest themselves in the given projects context, whether other risks are present, who will be affected, and how such risks can be prevented or reduced.

Beyond the preparation stage, during project implementation, the model can be further used to construct an indicator list for: monitoring specific progress; identifying undesired or unanticipated effects; and eliciting feedback from the affected and host populations about specific variables, e.g., land repossession, health, housing, common property assets, services, or the recreation of social networks. In turn, *ex-post* evaluation research has a rich and promising territory for comparing actual results achieved in reconstruction with predicted risks and with the effects expected from the project's "re-development package." Beyond immediate applicability, findings from various independent sites can be easily compared for revealing best practices and crafting, possibly, alternative strategies.

For basic social research, the model's potential is vast as well. Hypothesis formulation and testing is obviously needed to assess the correlations between the model's variables under different circumstances: for instance, it can be hypothesized that adverse impacts on health or on nutrition will be less acute if the emphasis is placed not just on emergency medical relief but rather on community reconstitution; or that the use of scarce resources for restoring access to common property assets may have stronger effects than incrementally higher investments in housing; or that there are gender-related differences in risks. An important research direction may be to explore the relationship between the psychological and economic aspects of marginalization; and so on. The model's variables also facilitate multivariate analysis, and coherent organization and aggregation of findings either around the risk variables *per se,* or around the social actors variables, with many possible correlations. Further, as has been done in research on natural disasters (see the remarkable Drabek inventory; Drabek 1987), an inventory of findings and propositions about human responses to development-caused displacements, could be constructed and classified by type of social group, or type of development program, in a manner useful to further theorizing and model building as well as to practice.

Actual applications of the risks and reconstruction model have been already initiated by some researchers, with very good results. A study on "countering impoverishment risks" was done on the displaced people from India's Rengali dam (Ota 1996), measuring for each risk variable actual impacts, analyzing counter-risk measures, and also formulating specific recommendations about what needs to be done in practice. Another, much larger scale study on resettlement caused by seven different projects (dam construction, thermal plants, mining and industry) was carried out by the Institute for Socio-Economic Development (ISED) in Orissa on a sample of 31 villages and 441 households, with 2274 people, selected from among 95 affected villages with 1977 households. That study has used the modeling of key impoverishment risks as an analytical tool, producing new and comprehensive findings (see Pandey et al. 1997). These substantive findings, structured along the main impoverishment risks, are also a practical test of this conceptual framework under the demands of a large-scale field investigation.

The actual use, in practice and research, of the risks and reconstruction model for resettling displaced populations will certainly test its potential in many ways; it may change and improve it, and hopefully will enrich it further. Its key premise is that impoverishment through displacement is not inevitable or unmitigatable. After having done a great deal of field research and operational work on resettlement, I cannot emphasize enough the significant difficulties involved in actually preventing and mitigating these risks and in the arduous reconstruction of disrupted livelihoods and communities.

Yet forecasting impoverishment trends is important for initiating policy and practical measures that counteract undesirable outcomes. Failure to acknowledge and make known in a timely fashion the social risks inherent to displacement would allow them to unfold unimpeded in every case. Conversely, equitable policies and improved resettlement financing and implementation, with the participation of those affected, are apt to make possible the socio- economic reconstruction and development of resettlers' livelihoods.

References

Agnihotri, A. (1996). The Orissa resettlement and rehabilitation of project-affected-persons policy 1994: An analysis of its robustness with reference to the impoverishment risks model. In A. B. Ota & A. Agnihotri (Eds.), *Involuntary resettlement in dam projects*, (pp. 19042). New Delhi: Prachi Prakashan.

Appell, C. N. (1985). Resettlement of people in Indonesian Borneo: The social anthropology of administered peoples. *Borneo Research Bulletin, 17*, 1.

Appell, C. N. (1986). The health consequences of social change: A set of postulates for developing general adaptation theory. *Sarawak Museum Journal, 36*, 43–74.

Atteslander, P. (1995a). Social destabilization and the development of early warning system, Special issue on Anomie. *International Journal of Sociology and Social Policy, 159*(8/9/10), 9–23.

Atteslander, P. (1995b). Global development and the meaning of local culture—reflections on structural anomie. *International Journal of Sociology and Social Policy, 159*(8/9/10), 221–242.

Babboo, B. (1992). *Technology and social transformation. The case of the Hirakud multi-purpose dam in Orissa*. New Delhi: Concept.

Beck, U. (1990). On the way towards an industrial society at risk: An outline of an Argument. *International Journal of Political Economy, 20*, 51–69.

Cernea, M. M. (1986, February). *Involuntary resettlement in bank-assisted projects. A review of the application of bank policies and procedures in FY79-85 projects*. Washington, DC: Agriculture and Rural Development Department, World Bank.

Cernea, M. M. (1988). Involuntary resettlement in development projects: Policy guidelines in World Bank-financed projects. World Bank Technical Paper No. 80. Washington, DC: World Bank.

Cernea, M. M. (1990) Poverty risks from population displacement in water resources development. HIID Development Discussion Paper No. 355. Cambridge, MA: Harvard University.

Cernea, M. M. (1995a). Social integration and population displacement: The contribution of social science. *International Social Science Journal, 143*, 91–112.

Cernea, M. M. (1995b). Understanding and preventing impoverishment from displacement: Reflections on the state of knowledge. Keynote address, International Conference on Development Induced Displacement. University of Oxford, England. *Journal of Refugee Studies, 8*(3), 245–264.

Cernea, M. M. (1996a). Bridging the research divide: Studying refugees and development oustees. In T. Allen (Ed.), *In search of cool ground: War, flight and homecoming in Northeast Africa.* Boston: UNRISID.

Cernea, M. M. (1996b, June). Public policy responses to development-induced population displacement. *Economic and Political Weekly.*

Chambers, R. (1969). *Settlement schemes in tropical Africa.* London: Routledge and Kegan Paul.

Chambers, R., & Morris, J. (Eds.). (1973). *Mwea, an irrigated rice settlement in Kenya.* München: Weltsforum.

Costa-Pierce, B. A. (1996). Sustainable reservoir fisheries: An ecosystems approach. Draft, unpublished.

de Wet, C. (1995). *Moving together, drifting apart. Betterment planning and villagization in a South African Homeland.* Johannesburg: Witwatersrand University Press.

Downing, T. E. (1996a). Mitigating social impoverishment when people are involuntarily displaced. In C. McDowell (Ed.), *Understanding impoverishment: The consequences of development-induced displacement* (pp. 203–215). Oxford: Berghahn Books.

Downing, T. E. (1996b). Personal Communication.

Drabek, T. E. (1987). *Human systems responses to disasters: An inventory of sociological findings.* New York: Springer.

D'Souza, V. S. (1990). *Development planning and structural inequalities: The response of the underprivileged.* New Delhi: Sage.

Feeney, P. (1995, May). *Displacement and the rights of women.* Oxfam, Policy Department, Oxford.

Fernandes, W. (1991). Power and powerlessness: development projects and displacement of tribals. *Social Action, 41*(3), 243–270.

Fernandes, W., Das, J. C., & Rao, S. (1989). Displacement and rehabilitation: an estimate of extent and prospects. In W. Fernandes & E. Ganguly Thukral (Eds.), *Development, displacement and rehabilitation* (pp. 62–68). New Delhi: Indian Social Institute.

Galtung, J. (1994). *Early warning: An early warning to early warners.* Biel: Swiss Institute for Development.

Giddens, A. (1990). *The consequences of modernity.* Stanford: Stanford University Press.

Gopal, G. (1992, August). Participation of women in involuntary resettlement in selected Asian countries: operational issues and guidelines. Manuscript.

Guggenheim, S. E. (1994). *Involuntary resettlement: An annotated reference bibliography for development research.* Washington, DC: World Bank.

Hansen, A. (1990) Long-term consequences of two African refugee settlement strategies. *Paper presented at the meetings of the Society for Applied Anthropology, York, UK.*

Jayewardene, R. A. (1995). Cause for concern: health and resettlement. In H. M. Mathur (Ed.), *Development, Displacement and Resettlement: Focus on Asian Experiences.* Delhi: Vikas.

Johns, K. (1996). Report on resettlement program of the Aquamilpa Hydroelectric Project. Draft, unpublished.

Joseph, J. (1997). Evolving a retrofit economic rehabilitation policy model using impoverishment risks analysis—Experience of Maharashtra Composite Irrigation Project III. In H. M. Mathur & D. Marsden (Eds.), *Impoverishment risks in resettlement.* New Delhi: Sage.

Kaplan, S., & Garrick, B. J. (1981). On the quantitative definition of risk. *Risk Analysis, 19*(1), 11–27.

Kibreab, G. (1996, September). *Common property resource and involuntary resettlement.* Paper at the Oxford international conference on reconstructive livelihoods: new approaches to resettlement.

Koenig, D. (1995). Women and resettlement. In R. Gallins & A. Ferguson (Eds.), *The women and international development* (Vol. 4). Boulder, CO: Westview Press.

Lassailly-Jacob, V. (1994). Government-sponsored agricultural schemes for involuntary migrants in Africa: Some key obstacles to their economic viability. In H. Adelman & J. Sorenson (Eds.), *Refugees: Development aid and repatriation.* New York: Westview Press Boulder and York Lanes Press.

Lassailly-Jacob, V. (1996) Key issues in preventing impoverishment in land-based resettlement programmes in Africa. In C. McDowell (Ed.), *Understanding impoverishment: The consequences of development induced displacement* (pp. 187–199). Oxford: Berghahn Books.

Low, S., & Altman, I. (Eds.). (1992). *Place attachment.* New York: Plenum Press.

Luhman, N. (1993). *Risk: A sociological theory.* New York: Aldin de Gruyter.

Mahapatra, L. K. (1991). Development for whom? Depriving the dispossessed tribals. *Social Action, 41*(3), 271–287.

Mahapatra, L. K. (1994). *Tribal development in India, myth and reality.* Delhi: Vikas Publishing House.

Mahapatra, L. K. (1996). Good intentions or policy are not enough: Reducing impoverishment risks for the tribal oustees. In A. B. Ota & A. Agnihotri (Eds.), *Involuntary displacement in dam projects* (pp. 150–178). New Delhi: Prachi Prakashan.

Marsden, D. (1997). Resettlement and rehabilitation in India: some lessons from recent experience. In H. M. Mathur & D. Marsden (Eds.), *Impoverishment risks in resettlement.* New Delhi: Sage.

Mathur, H. M. (1997). Loss of access to basic public services. In H. M. Mathur & D. Marsden (Eds.), *Impoverishment risks in resettlement.* New Delhi: Sage.

Mathur, H. M., & Marsden, D. (1997). *Impoverishment risks in resettlement.* New Delhi: Sage.

Mburugu, E. K. (1993) Dislocation of settled communities in the development process: The case of Kiambere Hydroelectric Project. In C. C. Cook (Ed.), *Involuntary resettlement in Africa*. World Bank Technical Paper No. 227. Washington, DC: World Bank.

Merton, R. K. (1979). *The sociology of science: Theoretical and empirical investigations.* Chicago: University of Chicago Press.

Mougeot, L. J. A. (1989) Hydroelectric development and involuntary resettlement in Brazilian Amazonia: planning and evaluation. Cobham Resource Consultants, Edinburgh.

Nayak, P. K. (1986). *Resettlement at Rengali Dam.* Orissa: Bhubaneshwar.

Nelson, M. (1973). *Development of tropical lands: Policy issues in Latin America.* Baltimore: Johns Hopkins University Press.

Ngaide, T. (1986) Socio-economic implications of irrigation systems in Mauritania: The Boghe and Foum-Gleita Irrigation Projects. Thesis submitted for Master of Science (Land Resources), University of Wisconsin-Madison.

OED (Operations Evaluation Department, World Bank) (1993) *Early experiences with involuntary resettlement: Impact evaluation on Thailand, Khao Laem Hydroelectric Project.* Report No. 12131. Washington, DC: World Bank.

Oliver-Smith, A. (1994). Resistance to resettlement: the formation and evolution of movements. In *Research in social movements, conflicts and change.* Greenwich, CT: JAI Press.

Ota, A. B. (1996). In A. B. Ota & A. Agnihotri (Eds.), *Countering the impoverishment risk: The case of the Rengali Dam Project Involuntary displacement in dam projects* (pp. 150–178). New Delhi: Prachi Prakashan.

Padjadjaran University. (1989, March). *Environmental impact analysis of the Cirata Dam.* Padjadjaran, India: Institute of Ecology.

Pandey, B., et al. (1997) *Development, displacement and rehabilitation in Orissa 1950-1990.* International Development Research Centre, Canada, and Institute for Socio-Economic Development, Bhubaneswar.

Quarantelli, E. L. (1980). *Evacuation behavior and problems: Findings and implications from the research literature*. Columbus, OH: Disaster Research Center, Ohio State University.

Quarantelli, E. L. (1981). Psycho-sociology in emergency planning. *International Civil Defense Bulletin, 2,* 28.

Reddy, I. U. B. (1997). Involuntary resettlement and marginalization of project-affected persons: A comparative analysis of Singrauli and Rihand Power projects. In H. M. Mathur & D. Marsden (Eds.), *Impoverishment risks in resettlement*. New Delhi: Sage.

Rew, A. W. and Driver, P. A. (1986) *Evaluation of the Victoria Dam Project in Sri Lanka, Volume III.* Initial Evaluation of the Social and Environmental Impact of the Victoria Dam project, Annex J Social Analysis, Annex K Environmental Analysis. Mimeo.

Scudder, T. (1991) Development-induced relocation and refugee studies: 37 years of change and continuity among Zambia's Gwembe Tonga. *Journal of Refugee Studies, 6.*

Scudder, T., & Colson, E. (1982). From welfare to development of a conceptual framework for the analysis of dislocated people. In A. Hansen & A. Oliver-Smith (Eds.), *Involuntary migration and resettlement* (pp. 267–287). Boulder, CO: Westview.

Sequeira, D. (1994, January). Gender and resettlement an overview of impact and planning issues in bank-assisted projects. Draft paper prepared for the Bankwide Resettlement Review. Washington, DC: World Bank.

Shi, G., & Hu, W. (1994). *Comprehensive evaluation and monitoring of displaced persons standards of living*. National Research Centre of Resettlement, Hohai University.

Shihata, I. F. I. (1991). Involuntary resettlement in World Bank-financed projects. In *World Bank in a changing world* (p. 181). Amsterdam: Martinus Nyhoff.

Soeftestad, L. T. (1990, June). On evacuation of people in the Kotmale Hydro Power Project: Experience from a socio-economic impact study. *Bistaandsantropologen.*

Sowell, T. (1996). *Migrations and cultures: A world view*. New York: Basic Books.

Spiegel, H. (1997) Letters to the author.

Thangaraj, S. (1996). Impoverishment risk analysis—A methodological tool for participatory settlement planning. In C. McDowell (Ed.), *Understanding displacement: The consequences of development-induced displacement* (pp. 993–232). Providence: Berghahn Books.

Turner, R. J., Wheaton, B., & Lloyd, D. A. (1995). The epidemiology of social stress. *American Sociological Review, 60,* 104–125.

United Nations. (1995). *Copenhagen program of action adopted by the World Summit for social development*. New York: United Nations.

Wolfensohn, J. D. (1995, October). *Address at the annual meeting of the world bank and IMF*. Washington, DC: World Bank.

World Bank. (1990). *Involuntary resettlement*. Operational Directive 4.30. Washington, DC: World Bank.

World Bank. (1994/96). *Resettlement and development: The bankwide review of projects involving involuntary resettlement 1986-1993*. Washington, DC: World Bank.

World Bank. (1995a). *Project completion report Kenya: Export development project.* Report No. 13886. Washington, DC: World Bank.

World Bank. (1995b). *India—Project completion report India: Dudhichua Coal Project.* Report No. 13938. Washington, DC: World Bank.

World Bank. (1996). *China-Shuikou reservoir resettlement*. Draft of completion report. Washington, DC: World Bank.

Michael Cernea started working as assistant researcher in the Institute of Philosophy of the Romanian Academy in 1958, became principal researcher, defended his PhD in 1962 and became the Chief of the Institute's social research section soon thereafter. During the 1960s, he helped break the official publication on empirical anthropological research in Romania at that time by shifting the research section h led at the institute of Philosophy from general social philosophy to empirical sociological field investigations in industrial and rural sociology. He was invited as visiting researcher at the *Centre D'Etudes Sociologiques* in Paris (1967) and as Fellow in residence at the *Center for Advanced Studies in the Behavioral Sciences* (CASBS), Stanford, USA in 1970–1971. The European Society for Rural Sociology elected him as Vice-President (1973–1977). The Romanian Academy awarded Dr. Cernea the Vasile Conta Prize, and other prizes and distinctions for his research publications.

In mid 1974, Cernea emigrated to the United States, where he has since lived, taught and practiced for the longest part of his professional sociological and anthropological career. In August 1974, the World Bank in Washington, D.C. selected him as its first in-house sociologist, then as its Senior Sociologist, and Senior Adviser for Social Policy and Sociology from 1982 to 1997. Between 1998 and 2003 he was appointed as member of the CGIAR Science Council (the group of 16 International Agricultural Research Centers). Professor Cernea has also served as Senior Social Adviser to international organizations such as the UN, OECD, UNDP, ADB, CGIAR, FAO, BP, Chevron, etc. on social policy, development, cultural and poverty issues. He was elected as officer in various capacities for international and national professional social science organizations, including as Vice-President of *The Gusti Foundation* (Romania) after 1990. He has worked also for non-profit organizations, served as currently Director in the Board of PACT (USA), and was a member of the Board of Trustees of the Bibliotheca Alexandrina (Egypt) (2000–2008).

Open Access This chapter is licensed under the terms of the Creative Commons Attribution 4.0 International License (http://creativecommons.org/licenses/by/4.0/), which permits use, sharing, adaptation, distribution and reproduction in any medium or format, as long as you give appropriate credit to the original author(s) and the source, provide a link to the Creative Commons license and indicate if changes were made.

The images or other third party material in this chapter are included in the chapter's Creative Commons license, unless indicated otherwise in a credit line to the material. If material is not included in the chapter's Creative Commons license and your intended use is not permitted by statutory regulation or exceeds the permitted use, you will need to obtain permission directly from the copyright holder.

Muddy Waters: Inside the World Bank as It Struggled with the Narmada Irrigation and Resettlement Projects, Western India

Robert H. Wade

Narmada is a four letter word (Africa division chief, World Bank, 1995)

You believe that institutions change the world, Mr Bromley. I believe that infrastructure does. Come back in 20 years and we'll see who is right (Gabriel Tibor, chief of World Bank India Irrigation Division, late 1970s).

The important thing is that we *have* such a report, and can point to it. It will also be a very valuable source of facts and references. (Letter of half-thanks from Sardar Sarovar task manager to the author of the first environmental assessment of the project, 1988)

The Bank's resettlement policy is "an exaggerated response. The condition of equal livelihood in the new place is too stringent as a general rule. It is possible where land is abundant and where there is a good financial system (for example Argentina or even Mexico), but almost impossible—I would say impossible—in India and Bangladesh" (Ernest Stern, the first or second most powerful person in the World Bank from the late 1970s to his retirement in the mid 1990s, speaking in 1995).

If the Bank continued with the project "it would signal that no matter how egregious the situation, no matter how flawed the project, no matter how many policies have been violated, and no matter how clear the remedies prescribed, the Bank will go forward on its own terms"

This article is based on field work inside the World Bank (not on the ground in India) undertaken in 1995–96 for the World Bank History Project. It is an extended (three times longer) version of my account of Narmada in "Greening the Bank: the struggle over the environment, 1970–1995", in Devesh Kapur, John Lewis and Richard Webb (eds), 1997, *The World Bank: Its First Half Century*, Brookings, vol. 2. The latter publication had a small print run and neither Brookings nor the World Bank publicized it; indeed, for some years after publication the World Bank bookshop refused to stock it, on grounds that it was not published by the Bank. It has long been out of print. Since 1997 I have asked some 15 Executive Directors whether they know of the History, whether they have read any of it. Several said they had heard of it, one said he had read some of it. In Bank culture, the value placed on learning from the past is approximately zero. The present tense refers to the mid 1990s, except where the context makes clear otherwise.

R. H. Wade (✉)
Department of International Development, London School of Economics, London, UK
e-mail: R.Wade@lse.ac.uk

(Patrick Coady, US Executive Director, statement at the meeting of the Executive Board, World Bank, 23 October 1992)

* * *

The period since the Second World War has witnessed three global power shifts: one, from sovereign states relating to each other through balances of power, to interstate organizations which pool some sovereignty and enact collective preferences; two, from states to non-state organizations, including NGOs, enormously facilitated by the internet; and three, from West to East. The World Bank has been a microcosm of these shifts. This chapter describes the interplay between some of the agents: World Bank staff; World Bank top management; World Bank Executive Directors (representatives of member governments, who formally govern the Bank); Government of India and governments of states; Indian and international (mainly UK, US, Japanese) NGOs; and the US Congress. The context is the Narmada irrigation and resettlement projects in western India from the 1970s to the 1990s. The first of the projects (Sardar Sarovar) became the subject of a large-scale opposition movement, Indian and international, which ended up forcing the World Bank to take serious responsibility for resettlement and environmental sustainability in its projects worldwide, and to create an independent inspection facility to which people who consider their welfare net harmed by a World Bank-supported project can bring complaints direct to the Bank by-passing their national government.

Then in the mid 1980s the third set of actors—after staff and governments — entered the game: NGOs, at first largely American and largely pursuing environmental objectives. They exercised leverage via their influence in the US Congress and its control of American finance for the Bank. They selected particular projects for scrutiny, aiming to reveal publicly that the projects were having seriously damaging effects not admitted by the Bank, and thereby to convince the Bank's shareholders that it needed reform.

The first project to attract serious criticism of the Bank from the US government, US NGOs, and the US public—the first "bomb"—was Polonoroeste, in northwest Brazil.[1] At its core it involved paving a 1500 km road from the densely populated south central region into the sparsely populated Amazon. Beyond this, it intended to help establish the incomers in new farms and settlements, while also keeping them out of demarcated ecological and Amerindian zones. Starting in 1983 and continuing till 1987 US NGOs used Polonoroeste as their spearhead or trampoline for demanding changes in Bank policy. Suddenly the Bank found itself defined as the doer of harm and the teller of lies, and required to react to *outsiders'* ideas about how it should do its business. For an organization that had always prided itself on its service to humanity and unrivalled technical expertise, this was a bewildering experience. The Bank eventually suspended financial disbursements for the project in response to the NGO campaign and the evidence of environmental and social damage which the campaign unearthed—the first time in its history that it had suspended

---

[1] See Robert Wade, "Boulevard of broken dreams: inside the World Bank as it struggled with the Polonoroeste project in Brazil's Amazon", Brazilian J. of Political Economy, part 1, 36 (1), 2016, part 2, 36 (3) 2016.

disbursements on such grounds. It resumed disbursements only after it was satisfied that the Brazilian government had made real progress on its commitments. Hence the Polonoroeste project has a seminal role in the story of how the Bank—and global norms more generally—moved from saying "We are a development organization and environment is for some other organization to deal with" to saying "Our mandate is environmentally and socially sustainable development"; and also in the interwoven story of how it moved from saying "We are accountable only to our shareholders (member governments), and NGOs can convey their views to us only through the relevant Executive Director on the Board" to saying "We are concerned to reach out to civil society organizations and learn from what they have to say".

As the Polonoroeste campaign was winding down in the late 1980s a second wave of attack on the Bank got underway. The "image" of this second wave was the Narmada projects in Northwest India.

The Narmada Valley Projects constitute a basin-wide, inter-state development scheme to harness the Narmada river, seen as one of India's last "unexploited" resources for hydropower and irrigation. Indian planners in the 1960s and 1970s envisaged four mega dams and hundreds of smaller dams being built along the Narmada river during the following half century or so, making it one of the largest water resource projects in the world. The first of the big dams, called Sardar Sarovar, would be as high as a 45 story building and over a kilometer long at the crest. Its reservoir would stretch for 200 km, displacing some 40,000 households or 200,000 people. The canal at its head would be more than 200 m from one bank to the other, its network would extend for 75,000 km and irrigate almost two million hectares of arid land.[2] The network would remove some portion of the land of 68,000 households. From the beginning the staff in the India Irrigation Division—the most powerful and prestigious division in the whole of the Bank, because it lent the most—saw the Narmada projects as the chance of a life-time to promote a paradigm change in Indian irrigation, from the prevailing late nineteenth century paradigm to a late twentieth century one geared towards the needs of complex agriculture. They saw themselves as innovators with a strong concern for what they called "the environment".

The transnational resistance to the Narmada projects began as a "bottom up" social movement (in contrast to Polonoroeste), led by Indian NGOs working in the

---

[2]This is the claim in the project documents. Indian irrigation canals normally irrigate a fraction of the planned irrigated area, there being political advantages to claiming a bigger area to be irrigated than is feasible. Politicians and engineers stand to earn many times their salaries by agreeing to extend the "planned" irrigated area to include hitherto excluded villages, regardless of feasibility. Also, inter-state water sharing agreements are based on "area to be irrigated", regardless of intensity of irrigation. Hence a project of 50,000 ha that planned to grow three crops of rice a year would get no more inter-state water than one of the same size that planned to grow only one crop of rice. Better to claim a very extensive irrigation and worry about broken promises later. See Wade, "On the sociology of irrigation statistics: How do we know the truth about canal performance?", *Agricultural Administration*, 19 (2), 1985, pp. 63–79. For an analysis of the Narmada projects as a case study of the inadequacies of traditional cost/benefit approaches to project planning see Jack Ruitenbeek and Cynthia Carier, "Evaluation of Narmada projects: An ecological economics perspective", *Economic and Political Weekly* (Bombay), 26 August, 1995, pp. 2138–45.

Narmada valley. Their resistance sparked a campaign within India that drew unprecedented support from the middle-class public, among whom it signaled a profound shift away from Nehru's "hardware" notion of progress. The Indian campaign blossomed into the transnational alliance of NGOs that pulled in legislators from several Part I countries. (Part I refers to the richer, non-borrowing members of the World Bank, Part II to the poorer, borrowing members.)

Taking off just before the Bank's internal reorganization of 1987, the transnational campaign against Narmada stiffened Bank senior management's commitment to environmental assessment procedures and the creation of a large environmental complex. But the main effects came later. In response to years of pressure the Bank and Government of India canceled the Bank's involvement in the first of the big dams, Sardar Sarovar, in 1993—the first time the Bank had canceled a loan anywhere in the world on environmental or social (as distinct from financial or procurement) grounds. Earlier an independent panel, appointed by the Bank, had reviewed the Sardar Sarovar project and the Bank's role in it, and reached conclusions very detrimental to the Bank.[3]

The momentum of the NGO campaign led the Bank to accede to the demands of US NGOs, the US Congress and the US and Dutch Executive Directors that the Bank establish, in 1993, a permanent "independent inspection panel" to which outside groups could bring complaints that they have been harmed by the Bank's failure to follow its own resettlement and environmental policies.

The Narmada campaign also accelerated the Bank's agreeing to a policy of freer disclosure of information about projects under preparation. And it helped to solidify the change in the Bank's stance towards NGOs from illegitimate to legitimate interlocutors.[4] These important changes in the Bank's governance—making features new to the governance of *any* multilateral financial organization—were driven by the constantly boiling pot of Narmada. This chapter reveals the "underwear politics" of the project.

Entry Conditions

The Government of India (GOI) approached the Bank for help with the Narmada scheme in 1978, and in the same year the Bank sent a reconnaissance mission to determine an appropriate means for involvement. The Bank prepared the first stage

---

[3] *Sardar Sarovar: The Report of the Independent Review*, Ottawa: Resource Futures International Inc., 1992, also known as the Morse Commission Report. Cited as *Independent Review, 1992*.

[4] World Bank, "The World Bank's Partnership with Nongovernmental Organizations", Participation and NGO Group, Poverty and Social Policy Department, World Bank, Washington DC, May 1996. Lori Udall, "The World Bank and public accountability: has anything changed?", in Jonathan Fox and David Brown, *The Struggle For Accountability: The World Bank, NGOs, and Grassroots Movements*, MIT Press, Cambridge, chapter 11, 391–436.

project (Sardar Sarovar dam and canals) in 1979–1983; appraised it in 1983–1984; the Board approved a loan and credit in March 1985 for $450 million.[5]

On the Indian side several initial conditions shaped the trajectory of the project:

- The costs and benefits of Sardar Sarovar were spread very unequally between the three riparian states. Gujarat, where the dam was located, got the irrigation benefits, and the project had long been one of the top priorities of the Gujarat government. Madhya Pradesh (MP), where most of the reservoir was located, was home to most of the "oustees" (the convenient Indian-English word for those forced to resettle). Eighty percent of the 245 villages to be flooded were in MP. But MP got none of the irrigation benefits. MP's willingness to bear the costs of Sardar Sarovar was critical for the project going ahead. But it did not strongly want a project from which it received only a small share of the benefits in return for bearing most of the costs in flooded land and resettlement. It agreed to cooperate only in the expectation that the Bank would help fund a large upstream dam in MP from which it would derive most of the benefits.[6] The third state, Maharashtra, had a small share of the costs and a smaller share of the benefits. Maharashtra had no strong interest in the project one way or the other. [7]
- There was no superordinate agency above the state governments to take authoritative decisions. Both water and resettlement are "state" subjects in the Indian federation. The mis-named Narmada Control Authority had neither control nor authority. It was only a coordination body, without a presence on the ground beyond the regional city. Hence the Bank had to deal with the state governments separately, and the state governments often disagreed. They could not even agree on a joint fisheries protection plan for the Narmada river.

---

[5]At the time of the Bank's appraisal this amounted to 18% of the cost of the dam and power sub-project and about 30% of the water delivery sub-project.

[6]The Bank's main leverage on MP came via its willingness to finance the upstream dam, Narmada Sagar (subsequently renamed Indira Sagar). Yet as the Bank later discovered, leverage via Narmada Sagar turned out to be much less than it thought. Political power in MP lies in the eastern part of the state, Narmada Sagar lies in the west. Within the west, power lies with rich landlords, many of whom did not want Narmada Sagar because it would flood *their* lands (and others did not want Sardar Sarovar for the same reason). In short, the politics of MP were such as to create no strong constituency for either Sardar Sarovar or Narmada Sagar. Cultural differences between the states added to the difficulties of cooperation. Gujarat is known as one of the most "progressive" states in India, next door MP as one of the most "backward". Gujarat is to Massachussets as MP is to Louisiana, it is said. Other differences fed in. Gujarat is one of India's smallest states (outside the northeast), and one of the wealthiest. MP is India's biggest state, the size of Germany and Austria combined; its 66 million people make it one of the biggest in population, bigger than all European states except Germany; and it is one of India's poorest states (14th of the 20 main states by per capita state domestic product). For much of the time between 1979 and 1993 the three states were run by different political parties, so they lacked even a common party bridge.

[7]The distribution of electrical power was meant to compensate. Under the terms of the tribunal award (clause VII) MP was to get 57% of the net power, Maharashtra 27%, and Gujarat 16%. But power is less valuable to politicians than irrigation in an economy of this type. Besides, since the power plant would stand in Gujarat, the other states could not be sure that Gujarat would comply with the stipulated shares.

- Gujarat was well advanced in planning the scheme by 1978. It had even started work on the ground, that had then been halted by an inter-state water dispute, resolved by a federal tribunal in 1979 after 10 years of deliberation. When the Bank reconnaissance mission arrived the chief engineer for Gujarat dumped 18 volumes of plans on the table and said, "Here are our plans. We start tomorrow."[8]

On the Bank side, the new vice president for South Asia, David Hopper, an expert in Indian irrigation and agriculture, remained vice president during the critical first two-thirds of the Bank's involvement, from 1979 to 1987. Under him the chief of the elite India Irrigation Division was Gabriel ("Gabby") Tibor, one of the Bank's longest serving and most charismatic division chiefs, a decorated Second World War veteran and Israeli irrigation engineer esteemed by colleagues as brash, innovative and hard-charging, and with a direct line—it was said—to Bank president Robert McNamara.

Hopper and Tibor agreed—as did the Secretary of Irrigation, Government of India—that the Bank had for too long been helping Indian engineers to perfect nineteenth century British engineering design instead of upgrading to late twentieth century design standards. They worried that if Gujarat's plans were not changed Sardar Sarovar would reflect a late nineteenth century solution to a problem that twentieth century technology had long solved. Gujarat's design gave priority to making water flow at a speed that was neither so slow as to deposit silt nor so fast as to cause erosion. In the twentieth century, reservoir management could handle the silt problem and canal lining could handle the erosion problem. A canal with reservoir and lining should therefore give priority to the higher levels of water control warranted by the more intensive and variegated agriculture of the late twentieth century. But Gujarat's designs did not reflect this.

For Hopper and Tibor, the inter-state tribunal's award in 1979 was what one of them described as "an evangelical moment". *They wanted to seize the rare chance of Sardar Sarovar to make a beachhead of change in India's conservative irrigation establishment.* Conversely, they thought Gujarat's existing plans would be a disaster in the making; the resulting canal would have insufficient water control to avoid extensive water logging and salinity, let alone support a variegated agriculture. *Hence issues of seepage, drainage, and water control became central to the project's definition. In this limited sense the Bank, supported by the Indian irrigation secretary, gave great weight to "environmental" issues, and it baffled the Bank's project staff when the campaign later accused them of neglecting the environment.*

However, the Gujarat government stoutly resisted any Bank-required delay. The Finance Minister told the Bank, "I have got 30 crores [300 million rupees] from the Assembly for the project. You want me to stop it now? How can I justify the delay?"

People both in the Bank and in India took for granted that, provided the water logging/salinity problems were taken care of and the engineering brought up to late

---

[8] Per Ljung, Project Officer, interview, March 12, 1996.

twentieth century standards, the benefits would be so big that the costs did not have to be examined carefully. "If you drive out through the command area of Sardar Sarovar", said one of the project leaders on the Bank side, "you don't have to be a rocket scientist to see that the benefits of this project are absolutely huge".

India had no choice but to invest in big dams, hydro power and irrigation systems, they said. Some 15–20 million extra livelihoods had to be found each year in order to sustain the growing population. Some could be found in agriculture, *provided* there was irrigation and power. Some could be found in cities, *provided* there was water, sewerage, and power. Either water must be diverted from existing irrigation—displacing existing farmers and making them the *refugees of the future* on a scale that would dwarf the numbers who had to move because of the reservoir—or additional dams and canals must be built. And the expanded hydro capacity would allow electricity to be provided without the additional air pollution of coal-fired power stations. The Sardar Sarovar hydro station would generate a more than 10% increase in power to India's Western Regional grid.

The assumption that benefits would vastly outweigh costs shaped what the planners paid attention to. Hardly any analysis lay behind the claim that 30 million people would benefit from improved domestic and industrial drinking water supply, for example. The existing situation was so bad that just about everyone could be assumed to benefit, said the project planners. Against a recommended Indian norm of 50–60 l per person per day, and an average of about 20 l a day for people living in the poorer parts of cities elsewhere in India with "adequate" overall water supply, the people living in the poorer parts of the cities of Gujarat were getting less than eight liters (two gallons) a day. So when a Bank resettlement specialist asked project staff in the late 1980s about the effect of the project on the drinking water supply of villages downstream of the dam, they responded impatiently, "We are bringing drinking water to X hundred villages in Gujarat that have never had reliable supplies before". The benefits to the new villages were so obviously greater than any possible loss to the downstream villages that the calculation did not have to be made.[9]

Indeed everything except the physical infrastructure was neglected. In 1980 a newly recruited Bank staff member with a degree in regional planning talked to several people in the India Irrigation Division about the Narmada projects, with a view to joining the division in order to work on regional development. He decided against after seeing that the division had little interest in matters beyond the water works.

Underlying this orientation was an assumption in the India Irrigation Division and in the Bank at large that infrastructure was the solution to development problems. When institutional economist Daniel Bromley gave a seminar on irrigation institutions at the Bank in the late 1970s Division Chief Tibor said impatiently, "You

---

[9]William Partridge, interview, March 10, 1995.

believe that institutions change the world, Mr Bromley. I believe that infrastructure does. Come back in 20 years and we'll see who is right".[10]

The Bank's budgetary rules reinforced the assumption. The budget for project preparation related not to the *complexity* of the project, but to the size of the loan. A simple highway project would receive (roughly) the same project preparation budget as the same sized loan for a complex irrigation-and-hydro project. This apparently nonsensical practice reflected the difficulties of designing a more flexible budgetary system for the whole organization when the organization's bottom line was difficult to measure; and reflected more specifically President McNamara's drive to control the organization by means of simple coefficients linking inputs and outputs (not outcomes).

Resettlement

The national and international campaign against Narmada focused on resettlement more than environment. The resettlement problems that in the end forced the Bank out were inevitable as long as the project was not held either to the resettlement standards contained in the inter-state water tribunal's decision or to the standards of the Bank's own resettlement directive, adopted in 1980. Neither the South Asia regional staff nor any level of the Indian government gave priority to resettlement.

---

[10] I gave a seminar to the India Irrigation Division in 1981. The seminar was titled, "Institutional determinants of canal performance in India", and had been pressed upon the reluctant India Irrigation Division by people in the central Agriculture and Rural Development Department anxious to promote an institutional agenda as a complement to the engineering one. When the Irrigation people learned, the day before the seminar, that my "institutional determinants" included an elaborate system of irrigation corruption they panicked, and begged me to talk about other things. They said that the sociologist Michael Cernea was the Bank's corruption man, he took care of corruption issues, and if I wanted to talk about corruption I should do it under his auspices, not theirs. (Right up to 1995, when President Wolfenson arrived, "corruption" was a forbidden word across the Bank.) I persisted. I began the seminar by citing evidence of poor canal irrigation performance in India, and then started to describe the well-institutionalized corruption system as one of the main causes. Division Chief Tibor, seated in the central place, rose to his feet, made a harrumphing noise of disapproval,, and stormed out, slamming the door behind him. The others froze. Their discomfort worsened as I persisted in describing how the corruption system affected operation and maintenance. At the end the acting chair called for questions. Silence. Eventually a corpulent Pakistani irrigation engineer and Bank consultant spoke up. He wore two gold rings, a gold bracelet, and a Rolex watch. He protested that—though my account of large-scale irrigation corruption may apply to India—he had seen nothing beyond petty field staff corruption in his many years with the Pakistani irrigation service. With barely any more questions or comments the seminar came to a relieved end. One of the participants whispering as we left, "Methinks he (the Pakistani) doth protest too much". See Wade, "The system of political and administrative corruption: canal irrigation in India", *Journal of Development Studies*, v. 18 (3), 1982, 287–328; and "The market for public office: why the Indian state is not better at development", *World Development*, 13, 4, 1985, 467–97.

The standard Bank line on resettlement worldwide had been, "It is the government's job to provide cleared land at the site of an infrastructure project. It is the government's job to decide how to treat the displaced". Then came the Sobradhinho incident in the late 1970s. Sobradhinho was a major dam in Brazil whose construction and reservoir entailed the involuntary resettlement of over 60,000 people. The Bank was helping to finance its construction. There was no plan to resettle the people. The dam was completed, the water began to rise, the people refused to move, their imminent submersion could not be ignored, the army was sent in to evict them. Some Bank staff tried to draw internal attention to the problem but were told that resettlement was a domestic matter. Church groups began to write letters to McNamara, and McNamara was disturbed to find that the Bank had no resettlement policy. He indicated to the director of the central Agriculture and Rural Development (AGR) Department (Montague Yudelman) that the Bank should get something in place. Yudelman was already persuaded that the Bank needed a policy.

At the same time, Michael Cernea, the Bank's solitary sociologist, had become interested in forced resettlement (as distinct from resettlement of the voluntary kind, as in Malaysia's FELDA jungle settlements).[11] Cernea worked for Yudelman. Now that McNamara was interested Yudelman boosted his support for what Cernea had already quietly started, a review of the Bank's experience with forced resettlement region by region. The review was to lead to resettlement policy guidelines for project officers.

Cernea was chief author of the Bank's operational policy manual statement (OMS) on involuntary resettlement, issued in February 1980. This was the first policy statement to be issued by an international development agency on the subject. It said, among other things, that the Bank required a resettlement plan whose "...main objective is to ensure that settlers are afforded opportunities to become established and economically self-sustaining in the shortest possible period, *at living standards that at least match those before resettlement.*"[12] On the other hand, the Bank made clear that the cost for resettlement had to be born by local budgets; it would not lend for resettlement.

---

[11]Michael Cernea joined the Bank in 1974 as its first sociologist, having been professor of rural sociology in Romania. He is a Romanian refugee. Asked why he made such a crusade out of forced resettlement he replied that he considers himself an oustee.

In 1977 Cernea invited Thayer Scudder, one of the world's few resettlement experts and professor of anthropology at Caltech, to give a seminar in his newly launched sociology seminar series for Bank staff. They agreed the subject would be government-sponsored voluntary settlement schemes like Malaysia's FELDA and Indonesia's Transmigration. At the last minute Scudder changed the subject to something he was currently interested in, involuntary relocation, including Bank-financed dam projects like Kariba, Nigeria's Kainji, and Brazil's Sobradhinho. Cernea had not thought about involuntary settlement, and was intrigued by what Scudder said. With help from Scudder he began to review Bank projects region by region to see how forced resettlement had been handled. See Michael Cernea, "Social integration and population displacement: the contribution of social science", *International Social Science Journal*, v. 143, n.1, 1995.

[12]OMS 2.33, "Social issues associated with involuntary resettlement in Bank-financed projects", February 1980, para. 18.

Then, as today, the Bank had many policy directives and guidelines. New ones landed on the project officers' desks every month or two. The art of the project officer was to figure out which ones mattered in the eyes of management. Around 1979 and 1980, when the resettlement directive was being prepared and introduced, resettlement attracted some attention inside the Bank, and plans were prepared for a number of projects. But for the next several years little happened as project officers saw that *observance* of the resettlement directive was not being monitored. It joined the long list of directives that could be ignored. These years of fading resettlement concern were the early years of Narmada.

The India Irrigation Division, its attention focused on redesigning the infrastructure to late twentieth century standards, ignored resettlement completely. Not till 1983, as Sardar Sarovar was being appraised, did Michael Cernea discover that the appraisal mission's terms of reference made no mention of resettlement.[13] Yet the resettlement implications were enormous.

---

[13] Cernea had already lost a battle with the Indian Irrigation Division. He saw that a medium sized irrigation project in Gujarat had no resettlement plan, though many people were to be displaced. He protested to the project officer. The project officer ignored him, and Cernea threatened to bring the case to the attention of senior management. The project officer continued to ignore him, telling his colleagues, "We [the India Irrigation Division] will win, because they [senior management] need to disburse the [IDA] money". He was right. The Board approved the project flatly counter to the Bank's OMS on resettlement.

Cernea saw the documents for Sardar Sarovar in 1983 almost by accident. Not long before, he had moved offices and become the next-office neighbor of Fred Hotis, the Bank's irrigation advisor. Hotis had seen the earlier documents for Sardar Sarovar but had never thought of drawing them to the attention of Cernea, the resettlement expert. Cernea should have been involved, but it was not the irrigation advisor's job to involve him. One day in 1983 Hotis wandered into his new neighbor's office with the latest pile of Sardar Sarovar documents. They included the terms of reference of the Bank's appraisal mission. Hotis, as irrigation advisor, was required to clear the terms of reference of the appraisal mission *before it left*. And the Bank's OMS on resettlement said—by Cernea's careful design—"Overall design of the primary project and the proposed schedule for relocation should be completed *before the start of the appraisal mission*, making it possible to assess the various resettlement options and the stages for their implementation." "Have you seen these?", Hotis asked Cernea. Cernea saw that the terms of reference contained nothing about resettlement. He decided there and then to draw a line in the sand on Sardar Sarovar. His attention was extremely unwelcome to the project people, which was why they had gone to great lengths to keep the project out of his sight. Until then its preparation had gone smoothly enough for it to go to the Board on time, a hallmark of a successful Bank career.

When Cernea rang the division chief to ask about resettlement, the division chief (by then Tiber had retired and William Rodger, a British irrigation engineer, had replaced him) told him that the appraisal mission had already been in the field for a week—contravening both the OMS on resettlement and the requirement that the irrigation advisor sign off on the terms of reference before the appraisal mission set out (another example of the regional vice presidency beating the center). The division chief suggested that he would add resettlement to the already full agenda of the appraisal mission. The appraisal mission leader telegrammed back the news that the Indians said they would take care of resettlement. Cernea insisted that the OMS *required the Bank* to prepare the outlines of a resettlement plan before the appraisal could go forward. This led to a sharp discussion with the division chief. "Who are you, Michael, to tell me and the Government of India how to do resettlement? Don't you trust us?" Cernea replied that the issue was not trust. All he wanted was a resettlement plan as required by the Bank's OMS. Cernea said that he would have to advise his vice

Cernea launched his own crusade to get the India Irrigation Division to pay attention to resettlement. Using his own Agriculture and Rural Development Department's budget he hired a well-known resettlement expert, Thayer Scudder, to investigate the resettlement situation. Scudder was "appalled" by what he found.[14] Nothing had been done to inform villagers about resettlement options and rehabilitation packages. In both the federal government and the state governments he found virtually no-one dealing with resettlement.

All three states worried about the consequences of complying with the Bank's directive. The required level of compensation was very high: restoration to living standards that at least match those before resettlement, and "land-for-land" (compensation in land, not cash, for those forced to give up land, up to five acres, including those whose claim was customary rather than legal, these being mainly "tribals"). Compensation at this level in the Sardar Sarovar project, the governments feared, might set precedents for courts to apply *retrospectively* to the many hundreds of thousands of people already displaced by infrastructural projects, not to mention those to be displaced in future. MP was especially worried, because whereas Sardar Sarovar would be the last major irrigation and hydro project for Gujarat, for MP it was only the first in a line of Narmada projects within its borders. The federal government had limited leverage to make the states comply, because resettlement, like water, was a state subject.

The states began to play a game of "chicken", each aiming to do as little as possible for their own oustees in the hope that they would go elsewhere. MP, in particular, wanted its oustees to go to Gujarat. Under the terms of the water tribunal award Gujarat had to offer to accommodate oustees from other states and was meant to reimburse the other states for the resettlement costs of those who stayed behind. But the MP government had no confidence Gujarat would actually reimburse it. Maharashtra, too, sat on its hands until 1988–89. While playing this game all three states calculated that the Bank knew that insisting on its guidelines in Narmada would encourage people resettled in other Bank-financed projects in India, who got little compensation, to insist on the same. Surely the Bank would shrink from this Pandora's Box.

---

president that a resettlement plan did not exist and that the project was out of compliance with Bank directives. The division chief asked him not to. Cernea proposed a compromise. He would draft a memo to the vice president, he would copy it to the division chief, but he would delay sending it to the vice president. The division chief later rang him to tell him one of his staff was returning from Delhi shortly with a resettlement plan. Some weeks later, hearing nothing, Cernea rang the division chief. "Sorry, the photocopy machine in Delhi broke down. But the plan will come shortly." More weeks of delay. Then the project officer (Per Ljung) rang Cernea to say that a load of documents had arrived from Delhi, but no resettlement plan. Cernea said there would have to be a special "post-appraisal" resettlement mission. The project officer said he had no budget. Cernea proposed that he would use his own department's budget to send a resettlement expert, Thayer Scudder, to investigate and make proposals. Snookered, the project officer reluctantly agreed. Such cat and mouse games were routine between experts in the central complex and the regional complexes of the Bank, and Cernea was a champion.

[14]Thayer Scudder, interview, 3 November, 1995.

In this situation, Scudder recommended that the Bank get the state governments to agree on an "annual rolling plan" for resettlement instead of a comprehensive plan covering several years into the future. Cernea was very unhappy with this recommendation, seeing it as an escape hole. But Scudder saw it as only the beginning of a much bigger reorientation of thinking in India about development-project-induced resettlement, using Sardar Sarovar as the focus of a coalition to push for a national policy. The India Irrigation Division, on the other hand, was relieved by Scudder's recommendation, and henceforth tried to deal with consultant Scudder on resettlement matters rather than staff member Cernea.

In retrospect Scudder's "annual rolling plan" was a momentus recommendation. It encouraged the Bank to give away its biggest bargaining chip, project approval, in return for...very little. On the other hand, if Scudder had said, "Stop right here until a decent resettlement plan is ready", his report may have been quietly ignored and the project approved anyway. He made his recommendation in the knowledge that the Bank and the governments in India were not monolithic; he wanted to strengthen the hands of resettlement advocates inside the various organizations.

By the time of Board presentation in March 1985 the Bank had devoted just five resettlement-person-weeks to the examination of the social impacts of a project that forced the relocation of at least 200,000 people. But enough had been done by way of planning for the staff to assure the Board, with some truth, that "the measures embodied in the plan for resettlement and rehabilitation represented a significant advance over the practices of the past in India".[15] However, neither the staff nor the supporting documents said that the "plan" was, in fact, no more than a diluted version of the resettlement principles enunciated in the inter-state water tribunal's award of 1979. Or that the tribunal's award, being focused on principles of water-sharing, did not claim to set out comprehensive resettlement principles, and failed to mention some of the most difficult issues.[16] It fell far short of what constituted a "plan" in the Bank's own resettlement directive. The staff also did not say that

---

[15]Summary of discussions at the meeting of the Executive Directors of the Bank and IDA, March 7, 1985.

[16]The tribunal award was nevertheless important in resettlement thinking. It established for the first time in India the principle of land-for-land (as distinct from cash-for-land) and indirectly shifted thinking in the Bank toward the same principle.

The Independent Review chastises the Bank for ignoring "tribals". Bank policy for involuntary resettlement makes special provision for tribal people, and by the time of Sardar Sarovar appraisal the Bank had an Operational Manual Statement setting out these provisions (OMS No.2.34, *Tribal Peoples in Bank Financed Projects*, February 1982). According to Indian census data, a large proportion (perhaps half) of the dam and reservoir oustees are tribals, yet the project appraisal documents and the loan agreement make no mention of tribals. I do not emphasize this omission. The OMS on tribals, written by Robert Goodland in connection with Polonoroeste, has scant application to most of India. The poorest and most vulnerable people in the Narmada area are as likely to be scheduled castes as tribals. There seems to be no strong justification for dividing very poor people into different social categories and giving one of them, tribals, special attention. All Narmada's poor people were being treated as detritus, not just tribals.

India's practices of the past were generally disastrous, and fell far short of India's own legal requirements.

Hence, *for all that Sardar Sarovar was intended in the Bank to be the spearhead of a new irrigation paradigm in Indian irrigation the new paradigm did not, apparently, include resettlement.* That was a "social" issue. David Hopper, the vice president, was forthright in saying that resettlement was peripheral. "You can't make omelets without breaking eggs", he kept saying dismissively.

Resettlement After Project Approval

The Bank declared the Sardar Sarovar loan effective in early 1986. But then India's Ministry of Environment and Forests refused to clear the project for environmental reasons. This caused a hiatus in the project until the ministry issued a conditional clearance in 1987. In that year a resettlement mission went out to see what progress had been made in the meantime. It found that those villagers who had already been moved to make way for the dam were still languishing in resettlement villages on sterile land without even rudimentary infrastructure. On its return it recommended that the Bank threaten India with cancellation on grounds of its non-compliance with the resettlement agreement.[17] Weeks later the Bank's reorganization of June 1987 hit, and the main proponent of the cancellation threat, the project's lawyer, Carlos Escudero, by then a resettlement champion, was moved to work on banking in Indonesia, despite his three requests to be allowed to continue with Narmada. His transfer was a victory for the India Irrigation Division.

Yet by this time the wider resettlement climate in the Bank was changing. The Bank's senior management, Ernest Stern in particular (number two in the hierarchy), signaled that the Bank had to take resettlement seriously—thanks both to an internal review by Michael Cernea showing the Bank's poor resettlement record worldwide[18] and to the escalating Narmada campaign focused on resettlement. Like it or

---

[17]Formally, the recommendation was for suspension followed by cancellation, since Bank procedures require that suspension precede cancellation.

[18]World Bank, Agriculture and Rural Development Department, "Involuntary resettlement in Bank-assisted projects: a review of the applications of Bank policies and procedures in FY1979-85 projects", February 1986. The background is as follows. In 1985 Cernea, supported by AGR Director Yudelman, began a review of Bank resettlement work since the directive of 1980. He found that most Bank projects with significant resettlement were out of compliance, and that three quarters of the appraisals of projects with serious resettlement implications had been done by missions that contained not a single resettlement expert. He informed his vice president that many Bank projects could explode at any moment because of neglected resettlement. When the report landed on the desk of Ernest Stern, the senior vice president for operations, he was furious. "Why weren't these things flagged when these projects came to the Loan Committee?", he demanded. "Who was asleep at the switch?" The regional vice presidents pointed the finger at Cernea. Cernea went back into his carefully maintained files, and produced a sheaf of memos to show how he and a few other staff had tried to raise the resettlement issues without success. Stern thereafter gave his

not, the India Department therefore began to formulate what it called an "incremental" approach to Narmada resettlement, one that would avoid the need for a comprehensive (and time-consuming) plan. Several years remained before large numbers of people would have to be moved, which gave time for steady pressure on the state governments to yield actions that would *in the end* constitute compliance with the Bank's directive.

The incremental approach had drawbacks. First, it gave an excuse for never collecting the data necessary to get a clear overview of the scale of the resettlement problem. Second, as news spread of the compensation possibilities adult sons and anyone else who might make a claim raced back from all across India. So not only were there no good figures about the number of oustees at the start, the number claiming oustee status kept growing. Third, from the Indian government standpoint, the incremental approach looked like a constant shifting of goal posts, a continual imposition of new targets. On the other hand, the Bank's own resettlement experts—by now several in number—tended to see the incremental approach as an unscrupulous way for the Bank always to be able to declare "progress". One of them said, "If you keep lowering the goal posts eventually people can score touchdowns no matter what they do".

By the late 1980s the Bank was devoting serious resources to resettlement. First in Gujarat and then in Maharashtra some progress began to be made on the ground, though hardly enough to lance the gathering international storm. What caused the turnaround? In 1988, with the international campaign in full swing, a high-level resettlement mission went to India led by Senior Vice President for Operations Moeen Qureshi, the first time a senior manager had involved himself directly.[19] He was briefed intensively by NGOs in Washington DC before he left. (In the 1987 reorganization Qureshi replaced Stern and Stern was moved to be head of the financial complex. Had he remained in charge of operations these meetings with NGOs would probably not have occurred.) On his return Qureshi again had intensive private discussions with NGO leaders about what to do, including a two hour meeting with Oxfam's John Clark with only the acting director of the India Department present. They discussed a set of benchmark actions by the Indian authorities which would justify continued Bank involvement. In November Qureshi wrote a strong letter to the Chief Minister of MP imposing a series of resettlement-related conditions to be met by December 1988 and March 1989, and threatening to suspend disbursements in March 1989 if the conditions were not met.

In April 1989 another resettlement mission went out partly to monitor the actions called for in Qureshi's letter. Thayer Scudder joined this mission. He found the state governments still playing the game of chicken, making their own resettlement sites

---

support to resettlement. Cernea recommended that the Bank protect itself from public attack by issuing a follow-up to the 1980 OMS in the form of an Operational Policy Note, under his central vice president's signature, calling for observance of the original OMS. The vice president agreed, and the Operational Policy Note came out in 1986.

[19]Earlier in 1988 President Conable had visited India and met with Narmada activists to hear their story, but he was not operationally involved.

as unattractive as possible. The people in the early resettlement sites, who had been moved to make way for the dam itself, still languished, years later, in the tin shacks erected for them on their arrival. The shacks turned into ovens in the summer heat, and the settlements still lacked basic infrastructure such as wells.[20]

At the end Scudder wrote a long report to the head of the Delhi office's Agricultural Unit. He said, "In comparing the August 1984/September 1985 situation with the situation today, I believe there has been a serious *deterioration*".[21] He went on to call for permanent or temporary termination of World Bank disbursements. The head of the Delhi office's Agricultural Unit (who had traveled with him to some of the existing resettlement sites) incorporated bits of Scudder's report into the overall mission report *but reversed Scudder's conclusions—and then made Scudder joint author of the overall report.* He emphasised the progress being made at the level of policy and organizational arrangements (such as the establishment of land purchase committees and grievance procedures). He recommended that in light of the progress the threat of suspension in Qureshi's letter be withdrawn.

When Scudder saw the report he was appalled, and insisted that his name be removed. Then Scudder's own confidential report to the head of the Agricultural Unit mysteriously leaked to the Indian press, causing a sensation. Inside the Bank a witch hunt began to find the leaker. The head of the Agricultural Unit in the Bank's Delhi office was shocked to learn that even he was under suspicion, such was the paranoia. In the event, the Bank told Government of India that it was satisfied with progress on the ground, and withdrew the threat of suspension.

Soon afterwards it was discovered, to the embarrassment of the Bank's Legal Department, that the Forestry Act of India and the Ministry of Environment and Forests' conditional clearance given in 1987 both explicitly *excluded* the use of forest land for resettlement purposes, while the loan agreements with each of the three states specifically *included* forest land for resettlement.[22] Eventually, after more negotiations, a threat of Bank suspension, and the intervention of Prime Minister Rajiv Ghandi, Maharashtra agreed to waive the exclusion of forest land, which opened the way to 3000 oustee families being resettled. The Bank regarded this as the breakthrough it had been waiting for.

Yet deep resistance remained in the state governments and the Narmada Control Authority to the idea of the project being responsible for resettlement. Within the elite Indian Administrative Service, resettlement continued to be at the bottom of the prestige hierarchy. A posting as Resettlement Officer was a punishment.

---

[20]See Catherine Caufield, *Masters of Illusion: The World Bank and the Poverty of Nations*, Macmillan, 1997, especially chapter 1.

[21]Thayer Scudder, memorandum to Michael Baxter, April 29, 1989, emphasis added.

[22]The Bank's Development Credit Agreement with Government of India, May 19, 1985, says (sec.3.02), "the Borrower shall take...all such action as shall be necessary, including...the provision of forest land" for resettlement purposes. But the Ministry of Environment and Forests' clearance for Sardar Sarovar explicitly prohibits use of forest land for resettlement. The contradiction was not spotted—or not acknowledged—until the Maharashtra issue in 1989.

The unconcern with resettlement, even in Gujarat as late as 1992, can be seen in a submission by the Gujarat government to the independent review panel on the subject of the canal oustees (those whose land had to be acquired as right-of-way for the canal). The submission said that the Bank's requirements (land for land) were excessively stringent, that the Land Acquisition Act of *1894* gave adequate protection, and that in any case, "For such a large irrigation project, which is to benefit the community at large, the farmers have always been ready for *slight sacrifice*".[23]

The attitude on the Indian side was colored by the fact that about half of the oustees were classified as "tribals", who receive particular disparagement from caste Indians. The chief engineer of the project raged at Bank staff, "Why are you are so concerned about tribals? What they need is sterilization!"[24]

Environment

Long before the Tribunal award the Gujarat government had already chosen the dam site and the height of the dam, and had already started to build the foundations before being forced to stop by the inter-state water dispute. Experts in environmental assessment agree that the site and height of a dam are the two main variables determining its environmental impacts. With these decisions Gujarat locked in the parameters of the dam's environmental impacts before the Bank became involved.

The whole thrust of the Bank in the first several years was to redesign Gujarat's plans so as to make the dam and canal less likely to cause water logging and salinity. In that limited sense environment was central, though not called as such. Everything else that we might call environmental was neglected up to and beyond project approval. Robert Goodland, from the Bank's tiny, mostly "shop window", Office of Environmental Affairs, elbowed himself into two early missions. He mapped out a series of environmental studies required before a proper environmental assessment could be made. After these two visits the India Irrigation Division refused to allow him anywhere near the project again, and without its permission he could not go. The absence of environment work was even less of an issue inside the Bank than was resettlement, partly because, unlike resettlement, environmental assessments were not covered by even a weak Bank directive before 1984, and because the Office of Environmental Affairs was considerably weaker in the Bank's power structure than

---

[23] Cited in *Independent Review*, p. 206, emphasis added.

[24] A similar spirit was expressed by the education secretary for Uttar Pradesh in the early 1990s. He gave endless excuses as to why the state government had not undertaken the planning for the use of a large grant from a UN organization for primary schooling. Eventually the head of the Delhi office banged the table in exasperation and said, "Please, sir, tell me what is really going on here." He looked at her and said, "If we provide education for the children of poor people, where will *our* children get jobs?" Those who like to bracket India with China as emerging world powers would be wise to weigh the attitude of the chief engineer and the education secretary.

the Agriculture and Rural Development Department, where Cernea the resettlement champion sat.

At the time of approval in 1985 there was virtually no knowledge of: the state of forest cover in the valley, the environmental impact of forest loss (for example, on siltation in the reservoir), the impact of the project on downstream communities (for example, drinking water and fisheries), the effects on run-off into the sea and the risk of salt-water intrusion, the impact on groundwater, the impact of resettlement on the environment (including on the demand and supply of fuelwood, central to the success of resettlement).

However, a dated covenant did go into the loan agreement with each of the states saying that an environmental workplan would be prepared by December 1985 (after approval but before effectiveness). But none of the documentation indicated what constituted an "environmental workplan", beyond a few sentences calling for suitable training for staff and studies of fish, forest, wildlife, and public health. Nor did any of the Bank's project documentation (including the Staff Appraisal Report) mention that the project had not yet received clearance from the Ministry of Environment and Forests, which was required by both Bank and Government of India's rules of project approval. Earlier, in 1983, India's environment agency (then located within the Ministry of Science and Technology) had refused to clear the project because of lack of information about environmental aspects, and the refusal still stood when the loan was approved.[25]

Nor did the documentation reveal that *the calculations of the expected hydrological, irrigation and power performance of Sardar Sarovar assumed the existence of the Narmada Sagar dam upstream* to provide the required degree of water control. Either the benefits were greatly overstated, or the Bank was implicitly committing itself to a much bigger investment (Sardar Sarovar plus Narmada Sagar) than the documents said. A 1992 Bank study found that without the second dam the power production of Sardar Sarovar would be 25% less than planned and the irrigated area 30% less.[26] This was omitted from the Sardar Sarovar documentation, though well known to the staff. They connived at the pulling of wool over eyes.

At the Board meeting in 1985 to approve the project only one Executive Director raised worries about potential environmental problems. The staff replied that "although a full environmental impact assessment had not been completed, a *comprehensive first-stage assessment* had been conducted by the University of

---

[25] This exposed a routine breach of Bank procedures that had been going on for years in Bank-India dealings. The Bank's rules require that it receive a communication from the borrower stating its approval of the negotiated legal documents *before* the Bank brings the project to the Board (BP 10.00 annex J, 1994, which repeats a directive in force since long before Sardar Sarovar). Such documentation was not being received from India for any project. The government of India argued that the Bank could take the fact that it sent a negotiating team as sufficient evidence that the project had all the necessary clearances within India. The Bank had long acquiesced as part of its special relationship with India, on whom it depended heavily for borrowings and interest repayments.

[26] *Independent Review*, p.250.

Baroda and then examined by members of the World Bank appraisal team. That study covered public health, flora and fauna, fisheries, wildlife and archaeology and had determined that *there were no endangered species in the area*".[27] This so-called "comprehensive first-stage assessment" was in fact a short, general document dating from the early 1980s, that could not remotely qualify as an environmental assessment. (Robert Goodland had seen this document on his second visit, and described it as "high-school-level".) Notice how the staff covered themselves by describing it as "first-stage"; and they gave the impression that the environmental situation contained nothing to worry about by reporting as the sole finding the absence of endangered species in the area. The uncurious Board fell for it.

Why was the project declared effective when the dated covenant requiring an environmental workplan had apparently not been met? Because what constituted an "environmental workplan" was unclear. The project's lawyer, with no guidance, decided that the Indian side's short list of planned studies constituted a "plan". He signed off.

The India Department's position on environmental questions was based not only on the wish to avoid delays. It said that the likely environmental impacts simply could not be estimated so long in advance. What was needed was a mechanism to monitor environmental effects as the project developed and take mitigating actions as the effects showed up. It considered as mistaken the whole idea of requiring an environmental action *plan* of the kind that the Bank's recently introduced (1984) OMS on environmental aspects of projects could be taken to call for. Its interpretation of the phrase "environmental workplan" as meaning a list of forthcoming studies constituted the triumph of substance over process in its eyes.

Environment After Approval

In 1987 India's recently formed Ministry of Environment and Forests granted a provisional clearance on condition that the three state governments complete several environmental studies by 1989. The studies were tied to the construction schedule, so the compromise became known as the *pari passu* principle: environmental impacts were to be determined and mitigation measures put in place in concert with construction.

Also in 1987 the Bank took the first step toward a proper environmental assessment. The India Department hired as a consultant a California water expert with much experience of environmental assessments. He worked in the Bank and in India for a year and a half. But in the meantime the person who had commissioned him moved out of the project team, leaving him without an internal patron. Other members of the India Department regarded him with indifference or suspicion, as

---

[27]Summary of discussions at the meeting of the Executive Directors of the Bank and the IDA, March 7, 1985, para. 14, emphasis added.

also did the environmental specialists in the newly created Asia regional environmental division (who had no hand in his recruitment).

He found the whole atmosphere poisonous. When he presented the draft in 1988 the project officer skimmed it and looked at him with dismay, and protested, "We don't have a budget to deal with these things". Of the many people sent copies, only two replied, one of them being the person who had originally commissioned him, the other being the post-reorganization task manager to whom he was working. The latter sent him a note of thanks saying, "The important thing is that we *have* such a report, and can point to it. It will also be a very valuable source of facts and references."[28] The implication was that the report satisfied a formal requirement but did not entail any particular follow-up. Having identified many areas on which more analysis was needed the consultant wanted to continue to work on the environmental assessment, but nobody would hire him. He later commented, "It is amazing how hard it was to find money for such 'peripherals' in a multibillion dollar project!"

So his report, running to 300 pages, died.[29] However, once the regional environmental divisions (REDs) were formed in 1987 one person in the Asia RED became the "environmental contact person" for Narmada. He was a professional biologist who had headed the Asian Development Bank's small environmental unit before joining the Bank.[30] He set about persuading the India Department to commit itself to helping the state governments prepare an environmental workplan. The Canadian aid organization, CIDA, promised money.

In the end, nothing happened—again. The Canadians backed away in the face of the political heat enveloping the project. The project authorities and state governments remained unsympathetic, claiming that quite enough was known about the environment; and the state governments refused to cooperate with each other. The India Department thought that the Asia RED contact person should himself solve the problem of the missing environmental workplan. Instead he told the department that hardly anything had been done at the Indian end, that every piece of environmental data was suspect, and that recommendations about mitigation could not be made until detailed (and time-consuming) studies had been made. When they pressed him on what exactly the environmental workplan or environmental assessment would have to consist of, his replies were, in the word of the South Asia vice president, "gibberish". All the environment contact person did, in their view, was to produce unhelpful back-to-office reports like:

October 1988: "It is evident that many of the environmental components of the project are in disarray... It is still unclear ... what the environmental and social consequences of the projects might be....Opportunities are being squandered."

---

[28]Christoph Diewald to Don Levenhagen, 12 December 1988, emphasis in original. Interviews with Don Levenhagen, 6 and 8 November, 1995.

[29]Overview Environment Assessment—Sardar Sarovar and Narmada Sagar Projects—Narmada River Basin, India, March, 1989, World Bank.

[30]Colin Rees, one of the team of three that drew up the Bank's environmental assessment OD.

June 1991: "The Narmada Control Authority currently seems to have only marginal impact on the execution of the environmental studies and action plans, and beyond occasional meetings, has done little to help integrate the studies and plans with engineering planning and implementation".[31]

Worse, he began to call for changes in the dam so as to reduce the damage to estuary fisheries, and even to echo demands from Indian and international NGOs that the environment plan should examine *alternatives* to the basic design of the Narmada projects. This made the India Department apoplectic.

In early 1992 the consultant who had written the first preliminary environmental assessment several years before was asked to make a short update. He found the whole project disintegrating, with relations between people and organizations infused by poison all around. Most dispiriting, he found that almost none of the follow-up work that the states' environmental agencies had agreed to do in discussions with him in 1987–88 had actually been done; nor had the Bank put them under any pressure to do it.

Later, in 1992, while the independent review panel was at work, the Bank's India staff ranked Sardar Sarovar as having only "moderate" environmental problems. In the covering memorandum for the staff's report environmental problems are not even mentioned as possible obstacles to the planned acceleration in the construction schedule (though resettlement and health problems are so identified). Yet the provisional clearance granted by India's Ministry of Environment and Forests in 1987 had been conditional upon the completion of eight specific environmental studies by 1989. None had been completed by that time, and virtually none had been completed by 1992 when the Bank rated the project's environmental aspects as having only "moderate" problems. Nor was a plausible environmental workplan ready, 5 years after the start of dam construction above the foundations.[32]

External Pressure

In the late 1970s a community health organization called ARCH was working in the tribal belt of Gujarat, that covered the dam site.[33] When construction work on the foundations of the Sardar Sarovar dam began (initiated by the Gujarat government before the inter-state tribunal award) ARCH discovered that villagers had not been informed about the project. The future oustees only learned they were going to be evicted when government surveyors drove into the villages to mark out the future water line of the reservoir, below which loggers could strip the timber. When ARCH heard the World Bank was involved it asked its main foreign funder, UK-based

---

[31] *Independent Review*, p.228.

[32] Health aspects of the project were almost completely ignored throughout, by both the Bank and India, for all the obvious dangers of malaria and schistosomiasis.

[33] The full name was ARCH-Vahini, headed by Anil Patel.

Oxfam, for help. The head of Oxfam's campaign programs, John Clark, visited the Narmada valley in 1982 and decided to take up the project.[34] Oxfam began to organize a letter writing campaign to the Bank and to UK members of parliament, yielding hundreds of letters, to which the Bank sent a standard reply of the "You can be sure your concerns are receiving our full attention" kind. (At this time communication between Oxfam in Oxford, UK, and ARCH headquarters in the valley was by letter, a minimum of 3 weeks round trip if a motorcycle was standing by to take the letter from the regional town to the headquarters.) In 1985 Oxfam orchestrated the creation of an international Narmada campaign, involving NGOs from many countries, to press for better resettlement.[35]

Meanwhile another local NGO had come to prominence in the Narmada valley, later called the Narmada Bachao Andolan (NBA), translated as Save the Narmada Movement. It was led by a fiery, charismatic social worker named Medha Patkar, seen by some as a latter-day Gandhi figure. Patkar linked up with the US-based Environmental Defense Fund (EDF). There a new recruit, Lori Udall, took up the Narmada cause full time, encouraged by EDF's seasoned Bank campaigner, Bruce Rich (moved from the Natural Resources Defense Council).[36] Leadership in the

---

[34]Ironically, the very lack of controversy about Narmada at the time recommended it to Oxfam. The organization had been thinking of taking up another big dam project in India for inclusion in its portfolio of projects for the "Real Aid" campaign. But the other project was already embroiled in controversy, and Oxfam's Delhi office dissuaded John Clark from taking it on, so as not to be seen taking sides against Government of India. Oxfam, as an operational agency with projects of its own on the ground, had to be careful about opposing the government. So Narmada was included within Oxfam's on-going Real Aid campaign for poverty-focused aid, one of about 12 projects targeted for public attention. Gradually Narmada began to catch on with the Oxfam-supporting public in Britain, more so than the other projects in the campaign, partly due to the British romance with "tribals" and the fact that tribals were being displaced without compensation (having no formal title to their land).

[35]By 1984 John Clark and Oxfam had good covert contacts with the resettlement specialist and a few staff in the India Department. They monitored the status of resettlement as the project moved towards loan approval. They saw that their letter writing campaign was not having much effect. In early 1985 the Environment Liason Center, the United Nations Environment Program offshoot dealing with NGOs, organized an international conference on environment and development in Nairobi. Clark lead a workshop on Narmada resettlement. Afterwards he invited all the participating NGOs to campaign jointly for changes in Narmada. This marked the birth of the international Narmada Campaign. The campaign accelerated after loan approval, when it became clear that the agreement implicitly accepted that those entitled to compensation included only those with legal title, which meant that most of the tribals, who accounted for a majority of those to be displaced, would not be compensated (in practice, neither would many with legal title).

[36]Bruce Rich, in charge of the Environmental Defense Fund's international program and a leader of the Polonoroeste campaign, visited friends in India in 1986, as he had done several times before. He was then beginning to focus on the coal mining and power generation project called Singrauli as the subject of the next Bank campaign. Singrauli was a disaster in both resettlement and environmental terms, he thought, but no NGOs, Indian or international, were calling attention to it; whereas by that time Narmada was already getting attention. He thought his and EDF's biggest value-added would be Singrauli. "It was virgin territory", he later said, making a bad pun. However, one day during his India visit he met, by accident, Medha Patkar, the leader of the NBA. She appealed to him to take up Narmada. Rich was doubtful: EDF was short of staff, a campaign was labor-intensive, difficult to do both Singrauli and Narmada, EDF could make more of a difference in Singrauli, etc. But he was

international Narmada campaign shifted from gentle Oxfam in Britain to high-octane Udall in Washington DC. EDF began to use the Narmada case to make a broader attack on "development-as-practiced-by-the-World-Bank". On the ground, the NBA eclipsed ARCH and changed gears by early 1988. Instead of pushing for better resettlement it launched a "Stop the Dam" campaign. To many international NGOs Stop the Dam was more promising than Better Resettlement.

Patkar pressed Oxfam to declare whether it was for or against the dam, period. Oxfam refused to do so, and issued a statement saying why. It said that the dam would probably be built anyway, so oustees would need resettling; and that Oxfam was not qualified to judge whether and when large dams had a place in Indian development. Patkar pilloried the statement as "pro dam".[37]

Udall coordinated the international campaign in the period from 1988 to 1992.[38] First, she identified groups within the more important Part I countries which might support a Narmada/Bank campaign and gave them a collective name, the Narmada Action Committee. (The "committee" was no more than the name Udall gave to her address file.) Second, she prepared menus of actions they might take in the circumstances of their own countries: parliamentary or congressional hearings, public forums, press conferences, lobbying key officials, letter-writing campaigns. She especially encouraged them to contact their legislators and their country's executive

---

impressed by her, and promised he would include it in a list of projects to take up with the World Bank and with Congress but without spending much time on it. Back in Washington DC he discussed the matter with new EDF recruit, Lori Udall. Medha Patkar, a great letter writer, began to deluge Rich with mail, which Rich, no letter writer, passed to Udall. Udall began corresponding with Patkar. Patkar visited Washington DC in September 1987 to attend fringe meetings around the Annual Meeting of the Bank and the Fund. People who heard her speak were impressed by her forceful personality, including Udall. She began to devoted most of her time to Narmada. Shortly afterwards she visited the valley, was aghast at the enormity of the human rights and environmental damage that was about to be committed, and energized by the dedication of the activists. She was able to learn a lot about the project from Oxfam and Survival International, both of which she was in close touch with.

Survival International had become involved in late 1984 through staff member Marcus Colchester (later of World Rainforest Movement). Colchester, who had detailed anthropological knowledge of the area, took up some specific angles that the other NGOs tended to neglect, to do with the cultural aspects of the life of the "tribals" (burial sites, places of worship, relationship with the communities they were to be moved into). Later, as the project moved into high crisis and relations between ARCH and NBA worsened, Colchester was the one "international NGO" person to maintain working relations with both Patel of ARCH and Patkar of NBA.

[37] EDF and Oxfam continued to cooperate on some matters. Together with Survival International they persuaded Bank President Conable to visit India in 1988 and meet with Narmada activists. The three NGOs sent a joint letter to NBA and ARCH leaders urging them to set aside their differences and present a common position to Conable—to no avail. Conable did meet with the activists—at World Bank headquarters in Delhi, the Indian government refusing to allow a venue "on Indian soil". The EDF/Oxfam split deepened in early 1992 when John Clark left Oxfam to join the World Bank.

[38] See her account of the campaign in "The World Bank and public accountability: has anything changed?", in Fox and Brown (eds.), *The Struggle for Accountability*, chapter 11. A valuable account, except that it air-brushes ARCH, Oxfam and John Clark out of the picture.

director at the Bank. Third, she prepared information packs drawing on materials sent from NBA and other Indian activists. Throughout she was in frequent touch with the US executive director's office. The US Executive Director (ED), Patrick Coady, gave her full support.

Meanwhile, in a less visible way, the Bank Information Center (a Washington DC-based NGO which closely monitored the World Bank) and the Tuesday Group (a regular meeting of representatives of Washington DC-based development-oriented NGOs) kept track of the project. They pressed the Treasury to keep supporting the US ED and they maintained channels of communication between major NGO participants who refused to speak to each other directly (notably Udall, an active member of the Tuesday Group, and John Clark, not a member). And it was this group that especially saw *the tactical importance of Narmada being a partly IDA-funded project* (as Polonoroeste was not). The US Congress had more leverage over IDA spending than IBRD spending. By linking Narmada directly to the US IDA contribution they could more effectively get the Bank's attention. (IDA is the soft-loan arm of the World Bank, financed by grants from Part I governments—on which those governments can set conditions.)

The Bank's response to the gathering storm was to deny any significant problems, whether in Narmada or the Bank's environmental and resettlement work more generally. President Barber Conable personally replied to letters from some of the more distinguished letter writers. To all he said some variant of, "I appreciate your continuing concern, and can assure you that my commitment to environmental protection is shared by all of the senior managers in the World Bank. We are indeed proud of the achievements already in place, and I agree that we have done too little to publicize the good side of the Bank's efforts."[39] He included a 14 page "Note on Narmada projects and World Bank involvement". The note concentrated almost exclusively on a description of Bank policy on environment and resettlement, without saying whether the policy had been implemented in Narmada; and it talked of actions that "will be" taken in Narmada. Neither the letter nor the document acknowledged real problems.

Bank staff were under strict instructions not to have contact with the NGOs, not even those on the ground in the valley. Thayer Scudder recalls an incident from 1985 when he and other members of a resettlement mission were staying in a resthouse. Word reached them that the leader of ARCH was coming to meet them. The mission leader ordered them all into hiding on the second floor, and the ARCH leader was informed that the mission was elsewhere and sent on his way. Scudder later made secret contact with ARCH, involving a hair-raising midnight ride by motorcycle to a safe house in the back streets of a regional city, and ARCH supplied him with information which disproved the project authorities' assertion that insufficient private land was available for sale in Gujarat for oustees to be able to exercise any choice in the selection of their new land.

---

[39]Letter from Barber Conable to Randall Hayes (Rainforest Action Network) and Brent Blakwelder (Environmental Policy Institute), July 31, 1987.

In 1989 the US-based NGOs in the campaign persuaded a congressional subcommittee to hold hearings specifically on Narmada.[40] The hearings mark a watershed in international criticism of the Bank. Thereafter the *international* Narmada/ Bank campaign mushroomed. In response to the hearings six congressmen and women sent letters to President Conable calling for either a suspension or cancellation of the project, or otherwise face zero contribution from the United States to IDA. They said, "We believe that there is sufficient and compelling reasons [sic] that this loan should be canceled immediately". They continued, "As you know, the issue of replenishment for the International Development Association (IDA) will soon be before the Congress. We believe that this funding increase would be particularly difficult to justify to U.S. taxpayers unless the World Bank takes immediate steps to insure that all of the projects funded by IDA are in compliance with the stated policies of the Bank. Continued funding of the Sardar Sarovar project...raise [sic] questions about the Bank's ability to assure donor countries that minimal environmental, social and economic standards will be met in future IDA projects....*we believe it would be a gross misuse of public funds to consider an increased replenishment for an institution which has demonstrated its disregard for human rights and environmental concerns*".[41]

For periods in 1989 and 1990 the president received as many as a thousand letters a day from the UK alone. In May 1990 the Japanese government announced it was freezing its aid for the dam's turbines and generators. This was in response to pressure from Japanese NGOs which had mobilized against Narmada, the first time they had taken a concerted position on international environmental/human rights issues.[42] In June 1990 22 Japanese parliamentarians wrote to Barber Conable calling for the World Bank to suspend funding.[43] US, European and Japanese media began to carry stories on the campaign. *The New York Times* first carried a story

---

[40]The subcommittee was the House Subcommittee on Natural Resources, Agricultural Research and Environment, chaired by James Scheuer. The same subcommittee chaired by the same Scheuer had earlier played an important role in getting the Bank to suspend disbursements in the Polonoroeste project.

[41]Letter from Congressman James Scheuer et al., to Barber Conable, November 2, 1989, emphasis added.

[42]The chair of the congressional subcommittee, James Scheuer, was also convenor of GLOBE (Global Legislators for a Balanced Environment). GLOBE held a meeting in Washington DC soon after the Narmada hearings. The meeting provided an opportunity for NGOs to discuss the problems of Narmada and the World Bank with the legislators. Japanese legislators were especially active in GLOBE, and took a particular interest in Narmada because Japan was the biggest co-financier of Sardar Sarovar. The GLOBE meeting triggered much greater involvement by Japanese NGOs in the Narmada campaign. Friends of the Earth (Japan) and other Japanese NGOs hosted the first International Narmada Symposium in April 1990, which brought together some 500 activists, journalists and academics from many nations. The head of Friends of the Earth (Japan), Yukio Tanaka, demonstrated a determination to get the Japanese government to withdraw from Sardar Sarovar that left even Lori Udall in awe.

[43]Open letter to Barber Conable, President, World Bank, from "Members of the Japanese Diet", June 26, 1990.

about Narmada in 1989, in which it drew attention to NGO criticism of the Indian government and only obliquely mentioned the World Bank's role of what it called "limited support".[44] By 1992 *The New York Times* carried seven articles about Narmada, with increasingly direct criticism of the World Bank. It quoted a prominent Indian environmentalist saying, "The World Bank is one of the most unaccountable institutions on the planet. It doesn't consult local people. Unless local communities really come into their own and are given control, you are not going to be able to save land and recover our ecosystem."[45]

At the time of the Annual Meeting in September 1992 some 250 organizations from 37 countries signed a full-page open letter in *The Financial Times*, *The New York Times*, and *The Washington Post*, which said, "The World Bank must withdraw from Sardar Sarovar immediately". The open letter went on to warn that if the Bank continued funding the project in the face of the Independent Review (which had presented its report in June 1992) then "NGOs and activists would put their weight behind a campaign to cut off funding to the Bank".[46]

Internal Organization

Inside the Bank, project management was from the beginning centralized in Washington, as was true for just about all Bank project work. The Bank's Delhi office had no-one responsible for the project until 1986. The first project officer was an economist with training in engineering, a young Young Professional with little prior experience. A new project officer took over in 1984, an experienced irrigation engineer already working on the project (described by friends as "a dams man"). In 1986 he moved to the Delhi office. But even then all correspondence between him and Government of India had to be signed off by the chief of the India Agriculture Division back in Washington, until 1989. The project officer found himself wrestling more than full-time with problems of procurement, design and construction. He and others in the project team devoted intense efforts to bring the dam up to international standards. They also struggled to persuade the Indian engineers to adopt more modern techniques of canal lining, fearing that the existing techniques would yield a lining unable to withstand the force of the water. Looking back from the mid 1990s, they see that great improvements were made on the infrastructure side, which makes them all the more bitter that the Bank eventually walked away from the project.

---

[44] Barbara Crossette, "Water, water everywhere? Many now say 'no!'", *New York Times*, October 7, 1989, sec.1, page 4.

[45] Smithu Kothari, quoted in Barbara Crossette, "What some preach in Rio is not what they practice at home", *The New York Times*, June 15, 1992, sec.A, p.8. I thank Anne Fentress for this reference.

[46] For example, *The Financial Times*, September 21, 1992, p. 6.

Preoccupied with engineering problems the core people had little time for other things, and in any case they thought that problems like resettlement and environmental protection were minor compared to the benefits of getting the system up and running. They had no intention of pressuring the state governments to comply with the Bank's resettlement policy any more than they had to, believing the policy to be mistaken.

Their definition of priorities prevailed all the more because for much of the second half of the 1980s they were scarcely managed. Just as serious implementation began on the ground, when the project should have been intensively supervised, the Bank descended into the chaos of the 1987 reorganization. For more than 2 years many Bank staff were chiefly concerned to protect their own necks. Partly for this reason the India Agriculture Division—the division with shared responsibility for the Bank's most sensitive project by far and for the biggest agriculture/irrigation lending program in the Bank—had six division chiefs between 1984 and 1993, averaging about 18 months each. In the critical period from 1987 to 1989 three came and went in 18 months. The parent department had four directors between 1984 and 1990. The high turnover meant that during the 6 years that the project was the spearhead of a great campaign against the whole Bank the same two people were agriculture division chief and departmental director often for less than 12 months. This matters because incoming division chiefs and directors each took time to find out about the project (just one of many things they had to attend to). They encountered it as well established and took it as the project staff presented it. Across the Bank at this time there were many slips in projects because task managers, division chiefs and departmental directors were not paying attention.

Not until 1988 did the Bank institute any form of "crisis management", and even then the response was minimal. In that year, with the Narmada/Bank campaign rising, one person in the India Agriculture Division, Thomas Blinkhorn, was asked to take charge of *all* resettlement and environmental issues in Bank work in India, working directly to the director of the India Department. Blinkhorn came from a public relations background, with no experience in resettlement or environment, and his appointment illustrates how the India Department saw the problem as primarily public relations.[47] Right up to project cancellation in 1993, Blinkhorn was the only person coordinating the Narmada resettlement and environment work; but he did this as just one item in a bigger portfolio of tasks that included several other resettlement

---

[47]Thomas Blinkhorn was an American public relations specialist who in the early 1970s had worked as a consultant to McNamara on how to make the Bank more sympathetic to poverty initiatives. Then he joined as a staff member working on Africa, followed by a spell in Information and Public Affairs, in which capacity he helped the Bank handle the criticism over Polonoroeste. He came to the India Agricultural Operations Division in 1986, began to consolidate the position of resettlement and environment czar for the whole department, and moved to the front office of the director of the India Department in 1990, until 1993. There has been much speculation about why he remained resettlement and environment czar for as long as five years, given all the controversy that swirled around him both inside the Bank and in India and given the need for someone with a more delicate public relations touch than his.

and environment hot spots in India. He had no assistant. For several years his normal working day was 12 h.

Blinkhorn believed that Sardar Sarovar and the proposed upstream dam, Narmada Sagar, were good investments that were in danger of being blown away by ill-informed critics. He shared the project staff's skepticism of the motives and competence of the Bank's own resettlement and environmental staff, who were, said the project officer, "in a unique position of being able to communicate the non-optional, critical life-supporting need for development of the Narmada's water and power resources but....chose to work tirelessly to criticize the SSP [Sardar Sarovar Project] planning and implementation processes, and thereby contribute to delays while remaining ever mindful of setting up detailed criteria requiring bureaucratic manipulation—empire building—for which they were well suited."[48]

In the eyes of the Bank's resettlement and environment staff, Blinkhorn began to act as a gatekeeper confining them to the sidelines and doctoring their reports. When they wrote about bad conditions in resettlement villages he assured his superiors that he had visited the same villages and found conditions much better than they said. He complained to their own departmental directors about their "uncooperative" attitude. They in turn found his abrasiveness intolerable. "There was no problem small enough for Blinkhorn not to turn into a major one", said one. Another said, "Any news that might justify not going ahead was strongly unwelcome in the project line. Staff and managers would say, 'This afterall is India. We can't expect to solve problems except by muddling through.'" Their deprecation of India was untroubled by comparison with the Bank's own chaos of 1987–88 as it underwent the Conable reorganization.

Relations between the project people and the environmental and resettlement people got worse and worse. Since the two sides were not in the same division or department antagonisms could flourish as each dug in. By 1990 everyone was at each other's throats. The India Department blamed the Asia Regional Environment Division, the environment people blamed the project people, Bank staff blamed the Indians, the Indians blamed the Bank, the central government blamed the states, the states blamed the central government, the NGOs blamed everyone.[49] Relations between the project people and the NGOs were even worse, with the Bank attributing to them the worst possible motives. The project officer referred to "the extreme intellectual dishonesty and related pressure tactics of the NGOs". They were practicing, he said, "tactics well honed in western USA in the 60s and 70s". Their concerns about resettlement and environment were mere "*tools of delay* needed to

---

[48]Personal communication, Gerry Fauss, 14 January, 1996.

[49]In 1992 the Environment Secretary, Government of India, refused to meet with Thomas Blinkhorn, the India Department's environment and resettlement czar. Blinkhorn made an urgent request for a meeting, wanting to persuade the Secretary to undertake a National Environmental Action Plan, such a plan being required of all IDA-eligible countries as a condition of further IDA funding. It took a request from the South Asia vice president to the Finance Secretary to persuade the Environment Secretary to change his mind. He looked thunderous and drummed his fingers on the table throughout the meeting.

organize the world net of anti-large-dam believers into a formidable political block".[50] The Bank must not cave in to such dishonest people, the project staff said.

On the other hand covert relations between the resettlement and environment people and the NGOs were good. The project people, Blinkhorn above all, never realized that their efforts to block the views of the resettlement and environment people from senior management forced them to go outside the Bank to the NGOs once it became clear that the NGOs had better access to senior management than they did.

India's Crisis

Just as the Bank began to pick itself up after the 1987–88 reorganization India hit a severe macroeconomic and political crisis. By 1991 the crisis was so bad that "A default on [international debt] payments, for the first time in our history became a serious possibility in June, 1991", in the words of a government report. [51] In response the government committed itself to a far-reaching program of economic opening, hoping to restore the capacity to generate foreign exchange in a sustainable way. "Bankruptcy drove the reform process, not ideology", said one analyst.[52] The central government was keen to involve the Bank in finding a way out of crisis, promising in return drastic economic liberalization. This was the golden opportunity the Bank had been waiting for. For several years the macroeconomic and political crisis and then the opportunity for far-reaching liberalization crowded out senior managerial attention to other things, like Narmada, both in the Indian government and in the Bank.

At the same time, the crisis stiffened the senior management's resolve to keep Narmada going ahead, to avoid a showdown, precisely because so much was at stake in the liberalization agenda. A senior manager said, "At senior levels there was an overarching concern that relations with India were delicate, and that the consequences of failure in Narmada were so great that the entire India portfolio might be in jeopardy".

And so the core project people, led by the director of the India Country Department, [53] backed up Thomas Blinkhorn, and strongly supported behind the scenes by Ernest Stern, godfather of the special Bank-India relationship, acted as though marching to the German Army slogan, "Augen zu und durch!", Eyes closed and through!

---

[50]Gerry Fauss, op.cit., emphasis added.

[51]Government of India, Ministry of Finance, *Economic Survey 1991-1992*, Part I: General Review, New Delhi: Ministry of Finance, 1992, p.10.

[52]Swaminathan Aiyar, *The Economic Times*, 15 August 1997:5.

[53]Heinz Vergin.

The Independent Review

The Executive Directors found themselves thoroughly confused. The staff told them the project was OK. The NGOs said the Bank remained far out of compliance. In 1988 the Dutch executive director, Paul Arlman, began to take a particular interest in Narmada and convened a group of Part I country EDs to follow it.[54] They had to rely on what the India Department staff told them orally or in sanitized briefs; they had no access to back-to-office reports.[55] Some of them met with Oxfam's John Clark, EDF's Lori Udall, and the NBA's Medha Patkar. After the meeting with Patkar one ED commented, "When I hear what NGOs say about this project and then what the operations people say, it sounds like they are talking about two different projects".[56]

The group of concerned EDs was briefed by Scudder in 1990, arranged by Lori Udall. By that time Scudder had been back from his 1989 mission for a year—the

---

[54] The Indian executive director, though invited, did not attend these meetings until 1990. In addition to Holland, the participating EDs represented the UK, the US, the Nordic countries, Canada, Japan, Germany, Australia, Belgium and later Switzerland.

[55] One such meeting was held in March 1990. It was attended by the EDs from Holland, the US, and the UK, and by Senior Vice-president for Operations Qureshi and four other Bank staff. The Dutch ED opened the meeting by stating that "while he had confidence in the Bank managers and staff working on the projects and was aware that a certain amount of progress was being made in project implementation, he was nonetheless very concerned about other developments....these other developments included 'major interests' in the Part I countries, and increasingly in the Part II countries (including India), as well as active non-governmental organizations which either oppose or are very critical of the project. Eventually, these interests could draw the Bank into a situation in which the outcome would be unsatisfactory to the project and detrimental to the Bank as an institution." "The senior vice-president for operations responded by asking what might be done to lead to a more satisfactory conclusion. [He said he was in close contact with the project, and felt optimistic about project progress.] In the circumstances, he continued, it would be wrong for the Bank simply to abandon the project in its current inconclusive state. Our continued involvement and influence can help to ensure that those aspects that concern critics the most—resettlement and environment—will receive priority attention and careful and proper implementation.... The essential point, he continued, is that the Bank sets specific standards for project performance. It is then up to the governments to implement the project in accordance with these standards. If they don't, it is then relatively easy for the Bank to suspend or withdraw. However, if Governments are meeting the standards, making best efforts to implement projects satisfactorily, we have an obligation to work with them to see the project through to a satisfactory conclusion." (Thomas Blinkhorn to Distribution, March 14, 1990.)

Note the senior vice-president's sentence, "If they don't [implement the project in accordance with Bank standards], it is then relatively easy for the Bank to suspend or withdraw." In its public or semi-public defence, the Bank frequently draws attention to the sanction of suspension or withdrawal and its willingness to use it if circumstances warrant. The key, of course, is what circumstances warrant. As everyone in the room knew, the Bank has hardly ever suspended or withdrawn from a project on environmental or social grounds anywhere, and by 1990, the year of the meeting, had never once suspended or withdrawn from an Indian project. It was not "relatively easy" for the Bank to suspend or withdraw. Qureshi's statement was intended to reassure the EDs that the Bank was fully in control.

[56] Quoted in Lori Udall, "The international Narmada campaign: a case study of sustained advocacy", in William Fischer ed., *Towards Sustainable Development? Struggling Over India's Narmada River*, Armonk: M.E.Sharpe, 1995, p.206.

mission on which he had urged suspension on grounds that nothing short of suspension would force improvement in resettlement. His meeting with the EDs lasted three hours. The EDs were shocked by what he said, so different was it from the staff's story. Scudder asked the Board to order the Bank to stop disbursements. He argued that the Bank had never taken a tough stance on resettlement in any Indian project, and that doing so would send a signal not only to India but also to other countries with poor resettlement, like Brazil.

In 1990 Oxfam wrote a report on resettlement and environment in Narmada. The report said that there was good news and bad news: some progress in Gujarat, little progress in the other two states. The India Department (Blinkhorn) quoted the Oxfam report in its report to the EDs—but only the good side. Oxfam then sent a blistering letter to the full Board, giving the full text and highlighting how the department had sought to mislead the recipients. This was a triggering event in many EDs' conviction that Bank management simply could not be trusted.

In mid 1990 the US ED began to sound out the Director-General of the Bank's Operations Evaluation Department (OED) about undertaking a special review of Sardar Sarovar. The idea was greeted with unease all around, because it would take the OED too far from its mandate of reviewing completed projects.

Then at the end of 1990 Medha Patkar and the NBA led a "Long March" in which thousands of people from the valley set out to walk to the dam site where they planned to stop construction by means of a sit-in. They were stopped at the Gujarat border by police. Medha Patkar and several others began a fast-to-the-death. The fast injected new urgency. What would persuade Patkar to stop? She was demanding that the whole project be comprehensively reviewed, but the Bank would not agree. As she grew weaker and the Bank said nothing John Clark, Lori Udall and others made desperate attempts to convince the senior operational vice president, Moeen Qureshi, to announce a review. Finally, Clark in Oxford, England, spent an entire night on the telephone mediating between Qureshi five hours behind in Washington and Oxfam and other NGO activists five hours ahead in India. By the end of Clark's night, Qureshi agreed to establish an independent review of Narmada. Patkar called off her fast.

In the spring of 1991 a small number of EDs led by the new Dutch ED, Evelyn Herfkins, began to consider the membership and terms of reference of an independent review panel. There were no precedents to draw on. Herfkins used her by then well-established contacts with NGO people like Udall and Clark to get ideas. But since the independent review would be established by the Bank, the India Department's resettlement and environment czar, Blinkhorn, was made responsible for establishing it. He approached a number of prominent persons to invite them to head it. All refused. Meanwhile Conable, in the waning months of his presidency, was getting desperate; he needed someone fast. With support from Herfkins and the other interested EDs, he approached his former congressional colleague, Bradford Morse, who since leaving the US Congress had been head of the United Nations Development Program (UNDP). Morse was in poor health. But Conable prevailed on him to chair the commission while others did the work.

In June 1991 Conable announced that an independent review panel would be established, headed by Morse. Blinkhorn started to look for someone to head up the real work. By this time the Environmental Defense Fund's Lori Udall was, as he said, "practically camping in the living room", getting so many leaks out of the Bank that she was better informed than he was.[57] Udall started a letter writing campaign aimed at the Dutch ED Herfkins to persuade her to push for the appointment of Thomas Berger as the principal investigator. Berger was a well-known Canadian jurist and advocate of native American rights. He was also a friend of Udall's uncle, former US Secretary of the Interior Stuart Udall, who had subsequently worked closely with Berger in a major legal case on native American rights. Barbara Bramble, one of the trio that led the earlier NGO-Polonoroeste campaign against the Bank and now working behind the scenes on this one, had also worked with, admired, and advocated Berger. Herfkins proposed Berger. Blinkhorn interviewed Berger and recommended him, even knowing his reputation as a defender of indigenous people's rights and knowing that there were many tribals in the Narmada area, in order to show that the Bank was bending over backwards to be impartial. Morse agreed. Berger named conditions. He would receive a fee of $1500/day (an unheard of rate in the Bank for a long-term assignment, to which the head of consultants' services in the Human Resources department made the strongest possible objection), and he would pick his own team (whom he named). By this time it was August 1991. Conable and Senior Vice President Sandstrom were anxious to end the already long delay. They accepted Berger's conditions. He was appointed deputy chairman of the investigation panel.

The NGO community was delighted. Many in the Bank were dismayed. They observed that the panel members had little knowledge of development (Morse apart) and no knowledge of India. They saw the fact that the chairman had been head of UNDP as ominous. "Of course, anyone related to UNDP [Mr Morse] would not miss an opportunity to embarrass the Bank", said one.[58] Conable himself warned Morse that Berger and his team might, on the basis of their track-record in handling native American issues, pre-judge the issue. Morse reminded Conable that he had obtained a pledge of absolute independence. Conable backed off.

Once the core members of the Review were appointed they had frequent contact by phone with Udall, and on their first visit to the Bank met with her at their hotel for three hours. It was true, as their critics alleged, that they knew little about the Bank and less about India. She briefed them on such issues as how they could retain their credibility in the NGO world, which NGOs were fighting which, which were trustworthy, who was doing what in the Bank, and what rules of operation to insist upon vis-a-vis the Bank. Berger also spent a day with Clark and others at Oxfam. The team formally started work in September 1991.

---

[57] Thomas Blinkhorn, interview, April 3, 1996.

[58] Senior legal official to a subordinate, comment in the margin of a copy of the Terms of Reference of the Independent Review.

Its independence from the Bank was ensured by several rules that the review panel (after the briefings from Udall and Clark) had insisted upon:

1. Complete access to all project files from the Bank and from Government of India, and to Indian NGOs and the Narmada valley.
2. An extended period of time (originally 7 months, increased to nine).
3. An independent budget, initially of $400,000 that grew to about $1 million. (The budget came from the President's contingency fund.)
4. Independent publication of the results, without Bank editing.
5. No post-Review Bank employment of panel members.

Its terms of reference were limited to resettlement and environment, its task being to assess the Bank's performance in these two domains in relation to the Bank's own policies and loan agreements. The NBA initially opposed such narrow terms of reference on the grounds that many other aspects of the project had also been questioned. The Bank stood firm, and there was an indication that the Indian government had agreed to the review on condition that it be confined to resettlement and environment.[59] All the Indian state governments were angry that the Bank had created such a body. Gujarat, in particular, wanted nothing to do with it. The Bank had to use maximum leverage with the Chief Minister of Gujarat to obtain permission for the panel even to visit the state.

Ten months later, on June 18th 1992, the panel issued a 363 page report. The report concluded, first, that the Bank had been seriously out of compliance with its own directives on both resettlement and environmental analysis of projects; second, that "there is good reason to believe that the project will not perform as planned"—perform in the hydrological sense of getting the water to the expected areas; third, that adequate resettlement was unlikely to occur on the ground "under prevailing circumstances", because "a further application of the same [incremental] strategy, albeit in a more determined or aggressive fashion, would fail". Finally, it recommended that the Bank "step back" from the project. Essentially, it confirmed most of what the NGO campaign had been saying.

The Review also found that "the richest source of material about the problems with resettlement in India are in the Bank's own internal documents", making it all the more "perplexing [that] there seemed to be so little effort to develop a remedial *strategy* rather than confront one resettlement problem after another".[60] One Review member commented that if key people in the India department had listened to their own mission members and consultants the whole review exercise would have been unnecessary.[61]

The panel presented the Review to the Board shortly before its public release. The Board pressed Berger to explain what he meant by saying that the Bank should "step back" from the project. Suspend or cancel? Berger's reply sounded evasive, leading

---

[59] Udall, "The international Narmada campaign".

[60] *Independent Review*, op.cit., p. 53, emphasis added.

[61] Quoted in Udall, 1995, "The international Narmada campaign", op.cit., p.210.

to speculation that Conable made a deal with Morse that the Review could recommend anything *other than* outright cancellation (which Conable denies).[62]

The report caused outrage in the India Department. It showed that members of the review panel were completely unqualified for the job, knew nothing about development or India, approached their task with preconceived conclusions, were captives of the NGOs, and as outsiders to the Bank had fallen into the trap of interpreting its policy guidelines literally. The panel had interviewed *none* of the core project team, India Department members said indignantly.

On the legal side, the General Counsel and Legal vice president, asked by the EDs for an opinion on whether the Bank had legal grounds for suspension or cancellation, wrote a memorandum that did not clearly say one thing or the other.[63] But the chief legal counsel for the South Asia region wrote another memorandum setting out ample justification for suspension or cancellation.[64] When the General Counsel squashed this memo, it mysteriously leaked to NGOs, which circulated it to finance ministers and EDs. It became part of the grounds on which several EDs were later to support cancellation. Meanwhile other South Asia Legal Department staff pronounced themselves "shocked" by the magnitude of non-compliance revealed by the Review. The India Department retorted that they were "shocked " as in "cover your arse". They knew perfectly well the nudging and winking that had always gone on over India's non-compliance with Bank procedures, said the India Department.

Fortunately for the Bank, the report was released 4 days *after* the United Nations Conference on Environment and Development (the Rio Earth Summit) had designated the Bank as the key agency to implement "Agenda 21", an informal intergovernmental agreement on global environmental priorities and actions.[65] So in the same week in 1992 the Bank emerged from the Rio Earth Summit as international environmental savior, and emerged from a 10-month review looking incapable of addressing environmental and resettlement impacts in its own projects.[66]

---

[62] Author's interview with Conable, 1 April 1996.

[63] Ibrahim Shihata, "Remedies available to the Bank/IDA under the loan/credit agreements on the Sardar Sarovar projects", July 16, 1992.

[64] Ian Newport, Chief Counsel, LEGSA, to William Humphrey, Acting Director, SA2DR, August 7, 1992.

[65] Was it planned or fortuitous that the report was released just after the Bank had been identified as the lead agency for Agenda 21? I do not know.

[66] Udall, "The international Narmada campaign", p.201. For two contrasting assessments of the report see Thomas Berger, "The Independent Review of the Sardar Sarovar Projects 1991–1992", *Impact Assessment* 12 (Spring), 1994, pp. 3–20; and David Seckler, "The Sardar Sarovar project in India: a commentary on the Report of the Independent Review", Discussion Paper 8, Center for Economic Policy Studies, Winrock International Institute for Agricultural Development, Washington DC, 1992.

The Decision to Continue, and then to Cancel

In July 1992 the Bank sent a large (14 person) mission[67] to review the status of the Sardar Sarovar project. The mission leader was anxious to have a member of the Department of Economic Affairs (the department within the Ministry of Finance that handled GOI/Bank and Fund relations) accompany it on its visits to help mediate relations with the states. The state governments were deeply hostile to the Bank, believing it was trying to foist on them resettlement policies written in the land of make-believe. The state governments were also resentful of Delhi for doing so little to moderate the Bank's demands.

The India Department's environment and resettlement coordinator, Blinkhorn, arrived a week before the rest of the mission to prepare the way. He asked the Department of Economic Affairs to delegate someone to accompany the mission. The department refused; it wished the Review and the Bank's response to be strictly a Bank affair. The evening before the mission left Delhi to fly to Gujarat Blinkhorn telephoned a middle ranking official of the division of the department that handled Bank agricultural/irrigation projects (including Sardar Sarovar) to say that he had instructions from the Finance Secretary that she was to accompany the mission to Gujarat. She was alarmed, for she was new to the division and knew nothing about Sardar Sarovar, yet Gujarat officials would turn to her for Government of India's views. She tried to contact the Finance Secretary, but he was out of town. She decided to trust her instinct and stick with the decision that had already been made by the department: she refused to go. Later she learned that the Finance Secretary had not even spoken to Blinkhorn, let alone issued such an instruction. The incident became known in the top management of the Department of Economic Affairs, and further inflamed the department's mistrust of the Bank.

The mission was received with hostility wherever it went. Tensions in the valley were running high as rising numbers of protesters encountered rising numbers of police.[68] At one point human rights observers reported seeing mission members traveling through the villages of MP with an escort of 200 police.[69]

The mission leader concluded that the Bank should *suspend* disbursements, and recommended this in the Back-to-Office report. Instead of saying, "You have six more months to do things x, y, z" the Bank should say, "We'll suspend now and resume when you have done x, y, and z". None of the mission members, including those resettlement experts who had not hesitated to criticize the Bank's performance, wanted *cancellation,* because they were convinced that without the Bank being involved resettlement and environmental protection would be worse.

---

[67] Known as the Cox mission, after its leader, Pamela Cox, a member of the India Department who had not previously worked on Narmada. The other mission members also had no "ownership" of the project.

[68] Patti Grossman, "Before the deluge: human rights abuses at India's Narmada dam", *Asia Watch*, June 17, 1992.

[69] Udall, "The international Narmada campaign", p.217.

Suspension and cancellation are the Bank's heavy artillery, and their use is strictly in the hands of the senior management. Managing Director Stern [70] decided that the Bank would neither suspend nor cancel but continue for another 6 months, or more precisely, that the Bank would recommend this to the Board, for the Board had already, very unusually, asked to reconsider the Bank's involvement in the project. Stern and the senior management's argument to the Board was, "After a rocky start we have finally got a good partner in the Government of Gujarat, the Bank is demonstrably helping to improve the project, the project is potentially a very good one, of great importance to India as a whole, why cut off the branch we are sitting on, why abandon it in mid stream, what good would it do to anyone (most of all the oustees) to stop now?" And they repeated, "We mustn't cave in". The senior managers also had in mind the signal that suspension would send to international finance markets, at a time when India's recovery from the macroeconomic crisis was not yet sure.

For the September 1992 Annual Meeting the international NGOs ran the full-page advertisements in the three newspapers most widely read among the Annual Meeting delegates, warning that if the Bank continued funding Sardar Sarovar against the advice of the Independent Review then "NGOs and activists would put their weight behind a campaign to cut off funding to the Bank". The vice president for South Asia and other senior managers lobbied delegates to put pressure on their governments in favor of continuing the project. Several from countries whose executive directors later voted in favor of suspension told these officials, "We see the sense in your arguments, but we are obliged by the political situation to be critical of the Bank in public".

Also in September 1992 the Bank presented to the Board a document called "Sardar Sarovar Projects, Review of Current Status and Next Steps".[71] This interwove the Bank's reply to the Independent Review's Report with its own "action plan" for dealing with resettlement and the environment. It was to have been the work of a task force set up to reply to the Independent Review's report, with membership drawn from both the India department and the environment and resettlement complex, the *first* time in the project's history that such a task force had been attempted. The result was failure. The task force was paralyzed by disagreement, and in the end Blinkhorn wrote it himself to a murderous deadline, working directly to the vice president and to Managing Director Stern, consulting hardly anyone else.

The "Next Steps" document satisfied virtually nobody. Operational people in the India Department resented the fact that the people working on the project were not allowed to reply to the Review's report themselves, as a consequence of which the "Next Steps" reply was not as convincing a rebuttal as it should have been, they said. The lawyer for the project was also unhappy, saying that the action plan "is neither precise nor monitorable". He went on to say, "We seem to be moving away from a

---

[70] In the mini-reorganization of late 1991 Stern became one of three managing directors.

[71] Dated September 11, 1992.

situation where compliance or non-compliance of GOI [Government of India] and the states are measured against the legal documents, to a situation where it is unclear exactly what is being agreed upon and what commitments are being made by GOI and the states under the action plan".[72] Indeed, "Next Steps" was intended to be ambiguous, so as to allow maximum scope for a political determination of what should be done.

Other internal critics observed that "Next Steps" flew in the face of the Bank's ostensible objective of getting India to take more ownership of the project: the action plan had been drawn up by the Bank with no input from the government.

The review panel members were even more unhappy with "Next Steps". They claimed that the Bank had seriously distorted their findings—though their report was in the public domain for all to see. In October the chairman and deputy chairman of the Review, Bradford Morse and Thomas Berger, wrote to the president saying that the Bank's reply *"ignores or misrepresents the main findings of our Review....*[W]e do want to ensure that the senior decision-makers at the Bank are not left with an account of our findings that is at variance with what we wrote."[73] They went on to say that the Bank's presentation of its findings gave the impression that their report found the problems with the project to be much smaller, more tractable, than the report actually suggests. Panel members subsequently flew to Washington to meet with the Board.

The vice president for South Asia signed a two and a half page response to the Morse and Berger letter (copied to the Board), rejecting virtually all its claims.[74]

The Board met to vote on the fate of the project on October 23, 1992, a few days after South Asia's response to the Morse/Berger letter. The president, the South Asia vice president and other high-ranking Bank officials were in attendance. (This was

---

[72] Salman Salman, LEGSA, to Andres Rigo, Assistant General Council, Operations, September 15, 1992.

[73] Bradford Morse and Thomas Berger, to Lewis Preston, October 13, 1992, emphasis added. Here is an example of what Morse and Berger claimed to be Bank distortion of the Review's message. The Review documented the project's disregarding the environmental clearance procedures of both the Bank and Government of India. It stressed that an environmental workplan setting out a strategy for dealing with environmental problems was still not available in 1992, though legally required by the Bank by end 1985 and by India's conditional environmental clearance by 1987. The Bank answered that "there have been no severe environmental consequences to date because of study delays", and that an environmental workplan was "under consideration". Morse and Berger replied to the president, "Of course there has so far been... 'no severe environmental consequences'. The ...dam has yet to impound any water and the canal is not yet functional". The Bank's operational directives recognize, said Morse and Berger, that environmental planning must be done *before or in the early stages of construction* so that the design and implementation of construction can take account of the results. The Review, they said, had strongly criticized the Bank for accepting the *pari passu* principle of doing environmental studies on a timetable that ensures the studies are completed by the time the construction is completed. This is simply too late, they said. The Bank's summary of the Review had missed this fundamental point. As for an environmental workplan being under consideration, "This kind of 'consideration' has been underway in one way or another to no avail for the last six years", they retorted.

[74] Joseph Wood to Bradford Morse, October 20, 1992.

the third time the Board had met for an all-day meeting on the project since the Morse Commission began.) The South Asia vice presidency had prepared a series of "benchmarks" of what should be achieved on the ground over the following 6 months, to strengthen the case for extending the Bank's involvement by at least another 6 months. These benchmarks tied the rate of construction of the dam and canal to the rate of (improved) resettlement. Failure to meet the benchmarks would provide grounds for the Bank to pull out.

Bank staff present at the meeting remember it for the sheer vindictiveness of the executive directors. The Dutch ED, who had taken a coordinating role for the project within the Board and between the Board and the Bank, reminded the meeting that the Board had asked for an independent review because it felt it could not trust Bank management. The Austrian ED criticized Bank management for its strong-arm lobbying of the EDs to keep the project going. The US ED, Patrick Coady, accused management of a "coverup", noting that "what is at stake is the credibility of the Board". He went on to say that if the Board allowed the project to continue "it will signal that no matter how egregious the situation, no matter how flawed the project, no matter how many policies have been violated, and no matter how clear the remedies prescribed, the Bank will go forward on its own terms".[75]

The Bank's management gave as its core argument one that had by then become its standard justification for involvement in all difficult projects. Using almost identical language to Polonoroeste it said, "While it would be safe to restrict Bank involvement to those situations in which the Borrower had already established an exemplary track record, this would in practice mean foregoing opportunities for potentially more important change. A decision by the Bank not to get involved could well mean that the project in question will still proceed but under much less favorable circumstances".[76] It did not say, though this was in its mind, that cancellation would damage the Bank's reputation as an infrastructure lender in India and the rest of the world.

Much of the discussion concerned the benchmarks against which progress would be monitored. Some EDs raised the worry, already voiced by many NGO critics, that the benchmarks depended on the governments of MP and Maharashtra doing things they were disinclined to do, while the Government of India patently had little influence over them. Therefore, said the critics, the benchmark exercise was *dishonest* because based on an assumption that everyone knew to be false: that Government of India, which had agreed to implement the benchmarks, had influence over MP and Maharashtra and therefore that its sign-on meant something on the ground.

At the Board meeting the UK ED asked the key question: had the "relevant authorities" agreed to the benchmarks (meaning in particular had the *state governments* agreed)? The Indian ED gave an answer that left everyone unclear whether he meant yes or no or maybe. Managing Director Stern, in the chair, replied to the UK

---

[75] Quoted in Rich, *Mortgaging*, p.301.

[76] The quotation comes from the first draft of the Bank management's response to the Independent Review, dated June 23, 1992, p.12.

ED: "The answer is yes". The UK therefore cast its vote in favor of continuing. Until that moment the outcome of the vote had been in doubt. The US, Germany, Japan, Canada, Australia, and the Nordic countries had indicated their intention to vote for suspension. But they accounted for a minority (42%) of the vote. The UK's vote for continuing tipped the balance. The majority—including all the Part II countries—"wished to give the benefit of the doubt to the new Government of India and to acknowledge the recent efforts made by the Indian authorities"[77]. They therefore urged that the Bank should continue to disburse subject to a review against benchmarks 6 months on.

The fact that the Bank acted against the advice of the Independent Review—helped by the ambiguity in the Review's recommendation to "step back"—re-energized the international opposition to the project and to the Bank at large. On the ground construction progressed while resettlement lagged far behind. On the other hand, environmental analysis suddenly took off. In the 6 months following the independent review more progress was made towards the formulation of a regional environmental work plan than in the previous 6 years. Both the director of the India Department and key people in India finally accepted that the issue could not be fudged. This is a milestone in the Bank's environmental history.

A senior Bank manager admitted in 1993 that suspension in 1989 would have been a healthy "shock" that might have speeded up action on the ground to fix resettlement and environmental problems.[78] But the "shock" thesis was consistently rejected right up to 1993, in favor of the argument that incremental progress should be rewarded even if not sufficient to reach agreed deadlines.

At the end of March, 1993, the Board was scheduled to decide whether to continue. By then it was clear that the benchmarks set 6 months before, especially those to do with resettlement, would again not be met on the ground. South Asia Vice President Joseph Wood, who had strongly resisted suspension or cancellation since taking charge in 1991, became persuaded there was no alternative. Government of India and Government of Gujarat had indicated they would *not* say, "We will stop building the dam until these other matters are in hand". On the contrary, their attitude seemed to be, "Damn the NGOs, we are not going to submit to crybabies, we will continue to build the dam". They did not wish to accommodate the Bank's attempts to respond to world outrage. In any case, it had become blindingly obvious that the lack of unified decision making between the federal government and the states, plus the difficulties of cooperation between the states, meant the Bank could not count on Indian assurances. This argued against mere suspension, leaving cancellation as the only choice.

And cancellation now looked to be necessary in order to protect IDA from the continuing storm. For some years the finance complex of the Bank (which raises

---

[77] Chairman's summary, "India: Sardar Sarovar projects", Executive Director's meeting, October 23, 1992.

[78] Quoted in Hans Wyss, "Bankwide lessons learned from the experience with the India Sardar Sarovar (Narmada) project", May 19, 1993, p.5.

IDA money) had pressed the South Asia region to close down Narmada. A director in the financial complex asked Blinkhorn in 1991, "When are you guys going to close that project down? It is killing IDA".[79] The Board's decision to continue disbursements, coupled with the Bank's alleged misrepresentations of the Independent Review, lead the Narmada campaign to focus its attention on cutting off the $18 billion dollars for the tenth replenishment of IDA (IDA-10), then being negotiated. In the spring of 1993 Washington-based NGOs testified in Congress that they would oppose IDA funding unless the Bank (a) cancelled the loan, (b) undertook a complete revision of the Bank's information policy, and (c) created a citizen's appeals panel to give affected people direct access to an independent body to assess their complaints. This last is the embryonic idea of what became the Bank's Inspection Panel.

Representative Barney Frank, chair of the key IDA-authorizing subcommittee (the House Subcommittee on International Development, Finance, Trade and Monetary Policy) privately informed the senior management that he would refuse to authorize the US's $3.7 billion share of the IDA replenishment until these conditions were met. He was in close touch with the NGO leaders.

By March 1993 a majority of the Board favored cancellation. In the end, President Preston informed Prime Minister Narasima Rao that Narmada was jeopardizing IDA, and India was a major beneficiary of IDA.[80] The vice president for South Asia told the Indian government, "Either we cancel or you tell us you will not submit requests for disbursements". In the end the need to protect IDA outweighed worries about the Bank's loss of credibility as an infrastructure lender and the Bank's special relationship with India.

A few days before the Board meeting the Government of India announced that it would not ask the Bank for more disbursements. The central government was not unhappy to cancel. The project was generating too many headaches, and the benefits of Bank involvement went largely to Gujarat, not to the center. A senior Indian official said, "The project had become a cancerous tumor on the country's overall portfolio with the Bank".[81] Needing Bank help in publicizing India's market reforms, the government wanted embarrassing distractions like Narmada removed from the spotlight. Indeed, taking the moral high ground, the government explained

---

[79]This was the common view in the financial complex, but of course it was not shared by Ernest Stern, the senior vice president for finance for several years prior to the beginning of 1992.

[80]This is the paraphrase by a close participant. Rumors persist of a deal between Preston and Rao for the Bank to boost IDA disbursements to India through other channels so that India suffered no foreign exchange loss. It is not possible to confirm the rumor from IDA disbursements figures because the amounts disbursed year by year have complex and lagged determinants. There is a well-established principle that India gets about 18 percent of the IDA total, which works out to $800 to $1,000 million a year. (China gets another 15 percent.) Through the period of cancellation total IDA commitments to India held fairly steady. The chief problem for IDA and India has been to find enough projects to absorb India's 18%. At the end of FY1993 Stern was urging the India department, "You've got to get another $400 million [in project commitments] to bring India up to 18 percent".

[81]Quoted in "A tactical retreat to save face?", *Pioneer* (India), March 31, 1993.

that its decision reflected determination to upholding the quality of the planning and consultation processes even at the cost of not meeting the arbitrary deadlines agreed with the Bank 6 months before.[82]

In private Indian officials said that what the Bank had been doing was "not in keeping with the country's self-respect".[83] They claimed the Bank had been exercising inordinate influence given that it was contributing only 15–20% of the funds. And they recognized that the gap between Bank resettlement requirements and what India was able to deliver would almost certainly persist and be the source of constant future problems. Finally, the cost of cancellation was by this time not very high. The IDA (almost zero interest) component had already been disbursed, leaving the (almost commercial rate) IBRD funds to be canceled.

The leader of the main opposition movement, Medha Patkar, sent a message from a remote Narmada village saying the loss of World Bank funds was "a victory for thousands of struggling tribals and farmers in the Narmada valley".[84] The NBA then succeeded in getting the Supreme Court to halt dam construction in early 1995, until resettlement was carried out in line with India's and the Bank's policies.

Why Narmada?

Narmada became the second spearhead of NGO mobilization against the Bank, the second trampoline, not because it was bad compared to other Bank projects or because mistakes were made that were not made elsewhere. On the contrary. Like Polonoroeste, Sardar Sarovar was prepared by people who were idealists and innovators, who believed they were helping to make fundamental improvements in borrower governments' practice.

It became the second focus of attack because it had several characteristics that helped the organization of opposition: it involved the forced displacement of large numbers of people, many of whom could be presented as sympathy-arousing "tribals"; forced relocation could support a radical campaign to stop the dam; local opposition was well organized and led by a charismatic figure (Patkar); the international campaign benefited from unusually energetic and tenacious organizers (first Clark and Oxfam, then Udall and EDF); some Bank staff members and Bank consultants were severe critics of the way the project was being implemented and helped the external critics with inside information; and the local opposition to Narmada began to be noticeable around 1986, just as Polonoroeste was loosing its mobilizatory potential. Finally, location in India helped, because international NGOs

---

[82] In "Sarovar project: India foregoes World Bank aid", *Statesman* (India), March 31, 1993.

[83] Reported in "India not to seek further WB loan", *National Herald* (India), March 31, 1993.

[84] Quoted in "The World Bank cuts funds to a dam project in India", *The Independent* (UK), April 1, 1993. See also Steven Holmes, "World Bank restrictions prompt India to cancel dam project loan", *New York Times*, 31 March, 1993.

had good access to English-language information and because India's democratic polity and free press allowed opposition. If Narmada had been in China, Indonesia or Turkey it could not have been used as a spearhead.

The question then is not, "What did the Bank do wrong in Narmada that it did not do wrong in other projects?". This is to make the contrast with one line of Bank self-criticism, which says that Narmada suffered from serious "entry mistakes", such as poor resettlement planning or environmental assessment—with the implication that other Bank projects had better resettlement planning or environmental assessments.[85] Not necessarily.

What did make Narmada unusual is the timing that put it in a set of "hinge" projects. It was prepared, appraised and approved at about the same time as the Bank introduced quite new directives on "non-economic" criteria—resettlement and environment. These "noneconomic" criteria and directives were stoutly resisted inside the Bank by the operational people, as we have seen, including South Asia Vice President David Hopper. Their resistance, combined with ambiguity about the status of "directives" (as analogous to national laws or aspirational guidelines), allowed the busy project people to continue to prepare the project as they had prepared projects before the resettlement and environmental directives were introduced. And of course "consultation" with people of the valley was entirely neglected, for the Bank did not have any directives enjoining consultation, let alone experience of it.

India's federal structure made the Bank's implementation of these new directives all the more difficult, because resettlement and water fell under the heading of "state" subjects, not central or joint subjects; but the Bank could lend only to the central government, and could approach the state governments only via the central government, which had only limited influence over the states. (Indeed, the central government sometimes tried to get the Bank to put pressure on the states, thinking that the Bank had more leverage than it did.) The same point applies to all federal structures, including Brazil's.

The Bank's own quality control mechanism—review by central departments like the Agriculture and Rural Development Department and the Office of Environmental Affairs—was easily brushed aside. However, Narmada differed from Polonoroeste in that the central departments were much less involved in opposing it than they had been in Polonoroeste. The staff of the Agriculture Department did not raise alarms about it as they had about Polonoroeste, being sympathetic to large-scale irrigation projects.

The big exception was the person in the center whose job it was to look after resettlement, Michael Cernea. That resettlement was the single axis of center-region conflict within the Bank owes much to the combination of dogged Cernea in the center, a strong local resettlement movement on the ground, and later, a powerful international anti-Narmada movement focused on resettlement. Cernea decided in 1983 to draw a line at Narmada and force the South Asia Projects Department to

---

[85]Hans Wyss, "Bankwide lessons learned from the experience with the India Sardar Sarovar (Narmada) project", mimeo, May 19, 1993.

implement what he—with the backing of McNamara and his own Agriculture director—had only recently persuaded the Bank to adopt as a general resettlement policy.

Although at project approval in 1985 and project effectiveness in 1986 there were resettlement and environmental conditions in the loan agreements, few people on the Bank side or the India side thought they were more than cosmetic. Only later, once NGOs began to train their spotlights on resettlement, did operational people inside the Bank start to worry about these things, and then more resettlement than environment.

Lying

The problem became, "How does the Bank retrofit a project"? A project is in a sense no more than an agreement over the conditions for the use of borrowed funds. Once the agreement has been reached it is deeply problematic for the Bank to say, "Sorry, but our requirements have now changed, so we must change the agreement", or even to say, "Sorry, but we now have to observe these conditions that we all thought we didn't have to, so you must observe them too". Projects are path-dependent; the way they start imparts direction for years later, partly through the expectations of personnel, partly through the irreversibility of certain steps, and partly because the later addition of conditions (an environmental workplan and a slowdown in dam construction until the workplan can be implemented, for example) may entail huge delays to the whole project that need not have occurred had those conditions been met earlier.

Retrofitting is difficult. The effort to do so in Narmada as NGO pressure built up began to produce apparently deceitful behavior on the part of the operational staff. Their logic went like this.

1. We know things are not going well in the project.
2. But do we want to pull out or suspend?
3. No, it is potentially a damn fine project, and things will go better if we are in. Anyway, management would not allow a pull out, for country relations reasons. India is too big a borrower.
4. Therefore we need to justify staying in. The way to do so is to send reports up the hierarchy that things are going well or at least improving, making sure that if anything is said about things not going well the phrasing implies that they are minor or on the way to being fixed.

The trick is to make the aroma of words do the work that the evidence cannot. It is unlikely that anyone connected with Narmada ever said, "India needs this foreign exchange and we need India to borrow; therefore Narmada must go ahead; therefore we say what needs to be said to justify going ahead". Rarely if ever would people admit even to themselves, "This is wrong but we have to say it anyway". Rather the bias to optimism comes in the atmospherics. The staff could report up the hierarchy,

"The government has committed itself in this period to finish preparing 10 resettlement sites but only two have been done; and the government has failed to implement its policies on compensation"; or it could say, "The government has committed itself to prepare 10 resettlement sites, two have now been completed, another four are being planned, and the government is initiating major improvements in the policy framework". The second version justifies staying in. And a normative justification for going with the second version is always at hand; it says that the Bank should give heavy weight to what is happening *at the margin*, for the likely future course of events can be read at the margin. This is how the head of the Agriculture Unit in the Delhi office justified his reversal of Scudder's conclusions after the 1989 resettlement mission; Scudder, he said, was talking about the "average" level of performance, whereas he was looking at policy changes and performance "at the cutting edge".

Nevertheless, with Bank management insisting on good news, mission reports based on a few staff members' 3 day trip to a few accessible corners of the valley would seize upon any sign of progress, however small, and inflate it as a turning point. In one case in Maharashtra about 50 households, out of nearly 3000 eligible households, had moved to a resettlement site (the others had been persuaded not to do so by Medha Patkar). Of those about 30 had been issued with identity cards identifying them as resettlement beneficiaries, a strictly clerical operation of no difficulty. The mission report took the issuing of 30 identity cards out of 50 as a powerful indicator of progress on the ground, and ignored the fact that only 50 out of 3000 households had agreed to move. The mission leader was well aware of the deception. He saw himself as having no choice.

The NGO's information needs were, in a sense, the mirror image of the Bank's. NGOs had whole structures of communication in place just waiting to hear the bad news. Medha Patkar said to the Indian Administrative Service (IAS) officer in charge of Sardar Sarovar resettlement in Maharashtra after 1990 (whose diligence and determination is credited with turning around the resettlement situation there and subsequently lifting him from the Maharashtra resettlement dumping ground to a plum job at the World Bank in Washington), "It is good officers like you who are a problem for us". Likewise the journalists wanted bad news, for bad news makes good copy. The journalists rarely penetrated into the Narmada valley beyond the nearest village to the train from Bombay, where they would talk to a few activists and write about the dire things that were happening—according to the activists.

The lock-in became especially problematic after 1991 when real progress did begin to be made on the ground in Maharashtra (and earlier in Gujarat). By 1992 there was probably as much support among the tribals in favor of resettlement as against the dam. But the NGOs and the newspapers refused to report on this. The Independent Review team, presented with both negative and positive evidence in the field, put in all the negatives and left out most of the positives, in the opinion of the chief resettlement officer in Maharashtra. In particular, the Review team downplayed the strength of the pro-resettlement sentiment among tribals, he said. Meanwhile, all through this period, Bank management grew more and more desperate to find good news, and blurred even more the line between actual progress and hoped-for progress.

Why Not Suspend Before 1993?

One of the great questions about Narmada is why the problems were allowed to fester so long—why the Bank did not step back in the late 1980s, take a fresh look, admit serious problems, and suspend the loan? It is not that the senior managers did not know what was happening. Though the staff glossed the bad news the senior managers did have other sources of information, notably the NGOs. They knew of the gathering transnational NGO campaign and the hearings in the US Congress in 1989.

First, suspension of any project, anywhere, has high transactions costs for the Bank and for the relevant division. Procedures must be gone through that require intensive supervision both before the threat and after the threat in the build up towards the decision of whether to resume or cancel. But divisional supervision budgets are under tight pressure as division chiefs attempt to allocate more resources at the margin for project preparation. This gives them an incentive to shrink from suspension. Few brownie points are to be earned and many to be lost by not bringing the project to the Board.

Second, suspension of a project in India has particularly high costs. India has traditionally been one of the Bank's most valued customers. In Bank-India relations threats of suspension or cancellation are "not part of the tradition", in contrast to some other regions (notably Africa).[86] Both the Bank and India knew that the whole relationship might be put under strain if Narmada were suspended or cancelled. This became an especially serious consideration around the time of India's macroeconomic crisis in 1991, when the government promised far-reaching liberalization that the Bank was keen to support.

Third, resettlement would be better if the Bank were involved, even if not perfect. Suspension, it was argued, would only hurt the oustees. Could the Bank walk away from the most vulnerable people?

Fourth, the Government of India wanted the Bank to remain involved partly to augment its own limited leverage over the state governments.

Fifth, Sardar Sarovar was just the first of many projects the Bank would be involved in on the Narmada river, helping to grow its lending and its revenue.

Finally, Bank managers came to see Narmada as a test case of the Bank's resolve to stay in the business of infrastructural lending worldwide and to protect its autonomy from NGO incursions. Ernest Stern was well known for stressing that, "The Bank does not cancel because of *political* pressure". He would tell his subordinates, "Development is a treacherous business. You'll make mistakes. When

---

[86]Wyss, ibid., p. 4–5.

crises come you just have to hunker down and wait till the storm dies." The whole idea of the Bank doing "Public Relations", courting journalists and NGOs, appalled him. The Bank should be above that level, he said.[87] And so the bigger the Narmada campaign, the more the rallying cry inside the India Department became, "The storm will pass. We mustn't cave in."

All these factors indicate why the costs of suspension or cancellation looked to be very high and the benefits of staying in very substantial. Moreover, the India Department had what it considered a workable strategy:

1. Focus on Gujarat, the state with the most to gain from the project and the most capable administration, on the assumption that once things are done well in Gujarat this will put pressure on the other states to move as well.
2. Keep the project on a "short leash", with close monitoring of targets.
3. Go for incremental gains rather than insist on blue-prints in advance, on the assumption that, given the long gestation period, incremental gains will eventually add up to large gains. If the incremental approach led the Bank to be out-of-strict-compliance with some of its directives (for example, on resettlement or environment), too bad for the directives. No project is in full compliance; there are too many directives for full compliance to be realistic.

The Bank's incremental strategy in Narmada represented (in the eyes of both senior managers as well as project staff) the triumph of substance over formality, of realism over idealism.

Like the frog in the heating pot who doesn't realize until too late that the nice warm bath is becoming frog soup, the Bank faced an escalation too gradual for someone to say, "Let's rethink this project ". NGO pressure grew by degrees, and the NGOs making the criticism were British rather than American until 1987, therefore more easily ignored. The time to reshape the project was in 1984–1985, before loan approval and loan effectiveness. As the campaign began, the Bank's "shove off" response became something that then had to be defended. By the time the senior managers noticed that the water was very hot, they were becoming World Bank soup.

The high turnover of managers in the India Department during the second half of the 1980s contributed to their slowness to notice. Each new division chief and department director wanted several months to familiarize himself with the whole portfolio before making major decisions. He was inclined to accept the project as the project people presented it. All the more so because he knew that Ernest Stern, who remained de facto the most powerful person in the Bank even while senior vice president for finance, took a specially protective interest in the Bank's work in India, "his" country. Who in their right mind would go up against Stern if they did not have to?

It is also important that the Bank did not staff up a crisis management team. Even as the Bank as a whole came under sustained attack from the late 1980s through to

---

[87]From a source who worked closely with Stern during this time.

1993 almost nothing special was done inside the Bank to enhance its capacity to respond. With the partial exception of the India Department's environment/ resettlement czar, no senior Bank professional staff was assigned to take charge of the Sardar Sarovar resettlement project component, despite it being so contentious. The Bank at no time tried to get a serious *political* analysis of what was happening in the valley or in the state governments, relying on the seat-of-the-pants understandings of its own staff. The worse the crisis, the more the director of the India Department and his environment/resettlement czar hunkered down and made the decisions themselves, excluding everyone else in the department and answering only to their own superiors.

Their difficulties were magnified by the fact that relations between the director of the India department, German, and Ernest Stern, American of German origin, were bad to the point that they could not stand to be in the same room together; Blinkhorn and the South Asia vice president had to act as go-betweens. (The director had earlier been the deputy Treasurer of the Bank under Stern as senior vice president for finance, and his Germanic concern for correct procedures had clashed repeatedly with Stern's budget entrepreneurialism. The director had later been chief of staff for Moeen Qureshi when Qureshi was in charge of all Bank operations, which lead him into more fights with Stern.) Moreover, the director and his environment/ resettlement czar had to manage the crisis on top of normal workloads, and with no more than the normal budget for supervision of a project of this size. The thinness of Narmada crisis management is striking testimony to rigid personnel and budgetary systems.

In particular, *the Bank did not try to lift decisions about the future of the project out of the hands of those who had a vested interest in continuing.* Once it became clear that Bank-wide interests were at stake, the Bank could have appointed a Bank-wide panel to take the big decisions about Narmada, reporting directly to the president. It did not. This was not peculiar to Narmada; there were no precedents for such crisis management in the Bank, strange to say.[88]

Only twice did senior management above the level of the South Asian vice president have any "public" involvement in the project, both in 1988. The Qureshi resettlement mission of that year illustrates the problem. Qureshi himself was directly involved in setting the benchmarks against which progress should be judged. *But the later judgment of whether the benchmarks had been met sufficiently to justify lifting the threat to suspend was put back entirely within the South Asia vice presidency, in the hands of people who had a vested interest in not suspending.*

---

[88] A partial exception was the newly filling Tarbella dam in Pakistan in 1974. When it appeared likely to break, the Bank established a crisis room from where it monitored the situation minute by minute, with direct access to McNamara.

Legacies

Beyond bad blood and bruised egos, Narmada left several legacies. First, the Bank came to be more accepting of international NGOs as legitimate interlocutors. The growth of powerful NGOs able to get the ear of governments complicated the old theory that the Bank is responsible only to its shareholders and to the relevant government; so NGOs should channel their views via the relevant ED, not direct to management. Narmada demonstrated that the Bank ignored (some) NGOs at its peril. And the Independent Review, by confirming much of what NGOs had been saying about the Bank's performance, helped improve their image from unreliable "crybabies" to sources of expertise, information feedback, and possible political help that the Bank should use. (In Polonoroeste, by contrast, the many NGO criticisms were never brought together in one place and ratified by an independent body.) The Bank moved in this direction to the point where there was by the late 1990s a more routinized, more cooperative, less antagonistic relationship between the Bank and some NGOs than was true earlier.

Second, the Bank came to accept the need to ensure consultation with project affected peoples, often via NGOs. The Independent Review endorsed the idea that much of the mishandling of resettlement and environmental questions in Narmada was due to a lack of consultation with area residents. International NGOs and Part I governments redoubled efforts to get the Bank to insert consultative elements into its project procedures.[89]

Third, the Bank's environmental and especially its social establishment had a boost of legitimacy after the Independent Review's report in 1992. They became the organization's protectors against another Narmada. Country directors and division chiefs who had never before voiced much sympathy for environmental or social concerns began telling their staffs, "We must avoid another Narmada". The director of the India Department, post-Independent Review, kept telling his staff, "This is a changed Bank. We cannot continue to do projects in the old way." Several times he ordered his staff to classify their projects as "A" (environmentally sensitive) even when the regional environment division had agreed on a "B". The "A" ensured that the project went through a comprehensive environmental review.

Prompted by the Narmada experience the Bank reviewed the resettlement aspects of all projects active, world-wide, for the period 1986 to 1993.[90] The Bank's resettlement policy became widely known among project staff, as something they could no longer treat casually.

Yet many people in the Bank, including among its senior management, continue to think that the Bank's resettlement policy is, as Ernest Stern put it, "an exaggerated response". He went on, "The condition of equal livelihood in the new place is too

---

[89] See Working With NGOs: A Practical guide to Operational Collaboration Between the World Bank and Nongovernmental Organizations, Operations Policy Department, Washington DC: The World Bank, March 1995.

[90] See *Resettlement and Development*, Washington DC: World Bank, April 1994.

stringent as a general rule. It is possible where land is abundant and where there is a good financial system (for example Argentina or even Mexico), but almost impossible—I would say impossible—in India and Bangladesh".[91]

Nor does the boost in the legitimacy of environment and resettlement extend to rewarding those who tried to advance environmental and resettlement concerns from within the India Department. On the contrary. Those few people inside the department who became known as project critics have subsequently not been promoted,[92] while most of those in the direct line of responsibility for Narmada have been promoted. David Hopper, the South Asia vice president throughout the evolution of the project up to 1987, was promoted to senior vice president; his successor as regional vice president in the late 1980s, when the crisis erupted and when things might have been done differently, was promoted to be managing director; the two successive directors of the India department in the late 1980s were promoted to vice president; and the resettlement/environment czar was promoted to division chief.

Finally, the Narmada campaign gave leverage for two accountability reforms in the Bank. It accelerated the already growing pressure for a more liberal information disclosure policy. And it directly catalysed a resolution to establish a permanent inspection panel, which began operating in 1994 and for its first decade of existence was one of the most divisive issues on the Board, generally pitting Part II countries against Part I.

These are legacies within the Bank. On the ground the game described here has continued unabated to this day (meaning the mid to late 1990s). On one side are activists and some federal bodies pressing the courts and multiple review bodies to require that dam construction (especially the height of the dam, which determines the submergence area) must be constrained by progress on resettlement and environmental work; while on the other side are the construction organizations which continue, bulldozer fashion, to build the dam, almost as though the former did not exist. Meanwhile the construction of the distribution system and the drinking water pipelines has hardly begun. S. Parasuraman and colleagues write that "The progress made by the SSP [Sardar Sarovar Project] does not seem to be very different from India's experience with major irrigation and power projects: while main civil works somehow get completed, creation of the necessary infrastructure to realize benefits of the projects remain uncertain".[93]

---

[91] Ernest Stern, personal communication, June 1995.

[92] One of India's best known resettlement experts, Abdul Salam, worked as a local consultant on Sardar Sarovar resettlement from 1987 to 1989. Shortly after the 1989 mission's return to Delhi a meeting was held in the Bank's Delhi office to discuss its findings. Salam informed the meeting that on the basis of what he had seen for the past two years he considered the Bank's resettlement strategy a failure cloaked in hypocrisy. He announced his resignation from further work on Sardar Sarovar resettlement. Thereafter he was not hired by the Bank in any capacity until Cernea hired him to help with the resettlement review in 1993, and by 1996 had never been hired by the India Department. Subsequently, however, he has again been hired by the Bank.

[93] S. Parasuraman, et al., "Sardar Sarovar project: the war of attrition", Economic and Political Weekly, January 30, 2010.

Robert Hunter Wade is professor of global political economy at the London School of Economics and Political Science. He was awarded the Leontief Prize for Advancing the Frontiers of Economic Thought in 2008; and the American Political Science Association's "Best Book in Political Economy, 1989–91", for *Governing the Market: Economic Theory and the Role of Government in East Asia's Industrialization* (Princeton University Press, 1990, 2004).

His research has focused on the great "Wealth of Nations" question about how capitalisms generate material well-being and power in the world system—with an interest less in models and statistical techniques and more in the culture and "underwear politics" behind the big trends. This has entailed long-term fieldwork in places including Pitcairn Island, Italy, India, Korea, Taiwan, Iceland, and inside the World Bank and IMF. At the World Bank from 1984 to 1988 he worked in the Agriculture and Rural Development Department and then in the Trade Policy Division. In the mid 1990s he wrote "Greening the Bank: the struggle over the environment, 1970–1995", in D. Kapur, et al., 1997, *The World Bank: Its First Half Century*, Brookings, volume 2. In the late 1990s he worked as consultant to the Inspection Panel on its investigation of the Qinghai irrigation and resettlement project in western China.

He is the son of a New Zealand diplomat, educated at Wellington College, Otago University, Victoria University, and Sussex University. He has worked at the Institute of Development Studies (Sussex University), the World Bank, US Congress (Office of Technology Assessment), Princeton University (Woodrow Wilson School), MIT (Sloan School), and Brown University (Watson Institute). His many books and articles include *Irrigation and Politics in South Korea (1982); Village Republics; The Economic Conditions of Collective Action in India (1988), and "The Strange Neglect of income inequality in economics and public policy (2014)"*. In 1992, Dr. Wade's book *Governing the Market: Economic Theory and the Role of Government in East Asia,* was the American Political Science Association's Best Book or Article in Political Economy, and in 2008 he (along with Jose Antonio Ocampo) was awarded the Leontief prize in recognition of his outstanding contribution to economic theory that addresses contemporary realities.

Open Access This chapter is licensed under the terms of the Creative Commons Attribution 4.0 International License (http://creativecommons.org/licenses/by/4.0/), which permits use, sharing, adaptation, distribution and reproduction in any medium or format, as long as you give appropriate credit to the original author(s) and the source, provide a link to the Creative Commons license and indicate if changes were made.

The images or other third party material in this chapter are included in the chapter's Creative Commons license, unless indicated otherwise in a credit line to the material. If material is not included in the chapter's Creative Commons license and your intended use is not permitted by statutory regulation or exceeds the permitted use, you will need to obtain permission directly from the copyright holder.

From Onlookers to Participants: How the Role of Social Scientists Has Changed in India's Development in the Last 70 Years

Hari Mohan Mathur

In the 1970s, the long ignored social and cultural factors in development gradually began to gain recognition in the World Bank. This was no small change. It was significant particularly because till then the World Bank had a strictly economic orientation, and there was little understanding of social issues that often arise in development work and which also need to be addressed.

In the wake of the Bank's turning its face toward poverty reduction, an historic change took place inside the World Bank itself. This was the appointment of anthropologists and sociologists as regular staff, to help the Bank understand what it defined as the 40% poorest rural population. In 1974, the Bank created its first position of staff sociologist and Michael Cernea joined the Bank as its first social scientist, slowly followed by others. Thereafter, social concerns began receiving increasing professional attention in the Bank's approach to development. This was then reflected in its concern to prevent social disasters resulting from infrastructure projects. With the support of his managers, Michael Cernea then proposed and drafted the first resettlement policy in the entire international donor and development community (World Bank 1980; Cernea 1993).

Social Scientists and Development in India

The impact of this and other subsequent social policies adopted by the World Bank was felt globally. The new social policies changed the social science scene in India as well. The big potential of India's social scientists to work for development began to be used in very consequential ways.

H. M. Mathur (✉)
Council for Social Development, New Delhi, India

Mere Observers Prior to mid-1970, India's non-economic social scientists had no role in policy, planning of development projects, or implementation of resettlement, though their skills and knowledge were relevant for these purposes. With few exceptions, anthropologists were distant observers of the socially terrible effects left behind by development projects. They were called to do little else besides teaching and studying. Anthropologists were just not needed in India's major programs for development.

Active Participants The World Bank issued in 1984 another operational policy, the OMS 2.20 on Project Appraisal, which contained the innovation-prone requirement that all Bank financed projects should incorporate in their preparation process (pre-appraisal and appraisal) a professional sociological analysis and an institutional analysis to complement the one-sided traditional economic and financial analyses required by the Bank before. This recognition of development variables previously neglected resulted in a sudden demand to borrowing countries for preparing more completely their projects for Bank financing; in turn, India also needed to involve Indian anthropologists and rural sociologists in the project preparation teams for social surveys, demographic and cultural assessments, resettlement planning, impact evaluation analyses. From *mere onlookers*, they then began to become *active participants in development activities,* including resettlement.

Anthropology in Government The history of anthropological use in government programs in India were colored by its colonial status that ended when India became independent in 1947 (Vidyarthi: 1971). However, for the most part that history was confined to providing descriptive portrayals of tribal, caste, and minority groups, leaving to others the job of defining and promoting development. For example, the Anthropological Survey of India (an old institution established by the British colonial anthropologists in 1905) has been functioning uninterruptedly, but still remains focused on tribal ethnographies, as before. Academic anthropologists, too, have mostly continued to follow their interests largely around documenting the lifeways of tribal people and socially backward groups. Even most universities and independent researchers have chosen to follow the same path—so strong is the ethnographic research tradition that prevails even today, although more recently a dozen or so Tribal Research Institutes established in tribal dominated states are doing applied anthropological research on development issues of and for tribal people.

Role in Development Gradually, the role of anthropologists expanded to the field of development, which then mostly meant programs of community development and tribal welfare (Majumdar 1960). But even there, the opportunities to introduce social knowledge into development policies and large programs were very limited. Only a handful of anthropologists were employed in various development agencies. In early 1950s, D. N. Majumdar, an eminent anthropologist from the Lucknow University, was invited to serve on the Planning Commission's Research Programmes Committee. At about the same time, the Planning Commission set up a Programme Evaluation Organization to report independently on the performance of community development projects. The Commission went on to appoint anthropologist consultants. Similarly, S. C. Dube, a reputed anthropologist, was appointed to head the National Institute of Community Development. Some positions were also filled in at the Tribal Research Institutes (Mathur 1976). But the zest with which these development-oriented programs involving anthropologists were begun did not last long, and most soon lost steam (Mathur 1985).

Opportunities Lost The large dam era began in India with a bang. From 1947 onwards, dam building started in a massive way, and within a short time a number of big dams came up. "Nearly 900 big dams were completed between 1951 and 1982" (Khagaram 2004: 37). Among the first dams built were Hirakud, Bhakra, Chambal, and Pong Dam. The human displacement caused by these dams was on an unprecedented scale, depriving millions of their homes, their livelihoods, often even their identity.

Here was a chance for the government to utilize anthropological expertise to resettle dam-displaced populations. Not only were the agencies unwilling to hear about the problems stemming from projects, but even national planners and representatives appeared to be uninterested in consulting Indian social specialists who could have at least flagged some of the most likely ways that these projects adversely affect their constituents. Preparing a national policy on resettlement was also a task for which anthropologists were best fitted. However, their role was not considered; the policy was seen as too important a matter to be left to anthropologists. Instead, the government preferred its own bureaucrats and other technical experts for the job, many of whom lacked any understanding or field experience with the complex social issues that were involved.

Surprisingly, anthropologists had no role in even such simple tasks as surveys to collect data required for planning purposes and for the evaluation of resettlement outcomes. They not only did not participate in externally funded projects, but they were left out even from those that the government funded itself. The frightening fact, however, is that the government often went ahead building dams with no consideration of their possible adverse social impacts (Singh and Banerji 2002). Unfortunately, such a situation has remained unchanged till today. A case study of a dam project in Orissa vividly documents the disastrous consequences of such a callous attitude on the poor tribal people (Agnihotri 2016).

Exclusion of Social Scientists Often, the exclusion of social scientists occurred due to a plain desire of economists, bureaucrats and others to maintain their dominance in their organizations. In some cases, the cause of exclusion is also pure ignorance of the value and potential of anthropological knowledge for development work. There are also examples where anthropologists were brought in by organizations, but their expertise was not utilized for the purpose for which it was meant. For example, in 1995 the National Thermal Power Corporation (NTPC), under World Bank pressure, turned to social science expertise for assistance in easing obstacles to its resettlement plans and the increase of farmer protests. They hurriedly inducted anthropologists and other social scientists to fix the problem. However, the lack of clarity in NTPC on the role of anthropologists led to their use as mere additional hands to assist project officials in carrying out displacement in ways usual to the NTPC organization with emphasis on simple removal of affected people to new sites rather than on simultaneously reconstructing their livelihoods. Unhappy with their other job conditions, most anthropologists soon left the organization, and the contracts of those remaining were cancelled once the World Bank project ended (Mathur 2013, also Mathur 2006).

Criticism of Flaws Is a Service for Better Development Even when excluded from any role in government development projects, social scientists did not get passive and disheartened. They didn't start grumbling over the rejection of their expertise—an understandable response. Instead, they responded positively and turned their expertise to serve the cause of development in pragmatic ways. Anthropologists and other social scientists provided on their own free services to development agencies by writing about the projects that were performing poorly (and there was no shortage of such projects). They looked into resettlement failures through their critical social scientists' lens, offering constructive and detailed analyses that pointed out design or implementation flaws, together with the ways such shortcomings could be remedied. India's resettlement literature abounds in such constructive critical anthropological studies. Examples include the detailed studies by Roy Burman (1961) and Karve (1969), to mention but a few. These studies did create some awareness that anthropologists do have the knowledge and skills to improve resettlement. But this awareness came too slowly to change the hardened bureaucratic mindsets in the short-run.

The Narmada Controversy

In the beginning of the dam era, government was able to build dam after dam, evicting hundreds of thousands of people from their homes and livelihoods without strong opposition. The dam-impoverished people felt the pain, but they didn't openly express their accumulating anger. The affected people would take the paltry cash compensation on offer, hand over possession of their land for developmental uses, and move on to resettle at new places, often with drops in the quality of livelihood that lasted for generations (Mathur 1977). Opposition to dams was then almost non-existent. Gradually, things began to change as popular protests against dams surfaced from various Indian states. Initially, protesters' demands were simple—better compensation for losses—and the methods of protest were entirely peaceful. As time went by, though, initial protests got bigger and better organized, and, with the infusion of much CSO support, they also became better organized and more militant,

Although displacement has gone on in India for decades, the resettlement issue came to the fore in a big way when controversy over the Narmada dam projects erupted in mid/late 1980s. Sardar Sarovar, one of the dams on the Narmada river, was causing massive displacement and relocation issues. As documented by Robert

Wade's in his Narmada paper in this volume, cracks and contradictions between the three affected states created opportunities for new political alliances. Medha Patkhar, a tenacious activist, led a powerful campaign against the Narmada projects, primarily Sardar Sarovar, denouncing both the Indian Government's and the World Bank's violations of its own poverty reduction and resettlement policies. This turned into a rallying cry calling for the complete stoppage of its construction, not just a better resettlement package. The agitation rapidly snowballed into something never previously anticipated—a social movement that was demanding a total ban on the building of dams not only in India, but all over the world.

In June 1991, the World Bank's management, responding to this well organized and unstoppable protests, , appointed David Morse, formerly a head of the United Nations Development Programme (UNDP), Thomas R Berger, a highly reputed Canadian jurist, and Hugh Brody, a British Anthropologist, to carry out an independent review of the Narmada Sardar Sarovar Dam's social and environmental impacts, and on how India and the World Bank carried out their social and environmental responsibilities. On 18 June 1992, the Independent Review submitted its report on the Sardar Sarovar projects to the President of the World Bank. It confirmed the worst of the Narmada protesters' criticisms. The report concluded, that the World Bank resettlement policy was adequate, but the World Bank and India's central and state governments had ignored and violated it, and, by doing so, had violated the rights and destroyed the livelihoods of the affected populations, Morse et al. 1992: p. xii).

Impacts of the Independent Review's Indictment on India

India felt the impact of Independent Review's indictment directly. Following the success of protest against the Sardar Sarovar dam, strong protests against other dams sprang up in almost every nook and corner of the country. And no longer were the protests directed against dams alone; protests in other sectors, including industrial, mining, power, highways, and urban development also became the targets of NGO protests. In fact, against any project that caused displacement and ignored its resettlement obligations became their target. Today, no development project that fails to resettle displaced people adequately can escape the critical eye of one vigilant NGO or another.

The other consequences of the Independent Review include the following: Writing on resettlement issues has become something of a growth industry since the controversy over the Narmada dam projects broke out, intensifying long after the 1980s. Books, journal articles, conferences, and other research documents kept coming out. Examples include: Paranjpye (1990), Baviskar (1996), and Dreze et al. (1997). India's resettlement literature became the largest in the world, and remains so today. The university departments of anthropology also saw the need to adapt their curricula to changed circumstances. With a rising number of students getting consultancy appointments on resettlement projects without any resettlement training or experience, most often with a mere degree in anthropology or sociology, forced them to include displacement and resettlement issues in their syllabuses. Consequently, the number of students pursuing resettlement as an optional subject because it opens up employment opportunities has steadily shown an upward trend. It is now quite common for students to select resettlement as a research topic for PhD in many other institutions, including even in such highly respected technical centers such as the Indian Institutes of Technology.

The most significant impact of protests, and the growing research output generated in its aftermath, though not immediately visible then, was slowly changing the mindset of India's bureaucracy. They began to see the need for a law for better planning of resettlement. For example, the slow process of formulating a national policy on resettlement lingering for a long time, now began to be seen as a matter of some priority, but it dragged through several weak versions in 2004 and 2007 that did not go down well with the public, the NOGs, and the social scientists. Eventually, in 2013 India's Parliament adopted a Law that for the first time brought land acquisition and resettlement within the same normative framework (GOI 2013), replaced the obsolete colonial 1894 Land Acquisition Act (Singh 2016). The extraordinary bargaining process and political battle for "the making of the 2013 Law" is described in detail in Ramesh and Khan's 2015 book *"Legislating for Justice"*.

Impact of the Independent Review on the World Bank

Following the Independent Review, the World Bank moved fast and initiated several corrective measures to improve the resettlement work in the Bank. Another key area where the need to eliminate weaknesses was seen as a high priority was to ensure strict compliance with all its other social policies too. Another major concern was to improve implementation of projects in India. These initiatives meant much for India's anthropologists, and sociologists, especially their role in development.

Implementing mandatory social policies, especially those related to the resettlement of those displaced, had opened vast new opportunities for anthropologists. But there were no takers for them, as the requisite expertise then did not exist on the scale required. In the beginning, the Bank attempted to carry out many of the resettlement and other poverty-oriented project assignments in India by sending out missions from its headquarters in Washington DC. Michael M. Cernea, William Partridge, Scott Guggenheim, Thayer Scudder, and Maritta Koch-Weser were among the staff and consultants who spent time working on resettlement projects in India.

The Bank, however, soon realized that it was not a practical or desirable solution to use the limited Bank staff from its headquarters to do the tasks that could well be done by local experts. But the lack of sufficient local capacity proved to be a big stumbling block. The first priority task, then, was to create it.

Building Capacity for Development Management

In India, development and resettlement issues emerged as a matter of overarching concern in the aftermath of Independent Review. Hence, the Bank turned its particular attention to equipping social scientists to capacity building for resettlement implementation, and took several measures, as follows.

(a) *Developing Resettlement Policies*: Until 2004, India had no national policy. (States had their own ad hoc guidelines to address the resettlement problem). In the absence of a national policy on resettlement, the Bank applied its own resettlement policy to all projects in India that it financed. The Bank moved further. It soon began assisting the preparation of resettlement policies for those organizations to which it made big loans. Examples of World Bank projects that supported sectoral policy development include the; Orissa Water Resources Development Project, Mumbai Urban Transport Project, National Thermal Power Corporation Project, Coal India Project, and several others.

(b) *Hiring and Training National Staff and Short-term Consultants in the Bank's New Delhi Office*. In pursuance of its decision to build local capacity, the Bank created some staff positions for resettlement experts from India within the Bank's New Delhi Office. Consequently, Sam Thangaraj, IUB Reddy, Mohammad Hasan, S Satish, Shankar Narayanan were among those appointed to the Social and Environment Division of the Bank's New Delhi Office. This Division flourished under David Marsden, Elllen Schaengold, and others who followed them.

The New Delhi Office also engaged many local consultants on a short-term basis to carry out resettlement tasks as and when required. For example, they were employed to carry out a variety of tasks that included: social impact assessments, resettlement planning, implementation, evaluation, supervision, monitoring, preparation of project completion reports, assisting Bank's inspection panel, and so on. It is impossible to estimate in retrospect the number employed as short-term consultants, but the number must be huge.

(c) *Building a Resettlement Curriculum*: The scarcity of relevant training material was immediately recognized as a big hurdle in conducting this programme. No training material, no other publication existed, explaining involuntary resettlement issues for resettlement practitioners in an easily comprehensible way. The World Bank, at the very start, took a decision to commission such a publication consisting of a series of case studies on resettlement experience in different project types in India, which could be used for training purposes. As part of my own first assignment with World Bank, I worked to produce a casebook on managing resettlement caused by dams, mining and other kinds of projects.

(d) *Training for Resettlement Practitioners*: The next major step that the World Bank took to fill in the expertise lacunae was the launch of a training programme for planners, practitioners, researchers and NGOs involved in resettlement activities. In 1993, the Economic Development Institute (EDI) of the World

Bank, Washington, was assigned this responsibility for the entire world, but this particular training programme focused on India and China for the obvious reason—these two countries were causing the most resettlement issues. EDI appointed Gordon Appleby, an anthropologist, as the overall coordinator for the EDI training programme, with two separate consultants, one each for India and China. For India, I was appointed as consultant and served intermittently from 1995 to 1999.

Resettlement training workshops were initiated in 1994, in Hyderabad, and were then extended to most state administrative training institutes in India, including Udaipur (Rajasthan), Mysore (Karnataka), Bhopal (Madhya Pradesh), Pune (Maharashtra), Bhubaneswar (Orissa), Nainital (Uttar Pradesh), Kolkata (West Bengal), and also Mussoorie (National). One workshop was also conducted for industry manages in collaboration with the Confederation of Indian Industry, as the private sector's role in development was becoming increasingly important. By the time the EDI programme ended in 1999, it had produced a large pool of trained resettlement practitioners, trainers, NGOs, resource persons and a useful publication for training purposes (Mathur 1997).

(e) *Support to Training by Correspondence* The Bank's New Delhi Office also provided support to an Open University in New Delhi to run a correspondence course. With Shobhita Jain as the Director of this programme and Madhu Bala as her associate, the programme ran well and trained many in-service resettlement staff doing resettlement without any prior training.

(f) *The World Bank's Support to National Seminars*: The World Bank headquarters sponsored several resettlement seminars in India. These included the following:

Seminar at ISEC Bangalore: One such early seminar was held at the Institute of Social and Economic Change in Bangalore in 1979. The key presenter in this Seminar was Scott Guggenheim from the Bank who elaborated on Cernea's Impoverishment Risks Model. The seminar also came up with a set of recommendations for preparing a National Resettlement Policy. A summary of this seminar was later published by ISEC for wide distribution (Aloysius 1990).

Seminar on Impoverishment Risks, New Delhi: 1994, another important seminar was held in New Delhi. This took place at the initiative of David Marsden who was then heading the Social and Environment Division in the Bank's New Delhi Office. The seminar was focused on Cernea's Impoverishment Risks Model. Later, David Marsden, at Michael Cernea's suggestion, invited me to prepare a volume based on the papers presented at this seminar, which was published with the title *Development Projects ad Impoverishment Risks*.

The Simla Seminar on South Asia Region R&R Sourcebook; Ms Ellen Schengold, who succeeded David Marsden as Chief, Social and Environmental Division in the Bank's New Delhi Office, organized yet another important seminar in Simla in June 1998. The purpose was to familiarize the seminar participants with the World Bank's just published 'South Asia Region R&R Sourcebook'. Participants attended the Seminar from all over

India from a variety of backgrounds: government, research organizations, NGOs, and consultants. From the Bank headquarters, several staff members and consultants also came over to serve as faculty.

The National Seminar on the South Asia Region Resettlement & Rehabilitation Sourcebook: The Bank recently supported the Council for Social Development to organize a national seminar to discuss the draft Land Acquisition Rehabilitation and Resettlement Bill 2011. The objective of the workshop was to formulate comments and recommendations on the draft bill from the perspective of both the people affected by land acquisition and resettlement, and that of the land requiring agencies, and to send these to the government for their consideration while finalizing the Bill. The participants included experts from the Council and elsewhere, social activists, academics, representatives of project authorities and land requiring agencies, NGOs, serving and retired civil servants, and World Bank staff.

(g) *Participation in International Seminars and Conferences*—The Bank supported the participation of a large number of India's social scientists, consultants and NGOs in international conferences held at various places around the world. Examples include the following:

World Bank Seminars on Involuntary Resettlement in Bank-financed Projects in Asia: An International Seminar titled 'World Bank Consultants Seminar on Involuntary Resettlement in Bank-financed Projects in Asia' took place in Washington DC at the Bank's headquarters and also at Baltimore, Maryland in June 1990. Participants from several Asian countries attended this seminar, including participants from India, Bangladesh, Sri Lanka, Nepal, and Vietnam. This training seminar was designed to develop local capacity for managing Bank-funded and other resettlement projects. A volume jointly edited by Mathur and Cernea (1994) based on Asian resettlement papers presented at this training programme was later published.

The World Bank also extended support for Indian social scientists to attend international conferences organized by other professional organizations, where participants could exchange knowledge and build cross-country networks . Among these were: (a) Xth World Congress of Rural Sociology, held at Rio de Janeiro (30 July 5 August 2000), and (b) A session on 'Population Resettlement and Environmental Risks' which was part of the larger IAPS/Biblex Conference on 'Environment, Health and Sustainable Development', held at Alexandria (11–16 September 2006).

Overall Feedback on Training Workshops and Seminars: The feedback from participants from these training workshops and seminars can be summed up as follows: Participants were unanimous in their view that what they had learned was going to be of immense help in efforts to improve their performance on resettlement operations in India. In addition, they felt that such programmes provided an excellent platform for Indian social scientists to meet and interact with their colleagues from different projects, places and backgrounds. Among those who participated in these various seminars, included Aloysius Fernandes, Vasudha Dhagamwar and L. K. Mahapatra, Ramaswamy Iyer, N. C. Saxena, A. B. Ota, IUB Reddy, Balaji Pandey, Anita Agnihotri, Walter Fernandes, Enakshi Ganguli Thukral, Malika Basu, Achyut Das, S. M. Jammdar, S. Parasuraman and several others.

Enriching Resettlement Knowledge

Social scientists of India and the World Bank together have contributed enormously to the publication of research-based books, articles and other publications on resettlement issues. The research output carried out both in India and the World Bank is indeed very impressive and also of a high quality. The difference is that while literature produced in India is more rooted in on the ground situations, the Bank's contribution is more tilted towards the macro side, both complementing each other's efforts.

Much contribution from the Bank is relevant to the Indian situation as well. Cernea himself has contributed several chapters and articles to many publications in India. These include: Mathur (1985, 1994, 1995, 1997, 1998, 2006, 2008, 2016), Parasuraman (2000) and Jain and Bala (2006), among others. He also contributed to a number of articles in Indian journals including *Economic and Political Weekly* (1996, 2007), *The Eastern Anthropologist* (2000), and *Social Change* (2006). In addition, Cernea also jointly edited a couple of books (Mathur and Cernea 1995; Cernea and Mathur 2008)

In turn, many Indian anthropologists and sociologists have written for World Bank publications. They include: Behura and Nayak (1993), Mahapatra (2000), Fernandes (2000), Hakim (2000), Nayak 2000), Appa and Patel (1996) and Thangaraj (1996). In addition, Mathur (1977) prepared a publication based on resettlement experience in Rajasthan, which was published by World Bank/EDI.

Initially, most research in India was "damcentric". Later, as projects in other development sectors began overtaking dams as a major driver of displacement, the area of research expended to cover them as well. Examples include, dams (Ganguly Thukral 1992) industry (Dhagamwar et al. 2000), mining (CSE), urban (Modi 2009), highways (Mridula Singh), women and displacement (Mehta 2000), development impact on tribal cultures (Felix and Das 2010), and conservation in protected parks (Kabra 2018), among several others. Several specific resettlement issues too have figured prominently, and these include: Impoverishment risks (Mathur and Marsden 1998; Mahapatra 2000; Bharali 2015), Ethnography of land acquisition (Guha 2011), and, Social Impact Assessment (Mathur 2016).

Finally, a widely known contribution from India is the *Resettlement News*. Edited by Hari Mohan Mathur, it reports on current operational, research and capacity building work in resettlement from around the world. The aim is to disseminate practical experience, ideas and information among those working in resettlement agencies, development research centers and management training institutes. This newsletter is published twice a year in January and July, and is regularly uploaded on the INDR website (www.displacement.net).

Summing Up

The building of big dams began in India soon after India became independent in 1947. Big dams together with a number of projects in other development sectors that followed soon resulted in displacement, which was truly unprecedented and on a vast scale. Yet, resettling affected people remained a low priority in development planning. Initially, anthropologists who could contribute to resettlement effort were not involved in any such activity; their participation in government development programmes remained confined mostly to planning and implementing tribal welfare schemes. Anthropologists felt left out at their role reduced to that of *mere observers* of development. They gave expression to this frustration in the form of their analytical studies critical of the unfolding disastrous events.

Around 1970s, things took a turn for the better for India's social scientists when finally they got an opportunity to do resettlement as *active participants*, a significant change from being *mere observers* for so long. In India, the research findings by its own anthropologists also slowly brought about a change in the perception prevailing about the relevance of anthropological knowledge to development and resettlement, though this change was at a pace too slow to make any immediate difference to the situation. But the trigger that made the real quick difference was the Bank policy on resettlement, first issued in 1980, and the follow-up work undertaken to help turn the overall policy into operational procedures, skills, and practices. This created a huge demand for anthropologists who could help reduce the damage stemming from the problem of resettling displaced people.

The capacity required to couple field research with policy development and operational support to programs was scarce, and had to be built up almost from scratch. While NGO advocacy and demands for accountability continue to press for better standards and more careful consideration of the human costs of displacement, India's social scientists also worked closely with their counterparts in the Bank to build capacities and skills. While there is still a long way to go, this partnership succeeded in strengthening the required planning and management skills in resettlement and other social policies and projects in India, which has helped mitigate the worst effects of displacement and offered displaced communities a better chance at recovering their livelihoods and future prospects.

References

Agnihotri, A. (2016). Building Dams, ignoring consequences: The Lower Suktel Irrigation Project in Orissa. In H. M. Mathur (Ed.), *Assessing the social impact of development projects: Experience in India and other Asian countries* (pp. 75–86). Cham: Springer.

Aloysius, F. P. (Ed.). (1990). *Workshop on rehabilitation of persons displaced by development projects*. Bangalore: Institute for social and economic change.

Appa, G., & Patel, G. (Eds.) (1996). Unrecognized, unnecessary and unjust displacement: Case studies from Gujarat, India. In C. McDowell (Ed.), *Understanding impoverishment: The consequences of development-induced displacement* (pp. 139–150). Oxford: Beghahan Books.

Baviskar, A. (1996). *In the belly of the river: Tribal conflicts over development in the Narmada Valley*. New Delhi: Oxford University Press.

Behura, N. K., & Nayak, P. K. (1993). Involuntary resettlement and the changing frontiers of kinship: A study of resettlement in Orissa. In M. M. Cernea & S. E. Guggenheim (Eds.), 1993 Francesco, Oxford (pp. 283–306).

Bharali, G. (2015). The application of IRR model in involuntary resettlement research in India. *Paper presented at the SFFA 2015 annual meeting held in Pittsburgh PA*.

Cernea, M., & Mathur, H. M. (Eds.). (2008). *Can compensation prevent impoverishment? Reforming resettlement through investments and benefit-sharing*. New Delhi: Oxford University Press.

Cernea, Michael M 1993 "Anthropological and Sociological Research on Policy Development on Population Resettlement" in Michael M Cernea, and Scott E Guggenheim (Eds) 1993 Anthropological Approaches to Resettlement: Policy, Practice, and Theory Boulder, CO: Westview Press (pp 13–38)

Dhagamwar, V., De, S., & Verma, N. (2000). *Industrial development and displacement*. New Delhi: Sage.

Dreze, J., Smson, M., & Singh, S. (Eds.) (1997). *The dam and the nation: Displacement and resettlement in the Narmads Valley* New Delhi: Oxford University Press.

Fernandes, W. (2000). From marginalization to sharing project benefits. In: M. M. Cernea & C. McDowell (Eds.), *Risks and reconstruction: Experiences of resettlers and refugees* (pp. 205–226). Washington, DC: World Bank.

GOI. (2013). *The Right to Fair Compensation and Transparency in land Acquisition, Rehabilitation and Resettlement Act 2013*. New Delhi: Department of Land Resources, Ministry of Rural Development, Government of India.

Guha, A. (2011). *Special economic zones, land acquisition and civil society in West Bengal*. In H. M. Mathur (Ed.), *Resettling displaced people in India: Policy and practice in India*. New Delhi: Routledge (London and New York).

Hakim, R. (2000). The creation of community: Well-being without wealth in an Urban Greek locality. In M. M. Cernea & C. McDowell (Eds.), *Risks and reconstruction: Experiences of resettlers and refugees* (pp. 229–252). Washington, DC: World Bank.

Jain, S., & Bala, M. (2006). *The Economics and politics of resettlement in India*. New Delhi: Dorling Kindersley (India) Pvt Ltd., (Licensees of Pearson Education in South Asia).

Kabra, A. (2018). Dilemmas of conservation displacement from protected areas. In Cernea, M. Michael, & J. K. Maldonado (Eds.), *Challenging the prevailing paradigm of displacement and resettlement: Risks, impoverishment, legacies, solutions*. London and NewYork.

Karve, I. (1969). *A survey of the people displaced by Koyna Dam*. Poona: Deccan College.

Khagaram, S. (2004). *Dams and development: Transnational struggles for water and power*. New York: Cornell University Press.

Mahapatra, L. K. (2000). Testing the risks and reconstruction model on India's resettlement experiences. In M. Cernea (Ed.), *The economics of involuntary resettlement* (pp. 189–230). World Bank.

Majumdar, D. N. (1960). *Social contours of an industrial city: Social survey of Kanpur 1954-56*. New York: Asia.

Mathur, H. M. (1976). Anthropology, government, and development planning in India. In: D. Pitt (Ed.), *Development from below: Anthropologists and development situations* (pp. 125–138). The Hague: Mouton.
Mathur, H. M. (1977). *Managing projects that involve resettlement. Case studies from Rajasthan, India*. Washington DC: World Bank: EDI.
Mathur, H. M. (1985). Anthropology in government of India's development programmes. *Development Anthropology Network (Bulletin of the Institute for Development Anthropology, New York)*, 3(1), 10–13.
Mathur, H. M. (1994). *Resettling development-displacement populations: Issues and approaches. The resettlement of project-affected people; proceedings of a training seminar*. Jaipur, The HCM Rajasthan state institute of public administration.
Mathur, Hari Mohan 1995 The Resettlement of Project-Affected People: Proceedings of a Training Seminar Jaipur: The HCM State Institute of Public Administration, Jaipur
Mathur, Hari Mohan 1997 Managing Projects that Involve Resettlement: Case Studies from Rajasthan, India Washington DC:The World Bank/EDI
Mathur, H. M. (1998). The impoverishment risk model and its use as a planning tool. In H. M. Mathur & D. Marsden (Eds.), *Development projects and impoverishment risks: resettling project-affected people in India*. New Delhi: Oxford University Press.
Mathur, H. M. (2006). *Managing resettlement in India: Approaches, issues, experiences*. New Delhi: Oxford University Press.
Mathur, H. M. (Ed.). (2008). *India social development 2008: Development and displacement*. New Delhi: Oxford University Press.
Mathur, H. M. (2013). *Displacement and resettlement in India: The human cost of development*. London: Routledge.
Mathur, H. M. (Ed.). (2016). *Assessing the social impact of development projects: Experience in India and other Asian countries*. Cham: Springer.
Mathur, H. M., & Cernea, M. M. (Eds.). (1994). *Development, displacement and resettlement: Focus on Asian experiences*. New Delhi: Vikas Publishing House.
Mathur, H. M., & Cernea, M. M. (Eds.). (1995). *Development, displacement and resettlement: Focus on Asian experiences*. New Delhi: Vikas Publishing House.
Mathur, H. M., & Marsden, D. (Eds.). (1998). *Development projects and impoverishment risks: Resettling project-affected people in India*. New Delhi: Oxford University.
Mehta, Lyla (Ed) 2000 Displaced by Development: Confronting Marginalisation and Gender Justice New Delhi: SAGE Publications India Pvt Ltd
Modi, R. (2009). Resettlement and rehabilitation in urban centres. *Economic & Political Weekly, 44*(6), 20–22.
Morse, B., Berger, T., & Brody, H. (1992). *Sardar Sarovar: The report of the independent review*. Ottawa: Resources Futures International.
Nayak, R. (2000) Risks associated the landlessness: An exploration toward socially friendly displacement and resettlement. In M. M. Cernea & C. McDowell (Eds.), *Risks and reconstruction: Experiences of resettlers and refugees* (pp. 79–107). Washington, DC: The World Bank.
Padel, Felix and Samarendra Das 2010 Out of this Earth: East India Adivasis and the Aluminium Cartel New Delhi: Orient Blackswan
Paranjpye, V. (1990). *High dams on the Narmada: A holistic analysis of the river valley projects*. New Delhi: Indian National Trust for Arts and Cultural Heritage.
Parasuraman, S. (2000). *The dilemmas of development: Displacement in India*. Delhi: St. Martin Press.
Roy Burman, B. K. (1961). *Social processes in the industrialization of Rourkela*. New Delhi: Census of India.
Singh, S. (2016). *Turning policy into law: A new initiative on social impact assessment in India*. New York, London: Springer Cham, Heidelberg, Dordrecht.
Singh, S., & Banerji, P. (Eds.). (2002). *Large dams in India: Environmental, social and economic impacts*. New Delhi: Indian Institute of Public Administration.

Thangaraj, S. (1996). Impoverishment risks: A methodological tool for participatory resettlement planning. In C. McDowell (Ed.), *Understanding impoverishment* (pp. 201–252). Oxford: Berghahn Books.

Thukral, E. G. (Ed.). (1992). *Big dams, displaced people: Rivers of sorrow rivers of change*. New Delhi: Sage.

World Bank. (1980). Social issues associated with involuntary resettlement in bank-financed projects, OMS *2.33*. Washington, DC: World Bank.

Hari Mohan Mathur is Distinguished Professor, Council for Social Development, New Delhi. Earlier, as a member of the Indian Administrative Service (IAS), he has held senior positions in the Government of India, New Delhi, as well as in the State of Rajasthan, including as Chief Secretary in the State of Rajasthan. He has also been Vice-Chancellor of the University of Rajasthan; he has also been staff member and consultant on Development Management and Involuntary Resettlement issues to UN and international organizations: UNDP, UNDTCD, UNESCAP, UNESCO, FAO, World Bank, and ADB. He has served as Development Administration Specialist at the UN Asian and Pacific Development Centre, in Kuala Lumpur, Malaysia, and was United Nations Adviser to the Government of Uganda in Kampala. Professor Mathur has published in international scholarly journals, and authored or edited several books on anthropology, development and resettlement, which include *Anthropology in the Development Process* (edited with C. Haimendorf, NY: Humanities Press, Inc 1978; *Administering Development in the Third World* (Sage 1986), *Improving Agricultural Administration: Elements of an FAO Training Plan* (Oxford & IBH.1989), *Sociocultural Impact of Human Resources Development* (New York: United Nations/Bangkok: UNESCAP (UNESCAP/UNDP Publication No ST/ESCAP/1169,1992), *Managing Projects that Involve Resettlement: Case Studies from Rajasthan* (Washington DC: World Bank 1997), *Development Projects and Impoverishment Risks; Resettling Displaced People in India* 1998 Edited with David Marsden (Oxford UP), *India Social Development Report 2008: Development and Displacement* (New Delhi: OUP, 2008); *Can Compensation Prevent Impoverishment? Improving Resettlement through Investments and Benefit Sharing* (co-edited with Michael M Cernea, Oxford UP, 2008), *Displacement and Resettlement in India: The Human Cost of Development* (Routledge UK: London 2013), *Assessing the Social Impact of Development Projects: Experience in India and other Asian countries* (Springer 2016), and *Development Anthropology: Putting Culture First* (Lexington Books 2019).

Open Access This chapter is licensed under the terms of the Creative Commons Attribution 4.0 International License (http://creativecommons.org/licenses/by/4.0/), which permits use, sharing, adaptation, distribution and reproduction in any medium or format, as long as you give appropriate credit to the original author(s) and the source, provide a link to the Creative Commons license and indicate if changes were made.

The images or other third party material in this chapter are included in the chapter's Creative Commons license, unless indicated otherwise in a credit line to the material. If material is not included in the chapter's Creative Commons license and your intended use is not permitted by statutory regulation or exceeds the permitted use, you will need to obtain permission directly from the copyright holder.

Social Assessment and Resettlement Policies and Practice in China: Contributions by Michael M Cernea to Development in China

Guoqing Shi, Fangmei Yu, and Chaogang Wang

We are very pleased to contribute to this volume to express our appreciation for the collaboration with the community of social scientists, sociologists and anthropologists, working at the World Bank. Chinese social scientists joined forces with them on essential activities: development projects, research programs, academic conferences, training courses, and joint books. One of us, Guoqing Shi, has participated in the international symposium in Bieberstein, Germany, where this volume has originated.

We begin this paper with some historical information on our first contacts with the World Bank's social specialists. They started to work in China in 1986 to assist us in preparing World Bank-financed development projects for our country. Since then our interactions have expanded to address some of the most complex development issues. We will focus in this article on our collaboration in two such major development domains: (a) population resettlement and how to prevent the impoverishment of displaced populations—a big concern that in China emerged only in mid 1980s; and (b) the promotion of social research in support of development through the introduction of pre-project "social impact assessments," a demand that emerged in China from the State Commission for Planning in the early 1990s.

G. Shi
NRCR, Hohai University, Nanjing, Jiangsu, China

F. Yu
Gulou District, Nanjing City, Jiangsu Province, China

C. Wang (✉)
The World Bank, Gaithersburg, MD, USA
e-mail: Cwang3@worldbank.org

Infrastructure Construction and Population Displacement

Over the last 40 years, China has achieved a rapid rate of economic development by building up a modern infrastructure across the country: highways, railways, dams, power plants, airports, pipelines, and large industrial zones, as well as new urban infrastructure (housing, schools, universities, hospitals, hotels, markets, malls). This widespread development has also involved a vast amount of population displacement and resettlement. However, in the first three decades after independence, between 1949 and 1980, the state's approach to displacement and resettlement gave one-sided priority to technical infrastructure, without concern for the adverse impacts on the livelihoods of the people displaced (see Chen 2018).

These were openly recognized after the end of the 'Cultural Revolution' in 1980. New social policies were adopted to deal with the adverse impacts of rapid infrastructure construction. An important factor in this process was – also in 1980 – the decision of the PRC Government to join the World Bank. Membership in the Bank opened China's way to learn from the Bank's development policies and experiences (Shi 2010, 2015).

The first projects for which China requested World Bank financing were three hydro-power projects: Shuikou Dam, Ertan Dam, and Yantan Dam. In preparing these projects, the first new idea that China learned from the World Bank was about its historic decision to adopt in 1980 its policy for involuntary resettlement.

For the preparation and appraisal of the first Shuikou Dam Project, the World Bank sent its senior social policy advisor, the sociologist Professor Michael M Cernea, to explain the Bank's involuntary resettlement policy to the high level officials of the Fujian Province, and to officials from Beijing. The appraisal mission brought along the World Bank's two major policy documents on resettlement: the OMS 2.33 (World Bank 1980) and the Operational Policy Note on Resettlement (World Bank 1986). Both policy documents (World Bank 1984, 1986, 1994/1996, 2001) and other important papers (see Cernea 1990, 1991, 1997, 2000, 2004) were translated into Chinese.

During their long meetings over several days discussing the content of the new policy, the Chinese officials concluded that the objectives and requirements of those two policy documents were compatible with China's government, and therefore acceptable for implementation in the Shuikou Dam project. China agreed to develop a Resettlement Action Plan (RAP) to protect the livelihood of the over 80,000 people (both rural and urban) to be displaced and resettled by the Shuikou project. After several days, Michael M Cernea was informed by the Chinese officials that these policy principles would be included also in China's forthcoming new resettlement regulation, which at that time was under preparation in Beijing.

The implementation and outcomes of the resettlement component in the Shuikou Dam became indeed "the best practice" at that time for both the World Bank and China. After the Bank's approval of the Shuikou investment, Cernea continued for several years to observe and study the Shuikou experiment through supervision missions. He and the government derived information and lessons for applying the same Shuikou approach to other resettlement processes in the Ertan and Yantan project resettlements. For the Ertan Dam project, the Bank recommended that China invite a well known Norwegian scholar anthropologist, Frederick Barth, who accepted to lead a monitoring and advisory international panel that was of great help. (Barth 2003).

Overall, the resettlement processes at all these three projects marked big improvements compared to the resettlement processes carried out in tens of Chinese project dams completed before 1986. China's government's appreciation for the Bank's policy and staff expertise was also reflected in its request to the World Bank to appoint a panel of five senior staff members to advise the managers of China's Three Gorges Project in the final stage of Three Gorges resettlement planning, as well as to assist China in guiding the resettlement work of the Canada-Yangtze Joint Project (CYJP). Michael M Cernea was the resettlement expert in the Bank-China panel. During the following 4 years he made several field visits in the TGP resettlement areas and participated in the periodic meetings between China and Canada for the conduct of the CYJP project.

The work of the World Bank's resettlement specialists in China in the following years expanded., with other World Bank staff such as David Butcher, Dan Gibson, William Partridge, Scott Guggenheim, Maritta Koch-Weser, Maria Clara Mejia, Gorden Appleby, Richard Manning and many others becoming part of a growing community that could exchange ideas and experience. Our bilateral cooperation also expanded due to the employment by the World Bank of Chinese resettlement specialists like Chaohua Zhang, Youlan Zou, Chaogang Wang, Guoqing Shi, Shaojun Chen, Wenxue Yu, Songlin Yao, Zhefu Liu, Zongcheng Lin, Youxuan Zhu, Heping Gong, Ajiang Chen, Wenlong Zhu and others, either as World Bank staff members in Washington and Beijing, or as external consultants. They worked together both in China on large scale projects such as the Xiaolangdi Hydropower Project (with 200,000 people to be relocated, and the Wanjiazhai project, among others) or as consultants employed on Bank supported projects in other developing countries in Asia and Africa. This cooperation has been highly beneficial in achieving transmission of international experiences as well as leading to more substantive convergence between operational policies.

Research Based Knowledge and Resettlement Science: The Creation and Role of NRCR

Displacement and resettlement can never be conducted as standard copy-cat programs. Their inherent complexity and diversity is, in each case, amplified by differences in geographic and demographic contexts. This is why carrying out *both* basic and operational sociological and economic research is indispensable for satisfactory resettlement performance. In China, this truth is not disputed. Academic institutions in China consider the build-up of resettlement research, knowledge, and literature as the emergence of a distinct science sub-discipline: "*Resettlement Science*" (Shi 1995, 1999, 2009). A new masters and Ph.D program in Resettlement in

1988 was created in Hohai University and approved by the Academic Degrees Committee of the State Council in 2004.

Beginning in the early 1990s, China has increased its financing for multiplying institutional structures for research and training for resettlement. The first major step was the creation in 1992 of China's *National Research Center on Resettlement* (NRCR) at Hohai University, in Nanjing, which was entrusted with major tasks at both the national and the international scale. NRCR is directed from its creation by one of the authors of this paper, Professor Guoqing Shi. A number of trained groups for research and planning resettlement were established also within the administrative structure of each of China's Provinces. More recently, a new academic Center for Reservoir Resettlement Research, headed by Professor Yuefang Duan, was created at Three Gorges University, in Yichang.

Besides its basic and operational research responsibilities to develop new knowledge for operational work and for supporting new policy developments, NRCR is also tasked to deliver teaching and training to help create professionally formed specialists in this domain, prepared for working as state officials for jobs related to resettlement or as managers of project resettlement components. NRCR offers a BA program of majoring in resettlement knowledge. It also offers university-based *graduate academic training* in resettlement science and management, both at the MA and PhD levels. Both an English-language international MA and Ph.D. program in Resettlement Science and Management, and Resettlement Sociology as a sub-program of Sociology attracted dozens of students from Asia, Africa and America to Hohai University since 2013. NRCR faculty and graduate students are participating in development projects in China itself, and also in World Bank and ADB projects with resettlement components in other countries. Thousands of international and domestic students from different universities and institutes have read Michael M Cernea's articles and books and taken them as the degree thesis's references.

NRCR also conducts a broad publishing program of Chinese and international books on resettlement to disseminate knowledge on resettlement and on other development topics to specialists and to the public at large. For instance, during 1995–1998, NRCR and Hohai University Press took the initiative to translate and publish two books of theoretical, methodological, and policy studies on resettlement authored by Michael M Cernea; both books were edited by NRCR's Director (see Shi 1996, 1998). These books are regularly used for training by NRCR and in the provinces of PRC. NRCR is also regularly organizing and hosting international and national conferences on Resettlement with Development; e.g., a major International Conference on Resettlement and Social Development was hosted by NRCR and Hohai University in Nanjing, both in May 2002 and in August-September 2019.

The emerging resettlement science (Shi 2009) is now informing China's policies and laws, and it has influenced Chinese society, decision makers, planners, managers, practitioners, and academics. The most significant event is that China's Academy of Sciences (CAS) submitted in 2012 to the State Council of China a major report, titled: '*Report with Recommendation on Strengthening Research in the Disciplines Relevant to the Social Engineering of Resettlement*'. China's Academy is emphasizing that the expanding research and the knowledge accumulation on resettlement is evolving into a scientific discipline known as "resettlement science" that requires also a social engineering methodology for being applied in practice. As a consequence, in March 2016 "Resettlement Engineering for Water Conservancy" was introduced as one of 16 distinct disciplines that compose the Water Science and Water Engineering Group of Disciplines, accredited officially by the China's National Council of Sciences and by China's Academy of Sciences.

Based on national academic exchange demand, a new resettlement sociology committee under the Chinese Sociology Association was proposed by Professor Guoqing Shi of NRCR and established in 2008. It is only the second committee approved after 20 years since the Reservoir Resettlement Committee of Chinese Hydropower Engineering Association was founded in 1988.

The Goal of China's Current Resettlement Policy: Legislating the Resettlement with Development Paradigm

Deriving important legal and economic lessons from research on its own experiences since 1986, China made a continuous series of improvements in its legislation for resettlement. Beginning in 1985, the government decided to initiate a large-scale action for "resolving the remaining legacy from reservoir-caused resettlement" to be financed from a supplementary "special fund" of 240 mil. yuan annually (Duan 2018). This was a shift from the impoverishing practices during the PRC's first 30 years to a nationwide policy characterized in 2006 by China's State Council as the *resettlement with development strategy* paradigm (State Council of China 2006). Thereafter, China advanced the process of defining and implementing the new resettlement paradigm, which over time became more protective and development-oriented than the World Bank's OP/BP 4.12 policy in terms of normative protections and economic enhancements provided to involuntary resettlers.

It is important to explain the philosophy that prompted China's leadership to arrive at the *Resettlement with Development* resettlement paradigm. The central objective *of all of China's legislation* (not only of that about resettlement) is to provide development benefits equitably to the entire nation. However, the complexity of producing development involves also difficult processes, such as displacement of people, which in itself carries severe impoverishment risks, long-term losses and social upheavals, as described in the "Impoverishment Risks and Reconstruction Model" (IRR) formulated by Michael M Cernea.

Chinese researchers have adopted and used widely the IRR model and identified the presence of these risks in many projects. But if such risks and upheavals are so frequent in many displacement that are inevitable, why not use such displacements deliberately as an opportunity to plan the relocation not simply a geographic move, but also a social and economic reconstruction and step up? This paradigm is asking China's resettlement planners, practitioners, and managers to regard the need to displace people as an *opportunity* to create conditions for the overall advancement of the uprooted population as well, because lifting people from poverty is the ultimate goal of the country's policies and laws. Certainly, this requires investing more financing. But such investments are worth making precisely at this critical disruption moment because they reduce social discontent, alleviates temporary distress, and accelerates the planned development to which those people are fully entitled, and which they expect. This way, in essence the *Resettlement with Development* strategy rebalances the pains and gains of development between those who benefit and those who are suffering significant losses from displacement, enabling the latter to also benefit.

The core strategy change embedded in the new *Resettlement with Development* paradigm is to give considerably more attention to the economics, financing, cultural potentials and the logistics of resettlement planning. This requires improved preparation, and involves carrying out, well in advance of resettlement, detailed planning and design for everything needed in terms of community facilities, services, employment opportunities, and family houses at the relocation sites. But what is most important is that sufficient financing must be allotted for investing both *in reconstruction and* in *post-relocation development of resettlers*. This orientation places the foremost emphasis on preventing impoverishment by reconstructing a sound productive economic basis for resettlement.

China's determined shift towards resettlement with development has brought with it innovative solutions to the problem of managing large scale resettlement in line with the government's policy prescriptions. For instance, the **twin** Xiaolangdi projects (advocated inside the Bank by its own social specialists) that were implemented in 1994–2004, consisted of a *distinct project* for constructing the dam itself, plus a *parallel yet distinct project focused only on the relocation and resettlement* of nearly 200,000 people. The two projects were legally cross-correlated but each had a distinct management team that focused entirely on each-one's project, but cross-coordinated the timelines of the twin projects.

These two twinned projects were a major success of China and the World Bank. Both had immense budgets, US$3.5 billion and US$1 billion, respectively. And for China, this was not an isolated case. Cernea's approach to risk analysis is now widely accepted and used by Chinese scholars, resettlement researchers, and practitioners. For example, another very large scale resettlement in the Shiman highway project in Hubei succeeded in alleviating the pre-existing poverty and reducing the risks of creating new impoverishment; also, Liu and Bennett 2008; World Bank 2010). In the second phase of the Danjiangkou Dam Heightening Project, which displaced 345,000 people, most displaced households got the subsidies for new house construction and new, modern community facilities. Within the project's resettlement policy, each displaced person got the construction cost for 24 m^2 as a minimum payment.

Nonetheless, implementing each project consistently with the *Resettlement with Development* paradigm is not always an easy process. The above descriptions reflect the essential content of this paradigm, but creativity in its implementation is a constant requirement and challenge. Departures from this paradigm and transgressions of norms certainly also occur in various forms and degrees. Chinese and international scholars who research these projects often signal failures, not only successes.

China's *Resettlement with Development* model still has broad scope for improvement and being perfected, particularly outside the water sector. Implementation of the Resettlement with Development model is also encountering difficulties and distortions in the practices of some provinces, and various populations of displaced people often still face hardships. As some international experts have written, improvements on a larger scale are needed to broaden participation and response feedback mechanisms; to develop culturally adjusted practices for resettling ethnic minority communities; to conduct intense monitoring and evaluations; to establish reliable mechanisms for grievances; and to improve accountability (McDonald-Wilmsen 2009; McDonald-Wilmsen et al. 2011).

The experiences derived from development induced displacement and resettlement practice and the IRR model developed by Dr. Michael M Cernea were widely applied to other types displacement and migration practices such as climate migration, post-earthquake reconstruction and rehabilitation, ecological migration, environmental protection migration, conservation migration, poverty alleviation migration, preventing disaster migration etc. Since 2005, quite a lot of studies were conducted and have been published both in Chinese and English (Shi and Chen 2001; Yu 2002, 2018; Tang and Shi 2002; Shi 2011, 2015; Hu and Shi 2017; Xu and Shi 2017).

Development Impact Assessment Policy and Practice: The Evolution of Social Assessments in China[1]

China has increasingly relied during the last two decades on the useful tools of *Social Impact Assessment (SIA)* which under China's improved legislation must be carried out now for every Chinese development project.

The development of social assessment in China and its achievements are the result of the combined efforts of the Chinese government, international organizations like the World Bank, UK ODA and the Asian Development Bank, Chinese and international experts and scholars. It is a particular honor to be able to use our contribution to this volume in honor of Dr. Michael M Cernea to acknowledge his longstanding commitment to the development of social assessment in China and the

---

[1]This section summarizes the more detailed paper presented by Prof. Guoqing Shi at the Bieberstein Symposium and then also in Nanjing at the NRCR conference of March 2016 (see: Proceedings, Hohai Univ. Nanjing-Jiangsu , PRC, pp. 35–47).

role that he has played in helping Chinese social scientists develop policies, standards, guidelines, skills, and operational experience.

As a specialized subject, the methodology of project social impact assessment was introduced and practiced first in western developed countries.[2] Popularized widely after WW II, project assessments produced very useful results.[3] Initially focused mainly on environment and technical variables, over time the pre-project assessments were usefully broadened to include also social impacts the overall project assessment framework and have been adapted to serve various types of project proposals and the trends in different countries and to the needs of various development agencies. As a result, there is no uniform definition for social assessment. For example, in the USA it is called "Social Impact Assessment" (SIA). In the United Kingdom it is called "Social Analysis." In international development, the World Bank was the first to institutionalize the use of "sociological analysis" in the preparation and the appraisal of its Projects, introducing it in 1984 as a mandatory operational policy (World Bank OMS 2.20) and employing the concepts or "social analysis" since 1984 (Cernea 2015). In 1995, the World Bank introduced also the equivalent concept of "Social Assessment" (see chapter "The Direct and Major Operational Relevance of Social Assessments" by Jonathan Brown, this volume). All these terms refer roughly to the same methodological approach, though there are some slight differences in emphasis between them.

In China, social assessment became a comprehensive framework that fits comfortably with all of these definitions. While the contents for specific projects differ due to each project's different objectives, users, and socio-economic environments, the main purpose, methods and tools of social assessment tend to be similar for all projects. Chinese social assessments for development projects cover a set of key topics, which were mainly contributed and proposed by Professor Guoqing Shi, as follows:

- Social Impact Analysis (SIA)
- Stakeholder Analysis
- Social Risk analysis
- Social Adaptation and Acceptance Analysis; and
- Social Sustainability Analysis

By carrying out the above sets of analyses, social assessments in China cover the full project cycle. They include not just an upfront "assessment", but also the preparation of a social management plan with measures and options for reducing the main social risks and adverse impacts.

The introduction and uses of social assessment in China reflect the broader changes in our country's development strategy and how the national policy makers and planners began to attach importance to issues of social development; meeting the

---

[2]Wang Yaoqi (2001). Assessment of Investment Projects. Beijing: China Financial Press.

[3]Henk Becher (1997). Social Impact Assessments: method and experiences in Europe, North America and the developing world. London: UCL Press: 24–26.

people's basic needs were put forward as the main objective of development. Social assessment of investment projects came into use in China, and over time social assessments have become an integral part of the evaluation system of project management. While offering further an overview on how the new social assessment methods were taken up by China's officials and researchers, this paper will also discuss the contributions of the international community, and, in particular, Dr. Michael M Cernea's deep and longstanding engagement with China's development community for helping Chinese authorities and practitioners draw on global lessons as they developed their own vision and skills.

Compared to developed countries, China's interest in social assessment in China started relatively slow and late, since this became possible only after the abnormal years of the "cultural revolution". Even social research on investment projects in China began only in the mid-to-late 1980s, and developed only in the early 1990s. However, once launched, social researchers were able to conduct their work with high-level support.

The first major institutions that promoted the early research on projects' social assessment based on their own perceived needs were the *Institute of Investment of the State Development Planning Commission* and the *Institute of Standards and Norms of the Ministry of Construction*. Their work was strongly supported throughout by the very powerful State Commission for Development Planning. The initial results of this research were published as *"Theory and Methods for Social Assessment of investment Projects"* in August 1993. This inspiring book was the first monograph on Social Assessment published in Mainland China. It played an important role in spreading the idea, and in making known, the methods of SA.

The next key step in 1991 Sino-British inter-governmental cooperation project, supported also by the World Bank, was the first international technical assistance explicitly intended to build Chinese capacity for the assessment of investment projects. Two subtopics of this project were related to social assessment, namely: *Social Analysis on Investment* Projects and *Social Policy*. Their findings were published as the report on *"Guidelines on Social Assessment for Investment Projects"* in June 1997. It became one of the most influential monographs on social assessment for investment projects in China.

An important part of this China-UK cooperation project were the academic exchanges. During 1993 and 1994, China sent two delegations to the UK; the first consisted of five social researchers who conducted research on social assessment under the instruction of Prof. Alan Rew at Swansea University; the second group consisted of 20 high ranking officials from different line ministries who participated in 1994 in the UK in an Advanced Workshop on Social Assessment of Investment Projects. Further, in July 1995, the Government of China and the British Overseas Development Agency held in Beijing an "International Workshop on Social Assessment of investment Projects" to which China invited also the World Bank which delegated Dr. Michael M Cernea; from the UK, the participants were Elizabeth Croll, Peter Oakley, and Alan Rew.

This was the first time that an international workshop about SA was held in mainland China. Dr. Cernea introduced the second edition of his influential book

"*Putting People First: Sociological Variables of Development Projects*". Learning about this book, China's *Research Institute of Standards and Norms of the Construction Ministry* decided to translate and publish *Putting People First* into Chinese, in order to make it available broadly in China to development practitioners and researchers. The main part of the translation work was carried out by Dr. Chaogang Wang, one of the co-authors of this present paper.

All these developments marked the start of China's adoption and work on social assessment for investment projects. The books mentioned above were published in the form of academic works, which is to say, without the endorsement of any related government departments. Therefore, the social assessment methodologies of SA described in the books merely represented the views of the books' editors. However, despite the lack of formal endorsement, they were readily available for researchers, consultants and decision-makers. The books mentioned above have been the most influential monographs on SA for investment projects in China.

The fundamental principle of putting people first in development projects has been accepted at the senior-most level of the Chinese Government. In his speech at the Central Party School on June 25, 2007, China's President Hu Jintao stated that the core of the scientific development perspective consists of *"Putting People First"*.

Other government departments have in varying degree also done work on social assessment. The Planning Department of the Ministry of Water Resources and the Chinese Association of Water Resource Economics have jointly set up an expert group which has conducted systematic research on the theory and methodology of SA for water conservancy projects since 1990. In 1999, it published the first sectoral guidelines on SA for construction projects in China that are designed for a particular industry. Another example of the spread of social assessment is that the Civil Aviation Administration of China (CAAC), in 2000, also formally declared that analysis on regional and social impacts must become an important part of building new airport projects.

In 1999, the Chinese Ministry of Finance requested also the ADB for assistance in building capacity for social assessment to strengthen the planning, monitoring and evaluation of development investments. The focus of this capacity building was on poverty, gender, minority and resettlement risks analyses. It produced a draft Social Assessment Manual presented during a SA Workshop in Beijing in April 2002. The Manual was endorsed by National Development and Reform Commission and published in 2004. In October 2004, the International Workshop in SA on WB and ADB Financed Projects was held in Hohai University.

Since 2002, the Chinese Government has continued to develop its social assessment policy and guidelines and to request regular SAs for large-scale development projects. For example, comprehensive social assessments were conducted for the giant Three Gorges dam project, for the Xiaolangdi project, and for the ongoing South-North Water Diversion project, which currently is the largest water resources project ongoing in China and in the world. Between 2008 and 2010, China's urban sector also adopted detailed social assessment guidelines that integrate social assessment into urban development strategies, as well as making it a management tool throughout each stage of the urban project cycle.

In May 2007, the National Development and Reform Commission (NDRC) issued the *"Necessary Documentation for Project Application Reports"*. It requires that all application reports of development which are to be submitted for approval include Social Assessments. The status of the NDRC meant that social assessment had officially become a necessary part of application proposals for development projects. And the Chinese government's 12th Five-Year Plan for the National Economic and Social Development put forward that Social Risk Assessments would be required for all policies and key projects.

We have already signaled the significant impact that the Chinese translation of *"Putting People First"* had on the development of Chinese thinking on social impact assessment. As we emphasized in the first part of this paper, Michael's partnership with our research community has had a tangible impact on improving the lives of people displaced by large development projects. But just as important as Michael M Cernea's direct contributions to policy and projects was his role as a teacher and researcher dedicated to building up China's own national capacities. Since 1988, Michael joined an few intensive training workshops or gave guest lectures in China, where his lectures treated subjects such as how to prepare a resettlement plan, how to carry out vulnerability assessments, and what methods of monitoring would allow program managers to adjust plans to changing realities. These lectures were heard by a large number of Chinese officials, social researchers, practitioners, and students.

Of great significance for the increase of the Chinese leadership's requirement for using risk analysis in each pre-project social assessments was the 2012 decision of China's State Council to add to existing legislation on Social Impact Assessment a new mandatory pre-project analysis for investments in infrastructure: the analysis of political risks, specifically of *"risks to social stability"*, to be done as *a condition for approving any infrastructure project.* China's leadership has been aware and strongly concerned about the risks of social unrest, This expanded the conventional use in China of SIAs, to the pre-project identification of potential political risks, incorporating into project design measures and mitigations for the prevention of risks to social stability. This high level State Council decision confirmed again Michael M Cernea's regular argument about *the centrality* of pre-project risk analysis in every social assessment.

Dr. Michael M Cernea continued to make visits to Hohai University and the National Research Center for Resettlement, and he was appointed as Honorary Professor of Hohai University and international scholar of our Institute for Social Development. He also lectured at Three Gorges University in Yichang, supported its new Reservoir Resettlement Research Center, and was recognized for his scholarly publications and development work by being appointed as Emeritus Professor of TGP University.

For sustainable development and to promote exchange with International Society of Social Impacts Assessment, a new Industry Sociology Committee under the Chinese Sociology Association was established in 2014. The committee covered all academic research on social impacts caused by all types of development and industry. The SA as sub-branch of sociology in MA and Ph.D program was developed in Hohai University since 2005.

Conclusion

The social dimensions of development projects appeared as issues of central concern to China's national planners only after the 'Cultural Revolution', starting from the 1980s. In the ensuing 40 years there have been big, progressive changes in China's legal, planning, and operational approaches to the legislation and practice of population resettlement and social assessment.

China's knowledge and innovation have combined openness to learning from global experience with a practical emphasis on adapting what is appropriate and building up national skills and instruments. With national interest and a program to build China's own knowledge and skills, international cooperation was given the opportunity to have a very constructive function in China.

Dr. Michael M Cernea played a significant role in these developments, by his direct participation along many years in the planning and implementation of some of the China's largest development projects, by his sociological publications that influenced positively China's approaches to resettlement and to social assessments, and by devoting a good part of his work as the World Bank's Senior Adviser on social policies, and by his direct contributions as a scholar and a teacher to large cohorts of Chinese social scientists.

Acknowledgment The draws from the authors' paper at the Bieberstein Symposium, and at the NRCR Conference, March 2016, Nanjing (see Proceedings of NRCR, Hohai University) as well as from papers presented by Guoqing Shi at SfAA annual meetings in Pittsburgh (2015), Vancouver 2016, and at the World Bank, in 2014. Some information in this paper draws from studies by Shaojun Chen (2018), Yuefang Duan (2018), and Guoqing Shi (2018), listed in the references.

The authors also express their grateful thanks to Dr. Scott Guggenheim and Ms. Arielle Klein for their valuable assistance in editing and preparing this paper for publication.

References

Barth, F. (2003). *The preventable calamities of forced resettlement: Reflections on the on the Ertan hydro-electric project in China*. Egypt: Processed Library of Alexandria.

Cernea, M. M. (1990). Poverty risks from population displacement in water resources development. Harvard University-HIID: DDP 355; www.cabdirect.org/cabdirect/abstract/19916712675

Cernea, M. M. (1991). Involuntary resettlement: research, policy, and planning. In M. M. Cernea (Ed.), *Putting people first* (pp. 188–215). New York: Oxford University Press.

Cernea, M. M. (1997). The risks and reconstruction model for resettling displaced populations. *World Development, 25*(10), 1567–1589.

Cernea, M. M. (2000). Risks, safeguards, and reconstruction: a model for population displacement and resettlement. In M. Cernea & C. McDowell (Eds.), *Risks and reconstruction*. Washington, DC: World Bank.

Cernea, M. M. (2004). Impoverishment risks, risk management, and reconstruction: a model of population displacement and resettlement. In *UN symposium on hydropower and sustainable development, Beijing*.

Cernea, M. M. (2016). State legislation facing involuntary resettlement: Comparing the thinking in China and India on development-displacement. In F. Padovani (Ed.), *Development-induced displacement in India and China* (pp. 7–51). Lanham: Lexington Books.

Cernea, M. M., & Maldonado, J. K. (2018). *Challenging the prevailing paradigm of displacement and resettlement: Risks, impoverishment, legacies, solutions* (pp. 45–56). Abington, NY: Routledge.

Chen, S. (2016a). A study of poverty risks based on involuntary resettlement of Chinese village dwellers. In *Proceedings of National Research Center for Resettlement (NRCR). Hohai University, Nanjing*.

Chen, S. (2016b). Discussion of resettlement cost externalization of water resource and hydropower projects. In *Proceedings of NRCR, Hohai-University, Nanjing*.

Chen, S. (2018). *Cost externalization impoverishes resettlers: findings from hydropower projects*.

China Academy of Sciences. (2012). Recommendation on strengthening development-relevant research work on resettlement engineering. Proposal to State Council.

China International Engineering Consulting Company, revised English version edited by Bettina Gransow, & Susanna Price. (2007). *Social assessment manual for investment projects in China-turning risks into opportunities*. China Planning Press

Duan, Y. (2003). *Theoretical and practical study of reservoir resettlement compensation*. Wuhan: Huazhong University of Science and Technology.

Duan, Y. (2018). Investing in resettlement and benefit-sharing in China: new paradigm, approaches, challenges, and prospects. In M. M. Cernea & J. K. Maldonado (Eds.), *Challenging the prevailing paradigm of displacement and resettlement*.

Hu, Z., & Shi, G. (2017). *Risk management on perverting disaster resettlement*. Beijing: Science Press.

McDonald-Wilmsen, B. (2009). Development-induced displacement and resettlement: negotiating fieldwork complexities at the Three Gorges Dam, China. *Asia Pacific Journal of Anthropology, 10*(4), 283–300.

McDonald-Wilmsen, B., Webber, M., & Yuefang, D. (2011). Development for whom? Rural to urban resettlement at Three Gorges Dam, China. *Asian Studies Review, 35*(1), 21–42.

Ministry of Housing Construction. (2011). *The guideline of social assessment for municipal utilities construction projects*. Beijing: China Planning Press.

Ministry of Water Resources of PRC. (2009, July 31). Specification on planning and design of land acquisition and resettlement for construction of water resources and hydropower project. Beijing, China.

National Council of Foundation of Nature Sciences. (2016, March). China Academy of Sciences. *Water conservancy science and engineering*. China Development Strategy. Beijing, China: Science Press.

NRCR. (1994). *Proceedings of the international senior seminar on involuntary resettlement and rehabilitation*. Nanjing: Hohai University Press.

NRCR. (2016, March). *Proceedings of National Research Center for Resettlement (NRCR)*. Hohai University, Nanjing City, Jiangsu Province, PRC.

Padovano, F. (2016). *Development-induced displacement in India and China: A comparative look at the burdens of growth*. Lexington Books.

Shi, G. (1995). *Reservoir resettlement system planning theory and application*. Hohai University Press.

Shi, G. (Ed.) (1996). *Resettlement and Development: World Bank resettlement policies and experiences* (Vol. I). Translated from English by NRCR, Hohai Univ. Press, Nanjing.

Shi, G. (Ed.) (1998). *Resettlement, rehabilitation, development* (Vol. II). Translated from English by NRCR, Hohai UP, Nanjing.

Shi, G. (1999). Discussion on reservoir resettlement science. *Journal of Advanced in Science and Technology in Water Resources, 1*.

Shi, G. (2009). Discussion on resettlement science. In *Advances in water resources and hydraulic engineering: Proceedings of the 16th IAHR-APD congress* (pp. 1456–1462). Berlin: Springer.

Shi, G. (2011). *Resettlement rights and interests protection and government responsibility*. Jilin People Press.

Shi, G. (2015, March 30). Past and future of social safeguards: How did China learn from the World Bank's and international experiences? In *Presentation at SfAA Meetings, Pittsburgh*.

Shi, G. (2018). Comparing China's and the World Bank's resettlement policies over time: the ascent of the 'resettlement with development' paradigm. In M. M. Cernea & J. K. Maldonado (Eds.).

Shi, G., & Chen, S. (2001). *China resettlement policy and practice*. Ningxia People Press.

Shi, G., & Dong, M. (2003). A study on social assessment for investment projects. *Journal of Hohai University (Social Sciences Series), 2003*(2), 49–53.

Shi, G., Yu, F., & Wang, C. (2016). Changes and achievements in policies and practices for resettlement and social assessment in China between 1980s to 2010s: contribution by Dr. Michael M Cernea. *Proceedings of NRCR, Hohai University*, 35–47.

Standard and Norms Institute of Ministry of Housing Construction. (2014). *The social assessment manual for municipal utilities construction projects: cases of social assessment*. Beijing: China Planning Press.

State Council of China. (2006). Regulation for land requisition, compensation and resettlement from large and medium water conservancy and hydropower projects.

State Council of China. (2017). Decision of the State Council to Amend the Regulation on the Land Expropriation Compensation and the Resettlement of Migrants for the Construction of Large- and Medium-Scale Water Conservation and Hydropower Projects.

Tang, C., & Shi, G. (Eds.) (2002). *Resettlement and development, Proceedings of the international symposium on resettlement and social development*. Hohai University Press, Nanjing.

TGP Preliminary design. of Three Gorges Project Vol. IX; Inundation of reservoir and primary plan of relocating peoples' disposition draft.

World Bank. (1980). *Social issues in involuntary resettlement under bank-financed projects. OMS 2.33*. Washington, DC: The World Bank.

World Bank. (1984). *Project appraisal. OMS 2.20*. Washington, DC: World Bank.

World Bank. (1986). Operations issue in the treatment of involuntary resettlement. Operational Policy Note 10.08. Washington, DC.

World Bank. (1994/1996). Cernea, M. M., Guggenheim, S., Aronson, D., and van Wicklin, W. (Task Force) Resettlement and development: the Bank-wide review of projects involving involuntary resettlement 1986-1993. Washington, DC: World Bank.

World Bank. (2001). *Operational Policy/Bank Procedures. 4.12, Involuntary Resettlement*. Washington, DC: World Bank.

World Bank. (2010). China—Hubei Shiman Highway Project: ICR1409.

World Bank. (2017). *Environmental and Social Framework: Setting Environmental and Social Standards for Investment Project Financing*. Washington, DC: World Bank.

Xu, Y., & Shi, G. (2017). *Sustainable livelihoods of losing the sea fisherman*. Science Press.

Yu, W. (2002). Reservoir-induced resettlement and poverty reduction. In C. Tang & G. Shi (Eds.), *Resettlement and development, Proceedings of the international symposium on resettlement and social development*. Nanjing: Hohai University Press.

Yu, W. (2018). *Policy innovation of reservoir resettlement under urban-rural integration* (pp. 678–681). Social Sciences Academic Press (China). Nanjing: Hohai University Press.

Zhou, X., & Feng, X. (2002). Potential risks of poverty of rural resettlers of the Three Gorges. *Statistics and Decision-Making*, (2), 31–32.

Prof. Guoqing Shi, Chinese, in October 1959, Professor, Founding Dean of Public Administration School of Hohai University (2004–2016), Director of Social Development Institute (2002–) and National Research Center for Resettlement (1997–). He received Bachelor's Degree in Water Conservancy and Hydropower in 1982 and Master Degree in Water Resource and Hydrology in 1989, in Hohai University, China. He worked in TU Delft, Netherlands as the resource person and Team Leader in IWRM during 2000 and 2003. Visiting Professor in University of Melbourne in August 2014.

He is one of main creators and member of International Displacement and Resettlement Network (IDRN) in 2000, the Chair of Membership Committee and Member of Boarding Committee (2010–2012) of IWRA. He is member of Sustainable Hydropower Council and Chamber of Emerging and Developing Countries Committee of International Hydropower Association (IHA). He is also International Member of Committee of Expert of Turkey's Ilisu Dam and HEPP Project from 2007 to June 2009, the International Panel Member of Dasu and Tabeila 4th Hydropower Project in Pakistan since 2012. He is an senior adviser of Resettlement Development Bureau of Three Gorges Dam Project Constriction Committee under State Council since 1993, Adviser of World Bank, Asian Development Bank since 1994, Member of IASFM, Founding Chairperson of Resettlement and Migration Committee of Chinese Sociology Association (CSA) and Vice Chairperson of Resettlement Committee of Chinese Hydropower Engineering Association(CHEA) etc.

His Academic fields include Involuntary displacement and resettlement, social and economic assessment, social development, applied sociology, land resources management, demography, management science and engineering, water economics and Integrated Water Resource Management (IWRM) etc.

He has involved the preparation of national and regional resettlement policies and legislation, decision making process in resettlement planning and policy of a number of huge projects such as Three Gorges DHPP project (1.3 millions displaced people) , Xiaolangdi Dam Projects (200,000 PAPs) and Danjiangkou Dam Projects (345,000 PAPs) etc. and more than 50 development projects fund by World Bank and Asian Development Bank. He was engaged in Ilisu Dam in Turkey, Murum DHPP project in Malaysia and Dasu DHPP project in Pakistan as the international resettlement expert. He created the new Major in Resettlement Sciences and Management (Ph. D and Master) in China and is the first Professor in this science research field. He is well known expertise in Development caused Displacement and Resettlement in Asian and in the World.

He has compiled or written 20 books such as China Resettlement Policy and Practice, Theory and Application of Reservoir Resettlement System Planning, Resettlement and Development -Study on World Bank resettlement policies and experiences, etc., and released more than 400 articles. He has achieved 15 Advance Science or Social Science Awards at the level of national or province. He has got following titles successively, Special Award of State Council, Outstanding Teacher of Ministry of Water Resources, Model of Youth Researchers of Jiangsu Province, Outstanding Youth Scientists of Jiangsu Province, Youth Scientist Award of Jiansu Province.

Prof. Shi has supervised more than about 200 Ph.D. and master degree students which include a few international students from USA, Ghana, Lao PDR, Kenya, Nepal, Tanzania, Pakistan, Iran, Cambodia, Viet Nam, Cameron and Bangladesh, etc.

Email: gshi@vip.126.com. gshi@hhu.edu.cn, Mobile :+86 13305183575

Address: NRCR, Hohai University, 8 Focheng Road Road, Nanjing, Jiangsu, 211100, China

Fangmei Yu, Female, born in 1984, Doctor in sociology, Assistant Professor of Nanjing University of Posts and Telecommunications. Her work focused on policy evaluation, social assessment, agricultural development, poverty and social safeguard. She was awarded Bachelor of Management by Hohai University in 2007 and received Ph.D degree in Sociology in 2014. She has done a few research projects on resettlement and social assessment at National Research Center for Resettlement (NRCR), Hohai University, China.

Chaogang Wang worked as Senior Social Development Specialist at World Bank headquarters in Washington DC. He holds a PhD in management and has worked for various government agencies in China before joining the Bank in 2000. Over the last 25 years Wang has worked on various social development issues including involuntary resettlement, social impact assessment and management systems, stakeholder engagement, community participation, cultural heritage, gender equity, and indigenous peoples. He drafted the first Social Assessment Guideline in China applied to large-scale government financed construction projects. He prepared the first Guide for Local Benefit Sharing in hydroelectric projects. He is author or co-author of *Method and Parameters of Economic Evaluation for Construction Projects* (1993, Chinese), *Guideline of Social Assessment for Investment Projects* (1996, Chinese); *Appraisal of Development Projects in China: Theory, Method and Case Studies* (1997, in Chinese), *Economic Evaluation Method of Real Estate Project* (1999, Chinese).

Open Access This chapter is licensed under the terms of the Creative Commons Attribution 4.0 International License (http://creativecommons.org/licenses/by/4.0/), which permits use, sharing, adaptation, distribution and reproduction in any medium or format, as long as you give appropriate credit to the original author(s) and the source, provide a link to the Creative Commons license and indicate if changes were made.

The images or other third party material in this chapter are included in the chapter's Creative Commons license, unless indicated otherwise in a credit line to the material. If material is not included in the chapter's Creative Commons license and your intended use is not permitted by statutory regulation or exceeds the permitted use, you will need to obtain permission directly from the copyright holder.

Part IV
Retrospective and Outlook

A Retrospective: Michael M. Cernea (1934–)

Anthony Bebbington

'Development anthropology is a contact sport,' Michael Cernea likes to tell his students (Cernea and Freidenberg 2007). His career, from junior researcher in the Romanian Academy of Sciences in the early 1960s to joining the World Bank in Washington D.C. in 1974 as its first-ever in house staff sociologist, and then advancing there to the high level position of the World Bank's Senior Advisor for Social Policies and Sociology, is testament to this observation.

Cernea's has been a professional life characterised by constant high-stakes struggles over social development ideas within different bureaucratic and political settings. His has been a career where the thinking through of ideas, and the acting upon them, have been one and the same process. As a thinker in development, Cernea has to be understood as much in terms of his relationships to particular institutions as to development anthropology and sociology. Indeed, many might argue that Michael Cernea's most critical contribution has not been his intellectual work on the use of social science knowledge in crafting new social policies and designing development projects, or on the inherent risks of impoverishment in projects designed to reduce poverty; rather, his most critical and enduring achievements were the embedding of those ideas in World Bank policies and philosophy.

From the early 1970s to the late 1990s, Cernea contributed more than anybody in pushing the 'social envelope' at the Bank. He had the ear of Presidents and Vice-Presidents in the process, and from time to time was unrepentant in giving those ears a good chewing. He has been one of those quintessential reformists (and at times

---

I am very grateful to Michael Cernea for the interviews, materials and time he gave me during the preparation of this entry as well as for our conversations over the years. David Simon also graciously shared insights and information. An earlier version of this essay appears in D. Simon (ed.) *Key Thinkers on Development* (Second Edition, 2019). London: Routledge.

A. Bebbington (✉)
Graduate School of Geography, Clark University, Worcester, MA, USA
e-mail: abebbington@clarku.edu

small 'r' revolutionaries) inside the Bank recognised by outside commentators and analysts as critical to any form of progressive change in the institution (Fox and Brown 1998).

How far personal history determines subsequent careers is always a matter of interpretation but in Michael Cernea's case there are at least apparent continuities. He grew up as part of the Jewish community in Jassy (Iaşi), a Romanian town close to the Russian border. As a child, he watched and experienced the violent unravelling of that community in the face of anti-semitism and fascism (Simon 2019). Along with all other Jewish children in the community, he was expelled from elementary school. Shortly before, his father had lost his job as an engineer for being a Jew. During the pogrom of Jassy in 1941, "one of the worst in Romania's history" (Simon 2019), he witnessed mass killings and his father badly beaten and impaired for life. The experience of persecution and resettlement was visceral—he was forced out of his home twice, first as a result of the pogroms (when the family went into hiding) and then in the face of the advancing German army. The experiences left him politically active and sensitised and after the war he became a member of the Socialist Youth Movement and a young journalist. Though initially a supporter of the Romanian Left's rise to government power in the post-war years, over time he grew more concerned at the directions taken by the regime. His PhD thesis, 'About Dialectics and Contradictions in the Socialist Society' (University of Bucharest, 1962), in which he tried to document factually the persistence of contradictions, conflicts and tensions within Romania's allegedly homogeneous society and structures, reflected these growing concerns. That he chose such a topic also presaged strategies of enquiry later in life at the World Bank—strategies in which he aimed to change an institution by fighting dysfunctionalities and challenging its foundational ideas from within that same institution.

As would later be the case at the Bank, this strategy generated resistance and so—coupled with the effects of anti-Semitism in the Romania of the late 1950s—he had to wait 4 years simply to schedule the defence of his PhD. Still, by the time he made his defence, the effects of the Khruschev thaw had changed the political context in Romania again, and Cernea was finally able to address the topic that really moved him, peasant economic rationality, although not without political fallout. This early work (Cernea 1970, 1971) operated at the boundaries of anthropology, sociology and rural economics, exploring cultural dimensions of productive strategies, and the relationships between peasant rationalities and co-operative agriculture. This concern for the socio-cultural foundations of the economy would reappear later in a different guise in his sustained questioning of what he referred to as the 'economic reductionism' of the World Bank (see Cernea 1994 and below).

As the thaw continued, foreign scholars visited Romania in increasing numbers, a process that ultimately came to define a turning point both in Cernea's career (see his Malinowski Award lecture, Cernea 1996) as well as in the future that the World Bank was yet to have. Cernea was nominated by one of these visitors for a fellowship at the Center for Advanced Studies in the Behavioral Sciences (CASBS) at Stanford, one of the US's most prestigious academic fellowships. The politics behind Cernea being able to assume the fellowship were equally convoluted, but shortly before the meeting of Ceaușescu and Nixon (a meeting triggered by Ceaușescu's resistance to the Russian invasion of Czechoslovakia), Cernea finally received the visa allowing him to travel to California, albeit only in time for the latter part of the fellowship. His time there (1970–1) led to the distillation in English of his ideas on peasant society, but more importantly, to a friendship with US sociologist, Robert Merton, and a growing reputation in the USA.

The links between the year at Stanford, his initial contacts with the World Bank, and his being interviewed for a position in Washington were neither direct nor without major risks, but were very real. Whatever the case, in 1974—following a talk given at Bank headquarters on the role of the family plot in collective farms—he was offered a job. His position was to be the first sociologist to work in McNamara's newly created central Rural Development Division, a division that in many respects occupied the pivotal piloting role in McNamara's rural development-led approach both to poverty reduction (and, if more implicitly, to the taming of rural radicalisation) and to changing the Bank. Cernea took the Bank—much as he did Romania—as simultaneously an institution he worked (and largely lived) in, as an object of analysis, and as something he wanted to change. He believed that such change could come from the injection of sociological knowledge into the very foundations of the institution's way of interpreting and acting on the world.

In time, these convictions led him to study the Bank's project cycle in depth and explore the entry points for sociological knowledge in the processes through which the Bank designed and implemented its operations. As part of this project, he seized on the seminar as an instrument of institutional change and began inviting outside social scientists to speak to the Bank's staff on the different ways in which sociological knowledge and an awareness of the social dimensions of development could be brought into the project cycle. This cycle of seminars culminated in the book *Putting People First* (Cernea 1985), which—notwithstanding its focus on the World Bank—became one of the early foundational texts on participatory rural development. Cernea's introduction to the collection argued that the World Bank was in the business of financially induced development, but that for any such induced change to be successful it was imperative that the Bank understand the social structures that existed in the area of intervention and that could play the roles required of them in this process of induced development: echoes of Robert Merton's influence (Cernea 1985). Social science knowledge—and social scientists—were thus essential for the Bank, he argued (Cernea 1994).

This was a recurrent theme in his work: social science was to be conducted not for its own sake but for development's sake, and one of the key purposes of such social science was to challenge, constantly, the ideas underlying economists' and others' models of development. While the argument would be made intellectually—and Cernea has been a prolific writer—most strategically for him, it had to be made bureaucratically. If social science analyses were to have any teeth in the Bank, he argued that they had to be turned into bureaucratic instruments that made such knowledge a requirement of normal practice in the institution. Thus, another area in which Cernea contributed greatly was in developing and implementing directives and operational policies that required projects to have social appraisals. This contribution, if less visible to outside readers, was critical if any institutional change was to derive from his ideas. The easier part of this process was to generate the ideas and write them; the harder part was to get them through the Bank's approval process and then, once approved, keep them alive in the face of the constant pressure from other parts of the Bank to get rid of them.

The culmination of these arguments was a series of events beginning in late 1995 on the occasion of the Bank's formal recognition of Cernea's 20 years of working for the institution. At one of these events, he caught the new Bank President, James Wolfensohn, and made the case to him that social development had to be central to the poverty orientation that Wolfensohn was promoting. This led to a series of exchanges in which Cernea convinced Wolfensohn to create a social development task force that would report on the state of social development work in the institution. Again, negotiated and contested—'development anthropology is a contact sport'—this was a process that the Development Economics Vice-Presidency was able to contain and to some degree capture. But not entirely, for in 1997, and against the advice of the Bank's Chief Economist, Wolfensohn approved the creation of the Bank's first Social Development Department as part of the Bank's central vice-presidency for Socially and Environmentally Sustainable Development.

Cernea's work has also pushed the World Bank's thinking on the links between culture and development, on cultural patrimony and on the environment, on the concept of social policy and on articulating several Bank social policies. However, of most significance perhaps—both intellectually and also for human welfare—has been his work on involuntary resettlement, risk and vulnerability (Cernea and Guggenheim 1993; Cernea 1997; Cernea and Mathur 2008; Cernea 2018). Cernea joined the Bank during the period in which the large-scale infrastructure projects that would later bring the institution into such criticism, were being hatched. As early as 1978 he began elaborating guidelines for resettlement, which were subsequently issued under Robert McNamara as Bank policy (1980). Not long after came a sharp fight within the Bank over the provisions for resettlement in India's infamous Narmada Dam project. This became the seed for a review of the Bank's overall performance on resettlement during the first 5 years of existence of the new policy (Cernea 1986). A further product of this Bank-wide product was a subsequent paper, which integrated the original 1980 policy with the policy conclusions of the 1986 review, producing a stronger policy paper that further enhanced the initial policy and included operational guidelines, authored also by Cernea in 1988. This larger paper was also the first official Bank publication of its resettlement policy available publicly, and thus gained much more influence than the initial policy, which had been kept internal by the Bank (Cernea 1988, Bank Policy Technical Paper nr 80). This synthesis paper has been translated into many languages in different countries, including Chinese, Spanish, Turkish, Bahasa-Indonesia, Italian, and French and has had over a dozen print runs. If the 1986 review was critical, a later 1993–94 review of the entire Bank portfolio of projects causing displacement over the period 1986–1994 (Cernea et al. 1994) pulled even fewer punches. It systematically drew attention to the failures of the Bank to follow its own policy and highlighted what needed to be improved policy-wise and operationally. It also constituted one of

Cernea's key—empirically sustained—statements on the way in which development inherently brings risk to people at the same time as bringing opportunity.

The resettlement reviews were not anti-development statements, but they did make clear that development processes handled irresponsibly, without adequate social science insight, without adequate consultation and involvement of poor people, are likely to increase vulnerabilities, and very often for the poorest. The intellectual core of this argument was later captured in his 'Impoverishment Risks and Reconstruction Model' (Cernea 1997, 2001, 2002, 2004; Cernea and McDowell 2000) of the eight risks that he came to identify as inherent in the process of displacement: landlessness, joblessness, homelessness, marginalisation, food insecurity, loss of access to common property resources, increased morbidity and community disarticulation (Cernea 1997; also Mahapatra 1999). The model typifies Cernea's intellectual and professional project in that it offers a framework intended not only to help understand risk, but also—through identifying and making explicit such risks—to trigger a response to this risk such that it might be mitigated even before its effects fully manifest themselves. Its purpose is to be analytical, predictive and methodologically useful. It became a leading model used internationally in research and policies about development triggered involuntary resettlement (Koenig 2002).

Cernea's contributions to development are many, reflected in a long list of publications, advisory roles and academic honours. Perhaps the most important among them, however, was to have changed an institution through the sustained and forceful insistence on a few ideas: that social science knowledge is critical to development, that induced development will fail in any meaningful sense if ordinary people are not involved in shaping the forms it takes, and that the cherished disembodied concepts of so much development theory cannot be considered separately from the social structures in which they are embedded. These ideas became embodied in the World Bank in different ways. A strong, mutually supportive, occasionally fractious network of social scientists was recruited to carry this agenda forward in their work in different parts of the institution; many of the ideas promoted by Cernea and these social scientists were built into operational directives and policies, project designs, and in some cases fully fledged loans; and the continued efforts of Cernea and his colleagues helped to elaborate a sort of public sphere within the Bank in which these ideas became common currency such that, even if many task managers, country directors and others found them annoying, they could not easily contest them openly or brazenly.

Thought of slightly more analytically, what Cernea did was to lead the building of the ideational, relational and normative bases for institutional change. What did not change, however, and this obviously exceeded the capacities of any network of social scientists, was the political economy of the World Bank as an institution that is ultimately dependent for its survival on its chief financial contributors (for its concessional lending) and on the approval and repayment of loans. Consequently today, much more so than in 2005 when the first version of this essay was written, the long-term survival of Cernea's and his colleagues' impacts on the Bank is less certain.

The network of social scientists that carried Cernea's early ideas forward has now largely left the institution, and social science at the Bank has once again been rendered less powerful than it was in the 1990s and 2000s. Financially and politically powerful member countries, together with other epistemic communities within the Bank, push for the substantial watering down of the policies and directives that derived from Cernea's and colleagues' work. Cernea himself worries greatly about these reversals and came out publicly with a written criticism of the dilution of the Bank's safeguarding social and environmental policies, in which he argued for new ways of reinforcing them to protect the livelihoods and dignity of vulnerable people (Cernea 2018).

That said, *even if* there is a reversal in the shifts that Cernea helped win, to have changed the institution's practices during the three decades he spent there, means that his ideas, and his work, will have affected literally millions of lives forever.

Acknowledgement This essay was first published in the volume *Fifty Key Thinkers on Development* (Editor, David Simon, 2006), Routledge, Abingdon-Oxon, United Kingdom, and was updated in 2018.

References and Major Works by Michael Cernea

Cernea, M. (1970). *Two villages, social structures and technical progress* (in Romanian, senior author, research co-ordinator), Bucharest: Edit. Politica.
Cernea, M. (1971). *Changing society and family change: The impact of the cooperative farm on the traditional peasant family*. Stanford, CA: Center for Advanced Studies in Behavioral Sciences.
Cernea, M. (Ed.). (1985). *Putting people first: sociological variables in rural development projects*. New York: Oxford University Press.
Cernea, M. (1986). *Involuntary resettlement in bank-assisted projects: A review of the application of bank policies and procedures in FY79-95 projects*. AGR, Operations Policy Staff, World Bank, February.
Cernea, M. (1988). *Involuntary resettlement in development projects: policy guidelines for bank-financed projects*. Washington, DC: World Bank.
Cernea, M. (1994). A sociologist's view on sustainable development. In I. Serageldin & A. Steer (Eds.), *Making development sustainable: From concepts to action* (Environmentally sustainable development occasional paper series No. 2). Washington, DC: World Bank.
Cernea, M. (1996). *Social organization and development anthropology. The 1995 Malinowski Award Lecture* (ESD studies and monographs series, no. 6). Washington, DC: World Bank.
Cernea, M. (1997). The risks and reconstruction model for resettling displaced populations. *World Development, 25*(10), 1569–1588.
Cernea, M. (2001). Eight main risks: preventing impoverishment during population resettlement. In C. de Wet & R. Fox (Eds.), *Transforming settlement in Southern Africa* (pp. 237–252). Edinburgh: Edinburgh University Press for the International African Institute.
Cernea, M. (2002). *Cultural heritage and development: A framework for action in the Middle East and North Africa*. Washington, DC: World Bank.
Cernea, M. (2004, September 22–23). The typology of development-induced displacements: Field of research, concepts, gaps and bridges. *Paper to the US National Academy of Sciences conference on the study of forced migration, Washington, DC*.
Cernea, M. (2018) Challenging the prevailing paradigm of displacement and resettlement. Its evolution and constructive ways for improving it. In M. Cernea & J. Maldonado (Eds.),

Challenging the prevailing paradigm of displacement and resettlement. Risks, impoverishment, legacies and solutions. Abingdon: Routledge.
Cernea, M. M., & Freidenberg, J. (2007). Michael Cernea 'development anthropology is a contact sport' an oral history interview with Michael M. Cernea by Judith Freidenberg. *Human Organization, 66*(4), 339–353.
Cernea, M., & Guggenheim, S. (Eds.). (1993). *Anthropological approaches to resettlement: Policy, practice, and theory.* Boulder, CO: Westview Press.
Cernea, M. M., & Mathur, H. M. (Eds.). (2008). *Can compensation prevent impoverishment?: reforming resettlement through investments and benefit-sharing.* New York: Oxford University Press.
Cernea, M., & McDowell, C. (Eds.). (2000). *Risks and reconstruction: Experiences of resettlers and refugees.* Washington, DC: World Bank.
Cernea, M., Guggenheim, S., Aronson, D., & van Wicklin, W. (1994). *Resettlement and development. The Bankwide review of projects involving involuntary resettlement 1986–1993.* Washington, DC: World Bank.
Fox, J., & Brown, D. (Eds.). (1998). *The struggle for accountability: The World Bank.* Cambridge, MA: MIT Press.
Koenig, D. (2002). *Toward mitigating impoverishment in development-induced displacement and resettlement.* Oxford: Refugees Studies Centre, University of Oxford.
Mahapatra, L. K. (1999). *Resettlement, impoverishment and reconstruction in India.* New Delhi: Vikas.
Simon, D. (2019). *Holocaust escapees and global development: Hidden histories.* London: Zed Books.

Anthony Bebbington is Milton P. and Alice C. Higgins Professor of Environment and Society in the Graduate School of Geography, Clark University, Professorial Research Fellow at the Global Development Institute, University of Manchester, Distinguished Professor at the Facultad Latinoamericana de Ciencias Sociales-Ecuador, and Honorary Professorial Fellow at the University of Melbourne. He is a Director of Oxfam America and has also worked at the World Bank, the Overseas Development Institute and the International Institute for Environment and Development. He is a member of the National Academy of Sciences and the American Academy of Arts and Sciences, and has been a Guggenheim Fellow, a Fellow at CASBS Stanford, a UK Economic and Social Science Research Council Professorial Fellow, an Australian Research Council Laureate Fellow, and has received Distinguished Scholarship honors from the American Association of Geographers. His research, primarily in Latin America, has addressed: extractive industries and socio-environmental conflict; NGOs and rural social movements; poverty and rural livelihoods; agricultural development; and the links between development interventions and political economy. Recent books include: *Governing Extractive Industries: Politics, Histories, Ideas* (Oxford University Press, 2018, with others); *Subterranean Struggles: New Dynamics of Mining, Oil and Gas in Latin America* (eds., University of Texas Press, 2013, with J. Bury); *Social Conflict, Economic Development and Extractive Industries: Evidence from Latin America* (ed., Routledge, 2012); and *Minería, movimientos sociales y respuestas campesinas: una ecología política de transformaciones territoriales* (ed., Instituto de Estudios Peruanos/Centro Peruano de Estudios Sociales, 2011).

Open Access This chapter is licensed under the terms of the Creative Commons Attribution 4.0 International License (http://creativecommons.org/licenses/by/4.0/), which permits use, sharing, adaptation, distribution and reproduction in any medium or format, as long as you give appropriate credit to the original author(s) and the source, provide a link to the Creative Commons license and indicate if changes were made.

The images or other third party material in this chapter are included in the chapter's Creative Commons license, unless indicated otherwise in a credit line to the material. If material is not included in the chapter's Creative Commons license and your intended use is not permitted by statutory regulation or exceeds the permitted use, you will need to obtain permission directly from the copyright holder.

List of Publications

Michael M. Cernea

Books and Monographs, Published in English

2020: *"The Risks and Reconstruction Model for Resettling Displaced Populations"*. (original version in World Development 25 (10) :1569–1588; updated and enlarged version, in the present volume.)

2018: *Challenging the Prevailing Paradigm of Displacement and Resettlement: Risks, Impoverishment, Legacies and Solutions*. Eds. Michael Cernea and Julie K.Maldonado. Abington, NY (334 pp)

1996: *Social Organization and Development Anthropology: Bronislaw Malinowski Lecture*, SFAA-World Bank, Washington DC.

2012/13: *Monitoring of Population Resettlement in Cambodia's Railway Rehabilitation Project*:
Current Status, Strengths, Weaknesses, and Recommendations. Report to the ADB on the Findings of the Independent Field Review, Sept. 12–22, 2012, on Project nr. 37269-013. Manila: Asian Development Bank. Mimeo (unpublished, 54 pages).

(Commissioned by ADB as an independent mid-term expert evaluation; intended, at its start, for publication on the ADB's website, this study was nonetheless withheld from publication because Cambodia's Government threatened the ADB with terminating ADB's financing of this project, should the report be made public. ADB's management, itself critiqued in the study based on documents from the project's supervision files, yielded to this threat, and formally announced that *"The Cernea Report"* will not be released publicly. This decision triggered a broad international outcry, which made the then ADB President to issue a statement partially overruling the non-publication decision; he directed the

M. M. Cernea (✉)
Retired, World Bank, Bethesda, MD, USA

public release of the Report's recommendations, but not of the factual analysis that led to the recommendations.)

2011: *On the Front Line of Climate Change and Displacement: Learning from and with Pacific Island Countries.* Co-authors: Elisabeth Ferris, M. Cernea, and Dan Petz. The Brookings Institution—London School of Economics, Project on Internal Displacement. https://www.brookings.edu/wp-content/uploads/2016/06/09_idp_climate_change.pdf

2008: *Can Compensation Prevent the Impoverishment of the Forcibly Displaced People? Reforming Resettlement through Investments and Benefit Sharing.* eds. M.Cernea and H.M. Mathur. http://jrs.oxfordjournals.org/content/22/1/130.full.pdf+html (448 pages)

Ilisu Hydroelectric Dam Power Plant Project. Report on the First Field Visit of the Committee of Experts – Resettlement. Prepared by M.Cernea, Shi Guoqing, Turan Hazar on behalf of Euler Hermes (Germany), OeKB (Austria) and SERV (Switzerland). http://www.oekb.at/de/osn/DownloadCenter/projekt-und-umweltanalysen/Ilisu/Report-CoE-Resettlement.pdf

Institutions and Capacity Building for Resettlement in ILISU DAM w. Shi Guoqing, Turan Hazar and Yavuz Kir. Report on Second Field Visit of Committee of Experts Resettlement. Prepared on behalf of Euler Hermes (Germany), OeKB (Austria) and SERV(Switzerland). https://www.google.com/url?sa=t&rct=j&q=&esrc=s&source=web&cd=2&cad=rja&uact=8&ved=0ahUKEwj6ub-bprrQAhXixFQKHV8rAE8QFgggMAE&url=http%3A%2F%2Fm-h-s.org%2Filisu%2Fupload%2FPDF%2FAnalysen%2FZweiter_Bericht_Umsiedlung.pdf&usg=AFQjCNGCUyRwpzdnb-KLIe5iXguTDtJqTA&sig2=nbn5ZMK_rBFteMKtTzBeyQ&bvm=bv.139250283,d.amc

2007: *Training Manual: Risk Analysis and the Risks and Reconstruction Model in Population Resettlement* (The Training Manual consists of 220 power points usable for lectures)

2006: *Researching the Culture in Agriculture: Social Research for Agricultural International Development.* Editors M.Cernea and A. Kassam. Cambridge, Mass., USA: CABI.

2006: *Yemeni Fishermen and GEF's Red Sea Project: Local Benefits and Missed Opportunities.* w. John Soussan, Michael Cernea, and Khalid Al-Hariri,. Washington, DC: Evaluation. GEF

2001: *Cultural Heritage and Development: A Framework for Action in the Middle East and North Africa.* Washington DC: World Bank. (Policy Paper) http://documents.worldbank.org/curated/en/406981468278943948/pdf/225590REPLACEM1ccession0A2003100110.pdf

2000: *Risks and Reconstruction: Experiences of Resettlers and Refugees.* Editors, M. Cernea with McDowell, Washington, DC: World Bank. (487 pp.) http://documents.worldbank.org/curated/en/947311468739277702/pdf/multi-page.pdf

2000: *Cultural Heritage Preservation and Management in the MENA Region: M. Cernea,* Washington, DC: World Bank. (processed). http://documents.worldbank.org/curated/en/701491468110062716/pdf/NonAsciiFileName0.pdf

1999: *The Economics of Involuntary Resettlement: Questions and Challenges.* (ed.). M. Cernea, Washington DC: World Bank. http://documents.worldbank.org/curated/en/790851468773055283/pdf/multi-page.pdf

1998: *Resettlement, Rehabilitation and Development: Studies on World Bank Resettlement Policies and Experiences.* Vol. 2. Edited and translated in China by National Research Center on Resettlement. Nanjing: Hohai University Press.

1997: *Social Assessments for Better Development: Case Studies in Russia and Central Asia.* ed. Cernea Michael with Ayse Kudat. Washington, DC: World Bank. http://www.socialassessment.com/documents/KudatWorks/1997/SA%20for%20better%20devpt%20case%20studies%20in%20Russia%20and%20CA%20-%201997.pdf

1996: *Social Organization and Development Anthropology: The 1995 Malinowski Award Lecture.* Washington DC: World Bank. http://documents.worldbank.org/curated/en/319641468740410065/pdf/256200cover0pg0fixed.pdf

Resettlement and Development: Studies on World Bank Resettlement Policies and Experiences. Vol. 1. With a preface by Prof. Shi Guoqing. Edited and translated in China

1994: *Sociology, Anthropology, and Development: An Annotated Bibliography of World Bank Publications 1975–1993.* w. the assistance of A. Adams. Washington, DC: World Bank. http://documents.worldbank.org/curated/en/156001468739187063/pdf/multi-page.pdf

Cernea, Michael, Scott Guggenheim, Dan Aronson, and Warren van Wicklin III. *Resettlement and Development: The Bank-wide Review of Projects Involving Involuntary Resettlement 1986–1993.* (1994, reprinted in 1996). World Bank, ESSD http://documents.worldbank.org/curated/en/412531468766148441/pdf/multi-page.pdf

1993: Cernea, Michael, Scott Guggenheim, Editors. *Anthropological Approaches to Resettlement: Policy, Practice, and Theory.* Boulder, Colorado: Westview Press.

1991: Michael Cernea, *Putting People First: Sociological Variables in Rural Development.* (ed.). 2nd edition. New York: Oxford University Press. http://documents.worldbank.org/curated/en/161691468765016390/pdf/multi-page.pdf

Translations of the book *Putting People First* in other languages and countries:

Bahasa—Indonesia, 1988 *Mengutamakan Manusia Di Dalam Pembangunan: Variabel-variabel Sociologia de dalam Pembangunan Pedesaan*

Spanish—Mexico, 1995 *Primero la Gente: Variables sociológicas en el desarrollo rural*

Chinese—Beijing, 1998

Japanese—Tokyo, 1998

French—Paris, 1998 *La dimension humaine dans les projets de développement: Les variables sociologiques et culturelles* (Ed. Khartala, Paris)

1989: Michael Cernea *User Groups as Producers in Participatory Afforestation Strategies.* Washington DC: World Bank. http://documents.worldbank.org/curated/en/742751468739271216/pdf/multi-page.pdf

1988: Michael Cernea *Involuntary Resettlement in Development Projects: Policy Guidelines in World Bank-Financed Projects.* World Bank Technical Paper nr 80. Washington, DC: World Bank. http://elibrary.worldbank.org/doi/pdf/10.1596/0-8213-1036-4

1987: Michael Cernea *Non-Governmental Organizations and Local Development.* Washington: World Bank. http://documents.worldbank.org/curated/en/723711468739268149/pdf/multi-page.pdf

1986: Michael Cernea *Involuntary Resettlement in Bank-Assisted Projects: A Review of the Application of Bank Policies and Procedures in FY 79-85 Projects.* Agriculture and Rural Development Department, the World Bank: Washington, DC

1985: Michael Cernea *Putting People First: Sociological Variables in Rural Development.* (ed.). 1st edition. New York: Oxford University Press.

Michael Cernea *Research—Extension—Farmer: A Two-Way Continuum for Agricultural Development.* w. J.K. Coulter and J.F.A. Russell. Washington, DC: UNDP and World Bank. http://documents.worldbank.org/curated/en/957321468767065931/pdf/multi-page.pdf

1983: Michael M. Cernea *A Social Methodology for Community Participation in Local Investments. The Experiences of Mexico's PIDER Program.* Washington DC: World Bank. http://documents.worldbank.org/curated/en/547061468756574626/pdf/multi0page.pdf

1982: Michael M. Cernea *Agricultural Extension by Training and Visits: The Asian Experience.* with J.K. Coulter and J.F.A. Russell. Washington, DC: UNDP and World Bank. http://documents.worldbank.org/curated/en/615741468777254639/pdf/multi-page.pdf

1977: Michael M. Cernea *A System for Monitoring and Evaluating Agricultural Extension Projects: India.* with Benjamin Tepping. Washington DC: World Bank. http://documents.worldbank.org/curated/en/813081468765006764/A-system-for-monitoring-and-evaluating-agricultural-extension-projects

1973: *Considérations sur les Aspects de la Politique Agraire et de L'Évolution de L'agriculture Roumaine.* I. Berceanu, M. Cernea and O. Parpală. Report to the Bled International Seminar in Yugoslavia. Vienna, Austria: Centre Européen de Recherche et de Documentation en Sciences Sociales.

Selected Books in Romanian (1964–1974)

1974: *Sociologia americană: Tendințe și controverse. Convorbiri la Stanford între M. Cernea și sociologi americani (American Sociology: Trends and Controversies. Dialogues at Stanford between Michael Cernea and: Reuben Hill, Stanton Wheeler, Immanuel Wallerstein, John Kunkel, Alvin Bertrand, and Elliot Aronson).* București: Editura Enciclopedică (240 p)

Sociologia cooperativei agricole (The Sociology of the Agricultural Cooperative). București: Editura Academiei. (240 pp)

1973: *Cercetarea monografică a communităților rurale în sociologia din Romănia (The Monographic Research of Rural Communities in Romania'sn Sociology)* (processed). București: Institutul de Filozofie al Academiei

1971: *Sociologia muncii: resurse umane ale întreprinderii (The Sociology of Work: The Human Resources of the Industrial Enterprise).* w.M.Popescu and H.Ene. Buc.: Edit. Pol.

1970: *Două Sate: Structuri sociale și progres technic (Two Villages: Social Structures and Technical Progress).* Mihail M. Cernea, Henri H. Stahl, Gh. Chepeș and assoc. Buc. Editura Politică.

*Procesul de urbanizare în Romania—zona Brașov (Urbanization in Romania: The Brașov Area).*w. T. Bogdan, M. Constantinescu and P. Cristea. Buc.: Edit. Politică.

1969: *Sociologia culturii de masă (The sociology of mass culture).* M. Cernea, Editor) w. H. Culea, Stefania Steriade, and assoc : Editura Academiei.

1968: *Resurse umane ale intreprinderii industriale. (The Human Resources of the Industrial . Enterprise).* (Senior editor and coauthor). București: Editura Politică.

1967: *Sociologia muncii. Mișcarea inovatorilor (The Sociology of Work: The Innovators' Movement).* Mihail M. Cernea, Maria Micu and Victoria Dumitrescu. Biblioteca de Filozofie și Sociologie, Bucharest.

1964: *Profilul spiritual al clasei muncitoare. Cercetări sociologice de teren (The cultural outlook of the working class: an empirical sociological research).* w. H. Cazacu and Gh. Chepes (eds.). București: Editura Academiei.

Chapters in Books, Studies and Articles in Journals

2016: "The State and the Legislation on Involuntary Resettlement. Comparing the Thinking in China and India on Development-Displacement". In vol. Florence Padovani (ed.). *Development-Displacement In India and China.* Lanham, MD: Lexington Books, pp.7–51

2016: "Social Impact Assessments and Safeguard Policies at a Fork in the Road: The Way Forward Should be Upward, not Retreat". In vol H.M. Mathur (ed.). *Assessing the Social Impact of Development Projects: Experiences in India and other Asian countries.* Switzerland: Springer International publishing, pp vii–xxiv. http://www.springer.com/us/book/9783319191164

2016: "The controversy over safeguard policies"; Michael Cernea, w. Vinod Thomas and Rob van den Berg (https://www.devex.com/news/the-controversy-over-safeguard-policies-87679)

2015: "A Landmark in Development: The Introduction of Social Analysis of Projects at the World Bank. In vol: Susanna Price and Kathryn Robinson (ed.). *Making a Difference? Social Assessment. Policy and Praxis, and its Emergence in China.* Oxford, . UK: Berghahn Books, pp 35–59.

2015: The Economic and Moral Imperatives for a new Resettlement Policy, Vision and Stronger . Safeguards. Keynote Address at the Opening Joint Plenary Session of SfAA/INDR Conf. March, 24–28.

2015: "Thoughts while reading an innovative book". Foreword to vol. Ryo Fujikura and M. Nakayama (eds.). *Resettlement Policy in Large Development Projects*. NY: Routledge.

2013: "The Reconstruction Challenge in Development-Caused Displacement". Keynote Address presented at the International Conference on Development- Displacement and Resettlement. Univ. of Oxford/Refugee Studies Center. March 22–23. "Broadening the definition of 'population displacement': Geography and economics in conservation policy". In vol. H.M. Mathur (ed.). *Resettling Displaced People: Policy and Practice in India*. New Delhi: Routledge, pp. 85–119. http://www.tandfebooks.com/doi/view/10.4324/9780203814024

"Preparing for Resettlement Associated with Climate Change". w. A. de Sherbinin, M. Castro, F. Gemenne, and assoc. *Science* vol. 334, no. 6055, October, pp. 456–457. http://science.sciencemag.org/content/334/6055/456.full?sid=fa71d7da-58e8-4c76-a6f1-4a692f185b87

2010: "Financing for Development: Benefit-Sharing Mechanisms in Population Resettlement". In vol. A. Oliver-Smith (ed.). *Development and Dispossession: The Crisis of Forced Displacement and Resettlement*. Santa Fe: School for Advanced Research Press.

"Development-Caused Displacement and Resettlement: A Source of Knowledge for Designing Resettlement as Adaptation to Climate Change". Manuscript, Processed.

2009: "An Original Contribution to Country-wide Displacement Analysis". Foreword to vol. Alula Pankhurst and F. Piguet (eds.). *Moving People in Ethiopia: Development Displacement and the State*. Suffolk, UK: James Currey, pp. xxv–xxx. https://www.cambridge.org/core/books/moving-people-in-Ethiopia/FC950503F6F44561AADD383671736C0A#

2008: "The Development Potential of Cultural Heritage Endowments". In vol. A. de Trafford, F. Hassan and M. Youssef (eds.). *Cultural Heritage and Development in the Arab World*. Alexandria: Bibliotheca Alexandrina, pp. 111–144. Full Volume Available Free Online: http://www.bibalex.org/arf/en/GRA1106_DF_20081102_book.pdf

"Compensation and benefit sharing: Why resettlement policies and practices must be reformed". *Water Science and Engineering* (1):Nanjing,China. http://www.sciencedirect.com/science/article/pii/S1674237015300211/pdf?md5=7f92fe1002cb84fa0dbe7da1c54f56ad&pid=1-s2.0-S1674237015300211-main.pdf

Cernea, M. and H.M. Mathur:eds. *Can Compensation Prevent Impoverishment? Reforming Resettlement through Investments and Benefit-Sharing*. Oxford Univ. Press, (441 pages).

"Compensation and Investment in Resettlement: Theory, Practice, Pitfalls, and Needed Policy Reform". In vol. M.M. Cernea and H.M. Mathur. *Can Impoverishment? Reforming Resettlement through Investments and Benefit-Sharing*. New Delhi: Oxford University Press, pp. 15–98.

"Risk analysis and risk reduction: IRR – A theoretical and operational model for population resettlement". In vol. V. Desai and R.B. Potter (eds.). *The Companion to Development Studies.* Second Edition. United Kingdom: Hodder Education, pp. 476–481.

2007: "Financing for Development: Benefit-Sharing Mechanisms in Population Resettlement". *Economic and Political Weekly* XLII(12): 1033–1046. https://www.jstor.org/stable/4419387?seq=1#page_scan_tab_contents

"The Knowledge Benefits of Digging Deeply: Economic and Political Dimensions of Land Expropriation and Displacement". In vol. A. Guha. *Land, Law and the Left: The Saga of Disempowerment of the Peasantry in the Era of Globalization.* New Delhi: Concept Publishing Company, pp. vii–xv. http://www.academia.edu/3533867/Land_Law_and_the_Left_The_Saga_of_Disempowerment_of_the_Peasantry_in_the_Era_of_Globalization

"The Action Approach and Michael Cernea's Model". In vol. *Theoretical Perspectives in R&R.* New Delhi: Indira Gandhi National Open University, pp. 67–78, 105–118.

"Development Anthropology is a Contact Sport. An Oral History". Interview with Michael M. Cernea by Judith Freidenberg. Human Organization: Winter 2007, Vol. 66, No. 4, pp. 339–353. https://www.sfaa.net/files/5613/9613/2881/oral-history-Cernea-Freidenberg.pdf

2006: "Resettlement Management: Denying or Confronting Risks?". In vol. H.M. Mathur (ed.). *Managing Resettlement in India: Approaches, Issues, Experiences.* New Delhi: Oxford University Press, pp. 19–44. http://jrs.oxfordjournals.org/content/19/2/264.full

"Ethics and Economics in Resettlement Policy and Practice". In vol. S. Jain and M. Bala. *The Economics and Politics of Resettlement in India.* New Delhi: Pearson Education, pp. xi–xxi. https://books.google.com/books?id=O3I8BAAAQBAJ&dq=Ethics+and+Economics+in+Resettlement+Policy+and+Practice

"A redefinition of concepts in conservation policies. Population Displacement *inside* Protected Areas". In *Policy Matters* (IUCN) Issue 14, March, pp. 8–26. https://www.iucn.org/downloads/pm14_section_i.pdf

2006–2005: Cernea and Kai Schmidt Soltau "Poverty Risks and National Parks: Policy Issues in Conservation and Resettlement". World Development, Vol. 34, Issue 10, pp. 1808–30. https://www.google.com/url?url=http://scholar.google.com/scholar_url%3Furl%3Dhttp://www.eike-klima-energie.eu/fileadmin/user_upload/Bilder_Dateien/Jaeger_DokSpeicher/PovertyRisks.pdf%26hl%3Den%26sa%3DX%26scisig%3DAAGBfm3ApCJucUz5s02fuOVtIxeRym4Cyg%26nossl%3D1%26oi%3Dscholarr&rct=j&q=&esrc=s&sa=X&ved=0ahUKEwiP2KrrnM_QAhVCsFQKHbT4CIMQgAMIGygAMAA&usg=AFQjCNF6XjiXLtuQwt7y5n8AWLD7vXIndg

2005: "Concept and Method: Applying the IRR Model in Africa to Resettlement and Poverty". In vol. I. Ohta and Y.D. Gebre. *Displacement Risks in Africa: Refugees, Resettlers and Their Host Population.* Kyoto, Japan: Kyoto University Press, pp. 195–258.

2005: "The 'Ripple Effect' in Social Policy and its Political Content: A Debate on Social Standards in Public and Private Development Projects". In vol. M.B. Likosky (ed.). *Privatising Development: Transnational Law, Infrastructure and Human Rights*. Boston: Martinus Nijhoff Publishers, pp. 65–101.

"Studying the Culture of Agriculture: The Uphill Battle for Social Research in CGIAR." In vol. James McDonald and Laura Levi (ed.). *Culture and Agriculture*, vol. 27. no. 2. Berkeley, California: UP California. Copyright American Anthropological Association. http://onlinelibrary.wiley.com/wol1/doi/10.1525/cag.2005.27.2.73/abstract

2004: "Culture? ... At the World Bank ?! Letter to a Friend". Can be accessed at: http://www.cultureandpublicaction.org/conference/commentaries.htm

"The Promise of the Future: New Territories for Development Anthropology." Foreword to vol. Yasushi Kikuchi (ed.). *Development Anthropology: Beyond Economics*. Quezon City, Philippines: New Day Publishers, pp. iii–vii.

2003: "Making (achieving) conservation without impoverishing people: The End of Forcible Displacements?". w. K. Schmidt-Soltau. *Policy Matters* (IUCN) Issue 12. Durban, South Africa: IUCN Commission on Environmental, Economic and Social Policy. http://www.schmidt-soltau.de/PDF/Englisch/2003_Resettlement_Cernea_Schmidt-Soltau_Article_Policy_Matters.pdf

"Biodiversity conservation versus population resettlement: Risks to nature and risks to people." w. K. Schmidt-Soltau. Paper presented at The International Conference on Rural Livelihoods, Forests and Biodiversity. 19–23 May 2003, Bonn, Germany. http://www.cifor.org/publications/corporate/cd-roms/bonn-proc/pdfs/papers/t4_final_cernea.pdf

"The question not asked: when does displacement end?" *Forced Migration Review No. 17*, pp. 24–26. http://www.fmreview.org/sites/fmr/files/FMRdownloads/en/FMRpdfs/FMR17/fmr17.09.pdf

2002: "Developments in Applied Social Science—The World Bank Experience". In vol. E. Krausz and G. Tulea (eds.). *Starting the Twenty-First Century: Sociological Reflections and Challenges*. New Brunswick and London: Transaction Publishers.

Cernea M. & Ravi Kanbur *An Exchange about the Compensation Principle in . Resettlement;* Working Papers 2002-33, Cornell University, Ithaca, New York

"Risk Assessment and Management in Involuntary Resettlement". In vol. C. Edmonds and S. Medina (eds.). *Defining an Agenda for Poverty Reduction. Volume 1.* Manila: ADB, pp. 254–268. https://www.researchgate.net/publication/237607830_Risks_Assessment_and_Management_in_Involuntary_Resettlement

2001: Cernea and Serageldin "At the Cutting Edge: Cultural Heritage Protection through Development Projects." In vol. I. Serageldin (ed.). *Cultural Roots for Urban Futures*. Washington, DC: World Bank. Full volume available online at: http://documents.worldbank.org/curated/en/693441468769796497/pdf/multi0page.pdf

2000: "Repairing the World". In vol. Elvira and Mihai Nadin (eds.). *Jewish: Does It Make a Difference?* New York: Jonathan David Publishers, pp. 189–190.

"Risks, Safeguards and Reconstruction: A Model for Population Displacement and Resettlement". In vol. M.M. Cernea and C. McDowell (eds.). *Risks and Reconstruction: Experiences of Resettlers and Refugees.* Washington, DC: World Bank, pp. 11–55. http://elibrary.worldbank.org/doi/pdf/10.1596/0-8213-4444-7

"Some Thoughts on Research Priorities". *The Eastern Anthropologist (Special Resettlement Number)* vol. 53, no. 1–2, pp. 3–12. Restricted Access Online http://www.refdoc.fr/Detailnotice?cpsidt=1155009&traduire=en

1999: "Why Economic Analysis is Essential to Resettlement: A Sociologist's View". In vol. M.M. Cernea (ed.). *The Economics of Involuntary Resettlement: Questions and Challenges.* Washington DC: World Bank, pp. 5–27.

PDF file (forcedmigration.org)

or

Full volume available online at: http://documents.worldbank.org/curated/en/790851468773055283/pdf/multi-page.pdf

"Development's Painful Social Costs". In vol. S. Parasuraman. *The Development Dilemma: Displacement in India.* London: Macmillan Press, pp. 1–34. Restricted Access Online http://link.springer.com/chapter/10.1007%2F978-1-349-27248-8_1

"Brief Overview of the State of the Art in Social Research on Involuntary Resettlement". In vol. M.M. Cernea (ed.). *The Economics of Involuntary Resettlement: Questions and Challenges.* Washington DC: World Bank, pp. 28–49. Full volume available online at: http://documents.worldbank.org/curated/en/790851468773055283/pdf/multi-page.pdf

"The Power of Synthesis". In vol. L.K. Mahapatra. *Resettlement, Impoverishment and Reconstruction in India: Development for the Deprived.* New Delhi: Vikas Publishing House, pp. xi–xvi.

"Mutual Reinforcement: Linking Economic and Social Knowledge about Resettlement". In M. Cernea (ed.). *The Economics of Involuntary Resettlement: Questions and Challenges.* Washington DC: World Bank. Full volume available online at: http://documents.worldbank.org/curated/en/790851468773055283/pdf/multi-page.pdf

1998: "Impoverishment or Social Justice? A Model for Planning Resettlement". In vol. H.M. Mathur and D. Marsden (eds.). *Development Projects and Impoverishment Risks: Resettling Project-Affected People in India.* Delhi: Oxford University Press, pp. 42–66. http://www.cridlac.org/cd/cd_asentamientos_humanos/pdf/eng/doc14274/doc14274.htm

"Economics and the Private Sector: Open Issues in Resettlement Research". 1998 Elizabeth Colson Lecture. Univ. of Oxford, Queen Elizabeth House, Refugee Studies Programme. May 13. Processed (Unpublished)

1997: Cernea, M. "Hydropower Dams and Social Impacts: A Sociological Perspective", Social Assessment Series, Nr. 4, Washington DC: The World Bank.

Cernea, M. *African Involuntary Population Resettlement in a Global Context.* In "Environment Department Papers: Social Assessment Series, Nr. 45." Washington DC: The World Bank

Globalization and the Significance of the Private and Informal Sector in Development. Keynote Address at Seminar: Building Partnerships for Development. Luxembourg, September 29–30, 1997. Swiss Academy for Development.

"The Risks and Reconstruction Model for Resettling Displaced Populations". *World Development* 25(10):1569–1588. http://www.sciencedirect.com/science/article/pii/S0305750X97000545

"Sociological Practice and Action-Research On Population Resettlement (Part II)." *Journal of Applied Sociology*, vol. 14, no. 2 (see Part I in vol. 13, 1996).

1996: "Sociological Practice and Action-Research On Population Resettlement (Part I)." *Journal of Applied Sociology*, vol. 13, no.1 (see continuation Part II in vol. 14, 1997).

"Understanding and Preventing Impoverishment from Displacement: Reflections on the State of Knowledge". In vol. C. McDowell (ed.). *Understanding Impoverishment: The Consequences of Development-Induced Displacement.* Oxford, UK: Berghahn Books, pp. 13–32. http://documents.worldbank.org/curated/en/909961468740152010/pdf/multi0page.pdf

"Bridging the Research Divide: Studying Refugees and Development Oustees". In vol. T. Allen (ed.). *In Search of Cool Ground: War, Flight and Homecoming in Northeast Africa.* Geneva: UNRISD, pp. 293–317. http://documents.worldbank.org/curated/en/287241468766455768/pdf/multi0page.pdf

"Public Policy Responses to Population Displacements". *Economic and Political Weekly* XXXI(24): 1515–1523. http://repository.forcedmigration.org/pdf/?pid=fmo:2295

"Sociological Practice and Action-Research On Population Resettlement (Part I)." *Journal of Applied Sociology*, vol. 13, no. 1 (see part Part II in vol. 14, 1997).

1995: "Understanding and Preventing Impoverishment from Displacement". *Journal of Refugee Studies* vol. 8, no. 3. http://documents.worldbank.org/curated/pt/909961468740152010/pdf/multi0page.pdf

1994: "Population Resettlement and Development". *Finance and Development* nr. 9, Sept. http://documents.worldbank.org/curated/en/909961468740152010/pdf/multi0page.pdf

"Social Science Research and The Crafting of Policy on Population Resettlement". *Knowledge and Policy* vol. 6, nr. 3–4. http://link.springer.com/article/10.1007/BF02696288

"The Sociologist's Approach to Sustainable Development." In vol. Ismail Serageldin and Andrew Steer (ed.). *Making Development Sustainable: From Concepts to Action.* Environmentally Sustainable Development Occasional Paper Series No 2. Washington, D.C.: The World Bank, pp.7–9. https://crcresearch.org/files-crcresearch/File/cernea_93.pdf

1993: "Anthropological and Sociological Research for Policy Development on Population Resettlement". In vol. M.M. Cernea and Scott Guggenheim (eds.). *Anthropological Approaches to Resettlement: Policy, Practice, and Theory.* Boulder, Colorado: Westview Press, pp. 13–38.

"Disaster-related Refugee Flows and Development-caused Population Displacement". In vol. M.M. Cernea and Scott Guggenheim (eds.). *Anthropological Approaches to Resettlement: Policy, Practice, and Theory.* Boulder, Colorado: Westview Press, pp. 13–38.

"A Sociologist's View on Sustainable Development". *Finance and Development,* nr. 12, December. pp. 11–13. https://crcresearch.org/files-crcresearch/File/cernea_93.pdf

1992: "A Sociological Framework: Policy, Environment and the Social Actors for Tree Planting". In N.P. Sharma (ed.). *Managing the World's Forests: Conservation and Development.* Iowa: Kendall/Hunt Publishing Co. pp. 301–335. http://documents.worldbank.org/curated/en/345981468764737222/pdf/multi0page.pdf

"Retooling in Applied Social Investigation for Development Planning: Some Methodological Issues". In Nevin Scrimshaw and Gary Gleason (ed.) *Rapid Assessment Procedures: Qualitative Methodologies for Planning and Evaluation of Health Related Programmes.* pp. 11–24.

1991: "Knowledge from Social Science for Development Policies and Projects". In vol. M.M. Cernea (ed) *Putting People First: Sociological Variables in Development.* 2nd edition. New York: Oxford University Press, pp. 1–41.

"Sociologists in a Development Agency: Observations from the World Bank". In vol. M. Schönhuth. *The Socio-Cultural Dimension in Development: The Contribution of Sociologists and Social Anthropologists to the Work of Development Agencies.* Rossdorf, Germany: Druckerei Peter Schultz. pp. 28–38. http://documents.worldbank.org/curated/en/410061468740182958/pdf/multi0page.pdf

"Using knowledge from social science in development projects". *World Bank discussion papers*; no. WDP 114. Washington, D.C. : The World Bank. http://documents.worldbank.org/curated/en/920971468764672322/pdf/multi-page.pdf

1990: "Putting People First: Social Science Knowledge for Development Interventions". In vol. H.M. Mathur (ed.). *The Human Dimensions of Development: Perspectives from Anthropology.* New Delhi: Concept Publishing Company, pp. 3–40.

"Poverty Risks from Population Displacement in Water Resources Development". Harvard University: Development Discussion Paper No. 355. HIID. https://www.cabdirect.org/cabdirect/abstract/19916712675

"Internal Refugee Flows and Development-Induced Population Displacement". *Journal for Refugee Studies* vol. 3, no. 4. Oxford. https://www.google.com/url?url=http://scholar.google.com/scholar_url%3Furl%3Dhttp://www.academia.edu/download/34169715/Journal_of_Refugee_Studies-1990-CERNEA-320-39.pdf%26hl%3Den%26sa%3DX%26scisig%3DAAGBfm2ebpF_WrjQYSUBgPNuUEvZlaLVVA%26nossl%3D1%26oi%3Dscholarr&rct=j&q=&esrc=s&sa=X&ved=0ahUKEwjy_p3jp8zQAhXLzFQKHScfB4IQgAMIGygCMAA&usg=AFQjCNGLuPilBnxkipTzvWnAZq9YQqaqBA

"From Unused Social Knowledge to Policy Creation: The Case of Resettlement". Harvard University, HIID (Development Discussion Paper No. 342), May. https://www.cabdirect.org/cabdirect/abstract/19901883974

1989: "The Management of Common Property Natural Resources: Some Conceptual and Operational Fallacies". *World Bank Discussion Papers no. 57*. w. D.W. Bromley. Washington, DC: The World Bank. http://documents.worldbank.org/curated/en/548811468740174575/pdf/multi-page.pdf

"User Groups as Producers in Participatory Reforestation Strategies". Harvard University, HIID (Development Discussion Paper no. 319). http://documents.worldbank.org/curated/en/742751468739271216/pdf/multi-page.pdf

"Foreword." In vol. Adam Koons, Beatrice Hackett, John P. Mason (ed.) *Stalking Employment in the Nation's Capital: A Guide for Anthropologists*. Washington, DC: The Washington Association of Professional Anthropologists, pp. i–iii.

1988: "Development Anthropology at Work". *Anthropology Newsletter* vol. 29, no.6. Washington DC: American Anthropological Association.

"Involuntary Resettlement and Development". *Finance and Development* vol. 25, no. 3.

1987: "The 'Production' of a Social Methodology". In vol. Elizabeth M. Eddy and William L. Partridge (eds). *Applied Anthropology in America*. 2nd edition. New York: Columbia University Press, pp. 237–262. http://documents.worldbank.org/curated/en/246361468739264007/pdf/multi0page.pdf

"Entrance Points for Sociological Knowledge in Planned Development". *Research in Rural Sociology and Development*. H. Schwartzweller (ed.). Greenwich: JAI Press. http://documents.worldbank.org/curated/en/518211468147838917/pdf/659280WP0Box360entrance0points01987.pdf

"Farmer Organizations and Institution Building for Sustainable Development". *Regional Development Dialogue* vol. 8, no. 2. Nagoya, Japan.

1985: "Sociological Knowledge for Development Projects". In vol. M.M. Cernea. *Putting People First: Sociological Variables in Rural Development*. 1st edition. New York: Oxford University Press, pp. 3–21.

"Alternative Units of Social Organization Sustaining Afforestation Strategies." In vol. M.M. Cernea. *Putting People First: Sociological Variables in Rural Development*. 1st edition. New York: Oxford University Press, pp. 267–293.

"Knowledge from Social Science for Development Policies and Projects". In vol. M.M. Cernea (ed.). *Putting People First: Sociological Variables in Rural Development*. 1st edition. New York: Oxford University Press, pp. 1–41.

"Involuntary Resettlement: Social Research, Policy, and Planning". In vol. M.M. Cernea (ed.). *Putting People First: Sociological Variables in Rural Development*. 1st edition. New York: Oxford University Press, pp. 188–215. http://repository.forcedmigration.org/pdf/?pid=fmo:3794

"The Social Actors of Participatory Afforestation Strategies". In vol. M.M. Cernea (ed.). *Putting People First: Sociological Variables in Rural Development*. 1st edition. New York: Oxford University Press, pp. 340–393. http://repository.forcedmigration.org/pdf/?pid=fmo:3798

"Is Anthropology Superfluous in Farming Systems Research?" co-authored w. Scott Guggenheim in *Farming Systems Research* vol. 4. Kansas State University. http://documents.worldbank.org/curated/en/286381468766805566/pdf/multi0page.pdf

1984: "The View of an American Historian on Romanian Sociology". In John W. Cole (ed.). *Society and Culture in Modern Romania.* Univ. of Massachusetts Press, Amherst Research Series 20. http://scholarworks.umass.edu/cgi/viewcontent.cgi?article=1030&context=anthro_res_rpt24

1982: "Indigenous Anthropologists and Development-Oriented Research". In vol. Hussein Fahim (ed.). *Indigenous Anthropology in Non-Western Countries.* Durham, North Carolina: Carolina Academic Press, pp. 121–137. http://documents.worldbank.org/curated/en/579001468740712071/pdf/multi0page.pdf

1981: "Rural Community Studies in Rumania". w. M. Larionescu, E. Springer and H.H. Stahl. In vol. J-L. Durand-Drouhin, L-M. Szwengrub and I. Mihailescu (eds.). *Rural Community Studies in Europe: Trends, Selected and Annotated Bibliographies, Analyses, Volume 1.* Oxford, UK: Pergamon Press, pp. 191–254.

(SCAN EXISTS IN CERNEA FILES AS A PDF)

"Modernization and Development Potential of Traditional Grass Root Peasant Organizations". In vol. M. Attir, B. Holzner, Z. Suda (eds). *Directions of Change: Modernization Process in Theory and Reality.* Colorado: Westview Press. http://documents.worldbank.org/curated/en/637331468766182209/pdf/multi0page.pdf

"Land Tenure Systems and Social Implications of Forestry Development Programs". Staff Working Paper nr. 452. Washington DC: World Bank. http://documents.worldbank.org/curated/en/519981468739491269/pdf/multi0page.pdf

1978: "Macrosocial Change, the Feminization of Agriculture, and Peasant Women's Threefold Economic Role". *Sociologia Ruralis* (The Netherlands) no. 18, pp. 239–250. http://documents.worldbank.org/curated/en/984471468146422560/pdf/REP98000Macros0eefold0economic0role.pdf

1976: "Cooperative Farming and Family Change in Romania". In vol. Bernard Faber (ed.). *The Social Structure of Eastern Europe.* New York: Praeger Publishers.

1975: "Social Organization of Pastoral Groups and Sedentarization in the Algerian Steppe". Staff Working Paper: AGR. Washington DC: World Bank.

Publications in Non-English Languages

2008: "Penser les risques sociaux du développement". In vol. N. Blanc and S. Bonin (eds.). *Grands barrages et habitants.* Versailles: Éditions Quæ, pp. 57–76.

2006: "Dimension humaine et développement: l'expérience des sociologues de la Banque mondiale." w. A. Marc. In vol. Jean-Pierre Gern (ed.). *Les Sciences Sociales Confrontées au Développement.* Paris, France: L'Harmattan, pp. 53–74.

2003: *Patrimoine culturel et développement: Cadre d'action pour le Moyen-Orient et l'Afrique du Nord.* Second Ed. Washington, DC: Banque mondiale.

2001: "Risques d'appauvrissement et développement: un modèle pour la reinstallation des populations déplacées". In vol. J.-F. Baré (ed.). *L'Évaluation des Politiques de Développement.* Paris: L'Harmattan, pp. 175–231.

"Hèritage, Famille et Communanté". In vol. N.L. Tagemouati. *Dialogue en Médina.* Casablanca: Editions Le Fennec, pp. 7–12.

1998: *La dimension humaine dans les projets de développement: Les variables sociologiques et culturelles.* Paris: Karthala.

1995: "Intégration sociale et déplacements de populations: la contribution des sciences sociales". *Revue Internationale des Sciences Sociales* nr. 143. Oxford-Cambridge: UNESCO-Blackwell Publ.

1991: *Primero la gente: Variables sociológicas en el desarrollo rural.* (ed.). México: Fondo de Cultura Econoómica.

1990: *Pemukiman Penduduk Secara Terpaksa Dalam Proyek-Proyek Pembrangunan.* Petunjuk Teknis Bank Dunia No. 80. Washington, DC: Bank Dunia.

1988: *Mengutamakan Manusia di Dalam Pembangunan: Variabel-variabel Sosiologi di dalam Pembangunan Pedesaan (Putting People First: Sociological Variables in Rural Development).* Translated by Basilius Bengo Teku. Penerbit Universitas Indonesia: UI-Press.

1976: "L'exploitation Familiale des Cooperateurs – Project Social ou Remanence Economique". In vol. Placide Rambaud (ed.). *Sociologie Rurale.* Paris: Ed. Mouton.

1969: "Transformations des Structures Familiales et Coopératives Agricoles". *Sociologia Ruralis* Vol. 9, issue 2, June, pp. 134–145.